The End of Kings

The End of Kings

A History of Republics and Republicans

William R. Everdell

THE FREE PRESS
A Division of Macmillan, Inc.
NEW YORK

Collier Macmillan Publishers
LONDON

The Free Press
A Division of Macmillan, Inc.
866 Third Avenue, New York, N.Y. 10022

Collier Macmillan Canada, Inc.

Printed in the United States of America

printing number

1 2 3 4 5 6 7 8 9 10

Library of Congress Cataloging in Publication Data
Main entry under title:

The End of kings.

   Bibliography: p.
   Includes index.
   1. Republics—History.   I. Everdell, William R.
JC421.E57   1983   321.8′6   83–48070
ISBN 0–02–909930–7

For Josh and Chris
and the other Saint Ann's students who helped
Liberis Rei Publicae

Titles are shadows, crowns are empty things:
The good of subjects is the end of kings.

—Daniel Defoe
The True-born Englishman

CONTENTS

ACKNOWLEDGMENTS

As this book has grown, I have come to agree with that old com-
plainer, John Adams. The "science of republican legislation," he
wrote, is "a kind of erudition which neither procures places, pen-
sions, embassies, chairs in academies, nor fame, nor practice in the
pulpit, at the bar, nor in medicine" (*Works*, 4:559). I think, however, I
would rather have the friends it has made me. Some of these I have
come to know and value entirely through their own writings, and I
have used the notes to explain how much. I would like to thank here
those to whom my debt is personal.

Many are my own students. Some are my teachers. J. Carroll Mc-
Donald introduced me to the Machiavelli of Croce 25 years ago, and
it stuck. John Walker's course on reason of state was my introduction
to the history of ideas; for his sins he has since been made a bishop.
James Billington, the historian of revolution, was my guide in the
history of conservatism and monarchism. Frank Manuel, whose
respect for the power of belief was unusual in his positivist generation, supervised my investigation of 18th-century apologetics, where
I first learned of the relation between evangelical protestantism and
republicanism.

It is my students, however, and not my teachers, who asked me

the hardest questions and thereby provoked the writing of this Brob-
dignagian answer. The classes of 1980 and 1981 at Saint Ann's
School, when they were in fourth grade, began the process by insisting that the sovereign of the United States was the president, and
by participating joyfully in the reenactment of the debates in the
New York State Constitutional Convention which I imposed on
them as a corrective. Other classes contributed after they got to high
school: the radicals of '75 and '76, the hopeless liberals of '77, '78, and
'79. Still others contributed, and are still contributing, by demanding
in sixth grade how a democracy could have executed Socrates, and in
seventh how any good could possibly come from religious war. It
would take another book to name them all. Three—Susan
Brockman, Lisa Goren, and Laurie Kaufman—long after graduation, read and criticized parts of the manuscript. Immy Humes not
only helped with the research on Gambetta but also recommended
an agent. Maud Harris found the manuscript a publisher.

The book has been with more than one editor, all helpful, ques-
tioning, and, happily, opinionated. Mike Stanford, Phyllis Seidel,
Charles Lieber, Wieland Schulz-Keil, and Linda Coverdale will be, I
hope, both surprised and pleased to see the final version, edited by
Joyce Seltzer. The book was written, however, almost all in one
place: the fourth floor of the Bobst Library at New York University,
to whose open-stack policy and hard-working staff I owe a great deal.

I owe no less to the brains, good will, and volunteer spirit of Anita
Halverson, Ann Rubin, Andrea Godbout, Laurie La Tourette, and
the late Mike Hershon, who typed parts of the manuscript and left
me alone after hours with their shiny new machines to type the
other parts. I owe more to my fellow historians, at Saint Ann's and
elsewhere in the Republic of Letters, who have read and criticized all
or part of the manuscript: Joyce Appleby, Darline Levy, Victor Mar-
chioro, Steevie Chinitz, Stanley Bosworth, and Ralph Engelman;
and to my colleagues who listened patiently to the ideas when they
were still too ill-formed to put on paper, among them Barbara
Everdell, most patient of all. It is my republican hope that they will
not be obliged to overlook errors or to defend views with which they
disagree simply because they have at last achieved the exalted status
of print.

WILLIAM R. EVERDELL

The End of Kings

1

Introduction

What a Republic Is and How It Was Mislaid in America

O<small>N</small> J<small>ANUARY</small> 27, 1970, Prime Minister Harold Wilson of Great Britain was greeted on a state visit to the White House by a guard of honor of White House policemen. The guard was dressed in double-breasted white tunics with gold braid and buttons, stiff plastic shakos decorated with the White House crest, and black holstered pistols hung from black belts buckled with the presidential seal. The policemen saluted "sheepishly" (said the *New York Times*), Mr. Wilson was diplomatically silent, but the President of the United States, Richard M. Nixon, was elated. The uniforms were his idea. As his aide Alexander Butterfield testified three years later, Nixon was fascinated by such ceremonial details as the salad or the seating plan at state dinners. The uniforms were inspired, said Nixon, by examples of ceremonial bodyguards he had seen during his European tour a year before.

Rather harmless, one would think; after all, Nixon's taste had never been his strong suit. Yet public opinion was outraged. Editorial writers in New York were echoed by those in Buffalo and Cleveland. Conservative Republican newspapers like the *Star* in Washington, which supported Nixon on almost everything, turned on him on the mini-issue of the uniforms. Why? A reaction so out

1

of proportion suggests that somewhere deep in the American psy-
che, the uniforms had touched a nerve. Which nerve was hard to
explain at the time. "German," wrote the *Star*. "Comic opera . . .
Ruritanian," snorted the *Times*. "Graustark . . . Student Prince,"
thought the Chicago *Daily News*. The writers all seemed to be
dredging for turn-of-the-century stage shows, works seldom seen
which made fun of central and southern European monarchies before the First World War. An odd sort of reference, but then, the
uniforms themselves seemed even odder, at least to Americans. Not
only "unusual," wrote the Detroit *News*, but "ghastly."

In fact the uniforms were monarchical, and they were offensive
because the United States is not a monarchy. From under layers of
forgetfulness, the writers had made contact with the lingering met-
aphors of an old idea; a smartly dressed bodyguard, for reasons both
symbolic and practical, cannot be allowed in republics like the
United States. The republican tradition, buried in 1970 by generations of changed practice and a national party that had no idea
what its name meant, was still alive enough to mark the ceremony
of January 27 for what it was, the personal display of the power of
a king. In the next three years, the United States was to learn how
much those Ruritanian uniforms portended. In a painful, almost
archaeological process, Americans began to learn, or rather to remember, that democracy does not in itself preclude monarchy. A
majority of all the people may easily choose to be governed by one
person, aided only by his appointees—the Palace Guard. Only a
republic is designed to prevent one-man rule, but though the United
States had been a republic for generations before it became a democracy, Americans had forgotten what it was.

What is a republic? According to the College Board (Social Studies, American History, Form 3DCB3, 1981) it is a government whose
central feature is "a representative system." To embed such a
definition in such a test, the testers must be about as sure as any
student of the humanities can be, either that the proposition is true
or that "everybody knows it." True or not, in the United States
"everybody," clearly, knows it. In May 1981, *Newsweek*'s house
Tory, George Will, wrote apropos of Massachusetts Proposition
2½, "legislation-by-referendum is contrary to the essence of republican government, under the principle of representation; the people
do not decide issues, they decide who shall decide."[1]

Now "representative government," even representative democ-

racy, is a very odd way to define republic. It cannot be found in
any of the writings of great republicans before the eighteenth century, and it cannot be found in more modern works except for some,
not all, of those published in the United States. Most of the world's
people, who use the term republic and its cognates in all languages,
mean nothing more by it than a state without a monarch, a simple
definition, but one which has the merit of fitting many more republics in world history than "representative democracy" can. The
Romans, who invented the word republic, might well have been
puzzled to discover that their remarkable political creation depends
on a principle which was not introduced into Western politics for
more than a thousand years after their own Republic fell, and which
the Greeks, who taught them politics, had hardly mentioned.[2] The
Romans had four different assemblies, but not one of them was
chosen according to a scheme or principle of representation.

The "representative principle" is found nowhere in Machiavelli,
who sums up for us the wisdom of the Renaissance city-republics,
and hardly at all in Harrington, Machiavelli's disciple, who was said
in the 1650s to be the only one in England who knew what a republic was.[3] Representation, like romantic love, was invented, in
the form we now understand it, in the Middle Ages. It is true that
it became a feature of the republics of the Reformation and afterward, and comes down to Americans in an unbroken tradition from
the first English Parliaments of the reign of Henry III; but representation and other medieval precedents held no charm for the men
and women who created the First French Republic in 1792, and
the republican tradition which descends from them finds representation a minor and even at times a contradictory feature.

The fact that representative government was ill-understood and
seldom practiced by the ancients was known to the classically educated Americans of the nineteenth century and bothered not a
few of them. Even Noah Webster, while dutifully recording the
"representative" definition of republic in his 1828 *Dictionary*, added
a plaintive footnote about how difficult it was to apply the definition to the beloved Greeks and Romans (the French, to Webster
and his fellow Federalists, were unmentionable).[4]

That such an unsatisfactory definition of republic might perpetuate itself in America is much easier to understand than how it
got started in the first place. Classical learning has waned continuously since the nineteenth century, making it harder and harder
for an ordinary citizen to carry an honest likeness of the ancient

republics in his mental baggage. The First French Republic, which renewed the ancient ones, is not approved of in the United States and is badly understood. Rightly or wrongly, Federalist views of it have prevailed in the public mind, which associates it with arbitrary executions, fanaticism, and an excess of democracy. Indeed, the very concept of representation has been made to serve as a buffer against what the right, since antiquity has called the "excesses" of democracy, and the more sophisticated of American conservatives have revived it in every reforming period in American history.

During the New Deal, when images of the First Republic and all her radical sisters were taken out for a fresh polish, outraged conservatives, by an adroit interpretation of representation, nearly succeeded in ending forever the ancient companionship of republicanism and democracy. Representatives, they insisted, were not a convenience for constituents but a bulwark against them. A representative in a democracy was bound, as the English reactionary Burke so elegantly put it, to serve the voters not with his "industry only, but with his judgement".[5] His membership in an unruffled elite would often, alas, require that "judgement" to differ from the view of the turbulent majority of his less privileged constituents. Such is the circuitous route by which republicanism, in the United States, has become democracy's patron and keeper. Since that time democracy, which was at the zenith of its popularity when America fought "for democracy" in World War II, has easily snubbed republicanism, and not even conservatives talk about it much anymore.

In this way, I think, has the American word "republic," like American "football," come to mean something different in America from what it means anywhere else in the world; but how did this particular definition get started in the first place? It must have been framed before Webster set it down in 1828, and it must have been done by a formidable authority. In fact, though there is no conclusive way of proving it, the culprit is almost certainly one of the real giants of American political thought—James Madison, Father of the Constitution and joint author, with Hamilton and Jay, of *The Federalist Papers* of 1787–88.

In Number 10 of the *Federalist* Madison wrote, under the Roman Republican name of Publius, the most read, the most quoted, and clearly the most influential of his many commentaries on politics. Among the eighty-five *Federalist* essays, it stands out immediately for the clarity of its argument, the conciseness of its expression, and the hint of prophetic zeal which underlies what passes in the other essays for an ingenious exposition of technical political science. In *Federalist* Number 10, the central metaphor is fire; the fire is faction, and faction was, for Madison and most of his contemporaries, the most dangerous of all threats to the infant United States. What is faction? It is, in Madison's words, "A majority or minority of the whole, who are united and actuated by some common impulse of passion or of interest, adverse to the rights of other citizens, or to the permanent and aggregate interests of the community."[6]

This lofty language does not disguise what is meant, two millennia of mobs and demagogues from sixth-century Greece to eighteenth-century America, all formed by the "most durable source of factions . . . the unequal distribution of property."[7] Madison was most afraid that the poor would take, by the majority rule which is the essence of democracy, the property of the rich. They had done so often in the past, as Aristotle pointed out, and had threatened, in Shays' Rebellion, to do so less than a year before. It would not do for Madison to put the argument against this evil on a polemical level. In the manner of Enlightenment writers, he tried, in fact, to put it on a level as abstract and as general as his extraordinary mind was capable of achieving.

He also tried to attach the argument firmly to the most unexceptionable political ideal available to his countrymen in 1787, and this ideal was the republic. He found ready to hand the terms of an old debate, familiar from Aristotle to Montesquieu, on the limits placed on ideal political systems by the size of territory and population; and, in the middle of the essay, came up with the quite novel statement that a representative system was not only a solution to the problem of reconciling democracy with a large state, but was in fact the precise characteristic which distinguished a republic from a democracy.

> The two great points of difference between a democracy and a republic are: first, the delegation of the government, in the latter, to a small number of citizens elected by the rest; secondly, the greater number of citizens and greater sphere of country over which the latter may be extended.[8]

If this were to be the case, the deduction would follow, with the Euclidean precision so much admired by the Enlightenment, that a republic was a democracy which assured "control" of "the effects of faction" without destroying "liberty," which was the principle cause of faction as air is of a flame.

Madison, who knew more history than most of his contemporaries and should have known better, was thus led into a definition of republic which was in serious conflict with most historical examples of the phenomenon, and the incompletely suppressed passion of his prose insured that his misdefinition would never be forgotten. He repeated it in *Federalist* Number 14, written at almost the same moment, and compounded it by referring to the "confounding of a republic with a democracy," as if that were a solecism.[9] Some time later, writing on a different aspect of the proposed constitution in *Federalist* Number 39, he contradicted himself. Now a republic was "a government which derives all its powers directly or indirectly from the great body of the people; and is administered by persons holding their offices during pleasure, for a limited period, or during good behaviour."[10] This much more satisfactory definition, significantly, followed a short review of the historical instances. He even repeated it in *Federalist* Number 43, but he never corrected the earlier definition.[11]

One may imagine some discussions with Hamilton, whose state convention the papers were intended to influence, because Hamilton's definition of republic, found in *Federalist* Number 22, was the twin of Madison's second definition: a government whose "fundamental maxim" is "that the sense of the majority shall prevail."[12] In *Federalist* Number 52, Madison came near to recanting, recognizing that representation was "but imperfectly known to ancient polity" and substituting "confederated republic" for "republic" in *Federalist* Number 63.[13] Alas, none of this revision has affected the posthumous power of *Federalist* Number 10, or of its definition, which, given even the epistemology of political science, is unfortunate, and from the historian's nominalist standpoint has to be called an error of the first consequence.

If the cause demands that we go to a Founding Father for a definition of republic, we should go to John Adams, who was even less of a democrat than Madison, but a better historian. According to Adams, a republic was "a government whose sovereignty is vested in more than one man." He got this from Doctor Johnson, who, in his *Dictionary* of 1755, called it, more concisely, "government of more than one."[14]

Adams's definition has met with little success in America. Like Adams himself, it was far more successful in Europe. At the time the French founded their First Republic (and the Republican Party in the United States was left wing and democratic) republic was defined as *"gouvernement de plusieurs"* (government of several), as it still is in *Littré* and successor French dictionaries. French republicanism, democratic at the outset, has in turn set the tone for European republican thought, though not for American. Indeed in the United States, since the beginning of the twentieth century, the term "democracy" has ballooned so alarmingly that it has absorbed almost all that remained of the alternative meanings of the word "republic." There are many reasons for this, beginning with the fact that Adams didn't like democracy at all, and his party hated the French Republic. In our own time, war patriotism, centralization of power, and a tendency toward president worship (usually focused on Democratic presidents) have tended to identify democracy with the American way of life and the sovereign people with the quadrennial choice of the largest of its electorates, the president. The word "republic" is now used rarely, usually by conservatives and closet elitists in the same way that Madison used it in *Federalist* Number 10—to keep democracy at arm's length.

It is the premise of this book that Adams was right in his definition of that historical object known as a republic, and further that the citizens of what its founders called a republic may want to know what that object is. Knowing what it is, we may intelligently decide whether we still have one, and whether we should keep it or not, rather than letting it fade away. Having decided to keep it, it may be useful for us to know how to do so. After about 1860, when the notion of a republic faded from American political science, history has been the only discipline that could help with such projects.

Moreover, if we do decide that the United States is and should remain a republic, it will not be a waste of time to find some reverence for republics; and here again history is most helpful. We have long studied, revered, even monumentalized the skein of Western democracies that lead to ours. Nor is it in any way wasteful of our increasingly limited reserves of public affection to do so. Surely Americans are as much the heirs of Athenian, Roman, French, and other democrats as they are of the makers of any other political tradition; and no one has yet shown that Woodrow Wilson was wrong when he said that the only cure for the ills of democracy was more democracy. I think, however, that we are also heirs of a republican tradition, stronger still because it is older, and possibly in these times more essential to liberty. We must give Madison his due: a republic and a democracy are not the same thing. A state may be both, but more often in history states are either—or neither.

Democracy, strictly speaking, means the making of law and policy by a majority of all. The Greeks coined the word to describe Athens because, of all the states of Greece, Athens was the only important one in which all the laws were made by a majority vote of all freeborn male citizens. Over the centuries, the meaning of democracy has been expanded by extending citizenship, the vote, and the right to hold office to larger and larger numbers. We may credit Vermont with being the first state since antiquity to enfranchise poor men in 1790, and similarly France for enfranchising black former slaves in 1794, Wyoming for enfranchising women in 1869, and the United States at large for extending full citizenship to eighteen to twenty-one-year-olds in 1971. If we ever enfranchise dolphins or felons, the word for that too will be democracy.

The term is clearly powerful; the concept, both politically and geographically, expands continually. Democracy's expansion, however, has led many to assume, wrongly, I think, that democracy is the same thing as liberty. Civil rights, common law privileges, property rights, and laws protecting minorities are not undemocratic, to be sure, but democracy does not imply them, and democracy has repeatedly shown itself capable of destroying them. Madison's fear that a majority might confiscate property was not unfounded. The fear that a majority may abrogate rights is not irrational. In America some of the most concerted attacks on the Bill of Rights have been led by magistrates secure in the support of an overwhelming majority of the electorate, and the largest mandates in our history have gone to presidents like Harding, Lyndon Johnson, and Nixon, whose attitudes toward minorities were at best problematical. The First Amendment is, in fact, a minority privilege. Majorities have never liked it. Only with great difficulty can they be persuaded that they will not always be majorities and may someday need its protection. Other countries provide much worse examples. Dictators from Caesar to Hitler have enjoyed majority support for the denigration, even the wholesale extermination, of minorities wihin their states. History suggests that the wisdom of the people is not the wisdom of a majority, and that democracy, though marvelous, is simply not enough.

If not democracy, then what? With democracy on trial everywhere, some have found themselves disagreeing so profoundly with Woodrow Wilson that they have asked not for more democracy, but less. These are the elitists, or what the Greeks called aristocrats. Let us be ruled, they say, by the best, by those with the skills to do so. Just as a majority cannot decide the truth of the Theory of Relativity, a majority cannot decide the fate of a community. Majorities are by definition incompetent. To decide if God exists or whether $2+2=4$, says the elitist, you do not consult a majority. To decide whether the United States should nationalize medical care you consult doctors, senators, or insurance men. To decide whether to go to war in Vietnam, you consult the Pentagon, or the Council on Foreign Relations, the best and the brightest. Alas, as the examples suggest, elitism works best in mathematics. Political aristocracy has not done too badly in its time, but history has clearly abandoned it, along with Bismarck, Protopopov, the House of Lords, and the Grand Council of Venice.

If nothing else has laid aristocracy to rest it is the lively though shapeless political tradition known in America as liberalism. The liberal's commitment to equality of rights and equality of powers among citizens makes the idea of an elite, however chosen, noisome or ridiculous. His view, honorably rooted in the seventeenth century, that individuals come morally and historically first and states and societies second, makes ancient republics like Sparta just as unattractive as the more modern monarchies of Louis XIV and Hitler. No state, however constituted, is right to demand the unconditional obedience of its citizens, to endorse any particular value system, to promote or even to recognize class. What the liberals forget is that an equal individual is neither skilled nor sacrosanct enough to oppose the state that he and his fellows are supposed by liberals to have created. It is no accident that the first great liberal thinker, Thomas Hobbes, produced a vision of absolute monarchy in which all were equal in subjection. It ought not to be surprising that in pursuit of the goal of *de facto* equality, American liberals have desanctified the law and engrossed the state. Liberals and democrats are alike in the shock they invariably express when the powers they erect are turned against them.

Well, some say, let us have anarchy. Not, the anarchist hastens to add, no government at all (which is what the Greeks meant by the word) but government on the lowest possible scale, voluntary, temporary, and limited, a confederation of self-governing communities. Something not so different from the ideal vision of the nineteenth-century liberal. If, as Hannah Arendt so neatly defined it, the state is that institution in society with the monopoly of violence, let us apply the antitrust principle and replace the state by many states. One society, several little monopolies, each one directed by its intimate little local majority. Somewhere in the network there will be a safe place for anybody. Violence might even become obsolete.

It is a view which, unlike elitism, appeals enormously to Americans. It has even been suggested that all home-grown radicalism in America is fundamentally anarchist,[15] and surely the case is plain for Thoreau, Walt Whitman, the SDS, or even Bat Masterson. What other idea could link John Wayne and Norman Mailer? So congenial is this view that it lurks in the back of our most responsible minds and often comes out in speeches by entrepreneurs to the Junior Chamber of Commerce. Fundamentally, it seems, the difference between the businessperson's "Get the government off our backs," and the Weatherman's "Smash the State," is only one of emphasis. Tempering democracy with anarchy seems so much more acceptable to Americans than tempering it with aristocracy that one is led immediately to ask why this should be so, a question not philosophical but historical and cultural. How did Americans become anarchists—government-resisters—at the same time that they were establishing a state in which government was more their agent than it was anywhere else on earth?

The answer, I think, lies in the capacity of the term "anarchist" to mislead. A European word, used by nineteenth-century American newspapers as a whip for immigrant radicals, anarchism, even at its widest definition, does not describe what Americans feel, at the unconscious cultural level, about the rights and wrongs of government. Certainly it is true, for example, that Americans are marvelous joiners, boosters, and selfless cooperators on the local level. In fact, in these activities Americans are the wonder of the world. It is not true, however, that they would want to replace state with local government, or abandon the army for a neighborhood militia, or replace General Motors with a string of producers' cooperatives. No, the underlying principle by which Americans judge government, in the absence of emergencies, is not smallness but balance. The American does not advocate destroying the irritating institution but cutting it down to size or matching it with another. Let General Motors match wits with Ford, or if the two are found to collaborate, let both tilt with the Federal Trade Commission and the Department of Transportation. In matters of government proper, let the three branches fight it out. Let states oppose Washington or parties each other. To take the classic case in which the United States was and still is to some extent unique, let all churches compete on a basis of absolute equality for the favors of God, government, and potential believers.

Such a prejudice, and most of the political solutions to which it gives rise, are not anarchist. They are instead what remains to us of a once clear vision, an inclusive paradigm, a rich body of political thought, and a long historical experience which we name by the Roman word republican. For the republican, the key to liberty is the balance of opposing forces, not, as for the democrat, the enfranchisement of all forces and the omnipotence of a numerical majority. For a republican, power to the people means perpetual institutionalized conflict.

This basic republican idea of conflict and balance provides the simplest approach to a complex political position which any American with his wits about him can still recognize as his own. A state which is highly democratic without being republican, the Second French Empire for example, he will immediately recognize as foreign to his political culture and an affront to liberty.

The United States was in fact a republic long before it was a democracy. Democracy, even in the form of universal male suffrage, did not come to a majority of states in the union until the nineteenth century. Many historians argue that this country did not become a democracy until after Reconstruction, when for the first time no state excluded the poor from voting (or, in theory, black men). By that time it had been a republic for more than fourscore years—and, in the minds of its founders, longer than that. It should not, therefore, seem strange that we recognize and respect republican principles when we see them.

A republic, however, is more than a state in which political forces are balanced and competitive. To begin at the beginning, a republic is a state without a king. Seeking a word to describe the new focus of political loyalty after they had expelled the kings, the ancient Romans found it in *res publica*—the public thing—a superior something which has ever since put the fragility of republics into the very name. In a republic one is loyal to the whole government, to each and every office, to the fundamental laws which keep them in being, to the society at large and to all its members. It is, as generations of peoples have realized, much easier to be loyal to individuals. It needs less abstraction. Indeed, many are not clever enough to be loyal to anything else. Moreover the rewards of loyalty to individuals have historically been, if not more tangible, at least more immediate. If leaders like Napoleon have been ungrateful, republics like Athens have been more so. They may impeach or exile a superbly competent public servant like Aristides simply on the grounds that they are tired of his ambition. In fact republics have an imperative to be ungrateful to the best of their politicians, for monarchy always threatens, and as long as the point is to prevent one office or officer from dominating, all offices must be equally independent and all officers equally respected.

This equality of office is one of the hardest things of all to achieve. Arranging for it is what makes the republican such an ardent constitutionalist, and such an obsessive political tinkerer. Monarchy requires no such advance arrangements. Monarchy is simple. One officer is chosen—by inheritance, by vote, or even by serendipity, like the Dalai Lama—and everything after that proceeds with no need of design. The monarch embodies the state. He can do no wrong. He is obeyed by all the other officers simply because they are his employees. If new offices are needed, the monarch creates them. The republic too hires officers and creates office, but to say so only begs the question, for the republic is an abstraction. People have to do it in the end.

In our own system, appointive offices are created by Congress and filled by the president. The offices of congressman and president in turn are created by the Constitution and filled variously by vote of citizens in states and districts. The Constitution itself, headed "We the People," was drafted by a coopted group of politicians from the Continental Congress, and approved by state conventions and legislatures. The conventions and legislatures were created by state constitutions, and one could go on. The republican, in short, is a maker of labyrinths. More Byzantine than the Byzantine monarchy are his structures for dividing sovereignty. Most of them are in this book. Together they prove that there are nearly as many ways to keep offices separate but equal as there have been republicans to devise them. In Rome, we shall see, each of two great classes had its own set of magistracies. To arm them, Romans invented, among others, the veto and the plebiscite.

From the most ancient of all republics, tribal confederacies in Greece, Israel, and pre-Roman Italy, we get the now obsolete idea of a Senate of heads of families. From medieval Florence and the limited monarchy of England, republicans have learned the technique of the independent geographical constituency. From the English Commonwealth come independent courts and judicial review, as well as the very concept of separation of powers; from it and from Athens, the idea of a constitution-making legislature. Athens by itself supplies the device of an executive board or commission, limited terms of office, the now disused idea of election by lot, and indeed, election itself. Confederations of independent states, another republican device called federalism, appeared in Greece and were revived by the United States. The written constitution was also largely on American contribution. To end a foreshortened list, the modern institution known as the parliamentary republic seems to have been contributed only a century ago by France in unwitting imitation of England. Republicanism is a kaleidoscope of institutions, all with the one purpose of preventing rule by one person. The seemingly simple objective has continually demanded the most bewilderingly complex of means.

Moreover, it will appear that none of these means is democratic. Though the republican usually, like the democrat, makes the people sovereign, almost all his devices are trammels on the expression of its will. For a pure democrat the only needful devices are a medium for the people to express itself and a tool for counting its votes. For a pure republican, the ideal would be to set up a different office for each citizen, held in rotation by every citizen, and kept separate by a number of devices greater than the whole number of citizens. A conservative republican, faced with the complexities of this structure of balance and with its fundamental need for order, will argue that the law, not the people, is sovereign. His is the dictum, "a government of laws, not of men," for though laws (at least since the Renaissance) are most assuredly made by men, those laws which establish the differing powers and duties of office must appear not to have been made by men, or at least, not easily changed by men. In the age when the gods were sovereign, republicans could preserve their constitutions by the liberal use of divine sanction. Nowadays, it must be proved that these constitutions, despite appearances, are effective at preserving liberty. Monarchy, even democratic monarchy, must be shown to be the enemy of liberty, and democrats need to be shown that devices which thwart the momentary will of a majority may in the longer run preserve the privileges and freedom of action of every citizen. This has never, in history, been an easy task.

In this book the republican tradition is traced from the Homeric and Biblical beginnings of Western civilization all the way to the Reagan administration. It argues that there were republics before the word was coined, and that plural leadership begins in the tribal traditions of Hellas and Israel at a time when shahs and pharaohs occupied the center of the stage. It shows how republicanism survived, particularly in Greece, and how it was reinforced in practice by the Romans, who subdued the Mediterranean world long before they submitted to the monarchy of emperors. Though the Roman imperial office survived as myth in medieval Europe and thereby abetted the revival of kingship, this book argues that republican institutions arose again in everything from medieval peasant villages to aristocratic councils and urban communes. These polities emerged to challenge monarchy in the cantons of Switzerland and in cities like Florence and Venice, beginning in the thirteenth century. The monarchy of Christendom itself, long rivaled by Holy Roman Emperors, was challenged in the fourteenth century by the Conciliar movement and in the sixteenth century by the Reformation, of which one branch, the Calvinist, emerged from the commune of Geneva and managed to forge powerful alliances among nearly all the various opponents of popes, kings, and emperors.

The book tries to trace how this combination, in the next century, severely threatened monarchy in France, limited it in Scotland, eliminated it from the northern Netherlands, permanently divided such would-be monarchies as the Church and the Empire, and provided a living alternative to the rising power of the monarchies that remained. On that alternative, in the 1640s and 1650s, the English Revolution drew. Though failing to establish a kingless commonwealth, this revolution permanently limited the power of the English monarch and provided the model for English revolutionaries in America in the following century. The United States of America, once established, helped inspire the French republics of 1792 and 1848.

Reorganized after 1865, the American republic also (together with the by now entirely constitutional monarchy of England) set patterns for the restored French Third Republic of 1870–75, a republic which has itself provided the model for nearly every republic founded since. The German Weimar Republic, it is argued, copied the forms imperfectly, but was in practice unwilling to bridle executive power or to vest such power in more than one magistrate. A similar unwillingness to divide or limit the presidency has led over the past two or three generations to a real threat to the republican institutions of the United States. This threat, of which Watergate was only the most recent manifestation, has been most consistently opposed by members of the senior branch of Congress.

There is nothing original in this book's view that responsibility and power gravitate to single executives in times of war or stress, or that democracy, perversely, often aids the process. The Greeks were already aware of the tendency, and it was a Greek historian, Polybios, who first applied Greek explanations of the fragility of republics to Rome. The framers of the American Constitution also fully understood the forces that might threaten their work, but modern Americans, deprived of the republican tradition, must face the stresses of Cold War, nuclear armaments, and universal democracy as if no free state had ever faced anything like them before. The least this book may do is show that American citizens need not go it alone, and that both diagnoses and remedies are ready to hand in the achievements of many ancestors both intellectual and political.

The reader will meet here, probably not for the first time, such luminaries as Solon of Athens and Samuel the Prophet, Calvin and Milton, William Tell and Niccolò Machiavelli, Thaddeus Stevens, Burton Wheeler, and Gustav Noske: republicans all, though in very different ways. Some, like Robespierre, were passionate and narrow in their republican faith. Others, like Gambetta, were broad and practical. Solon was a republican *avant la lettre*. John Calvin was a republican by default, and by imputation of his faithful disciples. Niccolò Machiavelli was a republican who, in what must have been frustration or despair, wrote a bible for tyrants. William Tell was a republican who probably did not even exist. Their biographies not only ornament the republican tradition and serve as emblems of the different republics they served; they also illustrate the different modes of republican practice and the snares that threaten this relatively unstable political form.

Can the republic survive? Can ours? Polybios himself did not argue that all republics are doomed to lapse into tyranny; but he surely would have held little hope for the survival of any republic after those who must maintain it have ceased to understand it. If republican solutions can be found to the great political problems of this century—the control of a world economy, of communication, of nuclear weapons for example—they will have to be found by people to whom the notion of republic presents itself not as a marginal concept like representative democracy, but as a deep, practical, and comprehensive political vision able to inspire once more the cry of "Long live the Republic!"

2

Samuel and Solon
The Origins of the Republic in Tribalism

O F THE MANY FORCES in human cultures which favor one-man rule, history itself is one of the most powerful. Because kings are interesting, kings are written about; and kings are interesting for the most down-to-earth of reasons—their freedom. Kings may build worlds of their own without having to resort, as poets must, to metaphor. They express themselves absolutely compellingly in the medium of flesh and blood. What monarchs want done, in short, is done; and whether it be decent as Hammurabi's laws, outrageous as Nero's homicides, or beautiful as Tutankhamun's coffin, it fascinates those of us who, not being monarchs, can only imagine such things.

The more ancient the history, the more kings are apt to dominate it. In Egypt little but the works of kings is left to look on. Before 1000 B.C. in most places, even chronology hangs on the reigns of kings. Most of what survives of ancient writing is dug from the ruins of their libraries, composed at their behest, or carved in the rock itself on their orders. That is why when one studies ancient history, even in a democratic age, it seems to be so ridden with pharaohs and dynasties. In fact, the royal bias of ancient history has gotten worse since the Rosetta Stone ushered in the great age of

archaeology in 1798. When no one could read hieroglyphics or cu-
neiform, the main sources for ancient history were the Bible of the
Jews, and Homer, the bible of the Greeks, and against all probability
neither of the two canons was at all kind to monarchy.

It is quite curious, in fact, that the written tradition of Western
civilization should begin in precisely these two societies, Israel and
Greece, where monarchy remained in question; tiny societies on
the far fringes of the great hydraulic monarchies of the ancient
world, who rebelled against the pharaohs of Egypt, the emperors
of Persia, the military tyrants of Anatolia and Assyria, and kept their
independence just long enough to write about it. There is no obvious reason why Egypt became a European province instead of
Europe an Egyptian one, and if the contrary had occurred, it is not
likely the modern West would read either *The Iliad* or the Bible.

"You Greeks are such children," said the indulgent Egyptian
priest to Solon of Athens in Plato's story.[1] He meant that Greek
culture was too young, the art of writing lost so often that history
went unrecorded and forgotten. Plato does not give Solon's answer.
Perhaps he said, with Tolstoy, "Happy people have no history."
Actually the Greeks had a very rich history, but like that of the Jews
it was a kind that is alien and unfashionable now and curious even
in Solon's time. Greek history was oral: the memorized, twice-told,
incantatory history of peoples who had not long ago been nomads,
following herd animals hundred of miles from pasture to pasture,
carrying their goods on their backs and their literature, weightless,
in their heads. When they finally wrote it all down, both Jews and
Greeks borrowed their letters from the civilized peoples around
them, but they were much too recently uncivilized themselves to
borrow much else from settled neighbors. The Bible and *The Iliad*
remained for them, as they have even for us, an inexhaustible
echoing well of precivilized values, not least among them the notion
that monarchs are not a blessing but a curse, that kings are not
divine, and that a loose alliance of independent clans is an ideal
form of state.

Because of this fortuitous chain of events, even the least educated Westerner knows that when Troy and Canaan fell, it was not
at the hands of kings but of many leaders, each with independent
authority. In each epic a whole people acts, sometimes in complete
contradiction to its Moses or Agamemnon. It might surprise him
to hear that both Troy and Canaan are reckoned now to have fallen
in the thirteenth century B.C., or that both stories were receiving

their final written form in the eighth century, but he knows that
the stories have important values in common that transcend the
long hostility between Jew and Greek. When a Jew and a Greek
make their historic stands against monarchy, long before a culture
arose that could know both sagas, and centuries before the very
invention of the word "republican," they could be confident that
the most venerable traditions of their respective peoples would give
moral support, and hopeful as well that the stories of what they had
done would enter the tradition.

The Jew (properly, the Israelite) was Samuel; the Greek (properly, the Hellene) was Solon. Each has the distinction of being the
first self-conscious republican in his society of whom we have nearly
contemporary written record and of whose actual existence we can
be reasonably sure. Each exemplifies no less the contribution of
these two seminal peoples to the foundation of Western republicanism.

Neither Samuel nor Solon, as we shall see, was entirely successful in the immediate task of forestalling a monarchy. In the long
run, however, their efforts bore fruit for both Israel and Hellas, notably for Athens; and in the very long run, for as long as they have
been read about by squirming schoolchildren from Milton and Machiavelli to Sam J. Ervin, they have provided the two principal
Western schemes for withstanding one-man rule. In all the republicans who came after will be found the echoes of Samuel's preaching and Solon's politics: the prophecy and praxis of the republican
tradition.

Of the two men, it was, appropriately, the prophet who came
first, probably in the eleventh century B.C. Samuel's appearance in
the Hebrew Bible is abrupt and problematical. He is called a *nabi*
(prophet) but he is not among the Prophets. He is called a *sophet*
(judge), but he is not in the book of *Judges*. He has title to a book
of his own, two books in fact, between *Judges* and *Kings*. It turns
out, however, that the books are not his at all, but for the most part
chapters of a unified narrative written a century after he lived by
a courtier of King Solomon. *I Samuel*, in which Samuel lives and
dies, has, it is true, pieces from a later eighth-century source, and
editors have fiddled with both books since the sixth-century Babylonian Captivity. In fact, one late editor made an inspired decision
to put Samuel's name where *Kings* had most likely been, but essentially the narrative is a whole work by a single author and intended, as were so many historical works of the ancients, to explain

and justify royalty. In fact, the object of this principal author of *Samuel* is to give the origin of the dynasty of David, the second and greatest monarch of Israel's five-hundred-year kingdom.

Even the so-called "court historian," however, cannot keep Samuel out of the story. After all it was Samuel who first plucked David from a shepherd's obscurity to be king, and it is by Samuel's agency that God takes the crown from Saul. He looms as the major character throughout the first book and appears even after his own death, from the bubbling cauldron of the witch of Endor, to condemn Saul to perdition. Perhaps it is a historian's conscience that constrains the court historian to report as well the two terrible sermons Samuel gave on monarchy. More likely, it is the eighth-century writer. In any case the diatribes against kingship in *I Samuel* 8 and 12 have echoed in our civilization for three thousand years. Behind a conflict of sources stands the sheer contradiction of a man, anointing kings with one hand and chastising them with the other, which insures that in Samuel we are dealing with the messy reality of a genuine historical figure.

Who was he? According to the history, Samuel was born in a way that in Israel has always been a sign of special grace. His mother, Hannah, like the mothers of Isaac, Joseph, Samson, and John the Baptist, had come to old age barren of sons. Among nomad women there is no greater curse. When Samuel at last arrived, Hannah dedicated him to the God Yahveh and gave him as a boy of three to serve Yahveh's priest Eli at the hill sanctuary of Shiloh in central Palestine west of the Jordan River.

Growing up in the service of Eli, Samuel would have learned as much about the history of his people as anyone could at that time. Shiloh was, in the eleventh century B.C., the nearest thing to a capital, and its priests as near to a national archive as Israel had. All the stories recorded in the Bible, from *Genesis* to *Judges*, were still unwritten, and Israel itself remained culturally much as it had been when it had arrived on the scene, driving Abraham's flocks perhaps, nearly a thousand years before, or when it had achieved religious self-consciousness with Moses in the thirteenth century. That is, Israel was not a nation in the sense we use the term today, but a *natio*, what an anthropologist would call a patrilineal association of clans and tribes.

Samuel knew this without reflection. He himself was a member of the tribe (*shebet*) of Ephraim, and by descent that made him, as he called himself, a son of Israel. Israel, or Jacob, was the son of

Isaac, who was in his turn the son of Abraham the herdsman. And
Israel had begotten Joseph, and Joseph begat Ephraim. Tiresome
but essential knowledge, these begats, the very rock on which all
nomad history is founded. Yahveh was Samuel's God because Yahveh had been God of Israel. He had given the land now called the
Palestinian West Bank to Abraham, and through Abraham to all his
descendants, numberless as the sand, Samuel among them. That
was why Samuel was there, that and the extraordinary events of
ten generations back when members of Israel, thought lost beyond
the desert border, had irrupted back into the land, invading with
fanatical assurance, and bearing with them new stories of Yahveh,
so awesome, so extraordinary, that no Israelite of any tribe could
doubt His power and solicitude.

These stories told of stone tablets on which Yahveh himself had
written the law in fire and thunder and which had been received
by an inspired (and clearly literate) descendant of the tribe of Levi
named Moses. They told of a generation's wandering under Moses'
leadership in a desert place so far from the beaten track that there
were no flocks and Yahveh himself had had to provide them with
food and water. They told of an escape *en masse* from forced labor
in distant Egypt, nearest of the great monarchies to Canaan, during which Yahveh had brought plagues on Egypt, parted a sea,
drowned a royal army, and killed every first-born Egyptian boy. No
nation of nomadic herdsmen had ever had a God like that, or ever
would again until Muhammed told the Arabs about Allah. All other
gods must clearly be false—not even subordinate, but false. Samuel
implicitly knew this to be true of the local Canaanite gods, Baal and
Ashtaroth, or the Philistine's Dagon. They were as false as the gods
of the Egyptians who had failed so utterly to protect the greatest
kingdom on earth. They were false because even though they continued to be worshiped, Yahveh had given the land of their worship-
pers to Israel, to Israel's twelve sons, to his numberless descendants.

Samuel knew about the tablets of stone. He had slept beside
them as a child. They were, in fact, in Eli's care, closed in an acacia
wood casket called the Ark of the Covenant and venerated not in
a temple but in a tent, the classic dwelling of nomads. Like Yahveh,
the tablets were rarely seen, and like everything else associated with
a God of nomads, they were movable. The Ark had been through
the desert with Moses, to Gilgal and Schechem in central Palestine
with Joshua (like Samuel an Ephraimite), to Bethel in the time of

Phinehas the Levite, and lay now at the holy place of Shiloh in the territory of the tribe of Ephraim. Each of the tribes descending from Israel had a part in the Ark. The tribe of Levi provided its priest (Samuel's tutor, Eli, was a Levite), and the other tribes, it seems, took turns providing honor and protection. By the tent of meeting, elders (*zechenim* or heads of families) of all tribes met at regular intervals to take counsel of Yahveh and with each other.

Hundreds of such assemblies are recorded from *Exodus* to *Judges*, some "national," some local, some misplaced in both categories by later editors. They were the nearest thing to a government of Israel in Samuel's time, just as they had been in Joshua's time. Their concerns were, first, defense against alien cultures and, second, enforcement of a primitive, largely oral law. Samuel would have known of one famous assembly, remembered with shame in Benjamite territory where he had been born, which had been summoned by the grisly but apparently customary method of dividing a body into pieces and sending one to each tribe. In this case the body was that of a human, a Levite's concubine whom some Benjamites had raped. The other ten tribes formed an avenging militia, sought the sanction of Yahveh at historic Bethel, and led by the southern tribe of Judah, killed thousands of Benjamites and laid waste their small territory. So many Benjamite women were killed that the tribe nearly became extinct and could survive only by a Sabine rape.

Such was politics for Samuel. As a sixth-century editor adds, following the savage story of Benjamin in *Judges*, "In those days there was no king in Israel and every man did what was right in his own eyes."

Embedded in the same book of *Judges* is a heroic poem which is one of the few things we can be sure that Samuel might have learned verbatim. Now called the "Song of Deborah," it seems to have been composed orally soon after the events it describes and only about a century before the three-year-old Samuel took up his abode at the Shiloh sanctuary. The "Song of Deborah" would impress any child. It is a victory song, full of blood, guts, and barbarian self-righteousness. "Most blessed of women," it says of the herdswoman Jael, because she drove a tent peg through the skull of the enemy general Sisera while he slept. In its verses the modern reader is brought as near to the world of ancient Israel, the world of the exodus and conquest of Canaan, as the written word can take him.

The kings came, they fought;
  then fought the kings of Canaan,
at Ta'anach by the waters of Megiddo;
  they got no spoils of silver.
From heaven fought the stars,
  from their courses they fought against Sisera.
The torrent Kishon swept them away, ...[2]

Israel, or part of it, met Sisera in about 1125 B.C. on the broad plain of Megiddo in northern Palestine. The people were led by a woman, Deborah, whose title was *sophet* or judge, and by a man named Barak, a war chief of the tribe of Naphtali. Neither was a lawmaker. Deborah summoned, and Barak led, a temporary force of militia raised from the tribes of Ephraim, Benjamin, Machir, Zebulun, Issachar, and Naphtali. Each tribal contingent was commanded by its own *nesiim* (elders or princes). Six tribes did not come, notes the poem with some bitterness. Reuben "tarried among the sheepfolds," Dan "by the ships," Gilead "beyond the Jordan," and Asher "sat still at the coast of the sea." Judah and Simeon are not even mentioned. This was obviously a world before conscription and taxation, a polity ruled by temporary "charismatic" figures, war chiefs and *sophetim,* on sufferance of a federation of tribes similarly ruled. Whether or not Samuel knew the poem, he lived in its moral world and its premonarchical politics were natural to him.

Young Samuel would also have learned the story of Abimelech preserved for us in *Judges* 9. Abimelech was a son of Gideon, the great sophet of the clan of Abiezer, who had defeated the army of the king of Midian so thoroughly that the tribes offered to make him their king. "I will not rule over you, and my son will not rule over you," Gideon had said, summing up the then political faith of Israel, "The Lord will rule over you." This paternal renunciation had not suited Abimelech. After his father had died, he had proceeded to get himself chosen king (*melech*) by the tribal elders at the ancient sanctuary of Schechem, the first Israelite we know of to bear this title. It is possible the very concept of monarchy entered Israel with Abimelech's question to the elders of Schechem, a question Samuel may have carefully considered himself. "Which is better," Abimelech had asked, "that all seventy of the sons of [Gideon] rule over you, or that one rule over you?"[3]

According to the story, Abimelech had then killed all his brothers but one, and assumed the kingship. The survivor, Jotham, had fled, uttering an unforgettable parable on monarchy. "The trees went forth to anoint a king over them," said Jotham. The olive, the fig, and the vine each refused the office, being happy where they were, but the bramble accepted with these words: "If in good faith you are anointing me king over you, then come and take refuge in my shade; but if not, let fire come out of the bramble and devour the cedars of Lebanon." After three years, the story continued, the elders of Schechem had at last seen the point of Jotham's parable. They toppled the tyrannical Ambimelech in a military coup. Like Sisera, Abimelech had died from a crushing blow to the head delivered by an angry woman.[4] "Uneasy," as one Bible reader wrote, "lies the head that wears the crown."[5] When Samuel became a man, and a sophet in his own right, he would make such notions immortal.

Leaders like Gideon and Deborah, and even to some extent Abimelech, were *ad hoc* chiefs—sophetim, not kings. The necessity that put them in the oral history was normally a military emergency, or a temporary league. Samuel took this for granted. Indeed, as he grew to manhood, Israel faced yet another such emergency, this time from the Philistines, a people so tough and persistent that David himself did not entirely conquer them. By their name, three millennia later we still call Canaan, Palestine. To Samuel, the Philistines, an immigrant European people, were pagans of the worst and least familiar sort. Unlike the still seminomadic Israelites, the Philistines dwelt happily in towns and worshiped a new god called Dagon, whom Samuel found particularly revolting. It was in resistance to the Philistines that Samuel was to find his life's work and Israel to succumb to the blandishments of monarchy at last.

For Samuel was one of those with an urgent and exact sense of right and wrong. He took seriously the vow of his mother Hannah which had "lent" him to Yahveh at birth. When he was still a boy of ten or twelve, Samuel had heard a voice calling "Samuel, Samuel," as he lay down to sleep near the Ark. Thinking it was old Eli, he ran to the priest three times saying, "Here I am," concluding finally on Eli's advice that Yahveh himself had called him. The fourth time he heard the voice, according to *I Samuel* 3, he waited for Yahveh's message, a prophesy which turned out to be as peremptory and exacting as anything even Moses had heard. "I tell [Eli]," said the voice, "that I am about to punish his house forever . . . because his sons were blaspheming God, and he did not restrain them. Therefore I swear to the house of Eli that the iniquity of Eli's house shall not be expiated by sacrifice or offering forever!"

With these words, Samuel's course in life was set. He was not a Levite and not a priest, but God had by the most direct and indubitable method of the times, taken the priesthood out of the hands of Eli's descendants and given Samuel the greater vocation of prophet. No doubt he felt satisfaction. He was a servant, an Ephraimite orphan. For years he had silently observed, at first hand, the rakish behavior of young Hophni and Phineas, Eli's sons and legitimate heirs to the priesthood. All the years he was growing up, these older ones had been extorting fresh meat from the bringers of sacrificial animals, sleeping with women by the tent of meeting, and no doubt joking cynically about the credulity of believers. None are inconceivable acts for hereditary priests, and the boy's reaction is completely conceivable.

Even greater satisfaction awaited Samuel on the day the Philistines attacked and the elders of the tribes decided to go into battle against them bearing the Ark itself from Shiloh as a talisman. On that day the doom of Yahveh was fulfilled, Hophni and Phineas were killed on the field, and Israel totally defeated. Worse, for the first time since it had received the tablets of stone in the wilderness, the Ark itself was captured, an event so dire that Eli fell dead.

Samuel now took charge. He assumed the office of sophet, summoned the tribal elders to Mizpah, and sacrificed to Yahveh. Then he set the army against the oncoming Philistines in a victory which settled the frontier for several years. Even the Ark was returned, with guilt offerings, for the Philistines blamed a plague on its presence. Nevertheless, the fright had been severe and the Philistines had by no means been destroyed—not, at any rate, as thoroughly as the house of Eli. When Samuel grew old and appointed his less able sons as sophetim, he was faced, symmetrically, with exactly Eli's problem. Thoughts of what might happen when he died appear to have panicked the elders, leaders of a social system which time and long settlement had weakened. The elders met with Samuel in his home territory of Ramah and asked him point-blank: "Behold, you are old and your sons do not walk in your ways; now appoint for us a king to govern us like all the nations."

The question had at last been put. Samuel's reply, preserved for us by someone who was most likely not Solomon's court historian, is the act for which he is now remembered. Together with the Jotham parable, it is the oldest antimonarchical document in Western literature, and crystallizes for the first time the reaction of a culture which had never known monarchy to the standard political system of ancient agricultural civilizations. It takes the implicit political beliefs of an originally nomadic tribal federation, where one-man rule was *ad hoc* and sporadic, and makes them explicit:

> This will be the manner of the king that shall reign over you: He will take your sons, and appoint them for himself, for his chariots, and to be his horsemen; and some shall run before his chariots.
>
> And he will appoint him captains over thousands, and captains over fifties; and he will set them to ear his ground, and to reap his harvest, and to make his instruments of war, and instruments of his chariots.
>
> And he will take your daughters to be confectionaries, and to be cooks, and to be bakers.
>
> And he will take your fields, and your vineyards, and your oliveyards, even the best of them, and give them to his servants.
>
> And he will take the tenth of your seed, and of your vineyards, and give them to his officers, and to his servants.
>
> And he will take your menservants, and your maidservants, and your goodliest young men, and your asses, and put them to his work.
>
> He will take a tenth of your sheep: and ye shall be his servants.
>
> And ye shall cry out in that day because of your king which ye shall have chosen you; and the Lord will not hear you in that day.[6]

Quoted endlessly by Puritan revolutionaries in the seventeenth century and American Whigs in the eighteenth, this speech has indeed made history, but it could not do so at the time it is supposed to have been given. The elders of Israel said, "Nay, but we will have a king over us," and Samuel, on Yahveh's advice, gave them monarchy for their sins. He led forth a Benjamite named Saul, gave him his blessing, and watched as the elders acclaimed him *melech* in the sanctuaries of Gilgal and Mizpah.

In vain, apparently, Samuel tried to circumscribe the powers of this new institution while it was in its infancy. In parts of the story, he refers to Saul simply as a chief (*nagid*) rather than as a king. He rails, too, against Saul's disobedience, setting a precedent for future priests as diverse as Gregory VII and John Knox. In the end, however, he failed to control what he had unwillingly created. All he was able to do finally was to replace king Saul by the more able king David.

It is unlikely that Samuel knew when he anointed Jesse's youngest son with holy oil that with that act he had lost his long battle to prevent or even limit the monarchy of Israel. Nevertheless, as the court historian faithfully tells us, little David had, by the end of his life, left little of Samuel's great prophesy unfulfilled. David created a taxation system, a census, a standing army, an appointed priesthood, and a royal bodyguard, the full monarchical apparatus against which even the revolt of a first minister and a favorite son could not prevail. David also put the herdsman's values to rest, literally, by capturing a capital city, Jerusalem, which no tribe could claim, and bringing the Ark there, which ended its wanderings for good. He assembled a harem, domesticating his enemies by the classic means of marrying their daughters to his power. Even before his accession he had prudently taken Saul's daughter as his first wife, after which he systematically (even the court historian is hard put to hide it) exterminated all Saul's supporters and descendants but one, a helpless cripple. He ended his own life as King of Judah, King of Israel, King of Jerusalem, King of Ammon, Governor of Aram (Damascus) and Edom, and Emperor (to use the Roman word) of Moab and Zobah.

Against these tremendous odds, however, Samuel's values stubbornly persisted. In the reign of David's grandson, the northern tribes broke away from the hegemony of David's tribe of Judah. Their monarchy, still beset by resurgent tribalism, became an unstable military despotism with ever-shifting dynasties and capitals. Even defeat and destruction by the Assyrians in the eighth century could not extinguish the stubbornly held values of the tribal republicans, though it did remove the name Israel from the map. When Judah, too, was defeated and exiled by the Babylonian Empire in the sixth century, monarchy perished completely, except as a Messianic vision. In the crucible of the exile, however, Israel survived; and it did so by redefining itself along lines first laid out by Samuel. Unity founded in descent and in faith reemerged to replace the lost unity of secular monarchy.

The fully developed theology which emerges from the exile and which can now at last be called Judaism leaves no room for *melechs*. Yahveh rules over the community called Israel wherever it is, however it may be governed. Kings He makes and breaks, demonstrating thereby His full power over them. In any nation they are instruments of His blessing, or more often, weapons of His wrath. As for Israel, whether or not it exists as a nation, it cannot cease to exist as a *natio*. There is monarchy in heaven, to be sure, for Jews are uniquely monotheist, but in terrestrial politics, republics are a fine thing. Whether one believes or not that it was God himself who proved to Israel that Samuel had been right, Israel thought so and thus made all Western religion in some sense republican.

The Philistines, who provided the original pressure behind Israel's demand for kings, were, ironically, tribal republicans themselves. The archaeologists' latest estimates place them linguistically and culturally with the Achaeans and Trojans of Homer's *Iliad,* and the wanderings of illiterate proto-Greeks over the eastern Mediterranean in the centuries after 1300 B.C. If so, they enter this story twice, and can claim some part in the making of a man whose place in the history of Greece is as secure as Samuel's in the history of Israel.

This is Solon of Athens, a politician of such consummate skill that his people named him to the list of their seven wisest men. Because he lived before the Greeks wrote history, we know no more about him than we know about Samuel who lived four centuries before. Like Samuel, he stood against monarchy, failed in his lifetime, and triumphed posthumously. Unlike Samuel, however, Solon claimed to execute not the will of the gods, but the will of the community and a will of his own. Solon was not a prophet but a politician. He learned from Homer what Samuel had learned from the Israelite tradition, that the heritage of his people was polyarchy, rule by many, but he went on to objectify the system and to develop the first of many practical means to preserve it. Since politics, even as a word, has come down to the West from Greece, we must call Solon an originator of republicanism even though he himself had no word for it.

We do not know when he was born. The eloquent Plutarch is his earliest biographer, but Plutarch wrote nearly seven centuries after Solon's death. Probably Solon reached maturity in about 620 B.C. at a time when Athens was a rather small *polis* or city-state, a dot in the newly expanding Hellenic world which had seeded the eastern Mediterranean from the great polis of Miletus on the coast of Turkey all the way to Syracuse in Sicily and beyond. Athenian democracy was as yet unknown and the brief Golden Age of Pericles, Sophocles, Plato, and Pheidias lay more than a century in the future. Solon's place, we learn, was to set the stage for all that.

Of Solon's education we know even less, but we can be sure of at least one thing: he was literate. Ionian Greece, of which Athens

was genealogically a part, had become literate a century before Solon by borrowing the *alpha-bet* from the same Canaanite people
that Israel had, and using it to write down *The Iliad* and *Odyssey*.
Solon knew the poems intimately. In fact, he was himself a poet,
and founder of the Athenian poetical tradition. To him, Homer was
the beginning of literature, and even more the beginning of wisdom, of politics, and of belief. Together with the classic tales of old
Athens—the rivalry of Athena and Poseidon, the legends of King
Theseus, and the rest of the oral tradition—they gave Solon what
sense he had of his place in the world and of his proper relationship
to the divine multitude on Olympus. However much his people,
the Hellenes, might now appear to be settled farmers, or even merchants, Solon knew them through Homer as patrilineal wanderers,
tamers of horses, who had followed their herds as closely as Abel
and Abraham. Danaeans, Argives, Achaeans, whichever Homer calls
them, remain, despite the most explosive disagreements, the same
people; no less so than the post-Homeric Aeolians, Ionians, and Dorians.

By Solon's time it had been more or less agreed that the common patriarch of all of them was Hellen, son of Deucalion, the
Greek Noah; and that the proper name of his whole people was
Hellenes. Settlement had not healed their divisions, and the jagged
peninsula they settled in created new ones; but even war could not
interfere with common language, culture, and ceremony. At Olym-
pia, as at Homer's Troy, peace was sacred while the Games were
on, and only born Hellenes could compete in them. Similarly,
though each polis had its god or goddess and Olympus was overrun
with deities, it was as clear to Solon as it was to every Hellene that
all of the reigning immortals had, like the mortal Greeks, one father,
Chronos. Presiding over the jarring councils of the gods on Olympus was Zeus, whom Homer called "cloud-gatherer," Chronos' son
and, indeed, his emasculator.

As for Solon's own polis of Athens, everyone knew at the time
that it had been founded by Erecthonios, who had brought the
horse to Attica, and by his grandson Erectheos, whom Homer called
the "high-hearted." Descendants of Hellen's son (or grandson) Ion,
the line of Erectheos was thus Ionian, kin to the Hellenic clans and
cities on the coast of Asia. Erectheos' descendants included Me-
nestheos who had led "fifty black ships" to Troy, Aegeus who had
given his name to the Aegean Sea by throwing himself into it, and

Aegeus' son Theseus who had gone as a slave to Crete, there to overthrow the monstrous tyranny of Minos and Minos' changeling son.

The title of the Erectheids was *basileus*, which we translate as sacred king, but which Solon might have understood differently. Homer gave each polis a *basileus*, but he gave none to Hellas as a whole. In their behavior they are like feudal lords, vassals perhaps of an absent monarch. Agamemnon, the *basileus* who leads the expedition, has power to confiscate a concubine from his fellow *basileus*, Achilles, but not enough to make him fight.[7] In *The Iliad* and *The Odyssey*, Hellas is governed through assemblies where the rule is murderous squabble. In assembly Achilles may call Agamemnon a "dog-eyed, deer-hearted sot," and even a common soldier may charge him with insolence. True, Odysseus, *basileus* of Ithaca, wallops the soldier for saying so, but as sovereign, Homer's Agamemnon is closer to Lewis Carroll's Red Queen than he is to Louis XIV.[8]

Hellas had no *basileus* in Solon's time. Even Athens didn't have one. In the eleventh century B.C., Kodros, last of the Erectheids, had died defending Athens against the Dorians. The story had it that since no one could be found worthy to succeed him, monarchy was ended. Since then Athens, like most of the city-states of Greece, had been governed by an aristocratic council called the Areopagos and an assortment of magistrates called *archons*, one of whom, called the *archon basileus*, performed the religious duties proper to the former patriarch. These offices were reserved for the heads of clans, called as a group the *Eupatridai* (well-fathered). Solon was one of them.

We now know that the stories Solon would have grown up with are not merely fabulous. Critical history, itself a Greek invention, has been increasingly kind to the oral tradition that educated sixth-century Athens. Minos really existed, not one king but a dynasty of despots who spoke and wrote Greek and whose title was not *basileus* but *wanax*. A *wanax* was a real king, not a war leader. Minos really had a labyrinthine palace on Crete, from which he and his appointees appear to have established naval supremacy throughout the Aegean Sea. His monarchy, and its successor monarchies like Pylos on the mainland, taxed and ordered with such professional efficiency that they could record nearly every chattel in the realm, down to the names of one poor subject's favorite oxen (Blacky and Glossy).

About the middle of the fifteenth century B.C. Minos fell, his southern Aegean capitals torn by earthquake, fire, and flood. It is in no way unlikely that a real prince Theseus of Athens figured in these disasters and helped to make permanent the fall of the Cretan monarchy. For more than a thousand years thereafter the word *wanax* fell into disuse and the Hellene cities maintained the independence gained at Minos' expense. Not until Alexander would they submit as a people to the rule of one person, and during a millennium of separate development, each Greek polis became so unique that Aristotle was able to define political science simply by describing about a score of them.

Thus, Hellas as a whole became a republic by 1400 B.C., and by 800 B.C. almost every individual polis had also become a republic. Why this happened is hard to specify at a time when the Greeks had lost the art of writing, but the closer one comes, the more the legends ring true. The limited monarchies of Homer's Agamemnon and Odysseus seem to have been the rule between 1400 and 1300 or so B.C. Invasions of less civilized (though no less Hellenic) nomads further reduced the scope of monarchy after that time.

The Ionians, who began this process by taking over Athens when it still paid tribute to Minos, were attacked by the still more nomadic Dorians in the twelfth century B.C. Athens held, but the Dorians were successful to the south and west. Other groups went further. The enormous nomadic movement brought Greek-speaking tribes as far as Egypt, the Caucasus, and Palestine by 1000 B.C. We might call this a barbarian invasion, but to the Hellenes a barbarian was one who said *bar-bar-bar* when he tried to speak Greek and none of these peoples had that problem. Their culture, in fact, is the one we find more than any other in Homer, a culture of ritual combat, reciprocal gift, kinship, patronage, and vendetta. The Greeks repeatedly returned to childhood, as the Egyptian explained to Solon, but in the process they also repeatedly renewed their tribal heritage, which was, like Israel's, deeply antimonarchic.

At any rate, by the time of the First Olympiad in 776 B.C., a century and a half before Solon, the lore of Greece was full of kings but the actual landscape, except for Argos, was bare of them. Sparta had kings, but always two at a time, which is not monarchy but dyarchy. The dynasties of Atreus, Erectheos, Cadmus, and Creon had vanished into time. In their place were councils of aristocrats like the Bacchiads of Corinth (originally a dynasty), the Penthelids of Mytilene, the Hippeis (horsemen) of Eretria, the Hippobotai (horse-herders) of Chalcis, the Spartiates of Sparta, and of course the Eupatrids of Athens.

Solon, however, was an exceptional noble. Ordinarily the clan heads' sense of hierarchy was so overdeveloped, and their sense of political alternatives so meager, that one is rightly uneasy about calling them republicans. The Hellene aristocrats make their first appearance in nonepic literature around 800 B.C. when the poet Hesiod complains of their ignorance, their abuse of working people, and their responsibility for the Iron Age in which the poet feels condemned to live. In the 700s B.C., the "cradle of democracy" is ruled by nobles. All magistrates, all military officers, all priests, are members of a small circle of the best families. All land is parceled out to them; all wealth beyond subsistence is concentrated in their possession; and citizenship in the polis itself is coming to mean kinship with them. This is the fully developed aristocratic republic, now almost extinct but for millennia typical of the governments of ancient and medieval Europe. Like Samuel's Israel, and Hellas as a whole, each polis had become a chiefless federation of clans (*genoi* or *phylai* in Greek) held together by their interspersed landholdings, by religious duty, and by rites too venerable, as yet, to analyze. The sacred fire, emblem of common, patrilineal ancestry, was kept perpetually burning on the *akropoleis* of a thousand cities, focusing ("focus" was the Roman word for this flame) the loyalty of a still tribal people. The system had lasted for centuries, and seemed as durable as the fires.

Durable, but not unchallenged, as Solon knew. The "well-fathered" were under attack in Athens and all over Hellas when Solon was growing up in the seventh century B.C. From Miletos to Syracuse, the aristocratic republics were threatened by a new form of one-man rule, called in Greek *tyrannia*. In an unprecedented self-propagating crisis, each Greek polis seemed to reach a peak of class conflict, dissolve into social revolution, and emerge with an unconstitutional dictator. Basileus was an inadequate term to describe these illegitimate despots. Except for Pheidon of Argos, they had neither the nobles' lineage nor their respect for law. Their power was absolute, independent of custom, constitution, and religion. Only among the oppressed and benighted Asians did such a thing exist as a monarch whose word was law. From these barbarians, real barbarians who spoke no Greek, the resourceful Greeks borrowed the word *tyrannos*. It meant, and still means, a leader in whom all the powers of the state are vested at once.

Always in the past, the polis' name, or the name of its god, had stood for all its inhabitants, its territory, its policies. In the seventh century, however, we hear a new address. Instead of speaking of the Corinthians, the ancient writers personify Corinth as a man, Kypselos or Periander. The city of Sicyon is referred to as Orthagoras or Kleisthenes, Epidauros as Prokles. Mytilene in Asia Minor has no policy but a leader named Pittakos does. The survival of the republics was much in doubt, and so was the survival of the republicans.

The conflict was a real one, having little to do with any competing idealisms. Aristotle wrote in the *Politics*: "The tyrant springs from the people, from the mob, and directs his efforts against the upper classes, to the end that the people may not be oppressed by them."[9] All later historians have echoed his judgment. Given the choice between republican institutions and social justice, Hellas was opting for justice—and populist monarchy. Tyranny was the means by which the rule of the knights of the eighth century was broken in the seventh and sixth. Though rule by the few survived and even prospered in Hellas, the events of this crisis period prevented it from ever again meaning mere rule by the heads of clans.

Why did this happen when it did? Essentially because Hellas was no longer in a very primitive stage. For one thing its armies had become democratized. Instead of a small band of mounted nobles leading a rabble of clients, the polis was now defended by the famous *phalanx*, serried ranks of equally armed, equally trained citizen infantrymen. Equal on the battlefield, militiamen demanded more equality in politics, and since they were armed they tended to get it.

No less important were the rise of colonization and commerce. Together with the invention of coinage, they created a new inequality of wealth and gave artisans and merchants a source of power comparable to the horses, land, and lineage of the knights. The lower-class resentment of Hesiod's time now faced two ruling classes instead of just one, and all were armed. Conflict became acute.

When the revolts of the nobles finally broke out, however, lack of any precedent made the stakes terribly high. The regime was incomparably ancient and the struggle against it correspondingly bloody. Then, too, as so often happens, the newly free soon yearned for new bonds. The revolutionaries demanded tyranny to end disorder, if indeed they had not already used tyranny to produce it. In order to carry through wholesale reforms like the expansion of executive councils, the opening of military commands to a new class, the separation of kinship from politics, and the redistribution of land, tyranny seemed the only alternative to class war. Stormy Mytilene had three unrelated dictators in a generation, overthrowing each other and exiling each other's supporters. Megara had years of anarchy. Of all the great cities only Sparta seemed to escape dictatorship. Sparta's tightly organized solution, however, despite its republicanism, soon came to remind so many Hellenes of the barracks or the anthill that they thought it worse even than tyranny.

Populist or not, tyrants soon showed themselves vulnerable to all the typical vices of monarchy. Once in control, the champions of the people began to delight in wealth, status, and power for its own sake. Efforts at reform at home soon gave way to dreams of empire abroad. Herodotos, whose bias against tyranny is the central theme of his *Histories*, tells how Polykrates of Samos was lured by the promise of gold to the court of the Persian governor of Sardis, who hung him on a cross as a monument to avarice. Why did Polykrates want the gold? Because, says Herodotos, he was the first since Minos of Crete to dream of a maritime empire in the Aegean, and he needed to finance a navy. Another imperialist, Periander of Corinth, followed up his conquest of Corcyra by castrating three hundred Corcyrean boys of good family and sending them to Persia as slaves. One might call this populism, but Gelo of Syracuse had not even that excuse when he conquered Megara. There he is said to have taken the common people—all of them—and sold them into slavery. "The masses," he is supposed to have said, "are very disagreeable to live with."[10]

With power and imperial ambition came the inevitable pettiness of absolutism. Kleisthenes of Sicyon ordered the Homeric festivals ended in his polis because Homer's Agamemnon was from Argos, and Argos was the enemy of Sicyon. As for Gelo of Syracuse, he refused to help Hellas against King Xerxes because he would not be allowed to command the joint army.

The tyrants, too, saw their interest in cooperating with each other against counterrevolution at home and the surviving republics abroad. Periander of Corinth, in Herodotos' famous story, sent to Thrasybulos of Miletos for advice on how to hold power. Thrasybulos took Periander's messenger into a wheatfield, said nothing, and systematically cut off the ears of the tallest stalks. The messenger reported back to Corinth in confusion, but Periander got the message anyway, find the best and destroy them.

Finally, tyranny may have been temporary at its beginnings, but it quickly became hereditary as tyrants indulged their natural desire to pass it all along to their kin. The first tyrant of Corinth was Kypselos. By the time his grandson Psammetichos began to reign sixty-five years later, hereditary rule must have seemed as inescapable as the tide. In Sicyon, the descendants of Orthagoras were still ruling after more than a century. Gela and Syracuse to the west were also ruled by dynasties for most of their postrevolutionary history.

In short, if any sixth-century Greek other than Solon had been inclined to write a history, he would have had to end it with the new monarchy. The remaining Greek republicans, most of them discredited aristocrats, could say only, along with their poet, Theognis of Megara:

> ... never dream
> (Tranquil and undisturbed, as it may seem)
> Of future peace or safety to the state
> Bloodshed and strife will follow soon or late.[11]

Against this background, around 600 B.C., the crisis came to Athens. Parties had already formed around the existing social classes. The regional "Coast" party, representing wealth, opposed the "Plain" party, representing birth. Even more extreme in its demands for reform was the "Mountain" party, from which Robespierre's Jacobins later borrowed their name. It represented, according to our best guess, the small farmers of Attica, most of whom cropped shares for great landowners. A classic oppressed peasantry, they sometimes sold themselves and their children for debt. The *horoi,* stone markers signifying mortgage, stood beside the earth of their ancestors and statues of the boundary gods, solid reminders of a permanent and exasperating dependence.

Tyranny had already been tried. In the 630s B.C., when Solon was a young man, an Olympic champion named Kylon had tried to seize the Acropolis and had been assassinated by members of a Eupatrid clan. Athens' republican institutions, in the hands of the "well-fathered" were under attack for generations of accumulated injustice. They seemed expendable.

And so, sometime in the 590s B.C., the partisans of tyranny came in secret to the man they thought best qualified, and proposed to him a plot to take over the state and put him at the head of it. This was Solon, a fine example of that most dangerous breed of politician, the disaffected aristocrat.

Solon must have been a unique figure already. Plutarch describes him as uniting four qualities seldom if ever found in one person: single-minded patriotism, an integrity proper to the haughtiest aristocrat, political genius, and a free-ranging intelligence that allowed him to entertain the most unprecedented ideas and strategies with coolness and deliberation. If it is true, as Plutarch insists, that he was "involved neither in the extortions of the rich nor the privations of the poor," then he must have been the only man in Athens who wasn't. Perhaps his aristocratic birth preserved him from the conflicts that centered around the new wealth. So cleverly did Solon play his hand that ancient writers were still debating, centuries later, whether he had been drafted for his magistracy or whether he had actively solicited it.

He was clearly ambitious. That is to say, he wanted the job of saving the Athenian state. He had an entire program of unheard-of measures in mind for accomplishing the goal. Yet, despite the fact that the program would be hard for all classes to swallow, and would require great power and prestige to force down the throats of his fellow Athenians, Solon genuinely wanted to administer it without violence and without becoming a tyrant. In this he was not only unique in Hellas, but the master of the art of politics. "Tyranny," he told his amazed and disappointed friends, "is a fine place in itself but there is no way down from it."[12] But the real question was how to avoid it.

To begin with, he would have to come to power constitutionally. Not an easy task. Though, as leader of an ancient clan, Solon was eligible for the nine archonships into which royal power was now divided, he could not be all nine at once. Nor could he hold any one of the archonships for more than a year, for the Eupatrids had not only divided the king's power in pieces but limited it in time as well. Moreover, the main power in Athens was not the *archon basileus,* who performed the rites, or the *polemarch,* who commanded the army, or even the "first archon," who drafted laws, but instead the whole college of former archons called the *Areopagos,* which proposed laws to the assembly (*Ekklesia*) and also applied them as a court. For Solon to reform the Athenian constitution without violating it, it was clear that he would have to be First Archon, dominate the Areopagos, command the Ekklesia, and do the entire job in a single year.

Such are the obstacles that a fully developed aristocratic republican constitution puts in the way of general reform. The division and subdivision of power continues in all dimensions as each new generation of clan heads indulges its mutual suspicion. The legislative process is paralyzed by the paradox that great power can exist while even the most ingenious cannot find a way to use it. The republic as a whole can have no tactics, only the long-term strategy of the class from which all the magistrates are drawn. Policy is their mutual interest, if any; and when there actually is a policy, it tends to be almost Olympian in its continuity, like the century-long program of the Roman Republic to destroy Carthage.

Yet Solon was determined to try to be both a republican and a reformer. Accordingly, that year, probably 594 B.C., he "ran" for First Archon, and was chosen by his peers no doubt in the mistaken assumption, carefully fostered by Solon, that as one of their class he would rebuild Athens to suit them. As he entered on his office there was a moment of suspended animation in Attica. Each class had that prerevolutionary expectation that it would be vindicated and made secure against all the others. Solon must have had the wit to anticipate and use this mood. In the end, he wrote proudly, *nobody* was satisfied:

> . . . *the people once placed*
> *Extravagant hopes in me, but now they are angry*
> *And look askance, as if I were their enemy.*[13]

He began with the peasants. At a sudden stroke he put through a cancelation of all debts on land and uprooted the *horoi* markers throughout Attica. The peasants gratefully baptized the law *seisachtheia* (shaking-off of burdens) and jumped *en masse* onto Solon's bandwagon. Eupatrids and newly landed rich were furious, but forbore for at least two reasons, the power of the masses and the fact that Solon could very easily have dispossessed them completely. In a grace note, Solon proved his own good faith by canceling a large land debt that was owed to him personally.

There were other poor people besides the peasants. Solon carried their support by changing the value of the *mina* from 73 to 100 *drachmas*, which incidentally is the first currency devaluation of which we have record. Large creditors, as furious as the landowners, went along because given their head the debtors might have cut off theirs. "In great affairs," wrote Solon, "you cannot please all parties," which for him was not a lament but a policy.[14]

It was probably at this point that the stunned Eupatrids handed over to their renegade member the remaining important offices of state. Solon now had full authority in all councils and complete rights to alter or abolish institutions. It was unconstitutional, and it was, for the moment anyway, monarchical. The republic was, for the remainder of the year, dependent for its survival on its judgment of one man's character. This was *aisymnetia*, which Aristotle called elective monarchy and what we would probably call Bonapartism. Fortunately, Solon was not tempted. Solon congratulated himself that:

> [anyone else], . . . would not have forborne nor stopped where I did
> Till he had shaken up the laws of the state
> And skimmed the cream for himself.[15]

Solon wanted only reputation and, being a poet, made his own.

Armed with his new powers, Solon proceeded to repeal the entire criminal code, which consisted of Draco's laws of the last century, whose severity has given us the word "draconian." He replaced it with a code of his own, not only more lenient, but more clever, with statutes that still testify both to his human understanding and to his penchant for novelty. His marriage laws required husbands to initiate sexual intercourse at least three times a month. The penalty in cases of impotence was for the wife to divorce and marry her husband's kinsman. A tribesman's law, that, like the one abolishing dowries, but perhaps he believed in love, too. It was Solon's legislation that first provided for the control of stray dogs, or made it mandatory to speak well of the dead; and it was one of his laws that first dealt justly with the silent majority. This one took the vote away from anyone "who, in the event of revolution, does not take one side or the other."[16]

The great centerpiece of the reform, however, was Solon's new "constitution." The Greeks did not have a word for this, and *politeia* does not quite describe the set of laws which define how all other laws are made. Most important of these were the laws defining citizenship, class, and class prerogative, and on them would depend Solon's hope of accomplishing lasting reform without destroying the republic. It was here that Solon took a leap in the dark and set aside the old kinship system in favor of one based essentially on wealth.

Every man born of free Attic parents was automatically a citizen of Athens. He was, just as automatically, a member of his clan and tribe. Solon now assigned him to an additional class based on his annual income. If he grossed five hundred measures a year or more (wet or dry), he was a member of the highest class, the *Pentakosi-omedimnoi* or Five Hundred Bushel Men. Middle classes he named *Hippeis* (Knights) or *Zeugitai* (Yoke-of-Oxen Men). The lowest class, with two hundred measures a year or less, he called *Thetes* (singular, *Thes*). Having made the new classes, he now opened the sacrosanct magistracies to the top three of them. Just by being rich, one could now become Archon, Treasurer, Tax Farmer, Secretary of the Areopagos, Prison Superintendent, Finance Secretary, or any of the innumerable and mostly ancient offices into which the original power of the king was now divided. It also meant that the ill-fathered rich would in a generation form a majority of the all-powerful Areopagos, because the Areopagos was co-opted from the ranks of former archons.

This was the ultimate betrayal of Solon's own class, the old aristocracy. By it, the principle of graduated plutocracy, rule by the richer, was introduced into the highest offices in the state. Even here, however, Solon refused to go all the way. In a by now familiar compromise, Solon kept the old tribal divisions and created a new executive council to represent them. It was called the Council of Four Hundred, since it had a hundred members from each of the old four tribes of Attica. We do not know how its members were chosen, but it is pretty clear that Solon meant it to placate the aristocracy, while at the same time drawing the second rank of clan leadership into a political role that had previously been exercised only by their superiors, the clan heads. This domesticated the counterrevolution and made it responsible. The Ekklesia would continue to check any tendency it might show toward arrogance, because whatever the Four Hundred proposed, the Ekklesia could still say no to it.

Solon went even further. The lowly Thetes, who had no political weapon beyond their vote in the Ekklesia, would not be able to prevent the return of oppression without some other office. Solon had barred them from the magistracies. Now he gave them the right to sit on juries in any court or case that required them. He also made all decisions in the magistrates' courts, which had no jury, subject to appeal in a special court called the *Heliaia*. The Heliaia had no judge at all. It was nothing but a monster jury of upward of two hundred Thetes. According to Aristotle, it was the mass popular juries of the Heliaia, more than anything else, that transformed Athens into a democracy. In three generations the Thetes were ruling Athens and Solon's merciful gesture had become the ultimate grant of democratic power.

Democracy, however, though it does not go badly with republics, never entered Solon's mind. He thought naturally in terms of class, and except for his imaginative leap from the old world of kinship into the new one of wealth, he was completely unsympathetic to the idea of equality. Like a reforming Victorian peer, he was happy to improve the lot of the lower orders yet blissfully unaware that some of the peasants might want to become peers on their own. It would be absurd to blame him for this, since his contemporaries were all as blind as he was. Blinder in fact, since they had already given Solon credit for the most farsighted act in their political history. Later generations would number him with Thales among the Seven Wise Men of all Hellas.

It worked. As the year of Solon's archonship drew to a close it was clear that despite political passions, his reforms were supported by enough members of each class to eliminate the threat of civil war. Asked if he had given Athens the best of laws, Solon would only say, "the best they would accept," but in the real world of politics it amounts to the same thing.[17] In fact the stage had been set for an economic boom that would last more than a generation, and Athenian primacy in Hellas.

There was nothing to do but resign. Astonishingly, he did so. The next year, probably 593 B.C., he confounded the hopes of his allies and friends by leaving office when his term was up; a final demonstration of the integrity that was both aristocratic and peculiarly Solon's own. The Hellenic cities had no provision, as Rome was to have, for emergency monarchies which the law took to be temporary. Here again the precedent was set by Solon of Athens.

He compounded this extraordinary act by leaving Athens for ten years. Plutarch reports that his motive for doing so was to avoid being asked to comment or enlarge on his own code, or, in other words, that Solon's belief in the sanctity of written law was such that he went into voluntary exile to save that principle. Solon could have given no greater witness to his faith in either the sanctity of law or the division of power. After all when Socrates was urged to go into exile a century later, he replied that leaving Athens was a fate worse than death.

The great republican made the best of his exile, turning it into a commercial and educational tour of the eastern Mediterranean.

Charming stories relate how he met Aesop, learned about Atlantis from the priests of Egypt, built a new city on Cyprus, and aroused the wrath of King Croesus of Lydia by denying that wealth brought happiness.

The famous story of Solon and Croesus also points to a final irony in the lives of both men which is an exquisite as any in Greek literature. The king gave the republican the grand tour, the story goes, but Solon was unimpressed by the luxuries of Asian monarchy. Fishing for compliments, Croesus asked if there ever was anyone luckier than he was. Yes, said Solon, and began naming them: a poor Athenian soldier named Tellus, two young brothers named Cleobis and Biton. . . . Enough, said Croesus, raging. Solon quickly explained himself. Tellus, Cleobis, and Biton had died happy. Croesus was still alive:

> The future bears down on each one of us with all the hazards
> of the unknown, and we can only count a man happy when the
> gods grant him good fortune to the end.[18]

It was Hellene wisdom, which Croesus really did not understand until many years later when the emperor of Persia attacked Lydia, defeated Croesus, sacked his city, and tied him to the stake. It is said that as the torch was lit, Croesus cried out three times, "Solon! Solon! Solon!" It is also said that the emperor of Persia then spared Croesus' life in order to hear the story. One wonders if the most recent monarch of Persia had ever heard it.

As for Solon, he returned to Athens, growing old, as he said, "always learning." But nemesis found him too. In one of the last remaining years of his life he saw the republic overthrown. It was, says Plutarch, in 561 B.C. Solon was in the square when a young reformer named Peisistratos, head of the old Mountain Party, arrived brandishing a self-inflicted wound and shouting that a rich man's conspiracy was out to assassinate him. As the mob gathered, Solon approached. He began to speak against them. "Son of Hippokrates," he roared at his political disciple, "this is not the Homeric way . . . . you are doing [this] to mislead your fellow citizens."[19]

No one believed him. The Thetes met in the Ekklesia and voted Peisistratos a bodyguard of fifty armed men. Solon rose and demanded the floor. Nobody listened. He turned to leave. Peisistratos took his bodyguard to the acropolis, seized it, and made himself tyrant for life.

Solon went back to the square, appealing to all who would listen to stop being foolish, take heart, and refuse to surrender their liberty. Tyranny, he said, was easy to stop while it was hatching, but took nobility and courage to destroy once it was full-grown. No one had the courage, except Solon. All alone he walked back to his house. There he took out his arms and armor, placed them on the street in front of the door, and declared, "I have done all that was in my power to help my country and uphold its laws."[20]

> We can only count a man happy when the gods grant him good fortune to the end.

Any Greek tragedian would drop his curtain here. A hero has been brought low and some divine principle demonstrated. History, however, is not so clean-cut as drama. According to Plutarch, Solon survived even this awful moment "still learning." Finding himself still alive, he first resorted to the Samuel pose of moral irreconcilability. Arms folded, he withdrew from politics altogether. He was old by now, too defenseless to imprison, and too much of a paragon to be anything less than a martyr dead. Knowing this, he spoke and wrote against the tyranny every chance he had, and scoffed at his friends when they warned him not to get killed.

A year passed and Solon continued hale, his persona ragged and fitting worse and worse. Peisistratos was a truly excellent politician, fascinating to a past master like Solon. For one thing, he was an unusually constitutional tyrant. He did not abolish the magistracies, he simply filled them with his own supporters. He left all Solon's laws intact. In due time Solon found himself accepting the tyrant's invitations to dinner. If Plutarch is to be believed, the old republican "actually became [Peisistratos'] adviser and approved many of his measures."[21] Never ceasing to learn as one grows old is an attitude that makes a terrible mess of martyrdom. Thus did the man who startled Hellas by refusing a tyranny end his life as a monarch's courtier.

Even in death Solon broke a rule. In an age when all bodies were buried, Solon is said to have had his body Homerically cremated and the ashes scattered on the island of Salamis. Perhaps, with his usual practicality, he meant to prevent his corpse being subject to what he knew would be a steady rhythm of praise and blame.

Was he a failure? Perhaps not. The scanty contemporary records show that for thirty years after his archonship Athens had no tyr-

anny. In the 580s B.C. it is true, there were years when there was
no archon at all, and one two-year period when an archon remained
in office past his term and had to be removed by force. Still, by 561,
when Peisistratos took power, the old struggles were much muted.
The mildness of the new tyranny shows that.

Moreover, it did not last. In 510–507 B.C. the heirs of Peisistratos
were overthrown by an aristocratic faction, the Alkmeonids, and the
restored republic lasted a hundred years. Solon's mark was on it.
The Alkmeonids were not able to restore the old tribal system, and
in fact had to eliminate kinship entirely from the political design of
Athens. Their divisions were based entirely on geography. With
some cynicism, the Alkmeonid leader Kleisthenes called the new
order "democracy," but the cynicism quickly went out of fashion.
In short order, the *demos* (people) quickly assumed and used the
power with which Kleisthenes had tried to patronize them, putting
an end not only to tyranny in Athens but also the aristocratic republic. Any citizen could now become an archon, and as often as
not, he was, since the choice was made by lot.

Once established, the democratic republic created for Athens
the reputation she has enjoyed ever since. In 490 B.C., she led the
Hellenic republics in the historic victory over King Darius of Persia.
Eleven years later, at Salamis, Athens halted the expansion of the
largest empire and the most classic absolute monarchy the world
had yet seen. This republican triumph was followed by what has
come to be called the Golden Age.

Nor did the democratic republic neglect the duty to tame its
magistrates. Great leaders were elected, used, and promiscuously
deposed whenever their ambitions seemed to threaten the public
thing. Solon had made magistrates impeachable and plotting tyranny punishable by death. Democracy added "ostracism"—exile for
any Athenian whom the republic, by majority vote, deemed un-
comfortable. This happened even to the victor of Marathon, Mil-
tiades, who was impeached, and the architect of Salamis,
Themistokles, who was ostracized. To get a stable magistracy, Athenians turned to the ten *strategoi* or generals, who had one-year
terms like everyone else, but who could be reelected if necessary.
This was the basis of the power of Pericles, the major politician in
the era of Socrates and Aristophanes.

In the end, the democratic republic of Athens was not overthrown by a magistrate, but in a way that Solon could not have
predicted or prepared against. The agent was the *demos* itself. Im-

perceptibly, the people of Athens succumbed to the classic temptation to rule the world, and initiated the political changes by which empire abroad leads to monarchy at home. They turned their allies into dependents, built a navy, attacked those who stood in their way, and reduced the public share of the fruits of victory. In 431 B.C., the *demos* overreached itself and ran afoul of Sparta while trying to checkmate Corinth. Sparta demanded that Athens restore the cities of Hellas to full independence. Athens refused and, to defend what had become her empire, began the war which has been called the suicide of Greece.

Nearly thirty years of the horrors of the Peloponnesian War made even Socrates despair of self-government.[22] In 404 B.C., Spartan victory and Athenian exhaustion brought tyranny back to Solon's city. This time the Athenians threw it off, but less than a century later, when King Philip and Alexander the Great defeated the Athenians at Chaeronea and the *strategos* Demosthenes fled from the battlefield, nothing was left of the supreme self-confidence of the republic. So Athens cheered when Philip called an assembly of the cities in Corinth in 338 B.C., assumed the hegemony of Hellas, and required each polis to agree never again to change its constitution. When the more successful imperialists of a later republic made Hellas into a Roman province in 146 B.C., they reserved for Athens (alone with Sparta in all of Hellas) the crowning irony of allowing her consitution to survive unchanged. It was an empty but filial gesture, amply justified by the closeness with which the history of the Roman Republic would parallel that of her Athenian ancestor.

In Israel the republic had succeeded, in the long run, by removing its monarch from present reality to an apocalyptic utopia. Prophecy energized it and prophecy preserved it. In the Hellenic experience, politics may seem less effective than prophecy, since even a politician of extraordinary gifts like Solon was never able to make an arrangement of political forces which could remain divided but balanced for more than a generation, much less for centuries. The long view, however, must assign the greatest importance to neither prophecy nor praxis, but to the living tribal tradition which managed, through Israel and Hellas alike and against the longest of historical odds, to form the political culture of the West.

3

From Brutus to Brutus
The Rise and Fall of Rome

WHEN ATHENS elected Solon in 593 B.C., Rome was a turgid, aggressive little city-state of uncertain origins and prospects. She was about a hundred and fifty years old and living, like many non-Greek upland cities, under a monarchy similar to those of Dark-Age Greece. Her dynasty was foreign—Etruscan, not Latin—but it held the same place in Rome's political life as the house of Erectheus and Kodros had held in that of Athens. Kings remained kings by noble consensus. They led in war, initiated laws, and took first place in the public rites of Rome's religion. In concert with a council of clan heads called the Senate (from the Latin *senex* = old) and a ceremonial assembly of the clans called the *Comitia Curiata* (from the Latin *curia* = brotherhood), they ruled the state for the benefit of its best families. The families, in turn, took care of numerous tenants, clients, and assorted hangers-on. Nothing in this was unusual. In fact, there would be little interest in studying the Roman example of city-state politics, except that Rome, unlike the rest, realized the old city-state dream of conquering all the others. Thus, it is the Roman Republic and not the Athenian that has become the classic example of the seductions of empire and of the effects of an aggressive foreign policy on republican institutions.

Nowadays, when all anyone seems to know about the Roman Empire is that it fell, comparisons are constantly offered between the Romans and the Americans which have little to do with historical reality. Most attractive is the one which assumes that the "fall of Rome," like the soon expected fall of America, was due to moral weakness and gross (preferably sexual) self-indulgence. The analogy would be less foolish if it were the case that Roman morality declined in the fifth century A.D., when the barbarians came. Actually, the first complaints about the city's moral decline were heard in the second century B.C. at a time when Rome was not falling but rising and there was as yet no such thing as an emperor. We live in a country founded by colonial gentlemen who not only understood Roman history but were fond of quoting it in Latin. Recently, the United States has produced a generation of leaders who do not even know that Rome was a republic and that it did not become a hereditary monarchy until the emperor Augustus gave up on the old constitution at about the time of Christ.

It is a real pity that this history is now so little known, for the analogies—the true analogies—between the Roman Republic and our own remain striking. Their hatred of monarchy was enduring, dating from the time they expeled their kings, and their belief in constitutional checks and balances was the product of years of practical experience. There are even individual events in Roman history which retain frightening immediacy, like the tale of the Gracchi. Two brothers, aristocratic members of the senatorial class, took office as champions of the poor between 135 and 120 B.C. First the older, then the younger Gracchus passed laws to benefit the poor and disenfranchised. First the older, then the younger one was assassinated.

The differences between the ancient world and the twentieth century are profound, but not profound enough to make these analogies cheap. The five-hundred-year experience of the Roman republic is simply too valuable to lose.

At the time of Solon, Rome was a kingdom. At the time of Augustus, 31 B.C.–14 A.D., Rome was again ruled by one man. These five centuries are the centuries of the Republic. History, with its curious flair for coincidence, has bracketed the era with two great republicans, one at the beginning and one at the end of this era. Both, as it happens, were members of the family of the Junii and both bore the cognomen of Brutus.

Thanks to Shakespeare and other vulgarizers, the name Brutus is still familiar to us. From Shakespeare we have an image of Caesar dying while Brutus strikes the most unkindest cut of all. We may know, too, that Dante put a Brutus in the bottom of the *Inferno* and that Michelangelo and Jacques Louis David did portraits of one or the other. Our image of the noble Roman, however, is rather tenuous, and many are unaware that there were two of them. The Brutus who helped assassinate Caesar and lost the ears of his countrymen to Mark Antony, is the last one. The Brutus who, in David's painting, presided over the execution of his sons is the first. Between the two lies much history: the conquests of Italy, Carthage, Greece, and Gaul; Cato and Scipio, Regulus and Cincinnatus; and the long strife-torn development of one of the most finely articulated constitutions in republican history. The first Brutus founded the Republic in about 510 B.C.; and the second killed himself in 42 B.C. after failing to save it.

Brutus the founder, Lucius Junius Brutus, was actually the nephew of the king he deposed, Tarquinius Superbus (Tarquin the Proud). Rome's last king was, says the historian Livy, a usurper as well as a menace. On his accession in 535 B.C., he had executed a number of senators who had supported the previous incumbent and threatened the constitution by taking capital cases away from the courts and foreign policy away from the Senate. Brutus was of royal blood and could easily have considered himself a beneficiary of this policy, but he had been alienated early.

Brutus's brother was one of the first aristocrats executed by Tarquin. The effect of this may be judged by the similar case of Lenin.

For some years Brutus bided his time by playing the fool. It was this form of low profile that got him the name of Brutus, which is Latin for stupid. Tarquin and his sons took regular advantage of their idiot relative's pose. They confiscated all his property and kept him about to amuse them. One day the king, faced with an extraordinary omen, sent two of his sons to question the faraway oracle at Delphi, and they took Brutus along for sport. Delphi was not to be addressed lightly, so the whole party took gifts, including Brutus, who brought a nice stick of wood. His cousins had a good laugh, and so did Brutus, for the stick was hollow and enclosed a rod of solid gold. In the sanctum of the goddess at Delphi, the two princes hesitantly asked their father's question, and one of their own in the bargain: which of them would be the next king?

From the depths of the cavern came the mysterious answer: 'He who shall be first to kiss his mother shall hold in Rome supreme authority.'[1]

While the princes were drawing lots so as not to have to fight over their mother when they returned, their half-witted cousin "accidentally" tripped and there, face down on the soil of Delphi, kissed Mother Earth.

The oracle would be fulfilled, but not by magic. Brutus needed allies. He needed, also, for Tarquin to make a misstep in his exploitation of fear and division in the Roman aristocracy. Judicial murder was not a sufficient outrage, but in this primitive, rigidly patriarchal society, rape and adultery were crimes without peer. Thus it was that, in 510 B.C. when Sextus Tarquinius, prince of the blood, took a fancy to the virtuous Lucretia Collatinus, the days of the monarchy were numbered.

Sextus attacked her one night after dinner in the house of the noble Collatinus, her husband.

> She was asleep. Laying his left hand on her breast, 'Lucretia,' he whispered, 'not a sound! I am Sextus Tarquinius. I am armed— if you utter a word I will kill you!' Lucretia opened her eyes in terror; death was imminent, no help at hand. Sextus urged his love, begged her to submit, pleaded, threatened, used every weapon that might conquer a woman's heart. But in vain; not even the fear of death could bend her will.[2]

This paragon did yield, however, when Sextus finally threatened to frame her for adultery with a servant. The next day, with Sextus gone, Lucretia summoned Collatinus, told him her story and, leaving the sequel in his hands, plunged a dagger into her heart. This superb gesture was followed by another. While the husband stood "weeping helplessly,"

> Brutus drew the bloody dagger from Lucretia's body, and holding it before him cried: 'By this girl's blood—none more chaste till a tyrant wronged her—and by the gods, I swear that with sword and fire, and whatever else can lend strength to my arm, I will pursue Lucius Tarquinius the Proud, his wicked wife, and all his children, and never again will I let them or any other man be king in Rome.'[3]

Those present took the oath and Brutus marched to the forum, which was packed, and gave a fiery speech about the evils of tyranny and Tarquin's viper brood. The king, who had been away on campaign, returned to find the city armed against him. Brutus meanwhile had reached Tarquin's army and turned it against him. The old king was checkmated. Once in control, Brutus called the comitia and instead of creating a new king, carried a law abolishing monarchy entirely. Two annual officials, *consuli,* were elected to inherit his power.

The consuls elected were Lucius Junius Brutus and Lucius Tarquinius Collatinus, and so it was that a feud in the royal family became an excuse for the founding of the greatest republic of the ancient world. Thus, says Livy, did the hatred of kings become the ruling passion of Roman politics.

Livy's story, of course, is pure legend. He wrote it down nearly six centuries after the event. Still, it is not the truth but what men remember that makes history, and Livy's Brutus is well-nigh unforgettable. One can catch echoes of his rhetoric in the Declaration of Independence and later in the speeches of Robespierre. The character, too, is eminently satisfying, one of the great turned worms of mythology, like Steinbeck's Lenny granted a sudden access of wit. The founder of the Republic is larger than life, a mythic figure with no shadows in his character and an utter starkness about his actions. When we read on in Livy and discover that a conspiracy to restore Tarquin was exposed later in the year, and that Brutus' two sons were involved in it, we are somehow not shocked that the old patriot should have been judge at their trial, or that he should have considered it his duty to watch his sons die. Who but the founding father could have set the Republic above his own children.

The historical reality behind this famous story is more difficult to grasp. Clearly Rome was ruled by its clan heads (*patres* = patricians) both before and after the revolution. Tarquin may well have been popular with the Roman underclass, which at that time included some propertyless laborers (*proletarii*) and a good many others (*plebs*) who owned land but lacked kinship ties with the senatorial clans. Solon's sort of reform, by which the rich were given access to the city's institutions and offices, had already been put into effect by a king, Tarquin's predecessor, in about 550 B.C. To satisfy the plutocrats, a new assembly, the *Comitia Centuriata,* had been provided in which the vote was given according to the amount of military hardware a citizen could lay on. Lesser aristocrats were kept happy by the continuation of the Comitia Curiata which went on choosing priests and ratifying laws. The Senate, unlike the Athenian Areopagos, retained both its powers and its franchise, still choosing members by coopting them from the upper aristocracy. Brutus and his fellow patricians did nothing to alter these arrangements in 507 B.C.[4] Everything but the monarchy remained the same. The plebeians and the proletarians gained nothing from the revolution and may in fact have lost.

The only thing the Republic did that was new was to hand over the royal religious functions to a *rex sacrorum* and invent the consulate, which functioned, except for annual elections, exactly like the dual kingship of Sparta. Consuls, like kings, could do anything they liked in the interests of Rome. Except within the city, they had power of life and death from which there was no appeal. They were supposed to consult the Senate when making policy and the Comitia Centuriata when making law, but otherwise the only check on a consul was another consul.

Fortunately, there always *was* another consul. Consuls were basically a republican device. They were a way of dividing power so as to prevent arbitrary tyranny. Consuls represented a fundamental faith that two magistrates were better than one, and that a short term gives less scope for mischief than a long one. Divided authority was inefficient of course: Livy says the Romans might not have lost the great battle of Cannae if one consul had not ordered an advance the day after the other one had ordered a retreat. Short terms, too, kept consuls from making policy and the Senate got this power by default. Untouchable while in office, a consul could be tried for malfeasance the day his term was over, providing many an edifying spectacle to the plebeian (later the proletarian) underclass. The Roman faith in divided and limited power, however, surmounted all practical obstacles. Over the next two centuries from 510 to 287 B.C., facing constant civil disorder as a result of the strife between the well-born patricians and the curia-less plebeians, Rome continued to apply the idea in an ever more successful search for compromise solutions.

These were the years when it seemed that Rome wished to accomodate every political crisis by adding another magistrate or doubling an office. If the plebeians demanded power, they too, might have a pair of magistrates: thus in 494 B.C. appeared the first Tribunes of the Plebs. If there were two praetors for the patricians, there had to be two aediles for the plebeians; later perhaps an aedile or two for the patricians. As the cycle continued, checks and balances multiplied. A consul could punish a tribune, but only if war had been declared and both were in the army outside the city. A tribune could veto (Latin for "I forbid") a consul, but only within the city. A tribune could be vetoed by any other tribune. The Comitia Centuriata could override the Senate but the Comitia Tributa could not. Pressing for eligibility to the great patrician offices, plebeian magistrates sometimes even vetoed military recruitment in time of war. Yet so firm was the Roman reliance on law and formal propriety that no violence ever resulted from this except a couple of fist fights.

When the enemy was at the gates and the army went on strike, the Romans did appoint dictators. In fact they invented this office, together with the word, in the first decade of the Republic. But even a dictator, with supreme unassailable power over every Roman, had to have a colleague (the Master of Horse) and their usual term of office was thirty days or less. Though there were scores of dictatorships in the first centuries of the Republic, none ever lasted more than six months.

The most famous of these dictators, still dimly remembered from the pages of Livy, was Lucius Quinctius Cincinnatus. Together with Camillus, Regulus, Scaevola, and Cato, he may serve us as an example of the evangelical simplicity and the stern devotion to the community that were characteristic of Roman political morality in this era. When called on to assume supreme power and save the state, Cincinnatus, says Livy:

> ... was working a little three-acre farm (now known as the Quinctian Meadows) west of the Tiber.... A mission from the city found him at work on his land—digging a ditch, maybe, or ploughing. Greetings were exchanged, and he was asked—with a prayer for God's blessing on himself and his country—to put on his toga and hear the Senate's instructions.... He told his wife Racilia to run to their cottage and fetch his toga. The toga was brought, and wiping the grimy sweat from his hands and face he put it on; at once the envoys from the city saluted him, with congratulations, as Dictator, invited him to enter Rome, and informed him of the terrible danger of the army....[5]

Cincinnatus was a patrician, but this austere peasant's honor could be found among plebeians too. Rome's conflicts took place in an almost unearthly atmosphere of reserve and restraint.

Finally the long "struggle of the orders" ended in complete victory for the plebeians. By 300 B.C. every magistracy of the patricians was open to them, including the dictatorship and the priesthoods, while few of theirs were open to patricians. More importantly, only six people were remembered as having lost their lives in the struggle, and four of them, Spurius Maelius (ca. 439 B.C.), Spurius Cassius (ca. 491), Marcus Manlius (ca. 384), and the decemvir Appius Claudius (ca. 450), died under circumstances that could be described as legal and constitutional. Appius, for example, died in jail. A fifth victim, Verginia, was killed by her father—a legal act—in order to keep her out of Appius' clutches. Only the sixth, a reforming tribune named Gaius Genucius who was found "dead in his room" in 481 B.C. was, says Livy, clearly the victim of patrician violence.[6]

Finally in 287 B.C., the dictator Hortensius carried a bill in the Comitia Centuriata which made all future actions of the plebeian Comitia Tributa binding on the whole citizenry of Rome. From the Comitia Curiata of 550 B.C. to the Comitia Tributa of 287 Rome had at last made the transition from government by clan to government by citizens. Plebeian and patrician were equal, every man had a vote, and no class differences remained except those between rich and poor or Roman and non-Roman. In the small, exclusive peasant community of Cincinnatus, neither of these distinctions could make much difference.

The Hortensian law capped a highly developed piece of antimonarchical machinery of which the vengeful Lucius Junius Brutus might easily have been proud. The constitution's checks and balances were, in fact, far more complex than our own. In 287, Rome had an executive composed of not less than twenty independently elected major magistrates: two consuls who could veto each other, ten tribunes who could veto each other as well as the consuls, and various praetors, quaestors, and aediles who were in theory their subordinates but whose independence was strengthened by separate election.

The legislative power, based like ours on the theoretical sovereignty of the people, was vested in no less than four assemblies, each elected on a different pattern of constituencies. The old Comitia Curiata, divided by families, still met to elect the *rex sacrorum* or confer *imperium* (executive power) on a magistrate. The prerepublican Comitia Centuriata, divided by wealth, elected consuls, praetors, and quaestors and retained the power to make law. Made supreme in 287 B.C., the Comitia Tributa, divided according to residence, made law, declared war and peace, and elected the tribunes and aediles. Finally there was the Senate, composed entirely of former elected magistrates, which issued advices (*senatus consulti*) to both the consuls and the assemblies on foreign and military policy. To ensure that all these assemblies would maintain their representative character and that members of the Senate would remain worthy despite life tenure, the Romans in 443 B.C. created the censorship, two magistrates with the uniquely long term of five years (later shortened to eighteen months). Their duty was to maintain and revise the *census*, or list of citizens, and to impeach members of the Senate.

The Roman judiciary did not have a separate existence. Most magistrates had judicial powers. Praetors held court in criminal cases, the Senate could censure, and the assemblies could impeach for malfeasance. Branches or functions of government, at any rate, were not seen by the Romans. Contemporary observers tended to follow Aristotle, analyzing the constitution in terms of its monarchical, aristocratic, and democratic elements. Thus, according to the greatest of contemporary political scientists, Polybios of Megalopolis, consuls, though dual, were a monarchical element, the Senate an aristocratic element, and the assemblies a democratic one. It was thought that the more these elements were mixed, the stronger and more stable the constitution would be.

Neither of these analyses into branches or elements is very helpful in explaining how the extraordinary edifice of the Roman republican constitution broke down over the next two hundred and fifty years. When despotism finally came to Rome, it was not through the agency of the "monarchical" consuls of Polybios or by the assertion of power by any of the twenty-odd executive magistrates over the assemblies and the law. It was, instead, a series of very modern agents, the successful generals or proconsuls who defied, defeated, and eventually buried the constitution while piously embalming its body. The generals, in turn, seem to have come directly out of the necessities of imperialism and the Roman people's drive to rule the world. A fatal dream, but one which, soon after 287 B.C., began to become breathtakingly true.

In 285 B.C., the *imperium* (empire) of the Roman people stretched from Rimini in the north to Naples in the south, a respectable territory for a militant city-state of the time but not so large as the contemporary empires of Pergamum, Carthage, or even Macedon. Acquired by years of uninterrupted war with obscure and stubborn neighbors, it was organized unsystematically and (for the times) gently as a league of allies in which Roman rights in a hierarchy of categories were extended to subject citizens. Subject cities essentially governed themselves, giving to Rome military aid and occasional tribute. There was no bureaucracy, no police, and no military occupation except in the form of Roman colonies sited and built by Romans near the league's frontiers. Older and nearer cities often had the full franchise for their citizens to vote and hold office in Rome, but no federal organization existed (in fact, Rome had fought a war in 340 B.C. to prevent federalism in Italy). The normal status of the cities under Rome's control was about the same as that of United States trust territories in the Pacific or of the Louisiana Purchase in 1803.

Then suddenly the world, which was then the Mediterranean Basin, took notice of Rome and Rome reciprocated. In 282 B.C. Thurii, which was a small Greek city on the Italian coast, called on Rome to help her defeat her neighbor Tarentum, and Tarentum, faced with a Roman declaration of war, called in Epiros, a still larger and more powerful city in mainland Greece. For the first time Rome was at war with an overseas power instead of a local neighbor. Under King Pyrrhus, Epiros won some battles—"Pyrrhic victories"— but withdrew in 275 B.C. When victorious Rome received the curious ambassadors of the faraway kingdom of Egypt in 273, the destiny of the Republic as a world power was set.

World War came next. As the Roman imperium advanced into Sicily it ran into the empire of Semitic Carthage, overlord of modern Tunisia, Algeria, Morocco, and Spain. There, in an epic struggle that lasted two generations, Rome gained total control over the non-Greek western Mediterranean, the base from which, in the next two generations, she would conquer the Greek east. On these years the great ancient historians Livy and Polybios achieve a dithyrambic climax.

For Livy, the Roman, it seems that the Republic here embraced her destiny. In 216 B.C., we see a great Carthaginian army under Hannibal ravaging central Italy. All Roman armies have been destroyed; the new navy, victorious in 241, lies impotently at anchor; the defeated consuls are back in the city, performing prayers and supplications; the defeated city is in mourning for its dead. Fourteen years pass, with Rome under constant threat, until the tide begins to turn. The Republic regains the offensive, her city and institutions intact, until, in 204 Scipio carries the war to North Africa itself. In 202, Scipio defeats the returned Hannibal at Zama in

Tunisia, one of the two or three truly decisive battles of ancient history. Rome wins and Carthage is reduced to insignificance. Spain, North Africa, Sicily, Corsica, Sardinia, and the Po Valley fall into the conquerors' lap. The western Mediterranean becomes *mare nostrum*—our sea.

For the Greek Polybios, the story is more universal: "The war with Hannibal was the most celebrated and longest of wars if we except that for Sicily [the first war with Carthage], and that we in Greece were obliged to fix our eyes on it, dreading the results that would follow."[7] Polybios was an eyewitness of Rome's rise. When he was twelve years old in 196 B.C., the Roman consul Flaminius defeated King Philip V of Macedon, liberated all the cities of his empire, and proclaimed "the freedom of Greece." When Polybios was old and beginning to write history in 146 B.C., the proconsul Mummius defeated the armies of the Achaean League of free Greek cities and looted, burned, and annexed the city of Corinth. Polybios went into exile in Italy, profiting by close study of the new colossus of the earth which the Roman Republic had become and musing on the future of his homeland. The purpose of his book, he wrote, was to discover how it was that under Rome's "single dominion nearly the whole world was overcome in less than fifty-three years, a thing the like of which had never happened before."[8]

In 146 Carthage, too, was burned to the ground. The city was leveled and its site poisoned with salt so that nothing would grow there again. This in response to the demands of a senator, Cato the Elder, a model of incorruptible rectitude, who ended every speech to the Senate, on whatever subject, by saying, "and besides I believe Carthage must be destroyed."[9] Not so strange a tale when we remember that Rome's imperialism had always been a product of her republican virtue, her aggressive simplicity, her altogether rural tenacity, in sum the virtues of Cato.

The empire, therefore, came along before the emperors. It was, in the Roman phrase the "empire of the Roman Senate and People," a conquest by aristocrats in the name of democracy. The men who led the Republic's armies were servants of the Senate and People of Rome (SPQR) elected by the assemblies, carrying out the strategy of the Senate, and returning obediently to the status of private citizen after leading their armies in triumph through the city. Conquest was the policy of the people, not of their leaders. Already in 282 the Comitia Tributa had passed a declaration of war against an express advice of the Senate. Not until much later would war-weariness finally catch up with the citizen-soldiers of Rome. Too late, apparently, for in 203 when the assembly was reluctant to declare war on Philip V, the Senate, its power swollen by the Carthaginian wars, was able to overcome their resistance.

Essentially, however, the ruling Republic of 146 B.C. had survived the experience of world war without much constitutional change. The Senate's power had greatly increased, but this had not come about through law but rather through the prestige acquired by the body responsible for Rome's complex and successful strategy. The tribunate had declined, since plebeians no longer needed to be defended against patricians and in fact formed with them a common aristocracy of officeholding families. The assemblies retained their sovereignty, and since they continued to be formed of independent citizen-farmers they remained responsible as well. Only a few straws in the wind could have indicated future crisis, as when Publius Cornelius Scipio demanded command in Africa and forced the reluctant Senate to give it to him by threatening to get it by vote of the Comitia Tributa if the Senate refused. It was also true that, although the one-year term for consuls had not been abandoned in the stress of war, the Republic had for the first time allowed immediate reelection to the consulate (214 B.C.) and extension of consular military powers *pro consule* for more than a year (327). At the same time, however, Rome had abolished the dangerous office of dictator (ca. 200) and increased the number of praetors (242, 227).

In hindsight, it seems that things other than the constitution itself, changes in the administrative system, in law, and in the fabric of Roman society itself were the real indicators of the future: taxes for example, the status of the army, and new ways of assimilating conquered territory.

Ancient war made a direct profit for the state, and the Romans had looted enough by the time of the conquest of Macedon in 167 B.C. that they no longer needed to tax themselves. For the next three centuries the citizens of the Republic lived tax-free off their new subjects. From Greece and Africa came free food for the poor, land for farmers, cheap slaves for the rich, and profitable tax-farming percentages for the bankers. In 241 B.C. the Romans acquired Sicily and for the first time in their history appointed a Roman magistrate to rule a province instead of planting colonies of citizens to defend an ally. By 146 Rome had seven provinces and from them each year returned seven very rich Roman provincial governors.

The enormous wealth of this empire, though theoretically acquired and held by the Roman people in common, fell out, as wealth so often does, in very unequal shares. It has been said that it is better in the long run for a nation to lose a war than to win it. For the winner, the temptation to try again is irresistible. Like a gambler you keep coming back, the stakes increasing every time, until you lose at last, worse at the end than at the beginning. Even if, like Rome, you are lucky enough to drive everyone else out of the game and gain the whole world, you may still lose your soul. In a commonwealth where a dictator had once plowed his own three acres and a general who had celebrated three triumphs could prefer boiled turnips to gold, there was now a division between rich and poor so great that twenty-year veterans of the citizen army could be landless proletarians and formerly destitute plebeians serve lark's tongues at a dinner party. Slowly but surely army pay, which was nothing but marching rations in 407, crept upward until the defense of the Republic had become the exclusive career of the poor. "How can we expect to save a city," thundered Cato the Elder in the 170s, "where people are prepared to pay more for a fish than for an ox!"[10]

A good question. In the comparative calm that followed the destruction of Corinth and Carthage, two aristocratic reformers tried to supply an answer. These were the famous brothers Tiberius and Caius Gracchus, each tribune in his turn and each in turn assassinated for trying to implement the old Roman principle that the gains of the Republic belonged to all its citizens. The Gracchi wanted to divide the public land and give it to poor citizens, to distribute the grain tithe of Sicily to the city proletariat at a supported price, and to take away judicial monopoly from the senatorial class. The senatorial class, like the patrician class of the early Republic, was not pleased by the Gracchan program. They called themselves *optimates*, men of the best, while the Gracchi and their allies were *populares*, men who pleased everybody. Class struggle had returned to Rome.

But this was class struggle of a new and particularly ugly variety. Where once the strife of orders had led to political invention and careful compromise, it now ended in assassination and civil war. 135 to 121 B.C., the years of the Gracchi, were, as in the Chinese curse, interesting times. Mobs in the forum, armed attacks on the Senate house, occupation of the plebeian-proletarian neighborhoods, and for the first time since the unexplained death of Gaius Genucius centuries ago, the killing of a Roman magistrate in the lawful performance of his duty. Finally, Caius Gracchus' head was turned in for its weight in gold (another first in Roman history) and order again reigned in Rome.

It was a perilous order. When the Senate attempted to justify the murder of the Gracchi, they invented a new constitutional law based on wartime experience, the duty of the consuls to "see to it that the Republic is defended from injury." But it is elementary that you cannot make a law to cover the breaking of a law. The rule of law, an invention often and without irony credited to the Romans, cannot survive *ex post facto*, for it is based on habit and expectation. Once the creators of law have broken it, no one can count on its protection. It has been superceded by power.

The assassination of the Gracchi was perceived by the Romans themselves as the turning point in their constitutional history. So it is still believed. Not fifteen years later came the constitutional upheaval of the Marian consulates. Thirteen years after that comes the first civil war and the Sullan dictatorship. Ten years after Sulla, the familiar names of Pompey, Crassus, and Caesar begin to appear in Roman annals and one can hardly escape the conclusion of Cicero, who witnessed all this, that the Republic's illness was mortal.

In the poisonous atmosphere created by the illegal violence of 133–121 B.C., party politics began to go to extremes unthinkable in the early Republic. The populares no longer trusted the optimates to be restrained by legal process. They demanded safeguards in the search for which they too were prepared to disregard the constitution. Sometimes a party would try to prop up one shaky law with another, a vain effort when each side remained ready to use extralegal force. Personal and familial ambition, always a mainspring of Roman politics, now ceased to serve the state and threatened constantly to subvert it instead. When in 107 B.C. a four-year guerrilla war in Numidia (Algeria) seemed to be going nowhere under the aegis of the optimates, the populares seized on Caius Marius, a citizen general, and elected him six times in succession to the consulate, in defiance of both the Senate and the constitution. Adored by the proletariat and by the army, Marius' very existence amounted to a threat of tyranny. Once his ingrained respect for the constitution under which he had been raised led him to retire as a

private citizen in 100 B.C. Eventually however, the years poisoned
Marius. In 88 B.C., when he was 69, he used his incomparable popularity to have a senatorial command in Asia taken away from the
optimate Lucius Cornelius Sulla and given to him by plebiscite.
This was not unprecedented, but Sulla's response was totally out
of constitutional bounds. Instead of giving up his legions, he simply
turned them around, took them armed into the city, and turned
out the offending magistrates. This, Rome's first military coup, occurred in 88 B.C. Truly the Gracchan chickens had come home to
roost.

Worse followed. While Sulla was away conquering Asia, partisans of the exiled Marius staged a countercoup and in 86 B.C. invited Marius back to Rome to take up his seventh consulate and to
share in a blood purge of pro-Sullan citizens. A reign of terror followed. As Plutarch wrote: "The sight of headless bodies thrown out
on the streets and trampled under foot excited not so much pity as
a general fear and trembling."[11] After Marius died, Sulla came back
from Asia with his army to return the favor. The heads of the Mar-
ians now littered the streets. Before they died in bed, these two
bloodthirsty old veterans had between them decimated the citizenry of the Republic. Sulla, less hidebound by tradition than his
enemy, had gone beyond mass violence into new attacks on the
constitution. With a saturnine smile, he watched the Comitia Centuriata elect him Dictator in 82, reviving an office unknown for
more than a century, and then proceeded to rewrite the entire political law of the Republic. He made tribunes ineligible for any other
office, abolished the censorship, established age limits for office,
and reestablished the law against immediate reelection. Giving the
Senate all initiative in legislation, Sulla vainly hoped to bring back
the political balance of the pre-Gracchan period, but he never explained how this might prevent new Sullas from rising.

Even Sulla, however, was enough of a republican to resign the
dictatorship after less than three years, an act by which Julius Caesar later said, he "proved himself a dunce."[12] When he died a private
citizen in 78 B.C., calm had once again descended on Rome and her
constitution was once again in a state of spontaneous remission.

Men did not forget, however, the wars of Marius and Sulla. Nor
did the longing for peace in the 70s obscure the precedents for violence set in the 80s. New demagogues rose and one by one the
constitutional laws of Sulla were repealed. One of the dictator's
youngest lieutenants became consul in 70 B.C., six years before he

would have been eligible under the law. His name was Gnaius Pompey. Another man, a young nephew of Marius whose execution Sulla had considered and rejected, began his consulate in 59 B.C. by threatening the Senate with the swords of the assembly and carrying its speaker off to jail. This man's name was Caius Julius Caesar.

Still another, a young man who at the age of three had seen his father unsuccessfully defend the Marian cause against Sulla and Pompey, and who was eight when Pompey had had his father murdered, did not become a consul. Instead he grew up in the congenial company of Greek philosophers and came to regard political action as a disagreeable necessity sometimes required to demonstrate a man's moral integrity. His name was Marcus Junius Brutus. When he died by suicide at Philippi rather than surrender to the man who was to become Caesar Augustus, his life became a tragic emblem of the extinction of the Republic. This second Brutus, Caesar's assassin, may in fact have been as great a maker of monarchy as his ancestor had been its destroyer. Having killed a friend, perhaps a father, on principle, he lived long enough to see that Caesar's death had only postponed the inevitable.

Brutus was a bookish fifteen when Pompey and Crassus repealed the Sullan reforms. Unlike most of the heirs of noble families he could look at the clash of faction with some detachment since he was not eager to take part in it himself. It did not fire him with ambition to see the Metelli win their umpteenth consulate or Caesar advance the fortunes of the Julii by serving as quaestor in Spain. He could see that the state was unsettled, not only by memories of coups and assassinations but also by a pervasive disregard for law.

In 70 B.C., the governor of the venerable province of Sicily was convicted of wholesale extortion. In 67, Pompey was voted a supercommand over the entire Mediterranean coast, with a mission to put down the pirates. In 66, this was followed by a command over the whole of the Near East, including the right to declare war and sign treaties of peace. It was easy to see that the governing bodies of the Republic were slowly but surely abandoning their responsibilities to proconsuls and demagogues. Popularity was the key to power, and popularity in turn could be bought. Thus Brutus may have heard the crowds roar their approval of Caesar when he laid on 320 pairs of gladiators to kill each other for their amusement in 65 B.C. He may have also witnessed the edifying spectacle of the two consuls-elect for 65 B.C. being tried and convicted of bribing their electors. An aristocrat like Brutus must have sneered at these populares. Democrats they may have been, if one accepts the proposition that bread, bribes, and circuses were all that the people wanted. Caesar, Pompey, and other democrats have them plenty of that. Men like Cato and Brutus showed, instead, a contempt for the people, but it seems in retrospect a more honest feeling than the demagoguery into which Gracchan liberalism had degenerated.

A steady escalation of illegality made it extremely hard for those who wished to serve the law as an end to use it as a means. Brutus, whose greatest act would have not the slightest pretense of legality, must have found it instructive to observe the fate of Cicero. As consul in 63 B.C., Cicero uncovered a conspiracy of dissolute young nobles to launch a popular coup against the Senate. To thwart it, Cicero decided to ask the Senate for the same dubious emergency power that had been used against the Gracchi. He got it, acted quickly, and publicly put to death those of Catiline's friends he could lay hands on. Five years later, when the danger had been forgotten, Cicero was quite legally convicted of denying these victims their constitutional right of appeal.

Brutus would have sympathized with Cicero. Though there was as yet no clear "first man in the state" (princeps), some of the leading contenders were beginning to strike at their lesser rivals. In 59 B.C., the three strongest of all, Pompey, Caesar, and Crassus, formed an alliance and simply divided the Republic between them. Caesar became consul. There he helped Crassus recoup his fortune, rammed through veterans' benefits for Pompey's army, and then got a command in Gaul so he could build up an army of his own. While Caesar was away the Senate at last began to realize how ludicrously impotent it had now become. Then it tried to enlist Pompey as its protector. In 52 B.C., with Rome reduced to chaos by rival gangs of political thugs, the Senate made Pompey consul all by himself. Sole consulship, unlike the dictatorship which it otherwise resembled, was completely unprecedented in Roman history. It even made Pompey nervous, for after only a few months he tapped his father-in-law to serve with him.

Pompey was a little like Marius, unwilling to use his loyal veterans or his extraordinary popularity in order to break the law. Time and again, when it came to the moment of truth, Pompey would pull back and wait with moonstruck vanity for the constituted authorities to abdicate to him. This small restraint in Pompey's makeup was absent from Caesar's; from Pompey and the others,

Caesar learned what means were necessary in order to seize the Republic. From their restraint he gained time to acquire these means himself. It is recorded that when Caesar illegally left his province in 49 B.C. to march on Rome, he hesitated "for a long time," but, Plutarch continues, it was his own reputation and chances of success that worried him, not the constitution.[13]

Caesar's crossing of the Rubicon into Italy on January 11, 49 B.C., could not have been a surprise to Brutus, or to anyone else who had his eyes open ten years earlier when Caesar ripped through the veils of precedent during his consulate. Cicero had once remarked, "When I notice how carefully arranged his hair is and watch him adjusting the part with one finger, I cannot imagine that [Caesar] could conceive of such a wicked thing as to destroy the Roman constitution."[14] Yet Cicero did imagine it, as horribly as Caesar had conceived it. In an agony of indecision and knowing there was little he could do, Cicero left Italy, where Caesar had quickly gained control, and joined Pompey and the senators in Greece.

Marcus Junius Brutus also left Italy that year, with less indecision than Cicero. He was thirty-six, and except for some semiofficial journeys abroad, he had taken no part in state affairs up to this time. According to the kinship and patronage politics of Rome, he might have been counted in Caesar's party. After all, Pompey had had his father murdered and, though the leader of the Senate, Cato the Younger, was his wife's father and his mother's brother, Caesar himself had been his mother's lover—possibly even his true father. Neither tie, it is said, bound Brutus, who was determined to try to put the Republic before private and family interests. Long before Cicero had made up his mind, Brutus sailed for the senatorial province of Cilicia, thence in 48 B.C. to the cockpit of the Civil War in northern Greece, so surprising Pompey "that he rose from his seat as Brutus approached and in front of all his officers embraced him. . . ."[15] Brutus' motives have not come down to us, but we may certainly infer that he was acting out of what he thought of as philosophical disinterest and profound conviction. It was high summer in Macedonia. The weather was steamy and Caesar's army was expected at any moment, but Brutus' mind was dwelling on the long term. He was always reading. On the night before the great battle of Pharsalus, the nearsighted doctrinaire was writing out a summary of Polybios, that masterful century-old analysis of the imperial Republic.

Caesar finally did come, and conquered. The republican leaders scattered. Pompey fled to Egypt and there died. Cato raised another revolt in North Africa, lost, and commited stoic suicide on learning of his defeat. Pompey's sons escaped to Spain, where Caesar defeated them at Munda. Of the last great generation of republicans only Cicero was left, and he, a trimmer of genius, made his peace with Caesar's new order.

Brutus too was spared. He escaped from Pompey's camp through a weed-choked swamp, wrote to Caesar, and received full pardon and friendship. Again, it is not recorded what Brutus' motives might have been for making up with the enemy of the constitution, the man who was by now dictator and consul for five years. He could have joined Cato in Africa or the young Pompeys in Spain. As he walked alone with Caesar, soon after the reconciliation, informing on Pompey, Brutus must have had some inkling of how pale a copy he was making of his stern and illustrious ancestor. A delighted Caesar not only brought Brutus into his party, but made him one of its leading figures, so that men often said he would be Caesar's successor.

What must Brutus have thought, serving as the first honest governor of Cisalpine Gaul in a generation, hearing the reports from Rome: Caesar reappointed dictator, Caesar sole consul, the Senate packed, the assemblies managed? How must the enemy of kings have felt when he helped arrange the dictator's fantastic triple triumph and the banquet to which he and Cleopatra invited the 20,000-odd citizens of Rome? Did Brutus resent it when, in the summer of 45 B.C., Caesar became censor, proconsul, and dictator for life, with tribunician powers thrown in? Did he realize, student that he was, that Caesar had now acquired all the important powers of every one of the great republican magistracies? As sole censor he could purge and pack the Senate and the assemblies. As tribune he could convene an assembly at will. As dictator he superceded both consuls, exercised judicial power without appeal, and could convene and prorogue the Senate whenever he pleased. As proconsul, he had the power of life and death over every member of the army outside the walls of Rome. By law, in 45 B.C., every resident of the Empire was no better than Caesar's subject.

It is said that Brutus was hampered by a genuine love for Caesar, which is understandable. Caesar was personally one of the most attractive despots in history. He could kill without remorse, but, unlike Sulla, he had a distressing habit of pardoning his enemies instead. Then too, he was highly literate, civilized, affectionate, and psychologically whole. His decisiveness, tenacity, and sensitivity won him recognition as both a military and political genius. He was even a modest man—or at least clever enough to appear so—for amid all these offices the title he preferred to use was the simple *imperator*, the soldiers' cheer for a successful general. In any case, we know that it was not until the fall of 45 B.C. that Brutus and other nostalgic republicans could see monarchy clearly in Caesar's actions.[16]

Something alien, Asian perhaps, now entered into Caesar's policies. The memory of Alexander the Great and possibly the experience of Cleopatra's divine monarchy in Egypt had given Caesar a fatal admiration for the trappings as well as the power of monarchy. How else to explain his erection of statues to himself, one in the temple of Rome's founder Romulus, and another next to the images of the seven kings of Rome on the Capitol? Any Roman patrician might erect a temple to the founder of his family, but when Caesar did it he was careful to suggest that the founder of his family, Venus, was also the mother of Aeneas and thus ancestor of Rome itself. Nor did Caesar neglect to place in this temple an image of his mistress the Queen of Egypt, the mother of his putative son Caesarion (both were then in Rome). To complete the family paradigm, Caesar had a compliant Senate declare him *Pater Patriae*, "father of his country," a title previously given only to the first king, Romulus, and to the three commanders who had saved Rome from Gaul and Carthage centuries ago.

Caesar toyed, too, with actual divinity as opposed to simple analogies. At the Roman Games, statues of Rome's gods were carried in procession. At the Games in late 45 B.C. there appeared yet another image of Caesar. He also erected a temple to *Clementia*, mercy, which, since Caesar was the most merciful man in Rome, soon held another of the ubiquitous statues and had become known as the Temple of Caesar and his Clemency. Then there was the business of the coins. Even Alexander the Great had never put his own head on a coin. Each ancient city featured its patron god or goddess on its coinage as Athens had Athena. Only in Egypt, where kings were gods, and in states like Macedon, where there had never been a republic, did rulers strike coins with the heads of living men and women on them. In 44 B.C., however, Caesar issued two coins portraying himself. On one, he was crowned with the imperator's laurel wreath, and on the other, in addition, he wore the cowl of chief priest of Rome with the title dictator for life. An image of

Venus on the reverse of these coins only made them more ominous, for Venus was the mother of Rome and of the Julii.[17]

Finally, in the winter of 45–44 B.C., Caesar floated some rumors of outright monarchy. First it transpired that Rome's old prophetic books had predicted that the Parthian empire, Caesar's next target, could only be conquered by a king. Then members of a crowd were heard to address Caesar as *Rex* (king). Caesar, politic as always, replied that he was not king but Caesar, but he listened very carefully for the reaction. Soon after came the famous festival of the Lupercalia when Anthony, Caesar's crony and the dictator's Master of Horse, placed a crown on his head. Let Shakespeare's Casca describe it:

> I saw Mark Antony offer him a crown—yet 'twas not a crown neither, 'twas one of these coronets—and, as I told you, he put it by once; but for all that, to my thinking, he would fain have had it. Then he offered it to him again; then he put it by again; but to my thinking he was very loath to lay his fingers off it. And then he offered it the third time. He put it the third time by; and still as he refused it, the rabblement hooted, and clapped their chopt hands and threw up their sweaty nightcaps, and uttered such a deal of stinking breath because Caesar refused the crown, that it had, almost, choked Caesar; for he swounded and fell down at it.[18]

The trial balloon continued with the discovery that crowns had been placed on two of Caesar's statues (they must have been easy to find). Two tribunes, incensed, tore down the diadems and indicted the man who had earlier called Caesar king. Caesar showed his hand by immediately deposing the tribunes. His haste was typical of the man, but for once it was disastrous. Rome still hated kings. This was the moment when Brutus began to receive anonymous letters from his fellow citizens calling on him to emulate his ancestor, and visits from the lean and hungry Cassius, urging him to lend his name to the conspiracy now forming against Caesar. "What the enterprise needed most of all was the reputation of a man such as Brutus, whose presence would, as it were, consecrate the victim and ensure the justice of the sacrifice by the mere fact of his participation."[19]

Brutus knew how much the plotters needed him. He held high office as praetor of the city and everyone knew him, despite his change of side after Pharsalus, as that rare, testy, and altogether unpredictable species, an honorable man. Finally, he convinced himself that principle demanded he kill his benefactor. He would rather die, he said, than acquiesce in a monarchy for Caesar. He embraced his old enemy Cassius, saw him to the door, and settled down to weeks of sleepless anguish, the combat of conscience and inclination. He would be the last man in Roman history to place loyalty to the constitution higher than loyalty to a friend and patron. That, at any rate, is what Brutus thought he was doing. That the act he contemplated was completely illegal and a horrendous precedent seems not to have entered his head. The deed as he saw it was morally difficult enough without this consideration, much more difficult than such deeds had been for his remote ancestors in a simple society with few alternatives.

When the Ides of March came, Brutus was there, walking with Cassius up the steps of Pompey's theater to attend the Senate meeting. Rumor among the plotters had it that Caesar's friends would this day present a resolution to make him king. The stage was set. Alas for Brutus' principles, the scene played out in Pompey's theater turned out to be as banal as a riot in the forum. It was a round-robin. A knife-wielding gang, lusting for blood, put twenty-three stab wounds into the dictator, made an end of his imperial ambition, and created a martyr (the word would soon be invented) to monarchy.

The rest of the story is all by Shakespeare out of Plutarch: Brutus' flat, "principled" speech to the Roman proletariat; the resistible rise of Antony, to whom the mob instead lent ear; the failure of the Senate to make use of its last golden opportunity; the arrival of Caesar's heir Octavian; and the havoc of the third civil war. Whether or not Brutus saw the ghost of Caesar in his tent as night fell at Philippi, he must have been dealing with many ghosts by then. Not the least, according to Plutarch, was the ghost of the Republic that he had loved more than Caesar. The first battle of Philippi, in 42 B.C., was won on Brutus' wing and lost on Cassius':

> But the day of the Republic was past, it would seem, and it was necessary that the rule of a single man should take its place, and so the gods, wishing to remove from the scene the only man who could oppose the destined master of the world, kept from Brutus the knowledge of his success.[20]

Because of this ignorance, Brutus gave battle again at Philippi, some three weeks later, and this time Octavian and Antony, allies of convenience, beat him.

With a few friends, Brutus escaped the battlefield. As night fell, they crossed a stream and stood in the shade of a tree. Looking at the stars, Brutus recited a line of Euripides from the books he knew so well. His principles now demanded that he commit suicide, but none of his companions had the stomach to help him. He did not blame them for this. On the contrary:

> . . . and as for Fortune; he blamed her only for his country's sake. He believed that fate had been kinder to him than to the victors, and not only in the past but in the present, since . . . the world would come to know that wicked and unscrupulous men who put to death the good and the just were themselves unfit to rule.[21]

Then he went off the Strato, a fellow scholar, and ran on his own sword, a last act of what he considered republican virtue.

It remained only to see which of the victors would become Caesar in his turn. Octavian inherited the name and the property of the murdered dictator who by now, by the grace of the Senate, had achieved his ambition to become a god. He took the west and left the orient to Antony. Quarrels grew, war was declared, and in 31 B.C. at the great naval battle of Actium, Octavian defeated Antony for good and ruled the world alone. On the body of a Republic now exhausted by civil war, Caesar's grand-nephew performed a faintly Frankensteinian surgery. Little in the constitution was changed, and indeed some very ancient customs were revived. However, sole pro-consular imperium, sole censorial and tribunician powers, and the power of the assemblies to make war and peace were all centered in Octavian, who now became Caesar Augustus *princeps rei publicae* (first citizen of the Republic). A decent man, he lived seventy-seven years and survived scores of assassination attempts, so that when he died the monarchy was so secure that even a Nero or a Caligula could not bring it into discredit, and so accepted that nearly eighteen centuries later there was still a Roman emperor in Europe and *princeps* (prince) had become the generic term of monarch.

Octavian did not, however, find the body of Brutus after Philippi. That was Antony's coup. In view of the famous story of Antony's debauchery in the east and his turning tail at the Battle of Actium to follow Cleopatra and sacrifice his character to his passion, it is not without some justice that Shakespeare gives to Antony the words of Brutus' epitaph: "This was the noblest Roman of them all." If it is indeed nobility to be strong enough to sacrifice simple human affections to that misty abstraction known as *res publica*, the public thing, then Marcus Brutus, and his ancestor as well, deserve the title. We would not now flatter a man by calling him no-ble. It could be argued too that nobility is like honesty or obedience to law in being something only aristocrats can afford. Still, it should be remembered that the Roman Republic found itself unable to survive without it, and that after it died, those for whom nobility was too expensive got little from the Caesars they loved that they had not already got from the Brutuses they hated—except a false respect.

4

William Tell

The Failure of Kings in Switzerland

SWITZERLAND NEVER HAS, as a nation, counted for anything. Physically soaring out of sight, morally and intellectually she has lain low and said nothing. Not one idea, not one deed, has she to her credit. All that is worth knowing of her history can be set forth without compression in a few lines of a guide-book. Her one and only hero—William Tell—never, as we now know, existed. He has been proved to be a myth. Also he is the one and only myth that Switzerland has managed to create.[1]

So wrote Max Beerbohm in "*Porro Unum. . . .*" Beerbohm was a monarchist, of course, and a very witty one. For some reason, however, he and his fellow turn-of-the-century dandies have established the political image of Switzerland, such as it is, in America and the rest of the world as well, with unintentional skill besides, for the image is its own prophylactic. Only a history of Switzerland longer than "a few lines in a guidebook" could possibly correct it. So Swiss history outside of Switzerland has been almost as funny an oxymoron as English opera, the Italian Empire, or, for that matter, the Swiss Navy. This is a pity, for, as descriptions by both John Adams and Machiavelli attest, Swiss political history is an epic, not a comedy; has very little to do with skis, cheese, clocks, banks, and yodeling; and stands, in fact, as a unique example of republican stability in the twentieth century.

Switzerland has been a fully independent republic for three centuries and a federal republic for five. Parts of the country have been under republican government for more than seven centuries without a significant interruption. Rome's five centuries and America's two or three seem paltry by comparison. Of all the republics in Western history only Iceland (A.D. 930–1983), Venice (ca. A.D. 800–1798), and possibly Sparta (ca. 800–146 B.C.) have outlasted her. If Polybios was right in thinking that the key problem in republics is stability, then Swiss history automatically becomes one of the most interesting of all, at least to other republics.

In fact, the story is quite astonishing. To begin with, Switzerland achieved republican government in the early Middle Ages, when kings were anointed, equality was inconceivable, and even heaven was a monarchy. Until 1332, she was purely rural, the only republic of this kind to survive the Middle Ages; and despite her cities she retains a rural character today. Not since Caesar has a monarch told the Swiss what to do.

To achieve her independence, the republic—or republics—of Switzerland outmaneuvered and defeated the most energetic of all medieval dynasties, the Hohenstaufen, and expelled from their Swiss homeland the fabulous dynasty of Habsburg. After this the republics briefly became a great power, but they failed to establish either a centralized state or a unified nation. After less than a century, they deliberately abandoned imperial expansion and substituted for it the policy of armed neutrality for which they have since become famous. When the Reformation added one more division to a seemingly hopeless disunity, the Swiss gradually made division into a virtue and based their patriotism on it. Only French bayonets in 1798 could impose a unitary republic on the Swiss, and only for five years. Only in Switzerland did Napoleon forbear to impose a central imperial bureaucracy. Only Switzerland, in 1815, had her neutrality permanently recognized, and of all European neutrals since, only Switzerland has never lost it. Finally, only in Switzerland did the world-wide revolutionary and civil strife of 1848 result in a permanent, conservative, republican constitution, a republic of republics, which presides today, somewhat miraculously, over a country with four official languages, two recognized religions, and the stubbornest localism in the civilized world.

Nor has Swiss republicanism survived only because Switzerland

itself is some mountainous, landlocked aboriginal place where an-
achronism flourishes and monarchs scorn to tread. Quite the reverse: Switzerland is at Europe's center, Rome's first conquest north
of Italy, a highway between the Roman capital of Christendom and
the German home of its emperors, a seedbed of Renaissance and
Reformation and a cockpit—even a battleground—for every division in the long, scarred history of Europe. She has been exposed
to every one of the temptations that beset the Roman Republic,
empire included, and survived them by conscious action in which
the luck of location or circumstance played little part. Indeed, one
of the greatest of all temptations in a republic is, as the examples
of Marius and Caesar show, great republicans; which makes the fact
that William Tell never existed edifying and turns Beerbohm's satire upside down. The President of Switzerland, who does exist, has
proportions so unmythic that most Swiss do not know who he is.
Like Tell, he is a stand-in for the many real Swiss republicans of
his time and place. Charisma loaded on a myth no longer has power
to unmake the constitution.

The Swiss have no Caesars of their own. They were conquered
once by an alien Caesar, Julius himself, in 58 B.C., and ruled by his
successors until A.D. 401. The symmetry is pleasant, for it was the
defeat of the Helvetii in the Alpine passes that began Julius Caesar's
military career. The career, in turn, made it possible for Caesar to
destroy the Roman Republic and inaugurate a millennium of monarchy to which the Swiss would eventually become the only exception. Nor did the Helvetii lose ingloriously. Like most barbarian
tribes then (and the Romans themselves before Romulus) the Helvetii were strongly opposed to the permanent hereditary rule of one
man; so strongly, in fact, that in the very face of Caesar's advance
they deposed and executed their greatest war chief, Orgetorix, because he had tried to make himself king.[2]

Rome's four-century rule in Switzerland was apparently tran-
quil, possibly because Rome ruled it as two provinces, Belgica and
Rhaetia, rather than one. We may take this as the beginning of Switzerland's classic response to another great republican temptation—
centralization. From the Roman division to the present time, Switzerland has largely overcome efforts to found political unity on some
principle—race, religion, or language—which might eventually be
thought more binding than common political interest. Though the
elites of both Roman provinces spoke Latin, the division into east
and west was linguistic in spite of them, which facilitated the later

occupation of the east by migrating "german"-speaking Alemanni in the third century. By the time Roman troops were withdrawn in 401, Switzerland was permanently divided, not even fully Christianized, reduced, in fact, long before the advent of feudalism to the characteristically feudal situation of self-sufficient agricultural villages not much different from the one where Heidi lived. The linguistic division was further confirmed when Charlemagne's grandsons each took one of the halves in the famous treaty of A.D. 843.

Like ancient Greece, medieval Switzerland favored division and self-sufficiency on geographic grounds. By and large, each mountain valley had to take care of itself. Winters much harsher than those in Greece reinforced separation. So did the fact that south of the Rhine and Rhône valleys, in the center of modern Switzerland, the classic farm had more haymow and pasture than wheatfield. Since it makes little sense to divide up a pasture among individuals, the whole village usually owned and regulated pastureland—especially the land up the side of the mountains which was snow-bound in winter.

Centuries passed. Charlemagne's empire fell into worse ruin than Caesar's, but the Swiss were left alone. By the time (about the twelfth century) when law and custom began to be written down again in the Alps, each of these little valley villages was being referred to as a *communitas*, in German, *Talgemeinde*, or valley commune. Some of them indeed would answer to no one except God or the Emperor, and neither of these worthies found it convenient then to make his will directly known in the Alps. Elsewhere the inheritance of Charlemagne had devolved into the hands of local lords. Thousands of farming villages which, like the Swiss, had been self-sufficient and communally run had fallen, not unwillingly, under the protection and jurisdiction of such lords. In central Switzerland, however, very few barons had penetrated and very few castles had been built. The usual landlord was a church or abbey, and the Talgemeinde were mostly independent. In different languages, each asserted the same political experience: the Val Camonica in 1164, the Blenio and Leventia around 1200, the Valsesia in 1218, to name only the earliest for which we have charters. The Swiss republic had begun. It had begun, too, on the smallest possible level of political organization and at the very moment when feudalism and monarchy were reaching their apogee.

These valley communes entered written history when they did, however, not because of the isolation of Switzerland but because of her centrality. The Holy Roman Empire formed by Otto the Great in the tenth century included both Germany and Italy. Switzerland was duly enclosed within it by 1032 and remained the controlling link between its two parts. Now Emperors came and went over the Alpine passes, and the valley communes acquired an imperial responsibility to provide homage and hospitality and to keep the passes clear. The Emperor rewarded them by taking them directly under his wing, out of the feudal hierarchy, and by guaranteeing their independence by written charter. In this way, whatever authority the great Saxon and Hohenstaufen emperors possessed outside their own domains was lent to the Alpine cowherds, in return for a little homage.

It was an unusual political position in the Middle Ages, and a marvelous one for the Swiss. They could thumb their noses at their theoretical overlords, the Dukes of Swabia, in the name of a greater lord. They could defy the more local feudatories like Zähringen and the Abbots of Fraumünster by appealing to an authority too distant to meddle in their internal affairs. Associations began among the communes, and these, in turn, grew and prospered until the Alps were checkered with leagues, cantons, and temporary alliances, none much larger than twenty square miles, and all governed much as the villages continued to be by committees of elected leaders. It was an excellent foundation on which to stand when, around the year 1270, the emperors themselves threatened to become the enemy of Swiss republicanism.

In the first stage the emperors became stronger. Late in the twelfth century, the best-known of the Hohenstaufens, Frederick Barbarossa (Redbeard), was on the throne. Not only was he probably the greatest monarch of the First Reich, he had a particular interest in Switzerland. In a relentless thirty-year campaign, Barbarossa crossed and recrossed the Alps to lead German armies against the cities of northern Italy. In the process of trying to break down the independence of the Italian cities, he was forced to grant a good deal of it to the Swiss villages through which he had to pass. His successors continued the policy, and for a while the Swiss took them for everything they had in the way of privileges.

Of course the relationship was dangerous. The later Hohenstaufen were committed to monarchy in a way their predecessors had not been. They got into the business of freeing communes from local lords because they hoped to control both lord and commune in the end. They were also Dukes of Swabia in their own right, and so could use in Switzerland whichever tie, feudal or imperial, might best serve their growing power. The Swiss were quite lucky when this greatest of medieval dynasties got into an unwinnable death struggle with the papacy in the thirteenth century. This added a third contestant to the local lords and emperors, and the Swiss could play all three against each other. They were lucky, too, when the great local baronial family of Zähringen became extinct in 1218. When the key St. Gotthard Pass was opened into the very center of Switzerland by 1230, the independence of even the largest valley cantons was pretty well assured. A desperate emperor in 1231 allowed Uri, the canton which controlled the Gotthard, to buy its way free of the Abbot of Fraumünster. In 1240, while he was busy besieging a papal city in Italy, the Hohenstaufen emperor granted full independence to another canton, Uri's neighbor to the northwest, which was to give both its name and its white cross flag to the confederation. The name of this canton was Schwytz; that of its disappointed overlord, County Rudolph of Habsburg. Thus did both names appear on the European stage together.

By 1268 the Hohenstaufen were extinct. The Habsburg bid lay in the future. For twenty years after 1250 there was no emperor in Germany to speak of, and the cantons of central Switzerland paid homage to no one at all. Independence and republicanism were, it might seem, assured. Even democracy, considering what we know about the communes' government at this time, is not an inappropriate word to use. Uri and Schwytz were calling themselves *Allmende,* that is, corporate or communal associations of free men. They seem actually to have met like Athenians to govern themselves. The assembly was called a *Landesgemeinde* and in it all men who were not serfs gave their assent to law and chose magistrates called *Amänner,* usually once a year. Some cantons, in fact, still govern themselves in exactly this fashion, which, if we date from the abolition of serfdom in the fourteenth century, means four solid centuries of male suffrage and direct democracy.

1250 to 1273 was a golden age perhaps, though we don't know very much about it. Then, in 1273, the Imperial electors chose an emperor from a new family, a family which was altogether Swiss and which was, in fact, the former overlord of the canton of Schwytz—the Habsburg. Now once again, in the person of Rudolph of Habsburg, the offices of feudal lord and emperor were united. Since the pope had withdrawn from these matters after extinguishing the Hohenstaufen, the independence of the Swiss communes had once again a single source and a single potential enemy, the Habsburg. In a few short years it became clear he was the enemy. By the end of the thirteenth century, tiny, divided Switzerland had embarked on a fight to the finish with the most tenacious dynasty of monarchs in European history, a fight which would last two centuries, and which, against all odds would be won not by the Habsburgs but by the Swiss.

Habichtsburg—the Castle of the Hawk—still stands on a high bank of the Aare River between Zürich and Basel in north Switzerland, a mute and empty symbol of the ultimate fate of an extraordinary family. Any argument for monarchy would have to deal with it. Philip II, who launched the Armada, was a Habsburg. So was Franz Joseph who began the First World War, and Charles V who ruled most of Europe and America at the beginning of the sixteenth century. The Swiss seldom visit the Castle of the Hawk and pay it no homage. When it was built about 1020, the seat of a minor churchman, it commanded the valley of the Aare south to the Lake of Lucerne. It might have commanded the world, but a century before, Charles V, the last Habsburg, was driven out of it, defeated by a peasant confederation which still survives and which the Habsburgs did as much as anyone to create.

The beginnings of this hundred years war of independence are as mysterious to historians as the mythic William Tell himself. All we know is that sometime between the year 1273, when Rudolph I became the first Habsburg emperor, and the year 1291 when he died, something unprecedented happened in the three cantons of central Switzerland (Uri, Schwytz, and Unterwalden) which command the Gotthard Pass and ring the Lake of Lucerne. We know for sure only that on August 1, 1291, Switzerland's Fourth of July, magistrates and freemen of the three cantons signed a perpetual alliance asserting their right to govern themselves in traditional republican fashion and to act together as a confederacy against foreign or servile governors. By the time the Swiss got around to writing the story down (in the *White Book of Sarnen* in 1470) legend had already got its start on what we confidently call historical truth. The Habsburgs were defeated. Because "everyone knew" how it happened, it may be we shall never know. Perhaps if we tell the story at the end of the history a case can be made for the special truth of myth, a truth to which history ought to aspire more often.

At any rate, the Habsburgs became the enemy and the cantons

allied against them, their first tentative step toward confederate government. Generation by generation, mounted armies of what was now called the House of Austria descended on Switzerland only to meet the pikemen of the forest cantons and be routed. On November 15 in 1291 a punitive expedition, led by the emperor's brother Duke Leopold, marched into Schwytz along the bank of Lake Aegeri to the tiny village of Morgarten. There the pikemen stood and did to the Austrian nobility what English bowmen had done to the French at Crécy. Not only Leopold, but the feudal hierarchy itself was massacred at Morgarten. After the battle, at Brunnen, the three cantons renewed their alliance in their own German language. Not yet a constitution, it was beginning by longevity to look like one; and in 1332, the adjoining northern town of Lucerne, fighting like all medieval cities for communal independence, joined it.

Lucerne was the first of many to join the alliance. For anyone who had something to gain from the Habsburg it was an ideal threat and often a good policy; for the forest cantons alone were unshakeable in their hostility to the dynasty.

They defeated the Habsburgs again in 1339 at Laupen near Berne. Berne, whose status as a free imperial commune had been at stake, was delighted with her temporary allies. In 1351, a quite large city commune, Zürich, joined the alliance with enthusiasm after an internal populist revolution. With allies of this temper, Zürich found herself able to beat off three Habsburg sieges in the next four years. The peasant commune of Zug, north of Schwytz, joined in 1352, left, was returned by the peace of 1355, and was invaded and liberated by the alliance once and for all in 1365. In 1353 the huge (by Swiss standards) city commune of Berne, whose status as an imperial free city was established anyway, joined the alliance. Five rural and two urban communes were now bound together with nothing in common but republican government and hatred of the Habsburgs.

Berne's motives in joining are instructive in dealing with later Swiss imperialism. She had a little colony of her own, the Bernese Oberland, which she did not allow political rights to and which the Habsburgs had announced they would free. Once that threat was removed, she turned coat and less than a year later was helping the Habsburgs beseige neighboring Zürich. Each member of this strange alliance, except the original three, seemed not to be interested in union and more in empire than independence. The city communes, largely aristocratic, did not much like the rural communes, which were more and more democratic. Without the constant threat from the Habsburgs, Switzerland could not operate as a unit. For a century it was only when the armies marched that the "confederation" could be said to exist. Yet the Habsburgs doggedly continued to march. In the summer of 1368, when Lucerne tried to conquer neighboring Sempach and Entlebuch, another Duke Leopold led an army south. On July 9, he encountered the allies at Sempach and lost not only the battle but his army and his life. It is here, says myth, that Arnold von Winkelried gathered the points of the Austrian spears into his chest and made a breach for his comrades in the Habsburg front line.

Two years after Sempach, Albert III marched an army south to avenge his brother (Habsburgs named Leopold now took to staying at home). Albert met defeat at the town of Näfels, just east of Schwytz, at the hands of an army of a few hundred herdsmen from the canton of Glarus; and Glarus celebrated by joining the alliance permanently.

The victories of Morgarten, Zürich, Laupen, Sempach, and Näfels, coming at regular intervals, may seem monotonous; but if the Swiss had lost only one of them their whole epic (which, one should remember, they did not yet know was an epic) would have probably come to an end. As it was, Sempach and Näfels stopped the Habsburgs. They gave up trying to regain their Alpine domains and concentrated their power on holding the two regions around Habsburg Castle and Lake Constance, which was now all they had left south of the Rhine.

Fortunately for the confederate future, the dynasty was still serious about this effort. Otherwise the famous Sempach Covenant of 1393, a particularly binding alliance of eight cantons, would have become, given their divisions, a dead letter. For the Covenant, together with the Habsburg enemy, was all there was of "Switzerland" in 1393. There was no regular assembly, no executive, no capitol, no treasury, no chancery, no registry of documents, not even a seal or a flag. Indeed if an alliance makes "Switzerland" there were at least four Switzerlands in 1393, for in the eastern Alps north of the Splügen Pass no less than three separate associations of peasant communes had grown up in the 1300s: the Gray League, the League of the House of God, and the League of the Ten Jurisdictions. There too the common enemy was a feudal lord or the Habsburg themselves, but neither the three nor the four were even diplomatically related until 1395.

So it is clear that the Swiss war of independence, which trailed to a close in the century after Sempach, was completely free of that complication called nationalism. The Swiss cantons fought for republican liberty and feudal independence, and they defeated a great dynasty; but they also fought their neighbors and fought each other, and they had as yet no state. The Greeks surely would have understood.

The "few lines in a guide-book" however, is by no means complete. In the next century, called the Heroic Age, the Confederation became both a political reality and one of Europe's great powers. Only the Swiss Guard at the Vatican is left, an almost comic emblem, to remind the world of Swiss imperialism; and yet the Swiss republic may owe its life to what happened between 1400 and 1516. It was then that the Confederation became, even in the minds of its members, a permanent arrangement, and like so many newly independent states, acquired an empire. Unlike other republics, however, the Confederation could not maintain its statehood at a level which would permit the extension of empire. It was militarily invincible, but only with great effort could it eliminate internal war, and it could not prevent conflicts between cantons beyond the confederate border. To solve their problem, the Swiss, who had been inhibited in their conquests neither by Christianity which condoned them, nor by the tragic examples of Athens and Rome of which they seem to have known little, were forced by their own disunity to abandon imperialism, and with it the possibility of Caesarism. This series of events may be unique in republican history.

Swiss statehood was not deliberate. Central institutions simply stole up on the confederates. For example, in 1411, after abetting Appenzell's war of independence with Habsburg and the Abbot of Sankt Gallen, the alliance made an ally of Appenzell. The Confederation had to be a single state in some sense because the language of the agreement makes it clear that Appenzell was not a new member of the Confederation but an ally of the whole Confederation. Before long other cantons would come in on this basis.

In 1415, also for the first time, the cantons together conquered a territory and began administering it in common. The territory was, in fact, the Habsburg homeland of Aargau, overlooked by the

Castle of the Hawk. Probably common occupation of any other territory would have been impossible—and even there the confederates were at odds for centuries. Still, this common aggression and
the permanence of its results drove the alliance ever closer to the
devices of central government.

How far the Swiss were from being a state in 1415 is shown by
what happened in 1436. When the baronial house of Toggenburg
became extinct in that year, Zürich saw a chance to take over the
Aargau completely. Not only did she leave the alliance, she joined
the Habsburgs in a war against it which lasted fourteen years. Both
were defeated, and at the peace of 1450 one can say at last that the
Habsburgs had been permanently driven from Switzerland and that
the Swiss state was inaugurated. The "perpetual alliance" ceased
to have exceptions. Cantons no longer turned coat.

Much like the Roman, Swiss energies turned outward with victory. Something of their accomplishment in defeating the greatest
monarchs in central Europe must have come home to them. They
marched ever further, north to German Swabia, west to French-
speaking Savoy and Burgundy, south toward the great cities of
northern Italy.

This was true even before the Toggenburg War ended. By 1416
a Swiss army had defeated the Duke of Milan. On August 26, 1444,
the French army advancing to the relief of Zürich met a small force
of picked men after six other cantons at Sankt Jacob an der Birs.
Outnumbered more than ten to one, this force proceeded to hold
the line until virtually every Swiss soldier was dead or wounded.
Within a month the French had withdrawn from the war, which
had begun as a conflict between separate cantonal imperialisms and
ended in a vindication of collective Swiss imperialism.

Soon after this the Confederation began annexing territory.
These new places were not members of the Confederation, or even,
like Appenzell, allies of the whole Confederation, but instead colonies or associated territories like the Bernese Oberland or the ancient Roman provinces. By 1468 the Swiss had control of the Black
Forest north of the Rhine, hegemony over the cities of southern
Swabia, and a foothold in Alsace. Meanwhile, Europe at large was
mulling over the lesson learned by France at Sankt Jacob an der
Birs.

The next great monarch to learn that lesson was Burgundy, a
major "new monarchy" of the fifteenth century which was then
contending with the French Valois and the German Habsburg for

the hegemony of Europe. Under that inspired dynast Charles the Rash, Burgundy ran into Bernese imperial ambitions in the western Swiss region of Vaud. Berne called on her confederates. On March 1, 1476, the armies met at Grandson and Charles the Rash was defeated. On June 22, Charles tried again at Morat and the Burgundian army, 20,000 strong, was destroyed as a fighting force. By 1478, Charles was dead and the Kingdom of Burgundy just about gone from the map.

The Burgundian War left the Swiss with so much loot that the Confederation nearly fell apart trying to divide it. It is as good an example as any of the strains put on what the Romans called "republican virtue" by a successful imperial war. The Swiss needed a saint to resolve this, a hermit named Niklaus von Flue. On December 22, 1481, Brother Claus's brief entry into politics resulted in a recommitment to the Confederation known as the Stans Agreement, and Swiss energies were once again directed outward.

Now the spotlight turned south, where the great dynasties had begun a century-long struggle for control of Italy. At the center was the great Lombard city of Milan, ruled by despot Giangaleazzo Sforza, a prize which stood just south of the canton of Uri and her lifeline the Saint Gotthard Pass. Habsburg and Valois devoted their full energies for three generations to this struggle. The pope took the field at the head of an army. Yet it was the Swiss who made the difference. When we look at the accounts of battle we see Swiss everywhere, and until the Battle of Marignano in 1515 all witnesses concede them the real military supremacy. It is their problematic sovereignty that disguises them. When Charles VIII of France opened hostilities with a promenade into Italy in 1494, he received the decisive help of some 6,000 Swiss troops. These were, however, mercenaries and not allies. When Louis XII renewed the French attack on Milan in 1499, the Swiss, again as mercenaries, fought on both sides. In fact the trade in Swiss got so bad that when the French encircled Duke Ludovico of Milan at Novara in April 1500, there were more than 7,000 Swiss mercenaries inside the city and another 8,000 outside it. The Confederation, such as it was, was not officially involved on either side, and the grim vision of Swiss killing Swiss for no more than money would certainly have come true had not the French recruiter bought Ludovico's Swiss out from under him for cash on the barrelhead.

The venality of this episode helped create Swiss patriotism by reaction. In 1503, an official assembly, a Diet, of twelve cantons agreed that mercenary troops would no longer have the sanction of the Confederation. From now on it would be alliance or nothing. There followed seven years of debate on who the Confederation might back and what its objective in Italy ought to be, beyond acquiring territory for itself or defending the more private empires of the cantons. Uri, for example, wanted the valleys leading from Milan to the Gotthard, and Berne wanted the Rhône valley then mostly controlled by the French.

The debate was very nearly decided by a Cardinal bishop from the Swiss colony of Valais in the southwest. In 1510, Matthew Schiner, a diplomat of rare talent, managed to bring the Confederation around to a policy whose slogan was the defense of the church. In practice this meant working for Pope Julius II and his ally the Duke of Milan. In 1512, 10,000 Swiss arrived as the army of a seemingly sovereign state, and were immediately and astonishingly successful. The same Swiss who had as mercenaries deposed two Sforzas in 1494 and 1499, and done it again for a price in 1500, restored Massimiliano Sforza in 1512 as allies. They also restored the independence of Genoa, returned Bologna to the Pope, secured the communes of Domodossola, Locarno, Lugano, Mendrisio, Valtellina, Bornia, Chiavenna, and Neuchâtel for the Swiss empire, and in a rematch at Novara in 1513, drove the French from Lombardy.

In that year of 1513, the Swiss dictated to Europe. One by one they had defeated each of the emerging dynasties of the Renaissance. Little imagination was required to see them as the coming Rome, and one Niccolò Machiavelli came close to this view in the book he was writing that year.[3] If the cantons had held together after 1513 and pursued a confederate foreign policy, it is hard to imagine what could have prevented the Swiss from driving the dynasts from central Europe just as they had driven the Habsburgs from Switzerland.

But the Swiss, unlike the Romans, were still a league when they began their empire, a confederation rather than a state. The western cantons, neighbors of France, did not like the Confederate policy. In September 1515, when François I renewed the French attack on Milan, the Swiss army emplaced at Marignano heard with consternation that the western cantons had accepted the French king's offer of a million crowns to withdraw from the war. The great battle, which began on September 13, had already been decided. The eastern Swiss fought for two days running. They left the field in perfect order with flags flying, but they had taken 8,000 casualties and they had lost. The Confederation had failed, the reputation of Swiss arms was tarnished, and the Swiss people had earned an undeserved but undying reputation as the most buyable people in Europe. As one of Machiavelli's comtemporaries wrote presciently: "I am among those who fear the Swiss but I have never believed they could be the second Romans. Consider the politics and history of past republics and you will conclude that a republic so disunited is not destined to make [imperial] progress".[4]

The Swiss reaction to Marignano, however, proved uniquely creative. It was too big to forget so it had to become either a source of pride or a source of shame. Determined to be proud of Marignano, the Swiss embraced a paradox and tacitly agreed that the whole reason for their union was the deep division that had led to the disaster of 1515. We, said the Swiss to themselves, are a nation because we are not a nation. We are one because we are many. Soberly, they repaired the Confederation and allowed their dream to empire to recede, concentrating their pride in their still great military reputation and in a last residue of the old mercenary tradition, the Swiss Guards of the Pope and of the King of France.

The divisions were all very deep: east and west, French and German, city and country, democratic and aristocratic. It seems almost unfair for history to have added a last and most murderous division which appeared within five years of Marignano: Catholic and Protestant. This was responsible for three more civil wars before the national constitution was established in 1848. And yet the religious division of Europe begun in the Reformation has a legitimate claim to having been invented in Switzerland. A founder of Protestantism, Zwingli, was Swiss; the most dynamic form of the new faith, Calvinism, originated in the new Swiss city of Geneva; and the famous solution to religious war, *cuius regio, eius religio*, was first applied in Switzerland in 1531. Most important, as we shall see in a later chapter, the republican style in Protestant church government began in Switzerland and was still having an effect when Jean-Jacques Rousseau, a Genevan, published his *Social Contract* in 1762.

It was the Reformation that laid the ghost of Swiss imperialism. Huldreich Zwingli, who began it with a sermon in the Zürich cathedral in 1519, was a veteran of Marignano and himself the last great Swiss imperialist. In what we must now call typical Swiss fashion, Zwingli checkmated himself. His plans for a vast Swiss-led Protestant empire in central Europe died with him on the battlefield of Kappel in 1531 at the hands of a soldier from one of the five Catholic cantons. The only solution to the movement Zwingli had led turned out to be the famous principle that the government of a place sets the religion of a place, which added one more unbridge-able division to the Swiss Confederation and one more source of that paradoxical pride in disunion which constitutes Swiss nation-alism. Perhaps the best symbol of what the Reformation did to Switzerland is the curious fate of Appenzell. A tiny canton to begin with, Appenzell was split into two concentric half-cantons, a circle and a ring, one Protestant and the other Catholic. *Cuius regio* could not be carried further.

Switzerland's retirement from international politics in the six-teenth century turned out to be permanent. So did its extraordinary confederate republic. Only the private empires of the cantons en-dured, minor affairs more irritating to their inhabitants than prof-itable to their owners. Switzerland's sovereignty and independence were recognized officially in passing at the conference of West-phalia in 1648, but Europe mostly left her alone. The creaky con-stitution of the fifteenth century remained in force and the cantons remained largely independent of each other without civil war.

Not until France led the democratic republican movement of the 1790s did Switzerland find herself the prey of a foreign power. A French army invaded her in 1798 and saddled her with one of those then-fashionable governments where all power was at the center in the hands of a mass-elected legislature and a national bu-reaucracy. It was Switzerland's first real written constitution but so little did the Swiss like it that hundreds died rebelling against it. In 1803 the chaos was so great that Napoleon himself felt constrained to step in. That year, in the Act of Mediation, the new Caesar showed his intelligence by giving the Swiss what he had refused to every other country in the French orbit—a republic acceptable to its inhabitants. In doing so he gave full cantonal status to most of the long-suffering confederate colonies like Ticino and Thurgau thus putting an end to the last shreds of Swiss imperialism. He also gave Switzerland a weak central government with an executive committee and a one-year rotating presidency which suited her traditions so well that she kept it when Napoleon was overthrown and Europe guaranteed her neutrality in 1815.

It only remained to have one last civil war, the *Sonderbund* war between Catholic rural cantons and Protestant urban cantons in 1847. So well did the Swiss manage this that the Confederate government, representing a majority of urban Protestant cantons, received the capitulation of the *Sonderbund* after only twenty-five days of war and a grand total of 128 dead on both sides.

With honor satisfied, the Confederate legislature appointed a commission to draft revisions in the constitution. In less than two months the commission came up with a whole new constitution, and by September 12, 1848 it was ratified by the cantons. It is now 130 years old, the oldest republican constitution in Continental Europe and the only survivor of that revolutionary year, 1848, when almost every country in Europe had briefly become a republic.

Americans should find this constitution instructive. In creating their central government the Swiss, like the Americans, found it necessary to have two houses in the legislature, one dominated by the cantons (states) and one by the people. They also found it imperative to set a three-hundred-man limit on the cantonal militias, so that the Swiss army, for the first time since 1512, was truly Swiss. Since this immediately created the danger of military tyranny, the Swiss constitution-makers provided that the army would not "stand" or have a commander except by act of the legislature in a military emergency. Also, unlike the Americans, the Swiss deliberately left the taxing power in the hands of the cantons (as it had been before 1787 in the United States) so that although there was a uniform currency, tariff, customs, and post offices, federal revenue would come by requisition from the cantons and could not until the twentieth century be raised independently of them.

The Swiss executive branch is of course the one that so amused Max Beerbohm. It consisted of a seven-man committee called the Federal Council, each member of which represents one of Switzerland's major divisions and heads a government ministry. All are elected by the legislature. The President of the Council, or President of Switzerland, is elected by the Council from among themselves. He stays in office for a year only and cannot succeed himself. Hence it is quite true that most Swiss don't know who he is, and for that reason alone he is about as safe as a functioning executive can be from the temptation that lured Caesar, Napoleon, and Cosimo de Medici to overthrow their constitutions. Moreover, though it is within the executive's power to make plans for the army, only the legislature can appoint a general for it and even the legislature would have trouble independently paying for it. The Swiss army remains as belligerent as it ever was in 1512, but it has never made a coup.

Thus Switzerland, one of the two oldest living republics, seems to be assured of several more centuries of both life and anonymity. The fact that, as Beerbohm noticed, it has no heroes may be the secret of that longevity.

Except for William Tell, who is a myth. But what a myth! His story, found in the *White Book of Sarnen,* was discovered and retold by the historians of the Romantic era, by a great playwright (himself a crypto-republican) Friedrich Schiller, and by an irresistible composer Gioachino Rossini, and is surely one of the world's great stories. As the Swiss national myth, it is the key to understanding all four stages in the history of the republic, whether it is the war against the Habsburgs in the fourteenth century, the acquisition and renunciation of empire in the fifteenth, the institutionalization of disunion in the sixteenth, or the formation of the federal republic in the nineteenth. Tell embodies all the values that Swiss history has selected for: orneriness, belligerency, independence, self-control, and intelligence.

As retold by Schiller, it goes like this. Albrecht of Habsburg, the son of Emperor Rudolph, sends delegates to Uri and Schwytz, whose mission it is to deliberately disregard the cantons' direct link to the imperial throne and reduce them, like Unterwalden, to fiefs of the house of Habsburg. Calling themselves imperial *advocati* (*Vögte* in German) they are to behave in practice like stewards of a private estate, landless employees of their lord, for whom all the local farmers and herdsmen could only be regarded as fellow dependents and indeed bound serfs. The last and worst of these fake Vögte are Landenberg in Unterwalden and Hermann Gessler in Uri and Schwytz. Myths though they are (Landenberg was probably not a man but a castle), they make superb villains. In each town they build castles garrisoned with non-Swiss troops. There they carry on luxuriously when they are not roving the countryside with hawks on their wrists, confiscating a freeman's house here, his oxen there, denying him justice, leering at his wife, or torturing his aged father. The people may have some rights, says Gessler, but:

> *This is no time to settle what they are.*
> *Great projects are at work, and hatching now.*
> *The Imperial house seeks to extend its power. . . .*
> *. . .This petty nation is a stumbling-block.*
> *One way or another it must be put down. . . .*
> *I will subdue this stubborn mood of theirs;*
> *This braggart spirit of freedom I will crush;*
> *I will proclaim a new law throughout the land. . . .*[5]

One hisses. The Swiss react by forming a conspiracy to overthrow Gessler and Landenberg and to repudiate the rule of their master Albrecht. In the middle of the night they arrive at a meadow called the Rütli, Switzerland's Independence Hall, in a neck of Uri territory between Schwytz and Unterwalden on the banks of Lake Lucerne. There in the torchlight the freemen of Switzerland jostle for precedence, make speeches, and, as dawn breaks, agree to a perpetual alliance (the unforgiving documents show that this was actually signed sixteen years before) together with a cleansing insurrection to take place during Christmas. William Tell, a lone hunter who, he says, is "not born to ponder and select," is not at the meeting—fittingly, since most of those who have met are, like Tell, mythical and so have not been there either.[6]

Meanwhile, Gessler, whose tyranny is as ingenious as it is melodramatic, has ordered a new castle built in Altdorf, the capital of independent Uri, and in the square before it he has his cap set up on a pole. [It]

> . . . *shall have like honor as himself,*
> *All do it reverence with bended knee,*
> *And head uncovered; . . .*
> *His life and goods are forfeit to the Crown*
> *That shall refuse obedience to this order.*[7]

Tell, who knows nothing of this, walks into the Altdorf square with his oldest son, ignores the cap which all others have been carefully avoiding, and is arrested for *lèse-chapeau*. Gessler arrives on horseback and, knowing and hating Tell, commutes his sentence on the spot. He orders Tell to take his crossbow and shoot an apple off his son's head. Tell, a good father, offers his life rather than shoot. Gessler replies, "Shoot, or with thee dies the boy . . . . 'Tis not thy life I want; I want the shot."[8] Tell has no choice and shoots, with results every child in the world must know by now; but he has taken more than one arrow out of his quiver. Gessler asks why the second arrow and promises Tell he won't be killed if he answers. Tell says the second arrow was for Gessler if the first had missed the apple. Gessler keeps his promise by arresting Tell and sends him by boat to prison. There is a storm. Tell, who is also a superb boatman, is unbound and given the tiller. He steers the ship to safety while the lightning flashes, and leaps to freedom on the opposite shore. He then beats Gessler to the Küssnacht Pass and there shoots him dead from ambush. The great insurrection is proclaimed on the spot, the castles are taken and burned, and every Habsburg bailiff is harried out of the land.

A superb story. Small wonder it is retold even in a day when it is known that the dates must be wrong, that almost all the names are made up, and that the same story appears in Danish legend nearly a century earlier. It is the story of a people who will not be told what to do, by a king or maybe even by their own community; a people stubbornly disunited, localized, even anarchist; a people capable of tremendous violence but trustful of each other's independence and integrity; a people above all incapable of bending a knee to anything—to a monarch, even to one of their own, and least of all to a hat.

5

Niccolò Machiavelli
The Florentine Commune

In a universe dominated by kings and popes and emperors, where it was a maxim of law that there was no man without a lord, the spectacle of Florence is like an exploding star. Here men acted as if there were no lords at all. Medieval Florence and her fellow free cities, from Antwerp in the north to Pisa in the south, defied not only their political superiors but the entire medieval vision of politics. From the moment they emerged from the ashes of the Roman Empire around A.D. 800 to the time they sold out to the "new" monarchies around 1500, they sat like strangers at the banquet of Christendom.

Emperor after emperor left their gates in consternation. Citizens of these places lacked morality. They paid their dues in gold and silver but refused the exalted status of vassal. The payment always felt like a bribe. Citizens inherited wealth, but not power. One never knew from one year to the next who was in charge of a city's affairs. At times it seemed as if the whole community was acting like a single person, at other times as if everyone in it were at war with everyone else. Never was there adequate respect, subordination, courtesy. It is easy to imagine the crowned heads who tangled with the cities shaking their heads and saying, "Chivalry is dead."

Of course, chivalry was not dead. Not yet. The great men of the cities often had no higher ambition than to trade their business for a barony and retire into feudalism. Men whom the cities had taught to read and write often spent their careers immortalizing the knightly code of careless honor, largesse, and war. Nevertheless, the city in the Middle Ages was a strange place, a mysterious refuge where serfs lost their masters and money talked.

Most of all, the medieval city was a seedbed of political republicanism. The territorial republic in Switzerland was a special creation of Alpine geography and a unique political status. The conciliar movement and similar assaults on monarchy were the creations of small elites willing and able to act together, seeking above all to limit rather than to destroy. The cities, however, were conceived in common and for seven centuries dedicated to the proposition that all magistrates need equals. It was the medieval cities that carried the republican idea across the great sea of medieval monarchy, first by practicing it, and then, in the Renaissance, by formulating it in theory for the first time since Tacitus and Plutarch.

These city-republics were not democracies any more than Rome was; the people did not rule. Only a minority of inhabitants could vote or hold office. Certain minorities were legally protected or given their own magistracies as the Roman plebeians had been. Elites of various kinds held, like the Roman patricians, strangleholds on one source of power or another. Citizenship was usually hereditary and speech was rarely free. Nevertheless, the plurality of power under a republican constitution made the cities more democratic than any other medieval polity except possibly the dependent peasant village. In the minds of the feudal lords of the earth it was quite mad.

How did this happen? How did it end? Did Florence, like Athens, have kings and mislay them? Did the Florentine republic, like the Roman, fall victim to Caesarism? Questions worth answering, but difficult ones. Because we have more raw data about Florence than about ancient Rome, her story does not emerge as smoothly. The history of the Florentine constitution alone is so complex as to be more often funny than sad. Still it seems that a great modern historian of the city (Hans Baron) is right: Florence was self-consciously, proudly republican by 1400. She gave us the Renaissance in that spirit, the deathless careers of Masaccio, Michelangelo, Donatello, and Da Vinci. Then, inescapably, there is the fact that in 1532 Pope Clement VII abolished the constitution and declared his grandnephew Alessandro de' Medici Duke of Florence. Thus it seems to have been at the hands of her leading family that the Florentine republic was definitively destroyed.

If the tale sounds familiar to a reader of Plutarch and Livy, how much more familiar must it have seemed to a Renaissance Italian for whom Plutarch and Livy were the basic texts of humanism; to a Machiavelli for example. In fact, it turns out that the leading theorist of republicanism in the Renaissance was none other than Niccolò Machiavelli. Known for centuries as the apologist for power, the author of the ultimate manual for monarchs, Machiavelli was also one of the last civil servants of the dying Florentine Republic and the author, in his *Discourses on Livy,* of a manual for republicans more comprehensive and more effective than *The Prince.*

John Adams read the *Discourses.* We do not. That is because, unlike John Adams, we don't know or care enough about the constitutional history of Florence. We know about Lorenzo and Michelangelo and Dante all right, and we have a vague impression of clever young men dressing in hose, carrying stiletti, and justifying ends by means. An operatic, Romantic, Anglo-Saxon image, it leaves out the fact that Dante was a political refugee from republicanism, Michelangelo an elected member of the Republic's Public Works Board, and Lorenzo de' Medici an unelected despot.

Let us then try to revive these hustling, unseemly, antic city-republics through the constitutional history of medieval Florence, the greatest of them all. On the way it may become possible to put the Medici family back into the context from which it emerged and to approach from a new angle the riddle of Machiavelli and the dilemmas and achievements of Renaissance humanism.

Petrarch used to write letters to Cicero addressed to Arpino, his farm south of Rome. Petrarch, like most of his friends, thought that the city-republics of northern Italy were genuine survivals from Ciceronian antiquity, the old city-states on whom Rome had built the Empire. It was a charming idea and a creative one, but alas for Petrarch's romantic soul it was not true. Medieval culture, having given us the jury trial and the university college went on to reinvent the city-republic, indeed the city itself, and not only in Italy.

Everywhere in Europe by 900, the cities had disappeared. In the

last centuries of the Roman Empire, taxes, bureaucratic incompetence, and cultural conflict, not to mention mugging and highway
robbery, one by one cut the links that held the old Roman cities
together, the goods and information whose exchange had made cities possible and desirable in the first place. By 900 or so it was literally necessary to start from scratch. The commerce and artisanship
that make a city out of a village, a castle, or a bishop's seat had to
be built up again from the simplest beginnings. The free and ven-
turesome citizens who inhabit cities had to be recruited haphaz-
ardly from the various rigid castes which had suited the autonomous
local economies based for many centuries on agriculture. Nor was
there any guarantee that the new city would be in charge of its own
destiny. Thus Paris was always considered as a kind of jewel box
belonging to the King of France. Similarly, Canterbury and Milan
belonged to their archbishops and Pisa to the Countess of Tuscany.
In the Middle Ages, no one, no group, could really be autonomous.
It was unthinkable even when it happened.

Ownership of their city by a member of one of the old castes,
however, was cramping to city people. They were essentially a new
class: Burghers, *borghesi*, burgesses, or, as they called themselves
with increasing pride in France, *bourgeois*, lived by a new morality
fundamentally different from that of the old agricultural hierarchy
and closer, had they but known it, to the habits of ancient Greece
and Rome. Finally, between the years 1000 and 1250 or therea-
bouts, the bourgeois managed to turn their own home-grown city
governments into autonomous institutions. Whether by bribe or by
revolution, they simply got rid of all the other authorities and declared their independence.

In Italy this medieval independence movement got started early,
for it grew up in an atmosphere of reduced authority. Feudalism,
with its hereditary vassals and subvassals, could only appear where
bureaucracy failed. In Italy, bureaucracy and its removable civil servants never entirely failed the way it did everywhere else before
900. Thus feudalism never entirely succeeded. The result was a politics so confused that even a weak and experimental institution like
the city could get under way early. Later, the confusion was pro-
longed by a crisis of authority three centuries long by which Italy's
two candidates for monarchy, the emperors and the popes, destroyed each other's strength in an epic struggle for supremacy. Italian cities were thus independent in fact from their beginnings in

the eighth century until the coming of the new monarchies in the sixteenth—eight hundred years of liberty.

How were they governed? There is very little evidence from the centuries before 1100. The best guess is that city governments began with the Dark Age equivalent of community groups and block associations. Someone, in that brutal era, had to keep the walls repaired and man them in an attack. Someone had to steady down the supply of food and water. In the market, any city's heart, disputes arose that needed quick, local settlement. And so, between a militia, a wall, a court, and a market, each city developed a government.

A republican government. Apparently the cities were republican from the very beginning and without exception as the one modern survivor, San Marino, still is. Their names for themselves was *commune* from the Latin for all together, and though they had leading families who strove for noble status, they seem to have had no one magistrate or family that was acknowledged first in the state. The Italian communes, like the French and Flemish, appear in history as sworn associations pledged to hang together in the struggle for independence against an overlord. At Verona in 945, they are called a citizens' council (*concio civium*). At Modena and Turin in the 890s they are even called a people's conspiracy (*conspiratio populi*). Given the power of the local bishop or count, no commune could achieve complete independence without this all or nothing solidarity.

By the tenth and eleventh centuries we find the Italian communes, especially those which had won their independence, governed by an executive committee of ten or so equal magistrates called, with becoming simplicity, "good men" (*boni homines*) and a chairman called "judge of the commune" (*iudex pro commune*). We also find a militia recruited by neighborhoods whose commanders are also and necessarily magistrates of the commune. Already the standard form of later republican government is visible: an executive committee of a dozen or less whose power is based on neighborhood militias and which is presided over by a single short-term chairman. This is the kind of government with which Florence emerges into history as an independent city-state, dominating eleventh-century Tuscany, and it is the basic form of all its many governments until the abolition of the republic in 1532. Whether Florence was struggling with the Count of Tuscany or the Bishop of Fiesole, or the emperor or the pope, her corporate independence and power would always be represented by an executive committee, captains and a chairman, whatever names they were called.

Only one authority was higher than this government, the *parlamentum*, Oldest legacy of the prehistoric commune, this was a general assembly of all the citizens of Florence, called to action in times of crisis by the cry "People and Liberty!" and the ringing of the great bell in the communal tower. Anything could happen in a parlamentum, especially in the early days before elites discovered how to manage them. The entire constitution could be revised in a day or two by a committee (*balìa*) elected for that purpose by the mob in the square. Too often it was. In fact, the number of balía-created constitutions in Florentine history has never been accurately counted and the instability of constitutional law in this little state was enough to make Brutus' head spin.

Far more stable were the power arrangements between social classes. It makes the job of counting Florentine constitutions easier if we leave out all that did not reflect a major change in these arrangements. This leaves us with four: the *podestà* constitution of 1207, arranging power among the aristocrats (*grandi*), the *priori* constitution of 1282, reflecting the triumph of the major gilds over the *grandi*, the *popolo grasso* (fat people) constitution of 1343 reflecting the rise of the minor gilds, and the *popolo minuto* constitution of 1378 under which the franchise was, briefly, the widest in the history of the republic. Four social changes does not seem much in two centuries, but in the Middle Ages it was a blistering pace. Many Florentines never caught up. Some, like Dante, suffered much by trying to buck the current. Social changes were painful. Even ordinary parlamentums left casualties, refugees, political prisoners, and assassinations in their wake; but at no time before the 1450s did the Florentines give up their goal of making a place in the state for all who had an interest in its affairs or a capacity to manage them. Like Rome after the Gracchi, Florence in the Middle Ages was an arena for the mortal competition of talented politicians.

It was so dangerous in the twelfth century that Florence's elite followed the example set by other Italian cities and in 1207 resolved to bring in a foreigner as chairman in order that he might better arbitrate between them. This was the *podestà*, so called from the Latin word for power. He was supposed to keep the Capulets and Montagues of the time from shooting at each other's fortified donjons across the streets of Florence.

The podestà was barely effective. When each great family stood against all the other grandi, a podestà might stand in the political center and play them off against each other. A few of the city's fortified castles might be disarmed, and (unsought dividend) a few Florentine bourgeois would escape being killed in crossfires. Most of the time, however, the grandi made alliances with one another, and often got down to a two-party system. When that happened the fur flew and the podestà could do little but hide, die, or resign. By such rough and ready measures the podestàs were prevented from becoming, like the Capets of France, hereditary monarchs by default. It also prevented strong emperors like Frederick II of Hohenstaufen from making the podestà into a royal bureaucrat and turning Florence, like Paris, into a crown jewel.

The office was apparently satisfactory to the townsmen of Italy. Men from the best families in the peninsula went into this carpetbagging magistracy as a profession. When classes below the grandi came to organize politically, they employed foreigners too, so that the first captain of the people (*capitano del popolo*) in Florence was an outsider, and not until 1282 was a hometown boy given the highest magistracy in Florence.

By then, Florentine politics was dominated by what is probably the most famous two-party system of them all, despair of generations of medieval history students, the Guelfs and the Ghibellines. So much of Florence's odd constitution derives from the Guelf-Ghibelline struggle that some effort must be made to explain it. It begins, according to the annals of Florence, in 1216, when a Buondelmonti jilted an Amidei and married a Donati instead. Then an Amidei got together with a Uberti to cut Buondelmonti's throat, and the war was on. Politics was very personal in Florence.

Soon this classic but forgettable feud merged with the world-wide struggle between the popes and the Holy Roman emperors which was already a century old and which, as we saw, had helped make the cities independent of both. Over the years, Florentine foreign policy had tended to oscillate sagely between loyalty to the emperor (Ghibellinism came from the name of an imperial fief in Germany) and loyalty to the pope (Guelfism came from the name of the man the pope wanted to put on the German throne). Since Uberti backed the emperor for reasons still best known to himself, and Buondelmonti backed the Guelfs for reasons equally obscure, the family feud and the political were enmeshed in each other.

For the next century, Florence was treated to the spectacle of assassination and wholesale ostracism carried out in the name, be-

lieve it or not, of foreign policy. Despairing of the central government and the podestà, each party eventually created its own
government, with its own executive, council, and captains. From
1250 to 1260, when the Guelfs held the city and the Ghibellines
were in exile, Florence was effectively governed by the six captains
of the Guelfs. From 1260 to 1267, when the Ghibellines ruled, Florence was governed by the six captains of the Ghibellines.

By 1280, the two parties had just about destroyed each other,
together with the class which had created them and the old grandi
constitution, but not before the Guelfs, during their decade of control in the 1250s, had made Guelfism immortal by conquering
Lucca, Pisa, and most of Tuscany for Florence. Florentine patriotism became Guelf thereafter, so that even a quiet-living cloth
merchant who hated the Buondelmontis of this world would still
fight for the pope, damn the emperor, and toast the *partè Guelfa*.

At first glance, there seems to be nothing republican in all this
except the plurality of chiefs among the grandi. A party system is
a useful safeguard in a republic but, especially when one party celebrates victory by exiling the other from the state, hardly an indispensable safeguard. A closer look, however, reveals two effects
which party strife imposed on the Florentine constitution for the
rest of its life, and which were instrumental in postponing monarchy for two centuries. One was the bringing of large numbers of
non-grandi into politics, and the other was the sentimental opposition to kings which Guelfism came eventually to stand for.

Hating the Ghibelline emperors meant hating monarchy.
Florentines obliged. Their animus eventually (even though Dante
disagreed) came to include all the inheritors of Caesar's mantle, the
whole idea of universal monarchy in Christendom, and Julius Caesar himself. A Guelf became a sort of medieval Whig, jealous of his
liberties, prickly as a cactus about local independence, and mortally
fearful of anything that smacked of absolute monarchy on any scale.
Finally in the 1390s, Florentines looked around them and began to
see their constitution no longer as a *modus vivendi* between competing families but as a deliberate and unique creation, the cradle
of progress, the palladium of Italian liberty, and an education to
Europe. The Renaissance had begun.

The second great effect of the parties was to politicize the artisans and merchants. In a life-and-death battle, neither group of
grandi could afford to neglect the able-bodied lesser breed they
called *popolani* or people. To bring them in, the grandi created in

their party governments an entire second string of captains, council, and executive, staffed by popolani. Soon after, the same institutions appeared in the formal constitution of Florence. By the 1270s, the podestà of Florence was seconded by a *capitano del popolo* and each had a council of his own composed of neighborhood and family leaders. Thus Florence more than doubled the size of its ruling elite and at the same time multiplied its magistracies beyond the capacity of any one man, however gifted, to control them. The republican habit was confirmed and extended. In a kind of mitotic ecstasy, Florence from 1250 to about 1450 multiplied offices beyond the capacity of the most respected historians to count them. Soon, the answer to every problem in Florence was to call a *parlamentum* and appoint a committee, preferably two. People even ran out of names for them and took to calling them ad hoc after the number of members they had, like the Seven of Food and the Ten of War. It was a glorious carnival of magistrates, all either elected or chosen by lot, or appointed by another committee. In addition, to make sure that no one would miss his chance to govern Florence, terms were set so short as to seem comical. In fact, at two months, the term of a Florentine *prior* is the shortest in republican history.

Against this background of ever-multiplying magistracies, Florence had her three social revolutions. Because of it, none of the three made any change in the basic Florentine theory of constitution making.When the popolo grasso dispossessed the grandi between 1282 and 1293, it was legally only a matter of adding a new twenty-eight-man captains' council, a new executive committee (the *priori*, composed of six leaders of the greater gilds), and a new presiding officer (the famous Gonfalonier of Justice). Thrifty souls, the Florentines did not dispense with either the podestà or the capitano del popolo. They simply hobbled the old executives with huge advisory councils.

The advent of the lesser gilds in 1343 required only the expansion of the priori from six to eight, and a slightly wider franchise for the other offices. Even the extraordinary failed revolution of the popolo minuto, workers and journeymen, in 1378 involved no new institutions. Instead a revolutionary parlamentum deposed the former priors, elected a new set, and lengthened the citizens' list.

The 1378 revolution only lasted a few months. Once back in power, the shaken mercantile elite of Florence quickly returned to more conservative franchises and stayed with them for most of the remaining century and a half of independence. So it is the 1343 constitution, established after the overthrow of an attempted dictatorship, which should be taken as the type of Florentine republicanism in its heroic age, and which should be seen as the object of the slow but steady attack of the Medici in the fifteenth century.

For an important constitution, the arrangement of 1343 is certainly one of the most Byzantine in history. It is far more complicated than the famous unwritten constitution of England. It provided for hundreds of public offices, almost as many as there were Florentines available to fill them. Election of these offices was equally complicated. Neither ancient nor modern democrats are equipped to imagine a system in which an elected committee might appoint another committee whose duty it was to draw up lists of candidates for committees, from which officeholders would be chosen by yet another committee. In essence, the system was not an electoral law at all but simply a way of getting every active citizen of Florence into office as often as possible and out again as soon as possible. Its effect was to shift power rapidly back and forth between the great families of Florence so as to prevent any one of them from doing any damage. To keep particularly dangerous families out of politics completely, the constitution gave the government power to define them as either grandi, or gildless, or Ghibellines, and declare them, under three thirteenth-century laws, barred from office (*divieti*).

In outline, the system looked like a truncated pyramid. On top was the Signory, six priors, and a gonfalonier, chosen by lot for a term of two months. Next came the prior's council, four militia captains, and three *boni homines* from each of the four city neighborhoods for a total of twenty-eight. The captains served four months and the good men three. Together these thirty-odd were the highest magistrates in the state, and also, by design, those with the shortest terms of office. For executive actions which required a bit more long-range planning, there were special committees, chosen *ad hoc* by lot and serving for a heady six months, like the Eight of Police (*Otto di Guardia*) or the Eight of War (*Otto di Balìa*). In addition there were offices such as tax assessor which had no parent committee but were unsalaried and elective like the higher ones.

Below the small executive committees were the podestà and capitano del popolo, each with a council of some two hundred fifty citizens all of whom served for a year. This had become a sort of legislature by 1343 and any law proposed by the Signory had to have a two-thirds majority in each of the two large councils.

All of the foregoing magistrates had powers which would now be called judicial. In addition there were special committees, like the Forty (*Quarantia*) or the *Mercanzia*, whose duty was to sit as courts in their special jurisdiction.

Such, inasmuch as we can generalize between parlamentums, was the government of republican Florence. It would seem just about impervious to tyranny. How could any one man gain control of all these offices? Bossism is prevented by lot election. A military coup based on the people's militia might have been possible, but when the Florentines gave up their citizen army in 1351 and switched to mercenaries, this danger too receded. Florence would have no Marius or Caesar. Set up as it was in the wreckage of Florence's only dictatorship (the one-year reign of Walter of Brienne in 1342), the Florentine system was confusing and inefficient but it was an unsurpassed weapon against one-man rule. It also managed to function in spite of credit collapse, family feuds, bubonic plague, and constant war with the cities of Tuscany. It survived an attempted coup in 1382 and a war with the pope in 1375. When, in 1390, the republic of Florence took on the despot of northern Italy, her constitution not only survived but was apotheosized.

The despot's name was Giangaleazzo Visconti. While Florence had been busy with constitution making, Giangaleazzo's family had parlayed an imperial appointment as vicar and podestà of Milan into one of the first Renaissance tyrannies. Self-made, intelligent, beneficent, cruel, and absolute, Visconti's regime would have seemed like the wave of the future to anyone looking back from 1532, by which time Venice was the only important republic that remained in all Italy and the triumph of the famous princely families of Sforza, Rovere, Gonzaga, or Este was complete. Visconti, moreover, was not satisfied merely to dismantle the Milanese republic, his ambition was to become monarch of Italy by systematically conquering the cities north of Rome. In more modern times, this too would seem inevitable and progressive; in fact, in the middle of the nineteenth century, a man with far less ability than Giangaleazzo (Victor Emanuel of Savoy) actually accomplished it.

Florence had the luck, however, not to know about the progressivisms of the glorious future. To the Commune, Visconti's policies looked like the crack of doom. A wave of patriotism buried the city's usual conflicts. Hostilities with the Tuscan cities were abandoned as Florence strove to create a defensive league against the common danger. Finally, as Giangaleazzo moved on Bologna in 1390, the Commune declared war on him.

It was hopeless from the start. Milan never lost a yard and the Tuscan League suffered desertion after desertion. Guelf France and republican Venice sat back to watch as Giangaleazzo moved nearer and nearer. Neighboring Pisa and Siena made Visconti their monarch in 1399, and Perugia in 1400. By July 1402, only Florence was left, the single republic of any consequence opposing the ripening Italian monarchy. A huge Milanese army stood poised on her frontier, fresh from its defeat of Bologna, first and last of Florence's allies. The city had few troops and little reserve of cash.

One would have expected surrender. Visconti's ability, the dream of Italian unity, the enhanced status of monarchy, were all trumpeted by his propagandists in every city. The republican cause was hopeless, and practical bourgeois all over Italy were not disposed to risk life and fortune to defend it. Nevertheless, the Signory of Florence never even debated surrender. Said one of the priors, simply, "We must go on, with courage."[1] They marshaled their small forces around the city and its hinterland and prepared for the kind of siege in which, under fourteenth-century rules, defeat would mean wholesale destruction and slaughter.

At this climactic moment Giangaleazzo Visconti was surprised by fortune. On September 3, 1402, he died of plague. Slowly his jerry-built empire fell apart and Florence was saved. Within a generation the republic had defeated Giangaleazzo's son Filippo Maria and established the independence of Tuscany. In 1440 she put an end to the Visconti dream for good by defeating Filippo's best army at the Battle of Anghiari (the same battle Leonardo was paid by the Commune to paint on its council chamber wall). Soon after, the Visconti themselves were thrown out of Milan. Florence's fifty years of war with the Visconti had been won by the republic. The David of Michelangelo had killed Goliath.

Of the thousands of wars involving Florence, this one is easily the most significant. Nothing so wonderfully concentrates the mind as having one's back to the wall. Convinced after Giangaleazzo's sudden death that God was a republican, Florentines of all classes, particularly the humanist intellectuals, discovered that the Florentine constitution was not a dull, much-mended *modus vivendi* but a work of providence and a work of art. It was, they found, riddled with the new values of the dawning Renaissance. Thus, in the minds of the new humanists, the old medieval city became the new Athens and the new Rome.

Poring over their precious pagan classics, men like Coluccio Salutati and Leonardo Bruni uncovered a parallel between Persia and Milan, between Philip of Macedon and Giangaleazzo Visconti. Monarchy had been the knell of classical culture once in Rome and now again in Italy. The secret of the Golden Age of Athens, announced Bruni in 1403, was the same as that of his own city of Florence: the energies of free citizens released by republican government.[2] Ghiberti, Brunelleschi, Donatello, and Della Robbia could not exist under tyranny.

Two generations before, in 1345, when Petrarch had discovered Cicero's letters, he had reproached Cicero for opposing Caesar and even condemned him for entering politics in the first place.[3] When Salutati discovered a new batch of Cicero's letters in 1392, at the height of the war with Milan, he hailed Cicero as a defender of republican liberty. It was, wrote Salutati, the duty of every citizen to fight for his commonwealth against subversion and tyranny.[4] According to Bruni, Caesar was not, as Dante had thought, the divinely ordained unifier and peacemaker of the world, preparing it for the coming of Christ. Caesar was instead a man of blood, an outlaw and a tyrant. Brutus and Cassius, placed by Dante in the icy bottom of the Inferno, were quite possibly heroes along with Cicero.[5] The ancient legend that Florence itself had been founded by Caesar was investigated by Salutati and discovered to be (as it was) false. Florence, he asserted, was founded by Sulla's veterans when the republic was still in being.[6] Excellent, echoed Bruni in his *Praise of the City of Florence* in 1404, for then, "the city of Rome saw her power, liberty, gifted minds, and the fame of her citizens in their greatest flower [and] still thriving was the freedom of which Rome was deprived by the most wicked thieves not long after this colony had been established here."[7]

Nor was all this scholarship merely words. Salutati and Bruni both held the post of chief secretary of the Florentine republic from 1375 to 1444. An unbroken chain of great humanist writers from 1375 to 1512 made this office the central source of republican theory for all of Italy. So eloquent was the *Cancellaria* that Giangaleazzo himself once called Salutati's propaganda the equivalent of a troop of paid mercenaries, and Florence became the acknowledged champion of republicanism wherever humanists were read.

No better proof could be given that monarchy was the wave of the future than the fact that gallant Florence had itself become a monarchy only a century after Bruni left the Cancellaria. In 1532, Tuscany was a principality ruled by the heir of the house of Medici and the city which Bruni had likened to Rome had met a Roman fate. How did this happen? Was there a flaw in the 1343 constitution? Something special about the Medici? Or was Polybios correct about those gloomy cycles: are republics simply mortal?

It seems, in retrospect, that we must blame the genius of the Medici most of all for the fate of the Florentine republic. Unlike the Bardi and Peruzzi, the Strozzi and the Pitti, or the Ricci and Albizzi families, the Medici saw that it was impossible under the Florentine system either to gain all the offices or to abrogate them by a coup. The Medici therefore adopted a policy new in republican history which was to manipulate the titular offices from a position on the sidelines. The modern analogy would be a city boss, but the analogy is misleading because bosses so seldom entertain a temptation to establish a dynasty and rule in public. Indeed, Cosimo de Medici, founder of the family's political fortunes, seems to have had no plans to make princes of his heirs. He himself was content to manage his party from a background position on the committees for diplomacy and the national debt.

Cosimo's object was probably no more devious than to keep himself from being thrown out of Florence by some other family. That had happened once in 1433, and it was only luck that five pro-Medici priors were drawn from the hat a year later and decided to recall him. After his return, Cosimo managed to have the offending Albizzi clan exiled and barred their allies from office. Such measures were traditional. Then, to prevent a recurrence, he devised his one truly brilliant constitutional innovation, a new committee which would fill the hat from which the names of priors and councillors were drawn. These ten *accoppiatori* were to be chosen for a term of five long years by a process which Cosimo was able to control himself. Very indirect but very effective—and very un-Florentine. Clearly the accoppiatori were more powerful than the signory they chose, yet their terms, instead of being shorter, were the longest in Florence. Florentines did not accept them easily either. They were abolished by parlamentums in 1454 and 1465. Medici loyalists restored them in 1458 and 1466 respectively, however, and such loyalists, thanks to brilliant face-to-face politics by Cosimo and his son Piero, eventually formed the largest party in Florence. When

Piero died in 1469, Medici ascendancy was so complete that a committee of six hundred formally petitioned Cosimo's grandson Lorenzo to lead the republic in the manner of his father and grandfather.

Florence was not yet a monarchy in 1469. Only a few signs existed that the Medici ascendancy was not like those of the Buondelmonti, the Donati, the Bardi, or the Albizzi of times past: the fact, for example, that the republic voted to Cosimo the epitaph of Julius Caesar (*Pater patriae*: father of his country), or the fact that Cosimo had supported the Sforza despotism against the Milanese republicans in 1450, or that he had, from his post on the diplomatic committee, engineered a general Italian peace in 1454 which favored Milan and sacrificed the interests of republics. Florentines were, alas, reassured when it was explained to them that the new lily on the Medici coat of arms was not the red lily of Florence but the white lily of Capet, granted to them by the king of France.

When we come to Lorenzo, however, the picture changes. He was no less brilliant and no less charming than his grandfather had been, but he was not so retiring. No modest bourgeois, he enjoyed his status. Powers that his grandfather had accumulated as an insurance policy Lorenzo used as a birthright. Cosimo had been extraordinarily careful to use his wealth privately, to dress down, and to cultivate an image as one of the boys. Lorenzo spent publicly like a prince, offered bread and circuses, and acquired the nickname of the Magnificent. The popolo minuto, of course, loved it all with vicarious passion. Lorenzo was neither cruel nor basely arrogant, but his self-assurance was a bit beyond what is expected of a republican aristocrat. A new generation learned almost imperceptibly that the game of politics had lost much of its savor when the only way to get into it was to join the party. The younger humanists gave up reading Plutarch and Livy and turned to the authoritarian idealism of Plato. They met with Lorenzo at his suburban estate and talked cleverly of the harmony of opposites.

The aging opponents of the Medici turned after repeated failure to the barbaric but logical means of assassination. Nothing better describes the state of the Florentine republic at this stage than the spectacle of old Jacopo Pazzi trying to call a parlamentum on the April day in 1478 when Giuliano de' Medici was stabbed in the cathedral. "Popolo e libertà!" "The People and Freedom!" he cried. He was answered—drowned out—by a slogan which translates roughly as "We want the Medici!" and nearly trampled by a hostile crowd.[8] Of course the popolo minuto would have gained little from a replacement of the Medici by the Pazzi, but they clearly no longer enjoyed the spectacle of political struggle between the great families. Loyalty to the abstraction of the republic had given way to loyalty to a man. Grateful for Lorenzo's survival, the Florentines now voted him the privilege of retaining, like Peisistratos of Athens, an armed bodyguard.

Encouraged by this kind of affection, Lorenzo carefully increased his control over the magistracies. Delighted with the accoppiatori, he made the device even more responsive to his will in 1470 by having the outgoing ten, together with the signory which they had chosen, elect the ten for the next five-year term. When a magistrate is chosen by his own predecessors the process is called cooptation. The old Athenian areopagos had been coopted, but this seems to be the first time cooptation had been tried in Florence. It was not the last.

In 1480, Lorenzo's men manipulated a parlamentum and created the first more or less permanent committee in the republic— the Council of Seventy. Not only did it sit indefinitely, it had an unprecedented range of powers. It coopted its members, presented short lists of candidates to the accoppiatori, and provided the members of the major executive committees already in existence. In 1490, the major powers of the republic were handed to yet a new cooptive committee with only seventeen members. The trend was clear. Lorenzo was proceeding toward monarchy by leaving the powers of existing offices unchanged and concentrating the power of election instead. Only Lorenzo's death in 1492 could halt this project. "We must conclude," wrote a historian who had seen this, "that under him the city was not free, even though it could not have had a better tyrant or a more pleasant one."⁹

Lorenzo's son Piero was only a fair tyrant, and never a pleasant one. Then, too, he made the mistake of fighting against the French king, patron of the Guelfs. Worse, he lost. On November 9, 1494, the priors locked Piero out of city hall and went into the streets shouting "Long live the people and liberty!" and this time Florence responded. A parlamentum exiled Piero, abolished the Council of Seventy, and called back from exile everyone who had opposed the Medici for the past sixty years. The atmosphere was jubilant and slightly crazy: very Florentine. The exiles and revolutionaries had none of the gravity of Brutus and twice his audacity. When the king of France entered Florence with his whole army to dictate surrender, the Florentine delegate, Piero Capponi, tore up the French draft and dared Charles VIII to order an attack. "Sound your trumpets," he said. "We will ring our bells."[10]

A Dominican friar, Girolamo Savonarola, rose in the councils of the revolution, declaring Florence to be the vanguard of a republican millennium, and the elect city of God Himself. Every major magistrate in Florence was spending his office hours drafting the new constitution, and all of republican history was reviewed for precedents, from Athens to modern Venice.

Eventually this second republic of Florence received a constitution largely designed on Venetian models by the evangelical Savonarola. It was resolved that the electoral powers of the Medicean Seventy and Seventeen would never again be held by so few, so they were given to a council so large that a simple quorum to do business was one thousand members. Commissions were hurriedly given to build a new meeting hall over the customs house, for the new Great Council was the largest committee in Florentine history—one of the largest, in fact, in all republican history. Membership was for life, but as in the Roman Senate, it was conferred on any who had been or would be elected to the highest Florentine magistracies, plus their descendants. It was therefore neither closed nor entirely cooptive.

This was the constitution under which Savonarola burned the vanities, defied the pope, and tried to make Florence into a holy city. In a series of electrifying sermons in the cathedral, Savonarola pictured the restored republic as a city upon a hill, preparing the way for a political and religious renewal of Christendom and possibly the second coming of Christ.[11] The tone and values of Savonarola's program can still be recognized in those of republicans as diverse as Calvin, Cromwell, and the founders of Massachusetts; but he was hanged and burned by the more worldly Florentines in 1498.

Looking back on it, however, Savonarola's Florence seems only a hectic episode, the last flame from a dying fire. A new constitutional law in 1502 brought back monarchical ideas in the figure of a new magistrate, elected but irremovable. So Piero Soderini was elected Gonfalonier of Justice for life. Even permanence, it seems, is not permanent, however, and Soderini's sentence ended in 1512. In August of that year a papal army financed by a Medici cardinal defeated the Florentine militia and entered the city in triumph. On September 16 a managed parlamentum restored the constitution of

Lorenzo the Magnificent in favor of a new Lorenzo, his grandson. The Medici claim to be citizen aristocrats was no longer mentioned. The new Lorenzo was a monarch in his own right: Duke of Urbino, if you please, by the grace of his uncle, Cardinal Giovanni, who had become in his own turn Pope Leo X. The return of the Medici was thus a result not of their mastery of the internal politics of Florence, but of their ability to make use of diplomacy to advance the status of the heirs.

This policy jibed beautifully with the new situation of the Italian cities. By 1500 they had lost the last shred of their diplomatic independence to a powerful combination of largely non-Italian monarchies and the long anomalous age of the free city was over. A French conquest had given Florence the chance to expel the Medici in 1494, and a Spanish one brought them back again in 1512. Fifteen years later, when Florence had a final opportunity to throw them out again, it was not a revolution in the city but the sack of Rome by a Habsburg army that provided the opportunity.

In 1527, Savonarola's constitution was restored with a one-year instead of a life Gonfalonier. It may have been the most workable and forward-looking constitution Florence had ever seen, but it could only exist as long as the unusual diplomatic conditions that produced it. In 1530, the new pope, a Medici, came to an understanding with the Habsburg emperor, and together they attacked Florence.

The last republic of Florence fought hopelessly but purely, impeaching one Gonfalonier for entering negotiations with the pope and electing Michelangelo to supervise the construction of siege defenses. It died fighting. On April 27, 1532, two years after military victory, Pope Clement proclaimed Alessandro de Medici Duke of Florence. No one, it seems, attempted to oppose this move by reminding the pope that on February 9, 1528, Florence had, in a last grand Savonarolan gesture, elected a king of its own: Jesus Christ!

Thus we remember the Medici, and forget the five-hundred-year-old republic to which they put an end. We associate all the great Florentines one way or another with Florence's Caesars, instead of with her Brutuses and Ciceros. Why? Because the Medici won, because Lorenzo really was Magnificent, and because, frankly, Florence never really had a Brutus, much less a Pericles. In Florence the republic was defended less by individuals than by families. The city's most memorable republican politician was a forbidding hook-nosed fanatic, and her most eloquent republican intellectuals were redolent of the ivory tower. All that is, except one. Into the office which had become, under Coluccio Salutati, the theoretical center of European republicanism in 1390, there came in 1498 a young assistant secretary named Niccolò Machiavelli.

Machiavelli was humanistically educated, but not fully a humanist. He look little interest in political ideas or rhetorical display. He was a technician, a practical politician (the unelected variety), and a diplomat, actually living the *vita activa* prescribed but only half-heartedly practiced by Salutati. It was the farthest thing from his mind in 1498 to formulate political theory in defense of the republic, however embattled it was. For the fourteen years he remained in the chancellery, he produced almost nothing but the required diplomatic reports, letters, and memoranda. If there was any trace in him of the tyrannicidal zeal of a Bruni, it is hard to find in any of these writings.

When Machiavelli, in the enforced leisure of exile, finally did come to write theory, he produced a book which has been a *vademecum* for tyrants ever since. A chilling book and still, after centuries, a thoroughly immoral one. He dedicated it to a Medici, the Duke of Urbino, and seemed to consider it part of a letter-writing campaign to get one of the Medici to employ him.

A very peculiar republican, Machiavelli; and yet it is certain that, willingly or unwillingly, he shared the republic's fate. When the Medici came in 1512, he went to jail, torture, and later exile. In 1527, when the republic was proclaimed in Florence for the last time, Machiavelli hurried back to the city to ask for his old job back. His death preceded the republic's by only a few years. When Florence was organizing its defense against the Medici in 1512, it was Machiavelli who resurrected the citizen militia of the thirteenth century, memorialized it as the secret of Rome's defeat of Hannibal, and got the city to raise it and send it against the Habsburg army. Last but not least, of all the books he wrote in exile, only *The Prince* is monarchist. All the other political works are sober but powerful manuals for republicans. Machiavelli was clearly many things, including a deliberate paradoxalist and a lover of power; but Machiavelli was beyond any doubt a republican partisan, a true descendant of a family that had given fifty-four priors and twelve Gonfaloniers to the Florentine republic. In his *Discourses on Livy*, Machiavelli wrote:

. . . cities never increased in dominion or wealth unless they were free. And certainly it is wonderful to think of the greatness which Athens attained within the space of a hundred years. . . . the general good is nowhere regarded but in republics.[12]

Livy's Roman republic almost becomes a utopia in Machiavelli's *Discourses,* so much so that at least one of the many learned men who have wrestled to understand Machiavelli has suggested that the monarchism of *The Prince* was a piece of pure deliberate irony, like Jonathan Swift's proposal that the Irish overcome famine by eating their children.[13]

It is probably much too late to recapture Machiavelli for the republican tradition. *The Prince* does not sound like a satire and it is taken straight in many a high-school class. Worse, the book is in fact not a satire, for Machiavelli never assumed that a preference for republics implied a hatred of monarchy. He was clearly more interested in public virtue and strength as ends than in either of the two means—monarchy and republic—by which a state might achieve them. Despite this, the *Discourses* remains one of the most powerful of republican books. In chapter after chapter of crystal-clear analytical prose, Machiavelli discloses and praises the politics of pagan republicanism, the values of men such as Solon, Brutus, and Scipio, the ethos of the societies which had produced them. Writing at the tail end of medieval Christendom, before Luther raised the stakes of belief, Machiavelli was as regardless of Christian morality as he was intoxicated by the classical ethic which had preceded it. "It was," he wrote, "necessary that the sons of Brutus should have been executed," for otherwise the Roman republic would have been stillborn.[14]

The love of fame, the strife of faction, above all the spirit of sacrifice to the state, all Christian sins since Saint Augustine, were for Machiavelli the salvation of the commonwealth. With the Roman historians he saw in Rome's expansion an indication of her health as a society. Like them he attributed the fall of the republican constitution to corruption caused by a pause in that expansion and a distribution of its gains among private citizens. Like Polybios, he saw in Rome's health and longevity as a republic proof that her constitution was successfully mixed and balanced against Fortune's turning wheel of decay and corruption. He praised Rome's citizen army because it was not, like Florence's, a mercenary force and because, before decay had set in, it had been a militia instead of a standing army. In fact, Machiavelli is probably the first thinker since the age of Augustus to advocate citizen militias on principle. The militia he devised for Florence panicked in its first engagement, but Machiavelli continued in *The Art of War* to view militias as a panacea.

As for Florence, which, wrote Machiavelli, "I love more than my soul,"[15] he made it the whipping boy of the *Discourses*. Derisory in war, unable to hold an empire, corrupted by inequality of wealth and an overdose of Christian kindness, Florence was the perfect example of a decadent republic. She was probably beyond redemption. Her Golden Age of literature, art, and scholarship was only a sign that her fourteenth-century *virtù* had left her. Or that it had never been there at all. Ungraced by public spirit, party strife in Florence could create nothing of value. In anguish, Machiavelli wrote, Florence "has gone on for the two centuries of which we have any reliable account, without ever having a government that could really be called a republic."[16] The amplitude, the unpredictability, the dizzying freedom of the medieval free city of Florence struck this late-coming humanist as a poor substitute for the austerity, relentlessness, and incorruptible virtue of Stoic Rome.

With such defenders it is no wonder the republic did not live long. It was abolished in 1532 by a Medici monarchy, and *The Prince*, published in that year, may serve it as an epitaph. Its five-century legacy, however, was preserved, summed up so oddly and backhandedly in the *Discourses on Livy*. Here the last of the Florentine humanist republicans, steeped in medieval republican practice, recreated the classical Roman republic, absorbed its values, freed them from medieval Christianity, and sent them on to the Age of Enlightenment for delivery to Adams and Robespierre.

6

John Calvin
A Republican Church

WHEN MACHIAVELLI DIED IN 1528, the pagan politics and brutal republican virtue he had recommended died with him. It was the century of the Reformation, and of the retreat of humanism. The text was the Bible instead of Plutarch; the model Samuel instead of Solon. The future of the republic depended on the survival, or the renewal, of backward-looking institutions like the barons and free cities of the north whom the Renaissance had barely touched. It depended on the establishment of a meaningful relationship between republicanism and an essentially medieval religious passion whose drive for uniformity and contempt for temporal politics made it the most unlikely bedfellow in republicanism's history. Here and there the liaison did happen—in Geneva, in the Netherlands, briefly in France and Scotland; but it is likely it would never have happened if it were not for the lethal effectiveness of that Samuel of the sixteenth century, a driven Picard prophet named John Calvin.

Almost nobody likes John Calvin anymore. In these times it is hard to understand how anyone ever did. Ascetic, imperious, convinced of man's depravity but jealous of his own dignity, a man deeply suspicious of even the little humor he had, Calvin is a rather

grim reminder of the inhumanity of the Reformation era and a hitherto overlooked patient for post-mortem Freudians.

This exalted Frenchman was, however, the most influential
leader of the European revolution we call the Reformation. To fail
to understand Calvin is to fail to understand that among the greatest forces in any revolution is the organizational skill, the other-
worldly conviction, and the more than human purity of revolutionary leaders. Moreover, Calvin's revolution was republican.
Without Calvin it would be hard to imagine the Reformation ending, as it did, in a century of international war, and a stalemate of
rival confessions; a stalemate so deep that this civilization escaped
definitively from the union of church and state that had threatened
it since Samuel anointed Saul.

There is no need to be a Calvinist to recognize that Calvin's
design for churches and his view of their relations with states
amounts to a renewal of classical republicanism. Nor does one have
to admire Calvin to agree that the Savonarolan fervor behind this
renewal is a major factor in the creation of the republic of the Netherlands in the sixteenth century and the English Commonwealth
in the seventeenth. Presbyterian, Congregational, Huguenot, Reformed, Separatist, and Puritan are all variations of Calvinism, and
the most significant differences between them have to do with
church government. Even modern revolutionary movements seem
to owe something of their organization to Calvinist precedent.

Like Solon, John Calvin was no democrat, but he was a genuine
republican, fervently when it came to the church, tentatively with
respect to the state. In his time, however, the overwhelming initiative lay with monarchy. The papal monarchy, to be sure, was on
its way out. The Reformation gave to what was, for all practical
purposes, Europe's medieval government the *coup de grâce*. Without Calvin and his movement, however, it is likely that the fall of
the papacy would simply have handed Europe over to the national
monarchies which, like France or Austria, could collect taxes, raise
armies, and direct bureaucracies better than the popes could. Such
monarchies had been in the wings since the fifteenth century—
"new monarchies" to use the historians' term, eager to pick up the
new tools of power which popes and Holy Roman Emperors seemed
unable to handle.

Despairing of discovering the moral fervor he considered essential to republican survival, Machiavelli, in *The Prince*, consigned the
future to such monarchies. Within two centuries the most success-

ful of them would be called "absolute monarchies." For many of
them, like Saxony and England, the Reformation made their task
easier, giving them control of the officials and property of the once
international church and clearing up the last medieval impediments
to sovereignty. In Switzerland, however, where Calvinism began, in
Scotland, and in the Netherlands, republican practice and republican thought prevailed. Moving from church to state, successfully
defending itself (even for a time in France) against triumphant monarchy, republicanism was an available experience when revolution
came to Europe again in the eighteenth century.

So much of this is John Calvin's doing that it seems niggardly
to reproach him for being unattractive to the twentieth-century
mind. From medieval Switzerland to eighteenth-century Europe,
the most beaten path is that of the followers of this French exile.
Whether or not he is forgotten as a theologian, as a republican revolutionary John Calvin is as alive as he ever was.

During his years in Geneva, from 1541 until his death in 1564,
Calvin was sometimes called the "Protestant Pope." He was not.
He did not want to rule and certainly never could have ruled his
movement as medieval popes had ruled the church. The papacy
that Calvin spent his life attacking was a paradigm of one-man rule.
At the height of the papal monarchy, Innocent III had raised armies, appointed most bishops, deposed kings, defined doctrine, and
levied taxes throughout Christendom. No monarch of the time was
more able to work his will. He even controlled the choice of a successor through the curious election system formalized in 1059 by
which cardinals named by previous popes formed an electoral College that named the next pope. More efficient and trustworthy than
the previous system (city politics in Rome) and elective after a fashion (election was, after all, the approved method of choosing kings,
bishops, and popes when the Middle Ages began), the College of
Cardinals had one major defect: It insulated the papacy from the
subjects it governed almost as much as hereditary succession would
have done.

There was a danger that popes might undertake programs their
subjects would not support, with money and arms supplied grudgingly or not at all. Spiritual powers are as difficult to exercise without the consent of the governed as temporal ones. More difficult
in fact, because the leaders of churches must set an even higher
example than the leaders of states. When Boniface VIII asserted in

a bull of 1302 powers that Innocent III had not hesitated to exercise a century before, he became the first pope to discover into what low respect the papacy had fallen. The French king called a council of French bishops, declared Boniface a heretic, and sent French troops to arrest him. In fury and terror, Boniface dropped dead soon after. Christendom was not outraged, but rather greeted the news with relief bordering on indifference. A few years later, the College of Cardinals was packed with Frenchmen and the whole papacy decamped from Rome to the French town of Avignon, there to grow in power, pretension, and efficiency, while Christians of all classes in every other country grew more and more embarrassed, resentful, or disinterested in the institution that had once been the focus of their loyalty. They called it the Babylonian Captivity of the Church.

Things got worse in 1378. Italian cardinals who wanted to move back to Rome elected one pope, and the French cardinals who wanted to stay in Avignon elected another. Each pope appointed cardinals and other officials, collected taxes, and called vainly for crusades against the other. It was a civil war without the catharsis of violence, bringing the papacy and every other value of medieval society into question, monarchy included. With chaos at the top, something very like the Reformation broke out at the bottom. Wyclif in England and Hus in Bohemia denounced all priests and called for a Biblical religion unsullied by courts or bureaucracies. Nor could anyone seem to stop the schism. Popes died but their colleges of cardinals went on forever, and each elected new popes. Desperate measures only made things worse. In 1408 dissident cardinals of both colleges called a council of bishops in Pisa which fired both popes and elected one of its members as Alexander V. Of course, no one resigned, and the result of Pisa was that Christendom now had three popes.

Possibly, after a century of this, the Church might have ended up governed by a Catholic Consulate or a committee executive as a confederation of dioceses; but the bereft Catholics of the fourteenth century didn't want a committee; they wanted their monarchy back. As they thought about the emergency, they drew on the more familiar precedents of medieval kingship. Just as it was up to aristocratic councils (like the English Parliament) to settle a disputed succession, it must be up to councils of churchmen to decide a disputed succession to the papacy. Indeed, lest as at Pisa the claimants deny a council's authority, it must be that the council is in the end sovereign and the pope is not. Going even further, to insulate any council from the effect of the appointment power of disputant popes, it must be larger than any college of cardinals, broader even than a synod of bishops. It must be an assembly truly representative of the entire Catholic Church—in other words, a General or ecumenical Council.

This theory, that a General Council was the locus of sovereignty in the church, was an extraordinary one. But for the emergency it might never have arisen. Pieced together from then minor sources, anti-Boniface canon lawyers like John of Paris or Henry of Suso, dissident scholastics like Marsilio of Padua and William of Ockham, the conciliar theory reached its full expression in works by an international galaxy of philosophers and legal scholars most of whom worked at the University of Paris in the years after 1378. Some of these, like Gelnhausen, Niem, and Langenstein remain obscure. Some, like Cardinals Nicholas of Cusa and Aeneas Sylvius Piccolomini, moved through conciliarism and on to other concerns, like the emergent humanism of which they remain great ornaments. Still others, however, like the great French scholars and successive chancellors of the University, Pierre D'Ailly and Jean Gerson, risked their lives and sacrificed their careers to solve the problem which Frenchmen like themselves had done so much to create in the first place. In November 1413, the propaganda of the University of Paris was answered by a call for a general council to meet in the Habsburg (later Swiss) city of Constance, midway between Avignon and Rome, to settle what had come to be called the Great Schism of the West.

A year later, on November 5, 1414, the fateful sixteenth Council of the western church met. Its secular patron was a pretender to the Empire and its clerical patron was one of the three popes, John XXIII; but its leader quickly turned out to be Jean Gerson. In March 1415, John XXIII saw which way the wind was blowing and fled Constance, hoping to take with him the Council's legitimacy. Gerson, however, was equal to this challenge. To the assembled councilors he preached a sermon excoriating the papal monarchy and affirming that no pope could disband this or any other Council. John XXIII was arrested and brought back to Constance under guard, and on April 6, 1415, the Council passed its most famous decree, *Sacrosancta,* affirming the sovereignty Gerson had so eloquently defended. By 1417 the Council had rid Christendom of all three popes. It had also decreed, in *Frequens,* that more general councils were to be convened at five-, seven-, and ten-year intervals.

Finally, it elected a new pope, Martin V, on the understanding that he would ratify the Council's work and agree to its sovereignty, which he did in a bull of February 22, 1418.

When the councilors left Constance in April 1418, the Catholic Church seemed to have become, for the first time since the see of Rome had asserted its primacy centuries ago, a republic. Its type was what would be called limited or constitutional monarchy. The pope was no longer sovereign but, in the words of Gerson's sermon, the executor of a power which only a council could define. His tenure was for life but a council had the power to impeach or depose him. Believing they had built for the ages, Gerson and D'Ailly went home to France, their scholarly careers cut short by unequivocal political acts. Neither lived to see the subsequent councils fail and the papacy triumph, in less than a generation, over all the work of Constance.

We can see now that Gerson and his fellow conciliarists were too moderate (perhaps the right word is conciliatory) to succeed. Constance condemned Wyclif for instance, executed Hus, and repudiated the tyrannicidal theories of John Petit. All three were the natural allies of conciliarists in any struggle for a reformed church, no less a republican one. Having deposed two popes, Constance also made the mistake of letting the third, Gregory XII, resign instead, and worse, to publish a bull "legitimizing" the Council. Last but not least, Constance left the College of Cardinals in existence. By not insisting that future popes be elected or at least confirmed by future councils, they gave the papacy institutional continuity greater than their own.

Councils met on schedule, it is true, but without the emergency of the schism they could not focus and lead. The Council of Siena dissolved itself in 1424, having accomplished nothing. When the seven-year Council met in 1431, its attempt to seize the initiative resulted in a long seesaw struggle from which the papal monarchy emerged splendid and triumphant. This Council met in the city republic (not yet Swiss) of Basel, but before it could act, the conciliar pope Martin V died and was immediately replaced by Eugenius IV.

Eugenius began his reign by officially dissolving the Council of Basel, which replied by declaring the pope contumacious. Negotiations eased the conflict and permitted the Council to continue, but battle lines were drawn. When Basel allowed parish priests to vote, and tried to appoint bishops, levy taxes, and put the pope on salary, Eugenius repudiated the *Sacrosancta* decree. Basel then impeached him. Eugenius was clever, however. He not only refused the summons, he summoned the Council to him, first to Ferrara, then to Florence, and finally to Rome. At the same time he neutralized the nations supporting Basel one by one with generous bilateral treaties.

In desperation Basel elected its own pope. Unhappily reminded of the schism, Christendom abandoned Basel, which dwindled to a junta and finally dissolved itself in the neighboring city of Lausanne in 1449. By 1461 the pope was none other than Cardinal Piccolomini, a former leader of the Council of Basel. So neatly coopted was this great humanist that he issued a bull that year called *Execrabilis,* forever prohibiting appeals from a pope to a council. There he drove his old ally Cusa, now a cardinal, weeping from his court.

So the papal monarchy was reestablished and the moderate republicans failed. Reform too had been put aside. Within the western church a deceptive quiet reigned for two generations. Renaissance monarchs and Renaissance popes wrote to each other about Livy and Cicero. Civilized intellectuals like Erasmus and More served monarchs and popes both, gently and occasionally calling for reform. None seemed aware that medieval conciliarism was still being taught at the University of Paris. None suspected the explosive energy that seethed below them, among the uneducated mass of Christians. When the republican church finally did emerge, a century after Constance, it would be led by the sort of people who could terrify Erasmus and make even Hus and Wyclif seem moderates by comparison. The Gersons of the sixteenth century, men like Montaigne, would spend a lifetime behind closed doors.

John Calvin was eight when Luther nailed the Ninety-Five Theses to the door of the church of Wittenberg; twelve when the great reformer defied the Emperor Charles V at Worms. He was a very good child, gently raised in the small town of Noyon in northeastern France by a father grown comfortable in artisanship and civil service, and a mother long practiced in both aristocratic manners and popular piety. He was also very bright, and his father decided to make a professor of theology out of him by sending him to high school in Paris. At fourteen, Calvin dutifully enrolled in the La Marche secondary school. La Marche, however, proved too relaxed for him. The next year he was enrolled in a semimonastic Parisian boarding school aptly named Montaigu (sharp peak), fasting and studying from dawn to dusk and taking a perverse satisfaction in a long array of disciplinary punishments. He remained there five years, generously supported by the revenues of church posts in Noyon which his father had obtained from his patron the bishop. In 1528, Calvin received his Master of Arts degree. By then the Reformation in Germany was in its eleventh year, with more than a dozen cities and states of the Empire officially Lutheran. Switzerland too was alight, with Basel and Berne following the lead of Zwingli's Zürich in that year. France, by contrast, was a backwater. Its Reformation consisted of a small group of humanist intellectuals in the town of Meaux, and a few isolated Lutherizers like Louis de Berquin, burned in 1529. Calvin knew little of them. Montaigu did not approve of humanism, still less of heresy, and Calvin did as he was told.

In 1528, however, Calvin's father, already secretary to the commune of Noyon, secretary to the bishop, and sometime attorney for the cathedral chapter, decided he wanted his son to be rich. He told him to abandon theology and become a lawyer. Calvin, of course, obeyed and took up his studies at Orleans, where for the first time his chronic indigestion and incapacitating migraine headaches appeared. But "Providence," as he called it, was in the process of "turning my bridle."[1] Beset with contradictory demands, the asceticism of Montaigu, the delights of classical literature, the piety of his mother, and the careerism of his father, Calvin found his way out. In 1531, he buried his father.

By 1532 Calvin had published a humanist commentary on a Latin classic (significantly, this was Seneca's plea for clemency to the emperor Nero). By 1533 he was a convert to the unsearchably omnipotent God of Martin Luther. In 1534, the year the King of France first began to burn protestants wholesale, Calvin returned to Noyon, said goodbye to his family, and resigned every one of the offices and stipends that his anxious father had so carefully accumulated for him through the cathedral of Noyon. He was twenty-four.

The man who took the road of exile in 1534 was painted in 1536. He had an angular face made longer by a fine lance of a nose and an incipient pointed black beard. From it, piercing from below high arched eyebrows, there appeared a pair of enormous almond-shaped dark eyes. He wore the graduate's round black hat with earflaps, a man of consequence and a man with a mission. Never, he would say proudly in later life, would he obey anyone but God. Never again would he be comfortable.

Calvin's first stop was the reformed city of Basel, conciliar in 1431 and Swiss since 1501. There he published the first small version of his summary of reformed theology, the *Institutes,* one of the most influential books ever written. Humanist in its exhaustive scholarship, lawyerly in the inexorability of its arguments, the *Institutes* was perhaps more deeply original in the asceticism of its style. It was totally organized. Not an extra word, not an overlong sentence, not a frivolous image in the entire book; and the nearest thing to self-indulgence was a signed preface threatening the King of France in the second person singular. When the French version of the *Institutes* appeared in 1541, a revolution was made not only in French but in all of European literature. Today Calvin's lovable French contemporary Rabelais cannot be read without footnotes. The deplorable Calvin is as clear as any Hemingway.

From Basel Calvin went briefly to Italy; then, making north for the Rhine city of Strasbourg, he stopped for the night in the newly independent city of Geneva. His old friend Du Tillet recognized him at the inn and told the local protestants, among them William Farel. Farel persuaded Calvin to stay and help them reform Geneva, possibly the last time a revolutionary party found a leader by threatening him with eternal damnation. Thus by chance, or as Calvin would put it, Providence, the city met its maker and the Calvinist revolutions began.

In a secular sense Geneva's meeting with Calvin was as providential as he said it was. In 1536 Calvin had no ideas on how to run a church, and, to judge by his Seneca commentary, no notable views on politics. It was Geneva's republican constitution that suggested both to him, and created a need to have them in the first place. Calvin hated public responsibility; indeed he wrote quite honestly that he would rather have died than lead the church of Geneva, which is no doubt why Farel had to threaten him with damnation (worse than death) to get him to stay there.[2] Without Geneva, Calvin would have remained a thinker.

What would Geneva have been without Calvin? For one thing, an independent, protestant republic. Geneva was not part of the Swiss Confederation, and would not enter it until the eighteenth century, but it was very much a free city in 1536, and thanks to a timely alliance with the Swiss republic of Berne, a very recent one. Until ten years before, French-speaking Geneva had been theoretically an episcopal city within the Duchy of Savoy (a duchy, by the way, which had been created for the man later elected antipope by the Council of Basel). Since 1424 it had been ruled jointly by the bishop and, through a deputy, by the Duke, both usually members of the same family. Conflict between either or both of these worthies and the city's elected commune had been chronic since the commune began in 1285, but in contrast to such cities as Florence or nearby Zürich and Berne, Geneva had been unable to secure its independence. Not until 1525 did events so favor the commune, but when, in December of that year, an assembly of citizens raised pikes and swore to independence, crying "Vive les Eidguenots!", Geneva got lucky at last. The Bernese alliance in 1526 kept the bishop at bay. His officials were replaced by two elected councils, the larger of which staged a coup d' etat against the duke in 1528. Finally, in 1533–34, the year of Calvin's conversion, the bishopric was declared vacant and Geneva was free.

The constitution of the new republic was not in the least unique. Like those of Florence and most earlier communes, it was aristocratic and plural wherever those principles could be applied. There was a *Conseil Général*, or general citizen's assembly, which had full powers and met twice a year, but of the 13,000 or so Genevans, only 1,500 qualified as citizen members and the assembly was content for the most part to be directed by the three councils. The *Grand Conseil* or Large Council chose its own members; the Council of Sixty was similarly limited; and the real government of Geneva, the Small Council of twenty-five, which met three times a week, consisted almost invariably of the ablest men from the ten to twenty leading families of Geneva. The system was very much like the vanished medieval communes of Calvin's native Picardy. Geneva's however was a living system. Calvin could see it at work, and through him the parochial old-fashioned constitutionalism set its stamp on states everywhere. All this because the Reformation and Calvin arrived in the newly independent republic within four months of each other.

On May 19, 1536, a General Assembly of 1,500 citizens of Geneva met in Saint Peter's Cathedral and with hands raised took a public oath to "live according to the Gospel and the Word." In August, when Calvin arrived, Geneva had a fresh and zealous republican government vowed to an as yet unorganized reformed church. It was natural that this church, as it came into being, would reflect both the zeal and the institutional shape of Genevan politics. In fact, the councils of the republic and the governing body of the new church could well have ended by being the same institution. The councils had by law inherited all the powers of the deposed bishop of Geneva, and most Lutheran city-states had already set a pattern of running their churches directly.

Calvin's first effort, in February 1537, to deal with the pressing problems of establishing a church was an uncharacteristically diffuse petition to the Small Council, which is now dignified with the title *Articles of Organization*.[3] He knew he wanted to pattern a church on the information in the biblical book of *Acts*, but he did not yet have a clear idea of how to distinguish the responsibilities of church and state. He could only begin with a request that the right of excommunication, essentially the right to admit or reject members, be confided to an elected body of pastors and laymen which would, in effect, form the governing body of the church of Geneva.

The councils were unwilling to grant this, and in fact did not definitively agree to it for twenty years; but they did accept the *Articles'* principle that any church of Geneva ought to be governed by a committee of ministers and laymen ("elders") one for each district in Geneva. They also agreed that church membership should be restricted to those who could make a confession of faith acceptable to this committee, and also that the responsibilities of the church, as opposed to those of the state, should be the same ones the bishop had had: preaching, morals, education, and the care of the sick and disabled. In these three principles we can see already the unique structure of the Calvinist churches. They would first of all be governed by both clerics and laymen, and they would be largely, but not entirely, self-governed. Second, their membership would always be exclusive. Third, their responsibilities would always include many functions essential to the state, but never so many that the church could become the state.

Or vice versa. Calvin and Geneva immediately entered on their characteristically tense relationship, soon to be duplicated in so many other states. Soon after the *Articles* were accepted a newly elected Small Council opposed what Calvin was doing under them. Then it threw Calvin out of Geneva. Three years later a new Small Council recalled Calvin and, threatened by damnation as usual, he returned. Geneva's politicians continued to pose serious threats to his system for a dozen years after that. No wonder. Once, when a member of the Small Council called Calvin an "evil Picard" over a glass of wine at a private dinner, the Church demanded—and got—

the offending councilor to tour the city, coatless and hatless, crying on his knees for pardon.

Yet Calvin, a member of the governing body of the church, was not even a citizen of Geneva until 1560. His loyalty to Strasbourg, where he spent his three-year exile, was greater. He became a citizen there in 1539, and he brought back from Strasbourg not only Idelette, his cipher of a wife, but Martin Bucer's system of having two clerical and two lay orders in the church, each charged with one of the four responsibilities described in the *Articles*. When he returned to Geneva in 1541, Calvin's republican vision of church government was pretty well fixed. He presented it to the Small Council almost immediately as the *Ecclesiastical Ordinances*, and the Council accepted them with very few modifications.

In the Ordinances we can see with perfect clarity the constitution that was to become so important a model for western churches and states. No Anabaptist anarchy or self-sufficiency for Calvin; no little conventicles of believers; no little vagaries of doctrine. This church was to be governed thoroughly. The central committee—"Consistory"—composed of both ministers and lay elders controlled membership by interview and possible excommunication. Proper behavior was forced on members by visits from local elders. Ministers controlled each other by thrashing out their disagreements once a week in meetings of their "Company." What they could not settle themselves the Consistory decided at *its* once-a-week meeting. Deacons appointed by the Consistory and teachers appointed by the Company controlled social services and primary education.

The entire structure had a coherence that was unique among Christian organizations in the sixteenth century, at least among those not governed by popes or princes. Like the more radical sects, it was independent of the state and transplantable, but unlike them it was durable and capable of being directed. No wonder Calvinism became such an ineradicable, international, revolutionary faith, or that some historians have taken to calling it an organizational prototype for the Communist Party.

Calvin's church, however, was built on the republican principle of collective leadership—Menshevik rather than Bolshevik, as we might say. Each group within it checked the other in some substantial way. No one, not even Calvin, exercised full executive power, and that was the way Calvin, according to the *Institutes*,

wanted it. Like the councils of Geneva, the councils of the church
were committees without a single leader, and all were composed of
members of differing constituencies and roughly equal strength.
Lip-service was regularly paid to the principle of popular sovereignty, too, and sometimes the church practiced what it preached.
Ministers had to be approved by their congregations, not just
coopted by the Company. As laymen, elders had to be chosen via
secular politics. In Geneva this meant appointment by the Small
Council, but as we shall see, Scots and French Calvinists were already making them submit to election by 1559.

Calvin's church was also extraordinarily independent of the
state. In reformed Basel, the town councils simply replaced the
bishops as autocrats. The result was republican but essentially medieval and did not greatly differ from the princely protestant
churches of England or Saxony. In Geneva, the church and the city
were parallel, separate, and interdependent. Theoretically, out of
thirty-one members of the Consistory, the Small Council chose
twelve and coopted two, while the other councils chose ten. Yet
the Consistory had no trouble at all differing with any or all councils. Much as each would have loved to, neither government could
get the other to do what it wanted. An elder might tell a magistrate
what proper moral behavior was; the magistrate could then tell the
elder what was legal. Elder and magistrate might even be the same
man. Conflict was frequent, public, and exhilarating. Consistories
excommunicated magistrates. Magistrates exiled ministers. Councilors purged elders, and elders purged councilors. Calvin himself
had written in the *Institutes* that one should passively disobey even
the state if it were wrong on religious matters. Thus every group
had its nose in everyone else's business. Geneva is still famous for
that.

After many years, Geneva and its church came to relate more
calmly. In 1555 the Councils finally conceded to the Consistory full
power to excommunicate. From that time, Calvin's church turned
outward and became, after the Peace of Augsburg, the number one
source of militant protestantism and the principal thorn in the side
of the European monarchies. In the banner years of 1559–61, the
great Calvinist churches of Scotland, France, and the Netherlands
were founded by men trained in Geneva. In Germany the Augsburg
settlement was upset by a new outbreak of civil war, provoked in
part by Calvinists, which would last well into the next century. Scot-

land converted wholesale and became in the seventeenth century the school for both old and New England. Her old ally France was nearly torn into its feudal pieces, like Germany; but in the end kings triumphed over both Catholics and Calvinists and built a throne for Louis XIV. The Netherlands was actually split in two, and in the north a new independent republic arose to defeat the pretensions of Habsburg kings.

It was Calvin's church organization that turned up at the center of all these events. Plenty of competing protestantisms had the necessary energy. Some were more fanatical, and many were far more disrespectful of the secular power than Calvin believed was right; but Calvin's church, calmly organized in the belly of the whale, proved it could subsist inside, outside, and even in spite of, the state.

When John Knox arrived in Geneva after escaping from the Catholic England of Mary Tudor, he was as amazed as any other visitor by the energy, austerity, and self-confidence of Geneva. This must be, he thought, "the most perfect school of Christ that ever was since the Apostles."[4] For him, as for every other man of his time, God was uppermost in mind, but he learned about more than Christ at Geneva. Returning to Scotland a jump ahead of Mary Queen of Scots, he began immediately to apply the lessons.

On May 2, 1560, a Calvinist revolt broke out. On May 11 the royal monastery of Scone was burned to the ground. On August 24 the Scottish Parliament, managed expertly by Knox and other graduates and disciples of Geneva, disestablished the Catholic Church and adopted a Calvinist confession of faith. The next year the church adopted Knox's constitution for itself, *The Book of Discipline*, and proceeded to elect synods, elders, and even ministers, the first Calvinist church to carry out the democratic possibilities in Calvin's *Ordinances*.

When Queen Mary arrived in 1561 she faced a *fait accompli* and Knox himself, who proceeded, with perfectly republican boorishness, to insult her to her handsome face. Seven years later, the Calvinists ran the poor Catholic monarch right out of the country. Later they would help run her Anglican grandson off the throne of England. Scotland never did dispense with kings entirely. In fact, when Mary's son James inherited the English throne in 1603, Scotland became part of the British monarchy. Nevertheless, Knox and the Calvinists checked the progress of new monarchy in Scotland to the point that no later king could establish absolutism there, and

wherever the influence of their precedent was acknowledged, monarchy became a pretty tame creature.

Established by the state, the Scottish Presbyterian Church, the
Kirk, became famous for being able to resist the state. It did so by
virtue of its independently elected governing bodies, and did so so
often that a theory arose about it, taking its departure not only from
Calvin, whose 1536 and 1539 *Institutes* had inconveniently branded
all political resistance as a sin, but also from the nearly forgotten
conciliarists of 1415.[5] Gerson, the leader of Constance, seems to
have been unknown to his fellow Frenchman Calvin; but he was
well known to John Major, who taught a conciliarist view of all government to John Knox at Edinburgh and to Calvin himself at the
Collège de Montaigu.

Both Knox and his fellow student George Buchanan wrote books
agreeing with Major that kings are made by the agreement of the
aristocracy and the people, answered by the king's coronation promises. They can be unmade the same way. An English friend of
Knox, Christopher Goodman, had made the same point in a book
published at Geneva in 1558. Another English exile, John Ponet,
had made the point as early as 1556. Why the Scots remembered
conciliarism while Frenchmen like Calvin never learned it may, one
supposes, be put down to the advanced state of monarchical
thought and practice in France. Whatever the reason, Knox and his
fellow exiles from the north were able to print, in Calvin's own lifetime and on Genevan presses, the key arguments for armed revolution.[6]

These arguments would, ironically, become most necessary of
all in Calvin's homeland of France. Within five years after the first
Geneva-trained ministers arrived in that advanced and Catholic
monarchy, a national consistory, the Synod of the Church of
France, had met under the king's very nose in the city of Paris. It
was May 1559; Scotland was already in revolt. Would France, too,
be forced by a republican church to become a limited monarchy?
The Calvinist organization there, speaking even the language of
Geneva, was more thorough and pervasive than it was in Scotland,
and the old feudal divisions were better exploited. All over France
local lords had been enlisted as patrons or elders of local synods, so
that, just as in Geneva, the leaders of the church were leaders also
of the state.

Since they were also leaders of the old feudal army, the church had a built-in military should the case come to violence. Within the year, at Amboise in northwestern France, the first blood was shed in what became a thirty-year civil war, now known as the Wars of Religion. Calvin, we know from letters, looked on with disapproval. He did not like the exemplary anarchy the wars threatened to bring to France, but he had, after all, buried in the newer versions of the *Institutes* a note about the right of inferior magistrates (nobles) to oppose a monarch.[7] Unable to be consistent perhaps, Calvin left the French church to use its own judgment.

Calvin was tired. In 1560 he had only four years to live—years wracked by migraines, kidney stones, tuberculosis, lameness, gout, and chronic indigestion. Already in 1556 he had had to be carried to the pulpit, only to abandon his sermon, shaking uncontrollably with headache. Carried home, he immediately began his favorite medical treatment, a two-day fast. A thoroughly healthy man might collapse under Calvin's normal day's work. He rose at five, dictated books or letters until the time came to give a sermon or a lecture, wrote or lectured again until the evening, ate his single meal of the day, took a fifteen-minute walk, and then went off to a council meeting. It is estimated that he had over three hundred correspondents, preached seven three-hour sermons every two weeks (286 a year), lectured on theology three times a week (186 times a year), and met with one governing council or other twice a week. He spent his spare time visiting the unfortunate or giving moral examinations to members of the church. His collected writings fill some sixty double-column folio volumes, and there is not a sentence in them that does not breathe the two passions of his life: the drive for order and clarity and the fear of God's unsearchable majesty.

For Calvin was a republican by default. The omnipotent and even capricious monarchy of God, which might save the most unlikely or damn a child, and which looms larger in each successive edition of the *Institutes*, was Calvin's substitute for any earthly kingdom, as it had been for paternal authority. All men were equal in impotence before it, minister and magistrate, kings no less than Calvin. Compared with it, all human governments were endurable, so that for Calvin, Samuel's warning seemed not a plea for republican government but a description of the usually necessary evils of all government. Government was one of God's more benevolent scourges. The republican kind was better for virtue, but not by much.[8] It took disciples like Knox to notice how shaky the argu-

ments were for supposing that the people, equals in abjection before God, were unworthy to oppose another damned human being
just because he was a king.

As his party prepared to run away with him, Calvin, the superbly
constituted party leader, finally succumbed in 1564. From his
deathbed he solemnly advised the members of the Small Council
to see that all citizens help preserve republican government by
equally respecting each other. To the ministers' Company assembled around his bed he apologized for having always been such an
angry man. But, he said "God will make use of this church."[9] Indeed He did. Already the French militant "Huguenots" passing in
and out of Geneva were arming themselves with the resistance theory of Goodman, Knox, and Ponet in preparation for the intensi-
fying struggle in France. In 1561 alone a hundred Geneva-trained
ministers had crossed the border. When Catherine de Médicis
turned on them all in the Massacre of Saint Bartholomew in 1572,
the books poured from the presses.

On the Right of Magistrates, wrote Calvin's successor Theodore
de Bèze, "by force of arms where that is possible, to offer resistance
to flagrant tyranny." For de Bèze the Calvinist nobles of France
were the successors of Brutus, the Roman tribunes, and the Swiss
communes. Law professor François Hotman fled his post in 1572,
leaving the manuscript of *Francogallia* behind him. Rewritten and
printed at Geneva, the book turned out to be a long proof from law
and history that the French monarchy was limited and elective. Finally Philippe Duplessis-Mornay, political aide to the Calvinist pretender to the French throne, produced a book that he wouldn't put
his name to and which even Geneva couldn't print, *Vindiciae contra
tyrannos (Defense against Tyrants).* Mornay wrote that not only were
the corps of magistrates bound to revolt but some or a few of them
could do it on their own. It was, he wrote, lawful for Israel to resist
Ahab, criminal for them not to. No less must the French Calvinists
attack and depose the Valois king. Private citizens too must obey
the magistrates and carry arms in the struggle; for it is not the king
but the people who are sovereign, and magistrates are the people's
lawful agents.[10]

Calvin would have been horrified at this overturning of the God-
given hierarchy of the universe, and for practical reasons he might
have been justified. The consequences of tyrannicidal thinking
proved to be too much even for the sixteenth century. Catholics
soon adopted the same views and the same tactics. The hapless

Henri III, caught in the middle, was assassinated, the first French king to die by assassination. Henri IV, Mornay's employer, succeeded Henri III but found it impolitic to remain a Calvinist. His conversion to Catholicism quelled an intractable revolt in the Catholic city of Paris and pacified the country. Fellow moderates, contemptuous of the regicidal republicanism of both sides, soon created a monarchy and a body of monarchical thought that made even constitutional kingship hard to think about. Henri IV was the first of the Bourbon dynasty. He too was assassinated, but his was the last tyrannicide. The Sun King, Louis XIV, was the third Bourbon. He reigned seventy-two years and died in bed.

By 1564, when Calvin died, Geneva-trained ministers had been in the Netherlands for seven years. Largely active in the southern provinces now known as Belgium, they had gone far enough to establish provincial synods and publish a confession of faith; but it didn't look like much beside the accomplishments of their coreligionists in Scotland and France. Nevertheless, it was in the Netherlands that Calvinism was to score its most remarkable political triumph: a brand-new republic with no monarch at all. The secret was that in the Netherlands Calvinism and revolution appeared as the allies of national feeling rather than, as in France, its enemies.

The fact made no less a difference then than it made in Switzerland in the 1300s. In fact, the enemy of national feeling was once again a Habsburg, Philip II of Spain, and the parallel between his loss of the Low Countries and his ancestors' loss of Switzerland is so close he ought to have known better. Once again, a Habsburg gained an empire but lost his own home. Philip's father Charles V had been born in the Netherlands and had loved them, but Philip preferred Spain and sent deputies to govern them. Local aristocracy of these provinces were first irritated, then disrespectful, finally rebellious, and eventually (it took three generations) victorious. To be fair to Philip, he might have avoided all this, but he was a stubborn man and he had a bee in his bonnet: heresy.

Whatever it cost him, Philip seems to have early decided, it was his duty to exterminate protestantism in his North Sea possessions. Once again, if (as seemed likely at the outset of his reign) the only protestants had been the anarchic Anabaptists, Philip might have got rid of them. Anabaptists disbelieved in violence, made perfect martyrs, and even better exiles. The Calvinists, however, put faith in self-defense and were the very devil to expel. Within a few years of their arrival they had built a relationship with governments so narrow that Philip hadn't a prayer of exterminating them without exterminating as well an important part of the Netherlands magistracy. The great city of Antwerp and sister cities like Ghent, Bruges, and Brussels all had Calvinist groups by 1566 that no one could uproot. Their reaction to persecution was inconveniently unlike that of the saintly (and dwindling) Anabaptists. In Antwerp that year, for example, they trashed the Catholic churches.

This combination of an aggrieved local nobility and Calvinist militants, supported by a rich and venerable medieval system of representative institutions—city communes, and provincial "Estates" or assemblies—was the brew that defeated monarchy in the Netherlands. Philip of Habsburg, for all his stubbornness and clarity of vision, was simply unequal to it. His first regent, Margaret of Parma, pleaded with him to withdraw his centralizing, heresy-hunting devices. Philip was imperturbable; the Inquisition must remain. The Netherlands nobility united in a remonstrance against Margaret. Philip fired her and sent an army under the terrible Duke of Alva. Again the nobility protested. With Philip's blessing, Alva executed the major leaders. Without the consent of the Estates, Alva imposed a sales tax. Netherlanders set dogs on the tax-collectors and closed their shops. Alva set up an unconstitutional court and burned more than six thousand protestants. The surviving leader of the Netherlands nobility, William the Silent, Prince of Orange and Count of Nassau, replied by converting to Calvinism. With Orange in exile, Alva occupied the cities, but in 1572 one of them, Brill, was recaptured by a motley fleet of pirate ships flying the lion pennant of the landlocked principality of Orange, and the war of independence was on.

Each side had a clear cause. Philip wanted centralized governmental control and uniformity of religion under an appointed hierarchy. The Netherlanders wanted provincial autonomy, and self-government in the areas of taxation, the church, and the military. They did not claim this in the name of natural right, but as a historic set of privileges implicit in the coronation oath and in the endless list of medieval insubordinations that had made them almost as great a trial to medieval monarchs as Italy or Switzerland.

The revolt spread from the rich south to the more Spartan north in the 1570s. Calvinism became a majority religion in most communes in Holland as it had not in Flanders. Here they were willing not only to die but to pay for independence. Haarlem, Leyden,

Delft, Holland, Zeeland, and Utrecht met to elect William of Orange *Stadhouder* or executive and to tax themselves at twice Alva's rate to provide him with an army. Philip replaced Alva with Don Luis de Requesens, Requesens with Don Juan of Austria. So unimpressed were the Dutch that they flooded their farms and sacrificed a harvest to lift the siege of Leyden. From 1563 to 1578 nothing Philip could do could compensate for his initial refusal to tolerate the Calvinists and govern through the medieval republican institutions of the Netherlands. Both grew stronger with each successive effort to destroy them. By the time Philip's fifth regent arrived, Alexander Farnese, Prince of Parma, they had become almost as modern in their power and efficiency as the monarchy itself.

Parma, however, was a cut above his predecessors. He was a good enough soldier to attract nobles to his service—charming, conciliatory, and trustworthy enough to command loyalty even after ten years of struggle. Militarily he did so well that he is generally credited with having held the southern provinces for Spain, and helping to draw the boundaries of modern Belgium. Some say that if the northeasters and the English had been only a little kinder to the Armada, he might have conquered the whole Netherlands and England in the bargain, but that probably goes too far. At any rate, it was only a year after his arrival that the lines between north and south began to draw tight. In January 1579, Parma presented the rebels with a loyalist union of the five southernmost provinces of Lille, Douai, Orchies, Hainault, and Artois. On January 21, led by William of Orange, the five northernmost provinces of Holland, Zeeland, Friesland, Utrecht, and Gelderland signed a perpetual alliance called the Union of Utrecht. Against all custom, perpetual it turned out to be. South of the border of Zeeland, all the remaining provinces eventually returned to Spain and to Catholicism. North of it, the two remaining provinces joined the rebellion and Calvinism. On July 22, 1581, the Estates-General, controlled by northerners, made it official in the following document:

> Therefore, despairing utterly of any means of reconciliation and lacking any other remedy or means of relief, in accordance with the law of nature and in order to preserve and defend ourselves and our fellow-countrymen, our rights, the privileges and ancient customs and the freedom of the fatherland, and the life and honor of our wives, children, and posterity, so that we may not become the Spaniards' slaves, . . . we have declared and declare hereby by a com-

mon accord, decision, and consent the King of Spain, *ipso jure*, forfeit of his lordship, principality, jurisdiction, and inheritance of . . . these Low Countries.[11]

Thus did the northern provinces become, in effect, a federal republic. Not until 1648 did the king of Spain finally agree to this declaration of independence, and with ill-grace, but for all practical purposes the republic of the Netherlands was a fact by 1600.

It was a great republic, the center of European intellectual and cultural life in the seventeenth century. Hals, Vermeer, and Rembrandt painted there. Spinoza, Huyghens, and Leeuwenhoek ground their lenses in Holland, secure in the knowledge that however strange their idle thoughts might be, they would not be jailed or burned for them. It was appropriate perhaps that one fruit of this long dour revolution should have been the work of Grotius— Hugo de Groot. Grotius saw the anarchy in the new Europe of national states, but instead of regretting empire or papacy, he proposed the groundwork of an agreed-upon international law, thus setting Europe on the long road to a federal republican substitute for the old monarchy of Christendom.

The republic of the Netherlands was not one of the enduring ones, however. The stress of the Eighty Years War did not fail to make a heroic dynasty out of the Oranges. William the Silent, whose relationship with the communes and Estates had been tactful and Cincinnattian in the extreme, was assassinated in 1584 for the price Philip put on his head. His heirs did not scruple to approve the execution of such antidynastic opponents as John of Oldenbarneveldt or the brothers De Witt, or, like Augustus, to accumulate republican offices.

The Dutch victory too was not of the sort that made them stop short at independence like the Swiss. Soon they made an empire in Asia, in Africa, and, at the mouth of the Hudson, in North America. The empire helped drive them toward centralized government, as empires will, and made them richer than the Romans. Rather quickly, even their dour Calvinist virtue failed them, and they went mad for tulips while monarchy burgeoned at home. By the nineteenth century Holland was officially a kingdom, ruled by the house of Orange. It still is; but the countless American places named Orange, Nassau, or Williamsburgh attest not to the crowns of the descendants of William the Silent. When the time came for Americans to declare their independence of George III, they not only honored the two-hundred-year-old phrases of the Netherlands declaration of 1581, but borrowed for good measure the name of the republic that made it: Vereenigde Staaten, the United States.[12]

This story has lasted three centuries, but its outlines are clear. To begin with, in 1300 Christendom was a monarchy. By 1600 it was not even a political unit. Of the states which grew up in its shadow, apart from the city communes, only two, Switzerland and the Netherlands, preserved the republic. Though conciliarism failed at the last instant to limit the pope's monarchy, later Protestantism succeeded in limiting the pope's writ, and Calvinists provided the means by which the backward-looking reformers and republicans could insure each other's survival.

As Geneva succeeded to Constance, Holland and Scotland succeeded to Geneva. After them would come Puritan England and America. John Calvin casts a long shadow.

7

John Milton
A Commonwealth of Saints

SOMETIMES a republic can be made as a result of social revolution on the grand scale. When the entire class structure of a society is plowed up in a single generation, when all dreams are suddenly spoken and every aspect of a culture is called into question, a republic may replace a monarchy simply because no simple unity is conceivable in a reality so hopelessly multiple.

Such was the great Puritan Revolution of 1641–60, the most consequential of all the many revolutions of the seventeenth century. Descendants of those who made it made our own revolution a century later; and at least if one measures by how deep it went, and by what it did to class and manners, property and value systems, the English Revolution was bigger than the American. In Western history there is nothing to compare it to except what happened in France from 1789 to 1815, in Russia from 1917 to 1921, or to the Protestant Reformation, of which it is often and justly considered the last act.

The republic which resulted, the Commonwealth of England, was no less consequential than the Revolution. It was both the last and grandest of the effects of political Calvinism and the first of the large, territorial republics of the modern era.

Of course, revolutions on this scale seem to make the question of monarchy or republic quite incidental. What can it possibly matter to an ex-baron begging his bread or a former shopkeeper commanding an army whether the sovereignty that brought him to this pass be exercised by one man or a thousand?

What indeed? And yet the French, the Russian, and the English Revolutions, like the American, all resulted in republican governments, and we have seen how the Calvinist Reformation went in that direction. In modern history monarchies have proved to be highly vulnerable to deep social revolutions even when, as in England, Russia, and France, the revolution ends by throwing up another monarchy. Most likely, this is not because such deep upheavals are ideologically republican, but simply because old monarchies are such huge targets. Simple men, who understand monarchy easiest and love monarchs best, know also, when things go wrong, exactly whom to blame. "It's all, all on the king," said Shakespeare's Henry V, and no wonder that his father's head lay so uneasy.

This sort of accidental republicanism is especially obvious in the great Puritan Revolution of 1641–60, because King Charles I, though physically small, was a target of barn-door proportions. By all accounts his father, James I, who reigned for twenty-two years, was not much better. Thus, by the time the House of Commons got around to chopping off King Charles's head in 1649, there had been forty-six years of Stuart egregiousness to provoke them. Then too, the English had gotten into a real habit during the Middle Ages of threatening, deposing, and even assassinating their kings. The hired assassin who ran a poker through Edward II, lengthwise, in 1327 began a butcher's bill that would eventually include, in chronological order, Richard II, Henry VI, Edward V, Richard III. Nothing in French history, even after 1789, can compare with this bloody record. In fact the French stigmatized the English for centuries as hot-blooded, politically unstable, and constitutionally insubordinate. "Magna Carta," they doubtless snorted, "What next, in the age of Louis XIII?"

The Stuarts agreed. Descended as they were from a French princess and the Francophile court of Scotland, harassed there by a Calvinist kirk and unruly Estates, they watched the development of absolute monarchy across the Channel with undisguised interest and worked diligently to promote it in England. They too desired earnestly to collect taxes without the consent of the Estates, rule their church as a department of state, make war and peace as it suited them, and employ Sullys and Richelieus and Mazarins to serve them. James I, that royal scholar, had written a book explaining all this.[1] Charles, in filial piety, read it. Both misread England, misread Shakespeare too, for that matter:

> . . . some [kings] have been depos'd, some slain in war,
> Some haunted by the ghosts they have depos'd,
> Some poison'd by their wives, some sleeping kill'd;
> All murder'd: for within the hollow crown
> That rounds the mortal temples of a king
> Keeps Death his court. . . .[2]

The worst Stuart misreading of all, however, was one which modern historians still make sometimes. They thought that England was a monarchy. This was a natural mistake for a Stuart. England did, after all, have a king and England had always had kings since Caesar discovered it. Moreover, no king had been deposed, no matter how violently or murderously, without a new king having been crowned. The best minds in fifteenth- and sixteenth-century England, however, would not have called England a simple monarchy. Henry VIII himself had not done so (at least in public). To the Tudor mind England was a mixed government, just like the one Polybios had discovered in Rome. The word they used was Commonweal, or Commonwealth, which roughly translates into twentieth-century English as the "general interest" or "public good," and which was for them an exact translation of the Latin res publica; in other words, a republic.

A republic with a king? Yes. Under an old and now forgotten use of the word republic, it was quite possible. Ancient Sparta, after all, had had two kings, and in Venice, an antipapal maritime republic much admired by Renaissance English thinkers, there was a doge who, once elected, ruled for life without a colleague. Besides, in England, as in republican Rome, Sparta, and Venice, there was a combination of monarchy, aristocracy, and democracy. Forms of rule represented by Consuls, Senate, and Tribunes in Rome were embodied by King, Lords, and Commons in England. A nice classical way of looking at the medieval hodgepodge and making a virtue of necessity, it was this combination of forms of rule which the educated English came to understand by the words republic and commonwealth.

By the time James Stuart succeeded to the English throne on

the death of his childless cousin Elizabeth in 1603, this idea of a Commonweath of England had become a very rich one. Elsewhere in Europe, for instance, the medieval idea of a state had depended on the institution of classes or "Estates." There were at most four of these: clergy, nobility, townspeople, and peasants. In England however, the idea of mixed monarchy eventually drew in the medieval division, so that often when a Tudor Englishman enumerated the estates of the realm he called them King, Lords, and Commons. Whatever divisions he found useful, it was the checks and balances between them that really charmed him. The image in his mind was of a team of horses beautifully trained to harness, or possibly a clock (Henry VIII had a passion for clocks) full of majestically interconnected weights and springs and cables.[3]

This idea of balance is what the hapless Stuart successors of Queen Elizabeth found so difficult to understand and so costly to ignore. They wished to be absolute, the way their French cousins were becoming. Failing that, they would have settled for an unquestioned freedom of action in certain key areas. Neither goal made sense when measured against the essentially republican ideals of Commonwealth and balance. Neither the Commons ("democracy") nor the Lords ("aristocracy") were willing to see their parts in the commonwealth reduced or the balance as they saw it altered. To pleas for simplicity they replied with a love of complexity. They wanted the government to remain a mixture of Aristotle's monarchy, aristocracy, and democracy on the one hand and the three feudal estates on the other.

Under the stress of later Stuart rule, many even developed yet a third notion of balanced government, the familiar idea of the separation of powers into executive, legislative, and judiciary. This idea, still one of the great touchstones of republican thinking, is the final state of that disagreement between the Stuarts and the country that broke out in the seventeenth century. It turned out that on this issue both sides were prepared to die. Thus, in 1642, civil war began in England, one army led by King Charles I and the other by the two houses of Parliament.

Parliament won in 1646, but Charles I refused to accept either his altered status or the increased demands of the forces which had defeated him. Finally in 1649, Parliament (what was left of it) had his head chopped off. Thus the Commonwealth of England became a republic such as Brutus would have recognized, and for the first time adopted the name commonwealth as its official title.

It was an extreme version of the old idea and its doom was clear. The Commonwealth's desperate search for a head settled in 1653 on the person of General Oliver Cromwell, MP, and the title Lord Protector (traditionally used in England for the guardian of an infant king). When Cromwell died in 1658 the Protectorate died with him and the son of Charles I was restored as Charles II in 1660. Eighteen years later a last Stuart try at absolutism was frustrated. Once again a king was deposed in England and succeeded by another king. Parliament established its supremacy within the mixed government in a tidier, wiser, and subtler way; the commonwealth as Tudors had understood it was permanently restored though without the name; and England was free to gain its modern reputation for serenity, stability, and balance.

Even today, the English sometimes minimize the hell England went through in the seventeenth century. Less than a century after 1641 they had already begun to read the peace of the present back over the violent past. Some of the English had very long memories, however—particularly the descendants of those remarkable men and women who crossed the Atlantic Ocean to escape the tyranny of Charles I and founded Massachusetts, Rhode Island, and Connecticut. To them, the men who had made war on King Charles, brought him to the headsman's block, and defended the kingless commonwealth were a constellation of antique heroes, fit to name cities after.

The names do not sound antique. Many sound funny, like Harbottle Grimstone and Bulstrode Whitelocke. Some are worn with familiarity, like Needham, Harrington, and Ludlow. Still others are unbelievable, like Praise-God Barebones. Most are very simple, like the Johns: John Eliot, John Pym, John Hampden, and John Lilburne. Most remembered, perhaps, of all the Englishmen who made war on Charles I was a poet who never killed anyone, the incomparable John Milton.

Milton's life is as good an example as one can find of the awesome power that politics can acquire over literature. Both before the Revolution and after it (when he wrote *Paradise Lost*) Milton seemed no more than a literary man of legendary learning and gentleness. But during the Revolution he was a fire-breathing prophet, a Marat, the conscience of the far left. His odyssey in search of republicanism is a commentary on England's own.

When Milton was born in 1608 in Bread Street, London, James

I had been king of England for five years and the political weather was fair. Milton's father lived an Elizabethan life as a London notary of comfortable and increasing income, writing music in his spare time and providing his son with the finest of Renaissance educations at Saint Paul's School and Cambridge. The boy, clever and delicate, began early to write the kind of poetry, pastorals and masques, which suited the sophisticated baroque taste of his age. Though drawn to Puritanism like many of his generation, he rejected the ministry for a literary career. On graduation from Cambridge he retired to his father's country houses in Hammersmith and Horton, and:

> ... devoted myself entirely to the study of Greek and Latin writers, completely at leisure, not, however, without sometimes exchanging the country for the city, either to purchase the books or to become acquainted with some new discovery in mathematics or music, in which I then took the keenest pleasure.[4]

After five years of this he took off on a literary grand tour of Italy and Greece. He was hardly an ideal candidate for revolutionary republicanism or sectarian militancy.

Suddenly, in 1639, as King Charles prepared to call his first Parliament in eleven years, Milton decided in Naples not to go on to Greece but to return to England. It was, he said, "base that I should travel abroad at my ease for the cultivation of my mind, while my fellow-citizens at home were fighting for liberty."[5] By 1642 he had written five thundering pamphlets against bishops. By 1649, he had twice placed himself, in print, on the side of King Charles's executioners and become, like Machiavelli, a correspondance secretary in the foreign office of the new republic. It was while doing this job that he lost the last of his sight in 1651. He was still promoting the republic when Charles II returned in 1660; in fact, he was jailed for it for two months and escaped execution only via a general amnesty.

Nor did this now blind republican ever abandon his conviction. When his masterpiece was published seven years after the restoration of the Stuarts, it was a Puritan epic with a title which has ever afterward been read as an elegy for the Commonwealth: *Paradise Lost.*

What was it that caught this fastidious poet and turned him into the voice of radicalism? One thing we can say is that the conversion was not as sudden as it looked. The political calm of Milton's youth was a very deceptive one. The team of horses, the mixed monarchy of the sixteenth century was straining at the harness. The estates were remarkably unstable in status and competitive with one another. Radical Calvinism, called Puritanism in England, was rising, and the so-called Elizabethan settlement—protestant theology with a catholic church organization—was coming unstuck. Calvinism and Conciliarism survived in the Stuart homeland of Scotland and the Wycliffism which had inspired Hus was still alive in England. Finally Parliament, and particularly the House of Commons, which Henrys VII and VIII had raised as a counterforce to the nobility, had begun both to understand its power and to mistrust its monarch's good faith. The war between king and Parliament had already begun.

There is an inevitability as well as an Englishness about this revolution. When Milton was six years old, James I convened his second Parliament. In the same year Louis XIII convened his Estates-General, which is the analogous assembly in France. Neither body cooperated with its king or passed any laws, and both were dissolved in a year; but the French were not to see another such convention until 1789. By contrast the English would see Parliaments in 1620, 1625, 1626, 1628, and two in 1640, all fractious, disrespectful, and in the end regicidal. Clearly, there was something special about Milton's kingdom that more than justified calling it a commonwealth. At a time when kings everywhere were rising above medieval arrangements, outflanking their estates, and becoming absolute monarchs, a unique and unbreakable net of restrictions was forming about the Stuarts.

The Parliaments of Milton's youth each marked a step in this process. When Milton went off to Saint Paul's at the age of twelve, James's third Parliament met at Westminster. Led by the great common-law jurist Edward Coke (with assistance from a young newcomer, John Pym), the 1620 Parliament began by impeaching three of the king's officers, including the Lord Chancellor (Attorney- General) and the Lord Treasurer. Thus they revived a practice almost unused since the fifteenth century by which the House of Commons could indict despite the king for official crimes not yet defined in law. The Parliament of 1620–22 also insisted on its right to debate foreign policy, traditionally the privileged business of the king alone.

James was seriously irked. Commons had indeed questioned his cousin Elizabeth about when she would ever get married, but never about war and peace. Unlike Elizabeth, however, James was not at war with Spain. In fact that was the whole trouble. The English liked being at war with Spain. Now that the great Thirty Years War was on between the Catholic and Protestant states of Central Europe; and James's daughter had been the first Protestant victim of it, it was clearly time to shoot Catholic Spaniards again. Yet there was James, cheerily signing treaties with the chief Catholic kings and even sending his son Charles to woo the Spanish Infanta. Commons, increasingly Puritan, suspected James of being a Catholic, or at least a fellow traveler. The thwarting, in 1605, of a plot by Catholic Guy Fawkes to blow up the Houses of Parliament had by now become a national holiday. Schoolboy Milton wrote a memorial poem about it every Fifth of November in the 1620s. No one could be soft on Catholicism in 1620. James, however, insisted that his policies would lead to a generation of peace, and anyway nobody was allowed to discuss them. He ordered the arrest of Coke and four other MPs for speaking out of turn, and dissolved the Parliament.

The issues of foreign policy and impeachment, familiar enough to us since Nixon, were but two strands in the net that was slowly enmeshing the English crown. In addition to the *sine qua non* of free speech, Parliament included among its rights the power to certify or expel its own members, cocreate all statute law, review all decisions of the royal courts, certify all accessions to the throne, investigate executive departments, and most important of all, to raise taxes—the power of the purse. Only the House of Commons could vote the king money, the source of his power. By tradition, such a bill had to originate in Commons, and behind this traditional claim was the hard fact that nearly all the tax collectors were MPs and most of the taxpayers were voters. When, in the late 1600s, Louis XIV created absolute monarchy, his secret was soon discovered to be the creation of a standing army paid by subsidies collected at its own gun's point. The King of England, however, had no such army. Worse, what army he did have consisted of local militias commanded and paid by the gentlemen who sat in Parliament.

What could an English king do but stay friendly with the House of Commons? His own traditional rights, in which most included the calling and dissolving of Parliaments, assent or veto to all their bills, the raising and commanding of the army, the making and unmaking of nobles, and complete executive responsibility for justice, diplomacy, and religion, were meaningless unless the House was with him. Powers more problematical, like his right to hire and fire judges, suspend habeas corpus, collect import duties, withhold privileged information, or force a loan from a subject, depended even more absolutely on the propaganda effect of a contented Commons. When James called his fourth Parliament in 1624, he found himself agreeing to war with Spain, and receiving from a gratified Parliament a healthy income from taxes.

This simple deal, typical of the Tudor period, which James was never quite stubborn enough to refuse, was impossible for his son and successor, Charles I—a man who, Milton was to write, "hath offer'd at more cunning fetches to undermine our Liberties and putt Tyranny into an Art than any British King before him."[6]

Charles was a shy man, charming in small groups but increasingly stiff and correct in large ones. A long face was accentuated by the fashionable pointed beard. Heavy-lidded spaniel eyes focused appealingly but obliquely in the middle distance, and a voice somewhat high and plaintive emerged from a delicate mouth. Behind them lay a fear of the strength of character in others which he knew he could not match, and the stubbornness and duplicity of a weak man out of his depth. Charles's brother-in-law, Louis XIII of France, resembled him a good deal, but Louis knew enough to back a great subordinate to the hilt. The nearest thing Charles found to a Richelieu, Thomas Wentworth, he found too late and threw to the wolves as soon as they set up a howl. To such a man went the honor of defending the prerogatives of monarchy in their hour of greatest trial.

One wonders if Milton, about to set off for college, could have seen at Charles's coronation the qualities for which he would condemn him twenty-five years later. Already, at his second Parliament in 1626, the honeymoon was over. The turbulent John Eliot was leading the house in an impeachment of Charles's favorite, the profligate Duke of Buckingham, and Charles could stop it only by dissolving the assembly before it would vote him a tax. This done, the only way he could think of to raise money was a forced loan, a method which squeezed by the courts but yielded far less in money than it did in resentment. Mistrust grew, and Parliament clearly had to be called again. When it met in 1628, Coke was in charge and the mood was defiant.[7] The Commons proceeded almost immediately to define the liberties and privileges of Englishmen in the great statute called the Petition of Right. Charles signed the Petition, binding himself not to use soldiers to intimidate his people, or to collect a tax not passed by Parliament, but instead of voting him money, Commons continued its attack. John Eliot closed in on Buckingham again; John Pym took aim at the Church of England; and finally the whole House insisted that the import duties which Charles had been collecting since he came to the throne, were included in the Petition of Right and thus unconstitutional.

On March 2, 1629, Charles sent the traditional Black Rod Usher to dissolve the Assembly. Forewarned, Eliot locked the doors, held Speaker Finch down in his seat, and in the next hour pushed through resolutions condemning the collection and payment of import duties, together with a change in religion, as capital crimes against the Commonwealth. The doors were opened, Parliament was dissolved, and Eliot and eight of his confederates went to jail. This was to be, Charles had determined, the last Parliament to sit in English history.

Milton came home with his AB degree some three weeks later. At Cambridge he had ranged himself clearly with the vocal Puritan faction. His best friend, Charles Diodati was off to enroll at the furnace of Calvinism, the University of Geneva, where his uncle, Giovanni, was a professor. Another schoolfriend named Gill had nearly had his ears cut off for toasting the death of Buckingham (a Puritan named Felton had stabbed the Duke just as the impeachment was gathering steam). Little of this appears in the elegies and pastorals Milton was writing at the time, or even in a letter to the unfortunate Gill, (though this may be self-censorship).[8] The tranquility into which the kingdom now fell was doubtless a congenial background for Milton's plan to write and study for the rest of his life. It was complemented by peace abroad, for Charles, who knew that the only way he could live on the few sources of income not controlled by Parliament was to have the smallest possible defense budget, had signed treaties with all his enemies by 1630.

"The happiest king in Christendom," he called himself.[9] His old enemies, Coke and Eliot, were dead by 1634. Eliot's former ally, Thomas Wentworth, had been tempted into the executive office and was turning Ireland into a gold mine for the king. The ingenious William Noy was digging up a score of farfetched medieval ways to raise revenue, including a masterpiece called "ship-money." By this device, all Charles had to do was declare a threat to national security, after which he could collect either ships or their equivalent in cash from every landowner in the kingdom. It was marvelous how regularly danger threatened the kingdom each year after the discovery of ship-money in 1634 and how paradoxically rare it was that the few ships ever built saw hostile action.

As far as the church went, Charles now resolved to make it uniform at the very lowest level, ceremonial, uncontroversial, and absolutely controlled by himself through his appointees the bishops. Neither he nor his erstwhile Presbyterian father had required great insight to see that the newer Calvinist elective forms of church government could not hold a candle to a good solid appointive hierarchy for keeping one's subjects in line. The Richelieu of this policy was the aggressive and efficient Archbishop Laud of Canterbury. He jailed the most outspoken Presbyterians, watched happily as little bands of Congregationals set off for the wilderness of Massachusetts Bay after 1630, and stood sternly by as the public executioner cut off the ears of the radical few.

The king might have done it. Twenty years of peace and steady collection of the prerogative taxes might well have created a habit, even among the legal-minded English, of letting the king govern the Commonwealth unaided, and allowing a true monarchy to replace king, lords, and commons. A few popular wars to enlarge the military establishment and presto! Absolute monarchy. The king, say the historians, made only three mistakes. First, he would not back Wentworth except at a distance (Ireland) where the great man's power couldn't help him. Second, he backed Laud too closely and gave Puritanism a new lease on life by persecuting it. Third, and most important, he got into a real war at last, an unpopular war too expensive to be covered by the profits of ship-money. By a whole series of ironies this war was against Scotland, the kingdom where his family had originated, whose crown he had inherited from his father, and which was, moreover, the only state in the world on which England could have made war without any ships at all.

And the cause of this fatal conflict? Sheer ineptitude. The king and Laud had decided in 1637 that it was time to have bishops in Scotland, and to dispense with the hitherto loyal—but, alas, elected—pastors and elders of the Presbyterian Church of Scotland.

Naturally enough, the Scots won. At any rate, they were successful enough to bankrupt King Charles in a few months. The eleven years of absolute monarchy were over in a trice. Parliament had to be called. It opened on April 13, 1640. Charles and Wentworth took one look at it and dissolved it on May 5. The Scots, seeing their king could not buy them off, resumed their advance into England. The king assembled the peers and asked for money. They temporized. The Scots advanced. In October, he promised them more money he didn't have and they stopped. Desperate, Charles called a new Parliament for November. It met in dour weather two days before Guy Fawkes Day, 1640 and sat for thirteen years. The commonwealth was reestablished but Charles I would not survive it.

Deep in the country, John Milton finally heard the noise of politics. His great elegy *Lycidas*, written in 1637, contains a famous oblique attack on the Laudian bishops.[10] Suddenly, Milton's commonplace book opens to topics like "king," "subject," "nobility," "taxes," "moral evil," and he begins to be struck as he reads by new facts, like the self-deification of the Emperor Diocletian.[11] It was the Bishops' War in Scotland that brought him back from his Italian journey, and the question of church government that turned the scholar of the 1630s into the pamphleteer of the 1640s. The apolitical poet had discovered that the future of his Puritanism lay ineluctably in political action.

What is this Puritanism that put such venom in the otherwise gentle Milton? Shakespeare's Puritan, Malvolio ("bad will"), dances onto the stage in act three of *Twelfth Night* smiling for the first time in his life. He is in love. The audience cracks up, now as it must have at the first performance in 1600. "Precisians," they were called, meaning nitpickers. Before they made a revolution, everyone knew that they stood for four-hour sermons and against robes, crosses, stained glass, and dancing on Sundays. "Sick of self-love" was Shakespeare's diagnosis. Did they think that because they were virtuous, there should be no more cakes and ale? Even in America, where for a while almost everyone was a Puritan, the Puritans have not fared well. Nowadays the engine that drove Milton from the library into the streets and John Winthrop to the snows of Massachusetts is rated as sullenness, inhibition, or hypocrisy. Upright has become uptight.

Since dead men tell no tales, few suspect how wild the Puritans were, or how central their doctrines remain. Their drive for longer sermons, for instance, was only a symptom of a deeper commitment to books and education. The attack on stained glass came out of a belief that God alone and neither man nor anything man had made should be worshiped. More importantly, large numbers of these English Calvinists believed that no man-made church government could bind the individual conscience or direct his relationship with God. Congregations were not geographical but autonomous intentional cells, associations of the saints. They were to be governed as a majority of them chose. They were to be associated through committees composed of elected officers, laymen included. Moreover, all these tightly knit communities, together with their highly educated elected leaders, who feared God and feared no man, believed themselves predestined by God to eternal life. They also believed that soon, such as themselves would begin the thousand-year reign of Jesus Christ on earth. No wonder that these ten thousand organized Savonarolas turned out to be among the most effective revolutionaries in history.

In the Long Parliament that began in 1640, "moderate" Puritans took over, led by John Pym, now a seasoned parliamentarian, and John Hampden, who had refused to pay ship-money back in 1635. They began by arresting Thomas Wentworth, and impeaching Archbishop Laud. To prepare their case, Commons committees subpoenaed privileged members and memoranda of the executive branch, the King's Council. By August 1641, Wentworth had been executed, Laud was in the Tower where Eliot had died a prisoner, and the entire House of Bishops had been impeached in a body. Six special royal courts had been abolished, and most of the new medieval taxes. On the march, Parliament had forced the King to agree never to dissolve it without its own consent, and never to let three years pass without calling another. At midnight on November 22, little more than a year after its first meeting, the Commons, urged on by Pym, passed by eleven votes the Grand Remonstrance, the nearest thing to a Declaration of Independence in English history.

The following year constitutional crisis became civil war. On January 4, King Charles walked dramatically into the House of Commons at the head of a "bodyguard" of soldiers, sat in the Speaker's chair, and produced a warrant for the arrest of Pym, Hampden, Holles, Haslerigg, and Strode. This time, however, the device of arresting the ringleaders didn't work. The "birds had flown," said the King, escaped downriver to organize a revolt in London. Empty-handed and beaten, Charles retired to the north, calling his loyalists to arms. Parliament raised its own army, and on October 23 the war began at the village of Edgehill.

It was a strange war, not least because the idea of a mixed monarchy held on throughout it. Parliament continued to assert that it was fighting the King in the King's name and for his own good. Members' minds boggled at the idea of treason against the sovereign. Nor was the King willing, in writing, to make war on Parliament. Polite fictions, suitable to the still medieval, precedent-ridden English political mind, covered the truly startling innovations which amounted to an abrogation of kingship. One by one the remaining constitutional powers of the King were assumed by Parliament. First tentatively, then firmly, it asserted the power to raise an army, command it, and raise taxes to pay it. It passed laws (carefully calling them "ordinances" to reflect the absence of the royal signature) and enforced obedience to them. It entered into negotiations with foreign countries, reconstructed the Church of England, and reshuffled the courts of justice.

Within the Houses, even more republican measures were taken. An executive committee of the House of Commons, called resoundingly the Committee of Safety, replaced the absent King and Council in the administering of day-to-day affairs and setting up the assembly's agenda. By 1644, executive power in both rebel states was wielded by a joint committee from the English and Scottish Parliaments, the famous Committee of Both Kingdoms.[12] No less remarkable, perhaps, was that Commons had been able to survive the deaths of its own leaders, John Hampden and "King" Pym, in 1643. At least where Parliament's writ ran, England had completely eliminated the single executive by 1644.

But no one dared say so. In 1643, the Commons expelled a member, Henry Marten, for seeking to depose the King and set up a republic. Unequivocal republicanism confined itself (without ever using the word) to debates on how to govern the church. Here both parties, Presbyterian and Independent (or Congregational), agreed that executives should be elected and that constituencies should be several and divided, differing only on the power of a federal authority to enforce uniformity on the constituent parts. Milton, who had begun his polemical career on this issue of church government, was able to move in the direction of the political republicanism he eventually embraced by first defending it in the church. In early 1641 he had been simply antiepiscopal. By 1642 he had moved through Presbyterianism to Independency. At least one of his friends belonged to no congregation at all: Roger Williams. In 1643, Milton brought this American original to his own publisher with a book (one of the very first) advocating toleration and free competition among religions. In 1644, Milton followed the Independent bias towards autonomy, division, and competition into the political issue of precensorship and wrote the still read classic defense of a free press, *Areopagitica*.

Episcopacy, or government by bishops, was officially abolished in 1646, but there was no assurance about its replacement. In fact, in 1646 there was no assurance about anything, for King Charles had been beaten at Naseby in 1645 and captured soon after, and no one could decide what to do with him. The *de facto* republic wanted Charles to recognize it and return to a powerless throne. Charles, though his word was now worthless, would not even promise such a thing. An emergent Leviathan, the victorious army, was camped in towns around London while its commander, Oliver Cromwell, negotiated for its unpaid wages. A republic which would not proclaim itself faced a society in turmoil, a devious king, and a power, the army, which could undo it in an hour. Uncertain times. Though in retrospect, England was never freer than in these years, few of the English enjoyed them, least of all moderates. Sectarian religious radicals, some claiming God's grace to sin with impunity, were in every parish. A strange countryman named Gerrard Winstanley was calling not only for republican government but for the abolition of private property. The most numerous and dangerous radicals, called Levellers, were so strong in the army that they took it on themselves to write a new English constitution giving the vote to every man who had a shilling in his pocket.

Finally on December 6, 1648, pressed to act by the mutinous army, Cromwell and his colleagues stationed an officer at the door of the House of Commons and removed ninety-six of its moderate, royalist, or Presbyterian members. What was left, the sixty-odd sitting members or "Rump," at last declared what had been true in fact for at least the last three years, that England was no longer a monarchy. All that followed depended on this declaration, and on the assumption that sovereignty—supreme power in the state—lay with the House of Commons and "the people represented therein."[13] It was now possible in law to set up a court to try the King of England for treason—betrayal of the sovereign—and to condemn him to death.

On the wintry day of January 30, 1649, outside the "former palace" of Whitehall, a man named Charles Stuart, "formerly King of England," was beheaded by the public executioner. On March 17 came the final step, abolition of all monarchy and proclamation of the Commonweath of England "without a King or House of Lords":

Whereas it is and hath been found by experience that the office of a king in this nation and Ireland, and to have power thereof in any single person, is unnecessary, burdensome and dangerous to the liberty, safety and public interest of the people, and that for the most part use has been made of the regal power and prerogative to oppress and impoverish and enslave the subject, and that usually and naturally any one person in such power makes it his interest to encroach upon the just freedom and liberty of the people, and to promote the setting up of their own will and power above the laws, that so they might enslave these kingdoms to their own lust, be it therefore enacted and ordained by this present Parliament ... that the office of a king in this nation shall not henceforth reside in or be exercised by any one single person. . . .[14]

A new great seal was struck, replacing King Charles's head with the multiple majesty of the members of the Long Parliament and the contentious motto: "First Year of Freedom by God's Blessing Restored."

The official republic, like the absolute monarchy before it, was to last only eleven years. Royalists called it the "Interregnum" (between kings), but not even royalists were able to forget it as thoroughly as they might have wished. Independents in America, by contrast, hung on the news from London, cheered the Commons speeches of Harry Vane, former governor of Massachusetts and co-founder of Harvard, reflected on the Westminster sermons of Hugh Peter, former pastor of Salem, Massachusetts, and told their children of their country's finest hour.

However heroic, however official, the English republic was a fragile product. Perhaps the terrible and irrevocable act of regicide fatally flawed the thing it was supposed to have created. In time, the Rump faltered, became ingrown and mean, lacking perhaps what Machiavelli might have called the paganism that alone breeds virtue. The Caesarism of Oliver Cromwell came all too quickly and failed just as clearly. England, perhaps because it had suddenly become so democratic, needed the monarchical focus, and the Tudor idea of a kingly commonwealth never quite died.

The tossing and turning of the republic did not, however, move John Milton. He had found his political position. So obvious did it seem to him that even the restoration of Charles II and the threat of execution could not bring him to trim it. All the classical reading of a Renaissance scholar pointed toward the excellence of a republican form of government. All the studies of a serious Puritan, including the Hebrew Bible, confirmed the truth of the injunction of God against kings in I *Samuel* 8, as did the discovery of Machiavelli's *Discorsi* and the visit to the Serene Republic of Venice, both of which he had made in 1639.[15]. Only a week or two after the execution of Charles Stuart, Milton published *The Tenure of Kings and Magistrates,* tenure which, he wrote, is held not of God but "of the people, both originally and naturally for their good and not his owne. . . ." Let Parliament then try Charles "to teach lawless Kings and all that so much adore them, that not mortal man, or his imperious will, but Justice is the onely true sovran and supreme Majesty upon earth."[16]

The prophetic rage of this tract was more than matched in the next one. Charles had been defended in a superb piece of propaganda purporting to be his own deathbed confession, *Eikon Basilike* ("image of the king"). Milton's answer, *Eikonoklastes* ("image breaker"), summed up all his Puritan hatred for idolatry—that sin of common people who, "exorbitant and excessive in all thir motions, are prone afttimes not to a religious onely, but to a civil kinde of Idolatry in idolizing thir Kings. . . ." Now Milton called down on Charles Stuart the judgment of an Old Testament God on King Ahab, "In the place where Dogs lick'd the blood of Naboth, shall Dogs lick thy blood, eev'n thine."[17]

The language might have been even stronger but for the fact that Milton had in March been appointed Latin Secretary to the Council of State, the republic's new committee executive, and may have felt restrained from private passion by a public commission. Milton was not, like that other foreign secretary, Machiavelli, a man of irony, urbanity, calculation, or dry resignation. He was more like Savonarola. He accepted his new post with pride and enthusiasm, eager to defend the republic whatever the cost to himself, pure in his devotion, and convinced the cause would be greater than his interest and ennoble his life. Given the job in 1650 of defending the Rump against the united hostility of European establishments, he wrote, in Latin, the *Defense of the English People Against Salmasius' Defense of Monarchy,* knowing he would lose the last sight in his one good eye doing the research for it. Until *Paradise Lost,* he considered it his greatest work. The tale is the more moving when we realize that Milton, even more than Machiavelli, knew the penchant of "the people" for monarchy and had seen the fragility of his own republic as far back as the debates of 1648. In *Eikonoklastes* he wrote:

People of England, keep ye to those principles [of piety, vertue, and honour], and ye shall never want a King. Nay after such a faire delivrance as this, with so much fortitude and valour shown against a Tyrant, that people that should seek a King, claiming what [Charles] claimes, would shew themselves to be by nature slaves, and arrant beasts; not fitt for that liberty which they cri'd out and bellow'd for, but fitter to be led back again into thir old servitude, like a sort of clamouring and fighting brutes.[18]

Milton's brutes, it seems, were the moderates in the House of Commons, but he was well aware, as a Calvinist, of the depravity of all men. Even the heroes of republicanism could be unreliable. We do not know what Milton's private reaction was to the events of 1653 when His Excellency Lord-General Cromwell, at the head of a troop of soldiers, rose from his seat in the Commons and said "Come, come. I will put an end to your prating. You are no Parliament. I say you are no Parliament. I will put an end to your sitting." As the troops cleared the hall, Cromwell picked up the Speaker's mace, the one John Eliot had held in place in 1629. "What shall we do with this bauble? Here, take it away."[19]

Whatever he thought, Milton remained at his post under the dictator. Cromwell had virtues equal to Caesar's and he was less calculating. He had refused the crown only twice, compared to the thrice of Caesar, and seems to have meant it. Like Caesar, he was unwilling to persecute. In an age of passionate intolerance, a quality which, in fact, had made the revolution possible, Cromwell made even Judaism legal. "I had rather Mahometanism were permitted amongst us than that one of God's children should be persecuted."[20] Indeed, one of the main reasons for Cromwell's dictatorial dismissal of his four Parliaments was their unwillingness to let sectarians alone. Milton no doubt approved of this, as he did of Cromwell's piety, his political talent, and his devotion to justice, if not to law. He hailed the Protector's expansionist foreign policy, dictated much of the vast diplomatic correspondence it required, and if he saw Caesar in it anywhere he kept his mouth shut. His sonnet to Cromwell appeals against a paid clergy but makes no mention of the subordinate dictatorship of the "major-generals," the Protector's peremptory dismissal of four parliaments, or the fact that Cromwell had brought back precensorship of the press in 1655.

Like Machiavelli and so many republicans before and since, Milton kept his blind eye on a strong and virtuous leader as long as an infant republic seemed to find no better security. Perhaps it was

not clear to Milton, in his darkness, that the English republic, like
the Roman and the Florentine, had brought back monarchy under
another name. He was not so much a believer in rule by an abundance of magistrates as he was a believer in pluralism, the rule of
law, and justice absolute and divine.

Turning to the writings of a now forgotten contemporary, James
Harrington, we can see the difference immediately. Harrington,
then described as the only man in England who could explain what
a "commonwealth" was, was also an admirer of Machiavelli and
Venice, but he did not believe that republics were sustained by the
virtue of those in power or their devotion to law. Instead, the secret
was the multiplicity of the powerful, the shortness of their tenures,
and the closeness with which their constituencies reflected the
amount of their property. Harrington, like Machiavelli, was an an-
alyst, at his warmest a utopian. Milton was a prophet, at his best a
visionary of the Kingdom of God. Having a king in heaven makes
it hard to take the earthly ones too seriously.

When Cromwell died in 1658, republicans of the Harrington variety had a brief moment of power. They designed constitutions by
the score, with senates, and assemblies filled by annual, biennial,
quadrennial elections, secret ballots, aristocracies of property, of education, democracies of freeholders, and whole arrays of curiously
titled magistrates.[21] Milton, retired as Secretary but faithful to the
last, joined the debate with a final pamphlet, titled in the new practical tone, *The Readie and Easie Way to Establish a Free Commonwealth*. For it, he borrowed a fair share of the clever new techniques,
a perpetual senate, federalism, and the principle of well-defined
constituencies and terms of office, the lack of which, many said,
had doomed the Rump.

Nevertheless, this little tract which he wrote in 1660 as the gay
young Charles II prepared to receive the thunderous acclamation
of the English people (including eventually the bright young Harringtonians) does not fall into the new opened field of political science. The passionate Puritan assurance of Pym and Hampden,
Peter, Barebones, and Cromwell thunders still in Milton. For it is
not bad laws that destroy republics. It is sin and stupidity:

> Can the folly be paralleld, to adore and be the slaves of a single
> person for doing that which it is ten thousand to one whether he
> can or will do, and we without him might do more easily, more
> effectually, more laudably our selves? . . . Is it such an unspeakable
> joy to serve, such felicitie to weare a yoke?[22]

Nor is it men who frame republics. It is God, who "deliver'd [us] from a king and not without wondrous acts of his providence."[23]

Paradise, he knows, is lost. Another grim Polybian circle is closed. He writes at last:

> What I have spoken is the language of that which is not call'd amiss *the good Old Cause*: if it seem strange to any, it will not seem more strange, I hope, than convincing to backsliders. Thus much I should perhaps have said though I were sure I should have spoken only to trees and stones; and had none to cry to, but with the Prophet, *O earth, earth, earth!* to tell the very soil it self, what her perverse inhabitants are deaf to. Nay though what I have spoke, should happ'n (which Thou suffer not, which did create Mankinde free; nor Thou next, who didst redeem us from being servants of men!) to be the last words of our expiring libertie. But I trust I shall have spoken perswasion to abundance of sensible and ingenuous men: to som perhaps whom God may raise of these stones to be children of reviving libertie. . . .[24]

With his much admired insouciance, Charles II pardoned Milton, who abandoned politics and returned to religion and poetry. Old, gouty, and blind, Milton died quietly in 1674. By then even the ardor of Massachusetts had begun to cool, and Milton found fewer readers every year. Among those readers, however, were some distinguished non-poets: Cotton Mather, Jonathan Mayhew, John Adams, the Comte de Mirabeau, and Maximilien Robespierre. In Milton and his fellow Puritan saints, the link between republicanism and apocalyptic self-righteousness had been, for better or worse, unbreakably forged. Their legacy to republicanism included everything from the legislative supremacy envisioned before 1600 to political localism, ecclesiastical pluralism, and, for the first time in history, judicial regicide.

8

John Adams and Benjamin Franklin
A Republican Union

 T WO CENTURIES the historians had been at work, yet in the Bicentennial year, the literate American still thought of a Whig as one who supported America and of a Tory as one who supported England. The argument between them, according to 1976 conventions, began with taxes and tea.

How sour old John Adams would be to see the point missed, and so narrowly. For him and his fellow Whigs, supporters of independence, the idea was not America versus England, but a republican solution to the traditional problem of subjects' rights and sovereign power. Until 1774 at least, the Founding Fathers were Englishmen. They defended the historic rights of Englishmen. The difference between them and Londoners was entirely in the way in which they conceived those rights.

In England there was a Tory for every Whig. In America, even Tories were lapsed Whigs. Nearly the entire right wing of the British political spectrum was missing in the American colonies, and the left wing there was correspondingly expanded. In England large numbers of voters still treated the monarchy with religious awe. In America the vast majority reserved their awe for the harmony and balance of the British constitution. Only a few in England had heard of Algernon Sidney's *Discourses of Government.* In America the book, a republican tract, was holy writ. Towns and colleges had been named Sidney. As Adams himself wrote in 1776:

> A man must be indifferent to the sneers of modern Englishmen, to mention in their company the names of Sidney, Harrington, Locke, Milton, Nedham, Neville, Burnet, and Hoadly. No small fortitude is necessary to confess one has read them. The wretched condition of this country, however, for ten or fifteen yrs past, has frequently reminded me of their principles and reasonings. They will convince any candid mind, that there is no good government but what is republican.[1]

We must be careful not to concede victory to the British, two centuries after the Peace of Paris, by casually adopting the British definitions of what once were fighting words. A real Whig, taking his title when he opposed the Stamp Act in 1765, is not a partisan of William and Mary, still less a revolutionary or a democrat. A Whig is a partisan of checks and balances, limited government. He wants the substance of republicanism and *in extremis* the word as well.

Prepared for this kind of surprise, let us take another look at the most successful republican revolution in modern history as it took shape in the hands of two remarkable Bostonians, John Adams and Benjamin Franklin. Both entered the maelstrom of revolutionary politics slowly and carefully, with full awareness of the appalling fragility of past republics and a Calvinist sense of human mortality and imperfection; but both entered wholeheartedly at last, believing, with their contemporaries of the Enlightenment, that law and even society itself could be improved by a tinker who knew his business.

When Algernon Sidney was led to the scaffold on Tower Hill on December 7, 1683, he was the last republican in England. Milton and Harrington were dead. The son of Charles I had been reigning for twenty-three years, to the general satisfaction of the new generation of Englishmen. When the aged Sidney was asked if he wished to address the spectators, he replied that he had made his peace with God and had nothing to say to man. He handed the sheriff a last writing in which he stated that he died for that *good old cause* in which he was engaged from his youth, and told the headsman to get on with it.

The good old cause was the Commonwealth. So changed was England since the 1640s that many did not know this. Five years after the execution, England deposed yet another Stuart king but the idea of replacing him with a republic never occurred to people. As the ax fell, Sidney's cause died bravely but vainly with him.

Among the king's subjects in America, however, the forlorn old traitor of 1683 became a martyr, a posthumous reputation which is one of the first important signs of a growing cultural difference between England and her North American colonies. Just as Jacobean English words like "sick" survived in America and vanished in England, so the Commonwealth view of the English constitution survived. By 1776, there had been a complete divorce. In America, a king was deposed who was not even a Stuart; and the idea of replacing him with another king was, if mentioned, denounced as insane.

The English were greatly confused by 1776. The Tudor idea of a mixed monarchy had become orthodox Whig doctrine. The notion of a kingless commonwealth was barely alive in the minds of a tiny radical minority—English readers of Tacitus, like Thomas Gordon, or spectacular rebels like John Wilkes. Few others cared what they thought and nobody, least of all the radicals, ever argued to eliminate rather than limit the monarchy. Americans, in a pattern by now familiar, steeped themselves in these ideas. They read and republished Gordon, Trenchard, and Molesworth. They named their children after John Wilkes. They read just about everything that emanated from the remnants of that Puritanism that had ruled in the 1640s, founded New England, and now wended its way to modest little chapels under the deprecatory title of Dissent.

Twenty-three years after the death of Sidney, Benjamin Franklin was born. In was 1706, and Boston was ruled by a Calvinist establishment less than three generations removed from John Winthrop and John Milton. Franklin's theology was not calvinist, and his humor wasn't either, but his moral and political culture were, and profoundly so. The same is true of John Adams, born in the same colony a generation later in 1735. Both men had the Puritan virtues of thrift, steadiness, learning, and industry. More importantly, they shared the Puritan faith in a self-selected society of men who, as equals before God, governed themselves by elected magistrates. Both, in short, were republicans.

So were most of the Founding Fathers. In fact, they were such strong republicans that when the Revolution came they would allow no one of their number to lead it. Adams was disgusted by the later adulation of Washington (a man he proposed because John

Hancock was getting too forward) and Washington himself was bothered by it. Modern students, however, are bewildered by the vast galaxy of nameless Founders and impatient to get on to Washington and a simpler, more hierarchical politics. To such, the choice of Adams and Franklin among the fifty-six signers of the Declaration of Independence seems justified only because they were both on the committee that wrote it. Also, Adams was president once and Franklin . . . well, Franklin discovered electricity.

In fact, as most people know, Adams was a rather poor president and Franklin did not really discover electricity. In fact, Franklin was a very good president—of Pennsylvania—and it may easily be argued that Adams's greatest achievement was the framing of the constitution—of Massachusetts.

Our present viewpoint not only obscures these achievements, and others like them, it makes it very hard to understand where the achievers came from. The Founding Fathers with all their talent and accomplishment did not arise in America because of a run of genetic luck or even something peculiarly apt in the American system of education. They came out of a society which prized a political career above nearly all others, directed its best minds toward elective office, and trained them fully by providing hundreds of such offices high and low in each of the thirteen colonies. Only the colonial governor and a few of his appointees achieved office in any other way. When Franklin was elected to the Second Continental Congress at the age of sixty-nine in 1775, he called himself a "printer, retired," but he had been for nearly eleven years the elected agent in London of the Pennsylvania legislature and for more than five the elected agent of the assemblies of Georgia, New Jersey, and Massachusetts. Earlier he had spent ten years in the Pennsylvania Assembly as a legislator himself, and he had drawn up the first constitution for the union of the American colonies more than twenty years ago.

Adams, a lawyer, was only forty when he arrived in Philadelphia, but he had been a member of the Massachusetts legislature (the General Court) for Boston and Braintree since he was thirty. All the other Congressmen had had similar careers. Each could easily have spent his life in elective politics without ever holding the same office more than a year. None, however, had seriously aspired to the highest office, colonial governor, which was not elective and whose incumbents seldom distinguished themselves. In a word, the Founding Fathers were equals. Republicans by inheritance, they had become republicans by training, tough on-the-job training in responsible politics. They were the products and survivors of parliamentary, not bureaucratic, procedures—clever, competitive, and well known to each of their diverse and demanding constituencies. The United States of America, which they named officially on September 9, 1776, and for which they drew up the constitutions of 1777 and 1787, was designed to perpetuate this fundamentally republican political culture and to set it definitively apart from the decaying whiggism of the mother country.

In the minds of the Founding Fathers, the American Revolution was not really about tea and taxes. It was about the future of the English constitution, which the colonists persisted in thinking of as a kind of republic. It was fear of decay and conspiracy that animated the revolutionary leaders, fear of a corrupt magistracy and unbalanced, unlimited government. They really believed, as the English Whigs did not, that the Stamp Tax, the Tea Tax, and the Coercive Acts constituted, in the words of the Declaration of Independence, "repeated Injuries and Usurpations, all having in direct object the establishment of an Absolute Tyranny. . . ." And the more one looks at their words, the clearer it becomes that to them the model of tyranny was the government of Charles I, of Sulla, Caesar, and Peisistratos. The more sophisticated among them, like Adams and Franklin, did not even see George III as a tyrant except for propaganda purposes. What they saw instead was a situation like that of Rome between the Gracchi and Caesar where the wealth of empire cheapened virtue, patronage replaced merit, election was at the mercy of money and influence, constitutional right quailed before power, and no legal remedy could be found to halt the decay of law. A tyrant would indeed come, but one who, like the Greek *tyrannoi*, would be a demagogue and a usurper. It all sounds a little extreme to us, but it is not surprising that anyone who had such fears would have thought that only a surgical separation from incurable England could insure a reasonable life expectancy for republicanism in the colonies—a longer ride on the high side of the cycle of Polybios.

Neither Adams nor Franklin lived long enough to see their fears for England proved groundless, but their old-fashioned philosophy of history cannot be proved wrong so easily. Indeed, both men, in the process of framing constitutions for both the states and the union, may have laid the groundwork for an American example of Polybios' circles. Moreover, they disagreed on the best method of creating a stable republic as deeply as they disagreed over whether or not to sleep with the windows open. Old Franklin, a fresh-air fiend who was in the habit of padding about his house in the nude, was one of the most radically democratic men in America. The constitution he helped write for Pennsylvania in 1776 gave every taxpayer a vote, scandalized American leaders for fourteen years, and was repealed as soon as he was dead. Adams, who feared the night air, was one of the least democratic of American republicans. The constitution he wrote for Massachusetts in 1779—powerful, centralized, and elitist—was a model for the conservative Constitution of 1787. It is, perhaps, something of the genius of America that when Franklin and Adams had to sleep in the same room together (on their way to talk peace with General Howe in the summer of 1776), Adams himself opened the window at Franklin's entreaty and, "leaping into Bed," was put to sleep by Franklin's extended lecture on the "real Cause of Colds."[2]

Compromise was this easy because, metaphorically speaking, it was unusual in revolutionary America for two magistrates to share a room. It was not necessary, even under the Federal Constitution of 1787, for a Philadelphian to agree to tolerate what pleased a Bostonian. Between the end of the Revolution in 1781 and the ratification of the Constitution, states were so independent of one another that they charged tariffs on the goods they exchanged with each other, coined their own money, and raised and supported their own armies. The difference between the constitutions of Massachusetts and Pennsylvania was glaring, but not, until 1787, an object of national concern. National concern was reserved for the creation of yet more states to join the loose-knit community, yet more theaters and offices for the rising politicians of the new Republic. Good fences made good neighbors, and politics made few bedfellows.

No country, with the possible exception of Switzerland, has ever been more fragmented than the United States of America was in the eighteenth century. No state, unless it be medieval Florence, ever had more elected magistrates. Even before the Revolution, America had the posts to train half the population in the delights of politics. Its reward was the production of men like Franklin and Adams. Their like has been rarer since this country ceased to value such divisions.

The celebrated shot had already been fired at Lexington when Franklin and Adams met for the first time in May 1775 in Philadelphia. Both had done much to load the musket. They had known of each other by reputation, had corresponded officially, and had moved in the same intellectual direction for many years. In each, a deep affection for England had died a lingering death. In both, New England was alienated from the old by a barely conscious projection forward of the Puritan Revolution. Though they were not friends and indeed never became friends, no one at the Second Continental Congress was the least bit surprised to see Adams and Franklin become the great moving spirits behind union, independence, and republicanism, or that they should have looked over Jefferson's shoulder when he wrote the Declaration of Independence.

No doubt it is true that there were too many great men in the American Revolution for an ordinary person's memory. If we remember them by their specialties (orator Henry, general Washington, financier Morris, propagandist Sam Adams) we can say of Adams and Franklin that none were more instrumental in defining the causes of the conflict with Great Britain, largely because they had been so careful to define it for themselves.

For Adams, a young lawyer of twenty-six, the key event in a long radicalization was the extraordinary argument of one James Otis, Junior before the Massachusetts provincial court in the case of Gray *vs.* Paxton. That was spring, 1761. As Adams sat in the Old Council Chamber in Boston, listening, he became too excited to take notes. For this earnest young man, ambitious and smelling of the lamp, who had read his Greek and Latin history at Harvard, taught it for a while himself, and who had discovered Milton at twenty-one and Machiavelli the previous winter, Otis came on like thunder and prophecy. Here he was opposing natural right and divine equity to the claims of the British government to search a subject's house at will. He was quoting Edward Coke and Selden on Magna Carta and the rights of subjects against the king. For the notes he forgot to take, Adams made up again and again. With each succeeding crisis and well on into his peaceable eighties, he returned to the Old Council Chamber like a convert to the place of his conversion. There, he wrote, "the views of the English government . . . and the views of the Colonies . . . were . . . brought to a Collision." "A contest . . . opened to which I could foresee no End . . . ." Adams saw in 1761, though perhaps not as suddenly as he later imagined, the difference in culture that made Algernon Sidney a fool in England and a martyr in America. "The child Independence," as he said, "was born."[3]

Franklin's love for England lasted somewhat longer than Adams's did. He had first visited London as a struggling, spottily educated printer of eighteen and liked it. In 1761 he was in fact living in London, enjoying its cosmopolitan delights and seeing to the interests of his adopted country of Pennsylvania. He was fifty-five and "retired." The kite, the stove, and the bifocals were behind him, as were *Poor Richard* and *The Pennsylvania Gazette.* He had recently received honorary degrees from Oxford and Saint Andrew's in Scotland, and he had just been elected to the Royal Society by his fellow scientists. "Was it not Well-known," he wrote, that the colonists loved England "much more than they love one another?" Franklin had, it is true, said some unfriendly things about British undervaluation of the charter of Pennsylvania in 1758, but they were mostly aimed at the Penn family. In 1761, he had hardly even heard about the dread writs of assistance. In 1765, while he sat in the galleries of Parliament waiting to lobby for Pennsylvania, he heard a languid debate on Prime Minister Grenville's proposal for a Stamp Tax. Four of his fellow colonial agents formally petitioned against the act. Franklin was against it, but all he did was to buttonhole his friends in the ministry. Franklin was still a Londoner, for London recognized, so he thought, the honor of a self-made man.

In Braintree, Massachusetts, however, Adams was struck with horror. The Stamp Act, he thought, was a deliberate effort to restrict the right of colonists to preserve their property and tax themselves. The "power of the purse" was to be taken away from its classic Whig repository, a local representative assembly. Adams drew up, on his own hook, a set of instructions against the Act of Braintree's member of the Massachusetts General Court. Forty other towns adopted the same instructions. Within the year Boston had elected Adams to the General Court and he was drafting its resolution against the tax. For the moment he avoided the Sons of Liberty and the mob violence orchestrated by his cousin Samuel, but he rejoiced at the mass resignation of the colonial tax collectors who were the objects of the violence. Adams tried hard not to be bloodthirsty, but he never thought of righteous anger as a sin. Possibly it was as an exercise in self-discipline that he defended the eight redcoats accused of the Boston Massacre. Adams was never as interested in condemning the tools of despotism as the theories that supported it.

Though both Franklin and Adams were the sort of men who get up steam slowly, by the 1770s both were convinced of the existence of a concerted effort to deprive British subjects, especially colonials, of the classic rights and antimonarchical devices secured at terrible cost in the previous century. More and more they saw the English governing class as venal, eventually corrupt, finally conspiratorial and despotic. Of the Townshend import duties, which had seemed such a concession in 1768, one of them, the tea tax, was a link in the chains of slavery by 1773.

Again and again, as if to provide them with an education, the British Parliament demonstrated its forgetfulness of the very principles on which as an institution it had staked its life in the seventeenth century. It proposed to pay the colonial governors and judges, taking this power away from the colonial assemblies. This made sense in England. To Adams and Franklin it was sinister. In such a system, they both knew, Charles I had fired Edward Coke. In such a system the colonial governors would become thirteen Charles I's. Such a proposal could be made only by men ambitious of despotism. The "judiciary" must be independent so as to check the "executive." The power to pay, which was the power to control, must be spread among as many magistrates as practical and put as close to the people as representation would permit. But, they said, Massachusetts was not represented in Parliament at all.

Mobocratic nonsense, insisted Massachusetts Governor Hutchinson (who had supported the Stamp Tax in 1765). And others noted that Massachusetts was far better "represented" by Benjamin Franklin, who was not an MP, than Bristol by Edmund Burke, who was, or Manchester, a large city with no MP at all. Franklin, like Adams, demurred. Absolute and direct representation, that odd American idea, had become the essence of whiggism as they understood it. If Boston were represented in the Massachusetts assembly and not, like Boston, Lincolnshire, represented in the British Parliament, it was despotism that Parliament should tax it, and evidence of a despotic conspiracy that Parliament should assert the right to do so.[4]

Final evidence of Franklin's arrival at the extreme Whig position came to Adams personally on March 22, 1773. In the mail was a small package for the Sons of Liberty (Adams was now a member) from Benjamin Franklin (who was by now agent for radical Massachusetts as well as moderate Pennsylvania). It contained private letters written by Governor Hutchinson after anti-Stamp Act mobs had trashed his house. No one knows exactly how Franklin got them, or more to the point exactly why he sent them. His own papers show that he still professed to be English and in favor of a reconciliation. Perhaps he thought bad faith ought to be met with bad faith. He must have known that his handling of the Hutchinson letters was the kind of thing we would now call an unauthorized wiretap, to which Adams and the Boston Sons would undoubtedly add political blackmail.

The letters were released. Hutchinson, his reputation irredeemably Toryized, was unable any longer to assert himself against Massachusetts Whiggery. Within a few months the Sons had defied his order in the Boston Tea Party and Hutchinson himself was in exile aboard a ship in Boston harbor.

The Tea Party charmed Adams. It was, he wrote, bold, daring, inflexible, intrepid, and sublime.[5] Unfortunately it had the effect of trapping Franklin into a position beyond conciliation. Franklin's part in releasing the letters became known in December. In January 1774, he had been summoned to present Massachusetts' case for dismissing Governor Hutchinson before the Privy Council. With his customary tact, Franklin had managed to get the hearing postponed to February 5, but news of the Boston Tea Party hit the London papers on January 21, giving the British government just enough time before the hearing to plan the humiliation of Poor Richard.

February 5, 1774 was the most decisive day in Franklin's life. Standing in the Cockpit (so the room was called), the sixty-eight-year-old, white- haired, self-made man, distinguished diplomat, and Fellow of the Royal Society was scolded like an apprentice for more than an hour by His Majesty's Solicitor-General. Always the optimist, he hadn't expected this. Never again, however, would he mistake the exquisite courtesy of the great for the manner of friendship between equals, nor ever again trust in the good faith of the British elite. Slow to anger, Franklin now achieved a rage so thorough, so sustained, and so radical that for the rest of his life the "most civilized man in America" was to be known as the Most Dangerous.[6] Don't pay for the tea, he wrote. Charge the British government for every tax you've paid, subtract the cost of the tea, and bill England for the balance. Don't pay for the tea: "By giving way you will lose every thing. Strong chains will be forged for you, and you will be made to pay for both the Iron and the Workmanship."[7]

Britain, however, wanted the price of the tea. Until it should be paid, Parliament voted (while the helpless Franklin looked on) to close the port of Boston and to revoke the General Court, town meetings, and colonial courts of Massachusetts. To enforce all these

acts they sent an occupying army. Adams, enraged, suggested a'
program of impeachments. Franklin lingered a year in England,
trying everything, but his heart was no longer in it. On March 20,
1775, Franklin visited his fellow scientist, the radical Whig Joseph
Priestly, and talked of America with tears running down his cheeks.
The following day he set sail from Portsmouth for Philadelphia, a
city he had not seen for ten years. When he stepped onto the dock
on May 5, the first news he heard was of the battle of Lexington
and Concord.

The next morning the Pennsylvania Assembly chose him as a
delegate to the Second Continental Congress, just opened, and
there in Carpenter's Hall the two revolutionaries met for the first
time. No one knows how it went. Adams, no less prickly than Franklin about being self-made, but thirty years younger, less traveled,
and far less celebrated, probably made the first move. It was his
second Congress and he knew the ropes. Adams, moreover, had
earned his spurs in Franklin's profession of journalism by publishing a magisterial brief for the rights of the colonists. Into *Novanglus*,
Adams had thrown everything but the kitchen sink, invoking Livy
against Tarquin, Hampden against bishops, Harrington against the
Roman emperors, Grotius against Philip II, Algernon Sidney against
Charles I, and Franklin himself against Governors Hutchinson,
Shirley, and Bernard. He had offered George III the title of King
of Massachusetts "gladly" if he wanted it—as long as he would govern in association with the Massachusetts parliament. Finally he
called on Edward Coke to prove that the British Parliament had
not even the right to govern Wales except by royal decree and Welsh
consent: so its title *a fortiori* was weak in Scotland, and nonexistent
in Massachusetts. To the assertion of such a title Adams called for
armed resistance. Thus, he protested, he was no republican, only a
Whig.[8]

Whether Franklin admired this effort we do not know. Franklin's humor was gentler, possibly because he had never learned that
much history. All he had written was a purported *Decree* of the king
of Prussia, expressing his claim to all lands colonized by the subjects
of his ancestors, the Anglo-Saxons, in North America.[9] At any rate
the two men plunged into work, Adams to the war committee where
he engineered the naming of Washington to command and agitated
for an official declaration of war, Franklin to the diplomacy committee, where on July 21 he made the first proposition to frame a
constitution for the United States. Both had given up on the rights
of Englishmen and were plotting independence. Adams's strategy

was to keep putting Congress up to calling the colonies states and recommending each to act as if independent and set up a new constitution. Then on June 7, Richard Henry Lee, an Adams ally, moved, "that these colonies are, and of right ought to be, free and independent states!" So much for the king. As the two Bostonians sat in committee, debugging Jefferson's Declaration, they must have felt impatient to begin the work now made possible, constructing a genuine republic.

Both Franklin and Adams had by now moved from the whiggism of limited mixed monarchy to outright republicanism. Adams, whose plan was already on paper, defined republic in terms which Franklin could easily subscribe to: "an empire of laws, not of men".[10] From this common ground, however, the two men moved in very opposite directions. Adams, steeped in all the history which forms the subject of this book, was bubbling with checks, balances, and safeguards. Franklin, more simply educated, had caught only one vision, sovereignty of the people. At seventy, he had become the first democratic republican in American political history.[11]

For Adams no one, least of all the whole people, was to be trusted with the exercise of ultimate power. Let this aristocracy check that one, this magistracy balance another, and all serve as counterpoise to the people, a dangerous group whose sovereignty was philosophic only. For Franklin the secret of an incorruptible republic lay precisely in the effective sovereignty of the people (at least all male taxpayers). Only give them the collective right to choose all magistrates and reelect them annually and it would be unnecessary to erect any other checks between the magistrates themselves. Adams was horrified and, always blunt, published as much, but he never blamed Franklin.[12]

In fact, the old man kept quiet and died before anyone quite realized just how amazingly radical he was. He was too tactful and too foxy to press his views in public. Long years in London had taught him the practicality of discretion and private persuasion. Far better to succeed than to publish or petition in vain. His colleagues, in turn were too tactful to tell a septuagenarian what they thought of him. They did, however, conceive the idea of sending him to France, possibly so they could debate the Articles of Confederation in peace. (They may have had the same idea about Adams in November 1777. The Articles had been approved, but Adams called them a mere "rope of sand." Soon after, he too was sent to France.)

Congress did not get rid of Franklin soon enough, however. He had the rest of the summer, and as it turns out September and October to get his ideas into some form and be useful. So he walked across the hall as an elected delegate to the Pennsylvania Constitutional Convention. On July 15 he was elected to chair the convention. By August he had helped write a good part of the new Constitution of the Commonwealth. By September 28 (with some time off for an inspection trip to Canada) he had achieved its acceptance by the Convention, signed it *Benj. Franklin Prest.*, and had a month left to pack for France.[13]

One look at this document was enough to stir Adams to both anger and emulation, but his time came later and he cut it thinner. He arrived in Boston from France aboard *Le Sensible* on August 2, 1779, was elected representative from Braintree to the constitutional convention of Massachusetts a week later, and was named to the convention's drafting committee on September 4. The committee reduced itself to a subcommittee of one—John Adams—whose draft was reported to the convention in October and accepted with a few revisions by the end of the year.[14] Adams, meanwhile, had got back aboard *Le Sensible* on November 15 and sailed back to France. The very tale makes you tired. Both men had put together their state constitutions in a matter of two months. Solon, who had had a whole year, would surely have admired such a performance. Americans may do the same, for these two republican experiments may well be their greatest domestic achievements.

In 1776 Americans had plenty of models for government, at least thirteen of which were voided by the Fourth of July. It was to the first experiments in state constitution making that they would look for guidance; and of those experiments, Massachusetts and Pennsylvania (with New York) were to be by far the most influential. That the Federal Constitution of 1787 was largely measured on the frame of Massachusetts must count as Adams's achievement. That the trans-Appalachian west took up and clove to the Franklin model, despite its 1790 repeal in Pennsylvania, is one of the very earliest tremors of the democratic earthquake of the next two centuries. That both constitutions were radically republican has helped bind this country for two centuries and more to a form of government which Aristotle judged the least likely to endure.

Basically, the Pennsylvania constitution of 1776, like the convention which drew it up, was a government by omnipotent assembly. The legislative power, which to all Whigs was the most important, was vested in a single house, the General Assembly of the Commonwealth of Pennsylvania, which not only made all laws but in addition elected the chief executive, or President, and had the power to fire Supreme Court justices and impeach any magistrate whatsoever. The President, elected annually like everyone else, had no veto. He was also responsible to an elected Council of Twelve of which he was himself a member, and which was required to keep written minutes which could be demanded by the Assembly at is pleasure. No doubt if they had known about the tape recorder they would have required all presidential conversations to be taped. The President was, it is true, commander-in-chief of the armed forces, but he could neither lead them in person nor appoint any of their officers below the rank of general. He was, in short, minatory. No Charles I or Thomas Hutchinson could have survived in such an office.

As for the Assembly, it was effectively checked or balanced nowhere except by the constitution itself on the one hand and the sovereign people on the other. Check by the people, however, was indeed awesome. First of all, every man twenty-one years old, owning some modicum of property, paying some pittance of taxes, and able to swear allegiance to Pennsylvania was a citizen, which was the widest franchise the world had ever seen. These voters elected Assemblymen (Councilmen, too) each and every year on a basis of strict representation of their numbers and location. They might monitor them as carefully and as often as they wished, for the constitution mandated that the Assembly doors remain open and all bills, votes, and debates be published once a week. No bill could become law before being presented to the people. Even if, after all this, constituents failed to discover and punish an Assemblyman's lapse, the officer would still have to resign, for the constitution prohibited him from being elected to more than four terms in any seven years.

The people even had a check on the sacred constitution itself. Its last section (not written by Franklin) provided a Livyesque Council of Censors, elected by the people for seven years. For one year it was to sit as a committee to judge whether the President and Assembly were keeping their constitutional noses clean. Then for the next six years it was to review the constitution itself and recommend amendments back to the people.

All in all, this was the most democratic frame of government in the world until copied in the letter by Vermont in 1777 and 1790 and in the spirit by the French National Convention in 1793. Its

dry prose still crackles with the optimism of 1776 and of old Ben
Franklin himself, as if he had said to himself, after centuries of poor
luck with governments, let us not despair of human goodness but
be bold and try the state of nature undiluted. At only two points
does the document, mindful of the classic doctrine that the virtue
of citizens determines the fate of republics, express any doubt of
the people's continued virtue: section 45, which urges constant en-
actment and enforcement of laws to prevent vice, and section 32,
which disenfranchises any voter who accepts a drink from a candidate.[15]

Adams, of course, was never an optimist—even about the
weather. "The People," he wrote, "are extremely addicted to Corruption and Venality, as well as the Great." The Pennsylvania constitution, and projects like it, he thought "Systems of Anarchy." He
seems, like everyone else, never to have been able to imagine that
Franklin, poker-faced, sleepy, and impossibly old, was the principal
author of this monstrosity.[16] If he had, he would have come to dis-
like him sooner than he did, but that feeling was postponed to 1778
in Paris. There Franklin shocked Adams by sexual complaisance
and silk waistcoats, not democratic radicalism. Adams, who sorely
missed his wife, sniffed and wrote:

> The Jews, the Greeks, the Romans, the Swiss, the Dutch, all lost
> their public spirit, their Republican principles and habits and their
> Republican Forms of Government, when they lost the Modesty and
> Domestic Virtues of their Women.[17]

Which is one way to look at it.

Adams did not try to prohibit vice in the Massachusetts constitution, however. His aim expressed a deeper pessimism. At all costs
the people were to be divided against each other, no less than the
branches of government, for history had taught Adams something
that Franklin, for all his experience, had overlooked: the natural
alliance between executive power—monarchy—and that popular
power—democracy—which it was so ideally placed to feed and focus. The Massachusetts constitution of 1780 is a full and masterly
display of republican devices borrowed from all epochs, designed
not to serve but to outwit a fallen human nature. Calvin and Machiavelli would easily have recognized Adams's frame of mind if not
his frame of government.

Adams began by dividing all voters into towns and counties and
requiring them to act through the existing local offices. Then, like
Solon, he divided them according to wealth. There were to be,

among the property owners, thousand-pound men, three-hundred-pound men, hundred-pound men, and sixty-pound men. The first could vote for anyone and serve in any office. Three-hundred-pounders could be anything but governor. Hundred-pound men could sit in the lower house but not in the upper. Sixty-pound men could vote for any of these offices but not run for them. Those with less than sixty pounds of taxable property (a distinct minority) were disenfranchised by the Commonwealth, as were, despite the views of Abigail Adams, all women.

Adams then set up the classic branches of executive and legislature; but here again he divided them against themselves. The legislature was bicameral, a Senate and a House of Representatives, and each could veto the other. The executive consisted of a Governor and Council, the former elected by the sixty-pound men and the latter by the Senate and house jointly. Again each had checks on the other and both had a veto on the legislature.

In the matter of the executive, Adams faced a dilemma. It was necessary for the executive to be nimble and vigorous in order to combat the anarchy which an excess of democracy occasionally produced. So he still believed when, as President of the United States in 1798, he signed the Alien and Sedition Acts at the cost of his future reputation. But what about that alliance of executive and people which he had long ago concluded to be a danger equal or worse. Adams's solution was to endow the Governor of the Commonwealth of Massachusetts with independence far beyond that of the President of Pennsylvania, and at the same time put greater power to check him in the hands of the aristocratic branch, the Senate and the Council. Thus the Governor had even less power over the army than the President and could neither appoint nor dismiss any of its officers. Those officers he could appoint had to clear either the Council or the Senate. Even if there were a Caesar there would be no Tenth Legion.

Last but not least was the judiciary. It was to be as independent as a perpetual salary could make it. Only justices of the peace had terms shorter than life. Only the concurrence of every other branch could remove the higher judges. Only the judiciary was immune from that great and comprehensive check on all the others, rotation in office and annual election. On that at least he was in complete agreement with Franklin. As he wrote in 1776, "there not being in the whole circle of sciences a maxim more infallible than this, 'where annual elections end, there slavery begins'."[18]

Finally came a set of clauses applying to all three branches, all of which may be distilled into one cardinal rule. No one may hold more than one magistracy at a time. This was the rule which, Adams thought, had kept monarchy at bay in Rome until Marius and Sulla had succumbed to temptation. Franklin's constitution shows a similar intention on this point, though less general and less explicit.

Beyond annual elections and separation of offices, only a provision for state support of education and the presence of a Bill of Rights link the Franklin and Adams constitutions. Nor is it at all surprising to find both documents prohibiting press censorship, closed courts, general warrants, and standing armies, when both authors had cut their political teeth attacking such things. Otherwise the two constitutions are, within practical limits, as different as two contemporary minds could devise. Strength at the center, a feature of both, expressed in Pennsylvania something very like Rousseau's "general will," while in Massachusetts it served as a fence against it. Franklin had believed in colonial union since 1754 and wished to establish it through legal simplicity. Adams was no foe of union but he feared both concentration and simplicity. He would have planted hedges in the Garden of Eden.

When the war was won, it was Franklin and Adams in uneasy harness who led the negotiating team that gained recognition and a treaty for the new country. Adams went on to become Ambassador to George III and Franklin went home to become president of Pennsylvania. Franklin seems to have been happy enough with his handiwork, but the national constitution, which Adams had helped Congress to write during Franklin's first year in France, continued to bother him. The Articles of Confederation had first displeased Franklin by excluding the representation of numbers. It was the union's lack of authority that most worried Adams.

Congress's inability to collect taxes and maintain a uniform commercial policy made Adams's diplomatic task monumentally frustrating. The President of the United States (in Congress Assembled) changed whenever Congress assembled or chose to elect a new chairman. The state department, Adams's boss, was nothing more than a protean congressional committee with doubtful status, an irregular chairmanship, and a staff of two secretaries. A man of Franklin's bent might have hailed irregularity as evidence of freedom. Adams did not. When, in 1786, the debtors of western Massachusetts took down the muskets they had used in the Revolution and declared war on the Commonwealth he had so carefully designed, Adams, in London, was not pleased; and when he heard of the project to write a new federal constitution for the United States, he wrote of it in unusually sanguine terms: "The convention of Philadelphia is composed of heroes, sages, and demi-gods, to be sure. . . ."[19]

Adams not among them. When the ambassador finally returned from Europe, the Constitution was already written and ratified. All the help the Framers had from him was his new book, *Defence of the Constitutions of America,* and the Massachusetts constitution of 1780 now seven years old and already venerable. They did use that constitution. James Madison, possibly the most intellectually influential of the demigods, kept it by him, though he was a Virginian, and Madison, with his usual scholarly *sitzfleisch* also read Adams's very long *Defence,* which turns out to be less worthy of oblivion than Adams expected. Madison could "find nothing new in it," but everything old was there.[20] Where else could he have located, in only three volumes, capsule descriptions of the constitutions of The Netherlands, Florence, Venice, Athens, and Sparta, plus, among others, Poland, Pistoia, Cremona, San Marino, Carthage, Argos, Crete, and eighteen separate cantons of Switzerland! Where else, too, could one find digests of republican thinkers from Polybios to Algernon Sidney, critiques of all of them, and conclusions as creative, foreboding, and oracular as this one: "There is no special providence for Americans and their nature is the same with that of the others."[21]

The Founding Fathers in Philadelphia shared the mood of Adams in London, despite the sunny presence in their midst of the now eighty-one-year-old Franklin. The document that emerged bore Franklin's mark in only two places, neither unique to him: the fillip it gave to union and the comparatively representative and democratic franchise it defined for the lower house of Congress. It would have its day in Jackson's time but in 1787, aged ten, the Pennsylvania constitution stood so low in the estimation of leaders now "older and wiser" that the oldest and wisest of them all was not able to raise it. Even Franklin was prepared to admit that the Massachusetts constitution was "one of the best in the World" and that the threat of *"excess of power* in the rulers" had become less worrisome than that of *"defect of obedience* in the subjects." So he wrote to Charles Carroll in 1789.[22]

Thus the famous federal Constitution of 1787 emerged looking very much like the Massachusetts one writ large. Framed at the high tide of a conservative backflow in American history, it is arguably the most conservative constitution ever written in this multiconstitutional country, certainly the most whiggish in its distrust of power.

The federal executive, for example, was the strongest in American republican experience, largely devised by James Wilson who had early been disillusioned by the constitution of his home state of Pennsylvania. The executive was given the veto, it was checked by no council or committee, it was very nearly made electable by the people at large, and unlike the Governor of Massachusetts it had full power to command and appoint, notably in the armed forces. The fact that it was given the disparaging and familiar title of President, meaning chairman, was the only gesture to men like Randolph and Gerry, who still feared monarchy. If Adams had been there he might have reminded them that Caesar had once been only a man's nickname and "prince" shorthand for "leading citizen," the title of Caesar's grandson. Adams, however, would most likely have let it pass, for he agreed with James Wilson that a strong executive provides a useful check on both aristocracy and democracy. As long as you don't let the people elect him directly, thought Adams, a president's power is on the whole a good thing. Besides, he had no nostalgia for the previous executive of ad hoc congressional committees under which he had toiled as ambassador.[23]

As for the other parts of the machine, all were, in theory, equal in power and each had powerful checks on the other two. In the process, however, of following the Massachusetts and New York examples, reacting against all-powerful legislatures like Pennsylvania, and because of the famous dispute between the large and small states over representation, the Convention came up with a bicameral legislature. In this way, although they did eliminate internal checks in the executive and the judiciary, giving them "unity and dispatch" with which to act against their competitors, they left that whig palladium, the legislature, divided against itself and hobbled, as Gouverneur Morris dimly saw, for the coming contest with the other branches. Asked whether the secret deliberations had produced a monarchy or a republic, Franklin said, "A Republic, if you can keep it."

Anyone, however, can second-guess the Framers now, with Madison's minutes and nearly two centuries of experience to guide him. The document has, as we say, stood the test for a long time. Only the constitution of Massachusetts, unrecognizably amended, has been in force longer, and very few other constitutions have survived, as ours has, twenty-eight amendments, a civil war, world power, and Richard Nixon. It has, moreover, added one more safeguard to the long list inherited from the Whigs and the Revolution: federalism.

This is the device whereby the national government is supreme but constitutionally limited in scope, while the state governments are inferior but by the federal constitution unlimited. To the balance between types of government and branches of government, federalism adds a balance between coeval *levels* of government.

The Greeks had tried this without much success. Adams thought it a solecism. Sovereignty, he thought, was indivisible, an odd blind spot for a man who had seen division everywhere and sown it himself. Actually the idea of federalism was first laid out by the diminutive egghead, James Madison, and the original of it is more likely a thirty-year record of Benjamin Franklin's practical suggestions, beginning with the Albany Plan of Union in 1754 and ending with the so-called Connecticut Compromise in 1787.

Defeated on many points in Convention, Franklin remained optimistic. Addressing the Convention as it prepared to adjourn, he wrote, "I consent, Sir, to this Constitution because I expect no better, and because I am not sure that it is not the best."[24] He knew it would, like a child, take on a history independent of its makers. It was designed, all the Framers knew, to prevent despotism, and to prevent it in whatever form it might take for at least a generation. Every power and faction, every office, every branch, every interest and party they could foresee had been comprehended and limited in some clause of the Constitution. As a whole it was to be the supreme law. Every American was ultimately to be governed by it and to it he was to give his ultimate loyalty. No magistrate, however charismatic, was to disobey it. No citizen, however ignorant, was to disregard it. No greater faith, I suspect, has ever been placed in words.

Franklin died in 1790 and the Pennsylvania constitution did not long survive him. The federal Constitution, however, survived ratification and went into effect in 1789. President Washington refused a crown and took office in New York. So did Vice-President John Adams, who was overruled in his view that Washington should be addressed as His Majesty. Adams was still a republican but already his obsolescent, Elizabethan, and pessimistic brand of republicanism was being sneered at. He would live to see it abandoned entirely, dying in 1826 after a bitter presidency and a little-honored old age. The very word "republican" was taken away from him. In 1787, Madison redefined it in *Federalist* Number 10 as a form of government in which the people are insulated from power by representatives, the view which has since prevailed and thus made enemies of republicanism and democracy. Jefferson in the 1790s called Adams a monarchist and founded the Republican Party to attack him, because, among other things, Adams defined "republic" in a way that included the kingdom of Great Britain.[25]

In retrospect, it seems true that Adams's view was old-fashioned. Aristocracy and monarchy, Polybios' terms, lost their meaning in his time and Adams never got used to the idea that democracy might be all that was left. Though it is clear that assuming the existence of aristocracy is not the same thing as favoring it, it is idle to exonerate Adams in this way and at so late a date. Nevertheless, his achievement stands. It is of a piece with his conversion in 1761 and his death on the fiftieth Fourth of July. Adams alone, of all the republicans in history, defined the beast correctly. A republic, he wrote to Roger Sherman in 1789, is "A *government whose sovereignty is vested in more than one person.*"[26]

Not bad for a vice-president.

9

Maximilien Robespierre
The Democratic Republic

T HE REVOLUTION THAT CREATED the First French Republic is one of the ten or so most crucial events in Western history. The revolutionaries themselves dated everything in history from the day in September 1792 when they abolished monarchy, and their hope and fervor on that occasion were no less than those of their remote ancestors who had hinged time on the birth of Jesus Christ. In the two centuries that have passed since, historians have modified their verdict but they have not set it aside. The whole period called "Contemporary History" is dated from 1789 and it is agreed that the French Republic of 1792 is the first democratic state of any consequence.

For Americans, it has seemed a period of high-pitched drama, and an uncomfortably serious and bloody one. From it dates the American fear of revolution, so paradoxically characteristic of a country itself founded by revolution. For Americans the resemblance between the Reign of Terror and modern totalitarianism is patent, the instability and French passion of the protagonists obvious, and an attitude has grown up that resembles most of all that of the English Whigs toward the American revolutionaries of 1776, ambivalent, stuffy, and patronizing. The best an American can muster is sympathy for the constitution of 1791—a limited monarchy like that of George III! Franklin would have wept.

This is the more ironic when we see that the French at all stages of their Revolution found America to be the most instructive of all contemporary polities. Relations between them were continuous. Borrowings were chronic. Lafayette and other noble veterans of Washington's army (also of Franklin's Masonic Lodge) were leaders of the Revolution in 1790. They saw America as the only state with a written constitution, and copied it. When new leaders, far more radical, arose in 1791–92, they saw America as the only modern republic and the nearest thing to a genuine democracy. In tribute they founded institutions with Anglo-American names, like Convention and Committee of Safety, to embody the sovereignty of the people in a kingless state. In the end they created a constitution as democratic as the Pennsylvania constitution of 1776.

It is this First French Republic, founded by the Jacobins, Girondins, and *sans-culottes* in 1792 and ceremonially ended by Napoleon in 1804, that changed the whole world of European politics and has inextricably associated revolution with republicanism in France and republicanism with democracy in Europe. It was able to do this because, of all the republics in the West since Rome, the French was the first to deliberately deny its continuity with the republics and commonwealths of the immediate past. Americans had invoked the Reformation and the English Commonwealth, and Adams had seen precedents in the history of Florence and of Switzerland. The French leaders, however, had learned more thoroughly the great lesson of the eighteenth century: the primacy of reason over history.

The French leaders not only avoided medieval or reformation precedents, they spent a large part of their time trying to get rid of them. Medieval communalism was all but extinct in France. Calvinism had failed in the land of its birth. France, in 1789, was a thousand-year Reich. Almost everything in the history of France pointed to absolute monarchy. Almost everything therefore had to be expunged. With the unbelievable courage of the Enlightenment, the revolutionaries bent themselves to the task of wiping out not only the millennial unwritten constitution but the laws, the social order, and even the calendar, the units of measurement, and the forms of courtesy.

Only one area of human experience could be left on the books to guide them: the experience of humanity before there were kings in France—before, that is, about A.D. 500. Thus the French leaders were not only the first to build a republic without contemporary materials, but also the last to make a revolution in conscious imitation of the classical world of Greece and Rome. For them there was almost literally no parent but antiquity. On the desks of the members of the constitution committee in 1793 were Plato's *Republic*, Aristotle's *Politics*, and Plutarch's *Lykourgos* and *Solon*. Saint-Just modeled his speeches on those of Lysander of Sparta, Vergniaud modeled his on those of Cicero, Robespierre on those of Demosthenes of Athens. Madame Roland carried her Plutarch to church instead of a missal when she was growing up. Jacques Louis David, the great painter, heralded the Revolution in 1789 by exhibiting a picture of Brutus after the execution of his sons. Certainly nothing so much explains the mentality that produced the Terror in 1793 as the conscious effort by republican leaders to adopt the value system of Livy's Rome. For if Brutus could sacrifice his sons to the Republic, no republican magistrate could in conscience spare his friends.

As Vergniaud, the guillotined Girondin, had truly said, the Revolution, like Saturn, devoured its children.[1] It has never ceased to inspire fear, and despite the religious zeal which it inspired as well, it was easily liquidated by a Caesar in only seven years. Yet it remains the great republic of modern times. Governed by an executive committee chosen by a national legislature, its magistrates successfully mobilized an army of half a million men, put down three different internal armed revolts, imposed national price and wage controls, and fought all the armies of Europe to a standstill in the single year of 1793. Before it expired it had republicanized the Low Countries, parts of Germany, and half of Italy; and had created republican revolutionary societies as far away as India and South Africa. It had made rabid republicans of the era's greatest painter (David) and its greatest composer, no less than Ludwig van Beethoven. France herself has been a republic since the Third Republic was founded in 1875 (Vichy is a technical exception) and when the monarchies collapsed after World War I, her constitution became a model for the states of central Europe.

Let us then lower ourselves down into the France of the First Republic and see it through the eyes of those exalted provincial lawyers and intellectuals, so many of them orphans, who killed their king and brought it into being. Because this was a true republic there were, as in the United States, a great many republicans. Indeed, the most prominent among them, Maximilien Robespierre, was guillotined largely for the republican crime of being too prominent—and aiming at tyranny. Perhaps more than any other, however, Robespierre embodies the ideals and values of the First French Republic. As a young man he exemplified the moral sea change that made republicanism conceivable and finally fashionable in Europe's oldest monarchy. As a politician he remained until the very last months of his life in the vanguard of reform. He deliberately sought the leadership of the *sans-culottes* of Paris, the most radical wind in the revolutionary hurricane. Lastly, since it was he who defined revolutionary government and was instrumental in setting up the Terror, it is around Robespierre that praise and execration of the Republic have swirled ever since. His execution came ten years before that of the Republic itself, but it has been easy to see it ending with him. It is certain that later leaders of the Republic could not match the zeal he displayed in its cause.

He was not a likeable man. Short, broad-faced, with the gimlet stare of a zealot, he dressed primly in broadcloth and cotton nankeen and spent an hour dressing and powdering his hair. One acquaintance described his veins as green. Enemies said he never smiled. Danton assessed him, living as a chaste bachelor in furnished rooms, as a man who had no balls. His speeches, well-constructed and resonant, were written down with care, and he read them through spectacles which otherwise sat on his powdered forelock. They were eloquent speeches, full of interest, but there is nothing more consistently displayed in them than an animus against conspiracy that would quickly be labeled paranoid today. In sum, he was a man of pale and terrible purity.[2]

His early life helps us to understand the politician of 1793. Robespierre was born in Arras in Calvin's region, northeastern France, in 1758. He was within four months of being a bastard and within six years he was an orphan, for his father, having sired three other children, abandoned them all and disappeared after Maximilien's mother died bearing the last baby. A tough beginning this, and one which created in the eldest son a small boy's vulnerability that lasted all his life. It made Robespierre suspicious by analogy of all monarchs. It also made necessary a precocious adult gravity and a hard-working responsible attitude toward life that almost precluded laughter and amusement.

He was not alone in the world. He was taken up by relatives and was himself the mainstay of his brother and sisters. He was sent to

Latin school where he, of course, drove himself hard; and he won a scholarship to the great Paris secondary school of Louis-le-Grand. There, he discovered the great mentors of his generation: Plutarch, Livy, and Rousseau.

The heroes of Plutarch and Livy were all that Robespierre wished to be and much that his father was not. Moreover, to a boy from the provinces who had only some talent, a small scholarship, and a large capacity for hard work to maintain his dignity in Paris, the society of early Rome, where the highest virtues were gravity, patriotism, and responsibility, and where no one had too much or too little, must have seemed like utopia itself.

It would be hard to imagine a city more different from the Rome of Cato and Brutus than Paris in 1774. Under a king who kept his own private whorehouse stretched a society with hundreds of legally enforced ranks, from dukes delighting in leisured amorality to starving beggars for whom the price of a single ducal suit of clothes could buy room and board for a lifetime. Robespierre was, of course, in the middle. Birth did not assure his status as it might a noble's; his class, the *bourgeoisie,* was the only one near the top which had no safety net and from which you could, like Maximilien's father, legally slip as far as the gutter. Moving up from the *bourgeoisie* was, by contrast, extraordinarily difficult. Even if you became a noble, practice would prevent you from becoming, say, a general or a bishop. Ancient Rome had had an aristocracy too, but few could have learned that from Livy, who always assumed that the well-born and the able were the same.

The last discovery of the young Robespierre was Rousseau, a modern philosopher whose distinctive contribution was to see the contrast between Plutarch and Paris more than a generation before anyone else did. Robespierre, like others of his age, read Rousseau as avidly as Rousseau, at the same age, had read of the ancient republics. When Robespierre went to Paris, Rousseau was in his sixties. His great books had been officially burnt when Maximilien was four years old, their author driven to paranoia and exile by the combined forces of church, state, and modern philosophy. The younger generation smuggled the books into their bedrooms, and Rousseau himself had sneaked back into France to live unmolested in the country around Paris. Robespierre saw him once before he died in 1778, his hair unpowdered, his face unpainted, wearing perhaps a republican fur hat like that of Ambassador Franklin. "The memory remains," wrote Robespierre in 1791, "a source of joy and pride. I contemplated your august features, and saw on them the marks of the dark disappointments to which you were condemned by the injustice of mankind."[3]

Who was this guru-like figure? First of all, Rousseau was not a Frenchman. By birth and early upbringing he was a product of Calvin's great republic, the Swiss free city of Geneva. He left Geneva to become an orphan and a wanderer when he was fifteen, but the city and its values never left him. In 1749, as he sat resting under a tree on the road from Paris to Vincennes, they burst upon him with such force that tears came to his eyes and all his characteristic ideas sprang fully formed into his head. In the *Discourses, Julie,* and *Emile,* he became the first philosopher since the Reformation to attack material progress and luxury in the name of morality and citizenship. He went on to insist that the increasing articulation and sophistication of society was also a step in the wrong direction.

In his last tract, the *Social Contract* of 1762, he outlined a utopia in which urban sophistication, material progress, social inequality, and intellectual heterodoxy would be repressed as permanently as a fallen human nature would permit. Of course this utopia was a republic. Indeed, except for its lack of social stratification, Rousseau's ideal republic was a mirror of both ancient Sparta and sixteenth-century Geneva. Here the people were sovereign, under a "general will" with which anyone who disagreed was either exiled or "forced to be free." Here all were austere, equal, incorruptible, constantly about the public business and ferocious against any who would make himself greater than his fellows.[4]

It is all enough to make Rousseau the father, if not of the First Republic, at least of the revolutionary sensibility, and certainly of the political faith of Maximilien Robespierre.

At any rate it seems so, for evidence is slim about the mind of a schoolboy. We know for sure only that he continued to follow the rules and do his best. He won lots of academic prizes. In due course he went on to law school, paternally passing his scholarship on to his brother Augustin, and, untempted by the capitol, returned to Arras to practice his profession. "There was," said a schoolmate, "nothing young about him."[5] Except a passion for justice. As a lawyer, Robespierre defended the rights of the poor, of women, and of others to whom his society gave the short end of the stick. In 1783, he defended a man who had had the temerity to set up a lightning rod, and sent a copy of his winning brief to Ambassador Franklin. In 1789, the year he was elected to the Estates-General, he was defending a man named Dupont against a *lettre de cachet* and calling on King Louis XVI to abolish the whole practice of arbitrary arrest.

The young, socially conscious lawyer was elected a deputy by the Third Estate of Arras and arrived in Versailles, the headwaters of absolute monarchy, on a beautiful May day in 1789. There he paraded with representatives of all the myriad ranks of French society before his king. Not one of the more than a thousand deputies was a republican. For these classically educated notables a republic was a state with no king, too utopian and impractical for anything but an ancient city-state. It was not a term which, as John Adams still understood it, could conclude constitutional or limited monarchies. Robespierre himself would still be denying he was a republican as late as July 13, 1792. What a majority of the deputies wanted, or came to want by the end of the fantastic summer of 1789, was a written constitution, civil rights, a national legislature, and a limited monarchy like England's. Such was their oath pledged on the Versailles tennis court on June 20, 1789, and such was the shape of the constitution passed by the assembly in 1791.

It was a clever, comprehensive document, engineered in wisdom and compromise. It began with an adaptation of George Mason's Virginia Bill of Rights called the Declaration of the Rights of Man. Its legislature was unicameral, supreme over the executive and the judiciary as the reformer Turgot in his letter on the Constitution of Pennsylvania, had said it ought to be. Nobility was abolished and property qualifications set; but the king remained on his throne, armed with a veto which (this had been settled in part over dinner at Ambassador Jefferson's) was to be suspensive only.[6] Under careful safeguards, his right was confirmed to appoint ministers and make foreign policy, and nothing else.

This constitution of 1791, dyed through and through with a whiggery both English and American, was celebrated even before its completion as one of the great works of the century. On the anniversary of the capture of the Bastille in 1790, tens of thousands of Frenchmen of all classes and regions gathered on the Champ de Mars in Paris (in Rome the assemblies met on the Campus Martius), singing the new song "Ça ira" ("It will go on," another coinage of Ambassador Franklin's), to cheer the king and Lafayette, embrace each other, and acclaim the permanent achievement of constitutional liberty. The constitution lasted exactly 367 days.

What happened? In Franklin's words, *ça ira*. It is a fact that the

French Revolution was really two revolutions. Only the first was
made in 1789. The second was made on the tenth of August, 1792
when the lower middle classes of Paris, armed and commanded by
their own neighborhood assemblies, marched on the Tuileries Palace and overthrew the monarchy. It was then that the Revolution
acquired its famous bloodthirstiness, then only that it became both
republican and democratic, then only that left-wing leaders of the
first revolution, among them Robespierre, embraced republicanism
and began to lead the new masses instead of trying to control them.
It was in that summer of 1792 that the Marseilles volunteers arrived
in Paris singing the song of Rouget de l'Isle that has become the
national anthem of republican France:

March! March!
That an impure blood
May quench the thirst
Of our plowed earth. . . .

There are a thousand reasons for the failure of the constitutional monarchy of 1791. One of them is not, as we have noted, the
republicanism of its leaders. It is a fact that the new Legislative
Assembly was staffed (by a law of Robespierre's recalling Cromwell's Self-Denying Ordnance) by men who had never served in the
old National or Constituent Assembly. Political novices, unused to
compromise, they found themselves deeply divided from the first.
A policy of the members from the Gironde which was designed to
unite them only divided them further—declaring war against the
émigré nobility and its protector Austria.

Essentially, however, the monarchy fell because of the people
of Paris and the monarch himself: the people because they gave
themselves a democratic republican government capable of acting
alone; and the monarch because, like Charles I, he refused to accept
his lot.

Louis was the first king of France to be deposed by his own
subjects. There were no Richard IIs or Edward IIs in French history, and never a Magna Carta. Not a few French kings had been
assassinated by fanatics, as is the custom in strong monarchies, but
never by organized opposition. By and large Louis brought this od-
dity on himself. His own family helped convince him, impractically,
that he had a duty to preserve the legal status of the nobility. His
own conscience resisted the religious settlement in the constitution. He delayed endlessly over signing measures which both as-

sembly and mass deemed essential. Once given the veto, he used
it so constantly and injudiciously that he soon acquired the nickname Monsieur Veto. It is clear from his letters that the vetoes were
only a small evidence of a deep hostility to the Revolution which
dated from 1789. Everything he signed he expected to be able to
repeal once the Revolution should have been defeated. In July 1790,
he embraced the constitution before thousands of cheering Frenchmen. A year later, on June 20, 1791, he left his palace in the middle
of the night to rendezvous with an émigré army on the German
border. He was never to be trusted again. Recaptured at Varennes,
he was brought back to Paris through streets lined with people, none
of whom made a sound. A year later, these same citizens destroyed
him.

Paris, unlike the rest of France, did have a habit of playing coy
with kings. She had frightened away Charles V with a revolt in 1358
and done the same to no less than Louis XIV in 1649.[7] She had
denied herself to Henri IV until he became a Catholic. But then,
as Henri himself remarked, she was worth it. In fact the first members of the endless Capetian dynasty of France had been Counts
of Paris when they replaced the heirs of Charlemagne back in the
tenth century. Nevertheless, Paris was dangerous. Though she never
governed herself in law, she had, like Florence, a long medieval tradition of neighborhood organization and self-defense, and she had
a fine martial coat of arms in red and blue.

On great days—*journées*—like Saint Bartholomew's or Barricades or Dupes, the armed bands would appear, too well-organized
to be spontaneous. In fact Paris in 1789 put on a journée that remains the national anniversary of France—and captured the Bastille. Almost everyone knows it was the fourteenth of July. Significantly, it was on July 13 that the voters of the Parisian third
estate established a permanent executive committee and raised a
city militia. Not until months after the fall of Robespierre would
Paris lose the independence gained on July 13, 1789. For five years
she governed herself as she pleased and for much of that time she
governed France. Louis went to Paris on July 17, there to be given
a cockade with the new revolutionary colors: red and blue for Paris
completely and ominously surrounding the old Capetian white.

By the end of 1789, Paris had a republic of her own, anticipating
the national one by three full years and destined to give new meaning to the old medieval word *commune*. She had by then executed
her royal governor, set up the National Guard of Paris, and created

a sovereign legislature of 120, later three hundred deputies, a couple each from the sixty electoral districts of March. Indignant at the king's residence outside the city, at a hostile court, and the high price of bread she had marched to Versailles in October and brought "the Baker" back to the old Tuileries Palace in the center of town.

By 1790 Paris was opposing the National Assembly because the property qualifications under the emerging constitution were too high to include most Parisians. An anxious National Assembly renamed her neighborhoods "sections," reduced their number and powers, prohibited demonstrations against the laws, and succeeded despite some left-wing opposition (including Robespierre's) in keeping low-income citizens out of the National Guard. But the Commune was irrepressible. Seeking the extreme left, she elected Danton, Pétion, and Robespierre to her leading magistracies when the likes of Lafayette and Bailly failed to be democratic enough. When the ministers of the Legislative Assembly in their turn tried to get Paris into line, the sectional assemblies swung into action. They opened themselves to all men over twenty-five, went into twenty-four hour session, founded a Committee of Correspondence, purged and replaced the executive committee of the Commune, raised the red flag of martial law, and at eleven o'clock on the night of August 10, 1792 sent their militia to overthrow both the Assembly and the king.

In the long sweep of history this is an astonishing event, a truly democratic mass movement that attacked the very idea of monarchy. It is odd because historians assume, not always wrongly, that the commoner the people the more monarchical they act. Artisans, shopkeepers, journeymen, peasant, and workers, having no time to do anything but make a living, are especially liable to leave politics in the hands of someone who impresses them. Illiterate, they worship heroes. Their culture, still medieval in the 1790s, approved of hierarchy, monarchy, violence, and ceremony. And yet, according to these same historians, the Paris sans-culottes were by no means a mob of thugs and beggars but respectable, hard-working citizens. They did not demand anarchy or mob rule. They wanted, it is true, very different things from the bourgeois of the assemblies, including fair, meaning fixed, prices for necessities like bread and soap; but their wants were well defined and not unreasonable.

Among these demands, it seems obvious, was republican government. Even those sans-culottes too ignorant to know the word republic had republican views of how government should work. They were not simply democrats, because although they believed fervently in rule by a majority of adult male citizens, they resisted, often heroically, any attempt to substitute for the actual majority a single leader, however charismatic, who would be chosen by such a majority. Long before the lawyers of 1789 had traced their tortuous path from Plutarch through Rousseau and Franklin to the republic, the Parisian sans-culottes had actually set one up and, to borrow a phrase, declared its independence of the king.

The forty-eight neighborhoods of the federal republic of Paris were the most inspiring place for radicals in the world. Twenty-four hours a day one could watch the sectional assemblies in action, purging and electing their representatives to the Council of the Commune at City Hall, ordering the pikes to be forged, denouncing local "aristocrats" and food speculators, voting instructions to their deputies in the Convention, and calling them to account if they dared to substitute their own judgment for that of their electors. Each of the forty-eight elected a Revolutionary Commitee, a Committee of Safety, a Police Commissioner every two years, a President every month, and an Executive Committee every two weeks! Fortunately it was legal, and customary, to get reelected, or most sections would have run out of citizens long before 1794. In short, Paris was by far the most hectic and thoroughgoing republic in the three centuries since the extinction of Florence.

How did it get that way? The only plausible explanation may be that medieval communalism, which lent greatness to cities like Florence, Venice, and Antwerp, did not completely expire in Paris but survived in the political culture of her common people to be revived with a vengeance in 1792. It is like all the other ideas such as fixed prices and summary justice, located there by historians and correctly labeled as medieval.

Whatever their source, the demands of the Parisians were carried to the nation on August 10, 1792 and by the winter of the following year—Year II of the Republic—had been implemented in full. There were a lot of them. Some are considered left wing even today. Many still sound dangerous and impractical. Taken together, however, they are the political program of the First Republic. Leading the list was the demand to set up the republic by getting rid of "Louis Capet" and calling a National Convention based on the sovereignty of the people to draw up a new constitution. This met on September 21, 1792 and promptly, on a motion of Collot d'Herbois, a Paris deputy, abolished royalty in France. Another demand was for "popular justice," the prompt trial and summary execution of enemies of the revolution under officials subject to democratic control. Paris had already done this on her own three weeks before the Convention opened in the bloody September Massacres. The Convention's reply was to establish the famous Revolutionary Tribunal in February, the Law of Suspects in the following September, and the terrifying Prairial Law ending due process in June 1794.

A third demand was for adequate supplies of necessities guaranteed by requisition and price controls. It was answered by a whole series of laws culminating in the General Maximum of February 1794, the first attempt at a controlled war economy in Western history. The Maximum foreshadowed still a fourth demand, for the equalization of property by progressively taxing the rich (this is now called the income tax) and confiscating the property of counterrevolutionaries. Robespierre was tepidly in favor, but the Convention, all of whose members had rather large amounts of property, waffled badly on this demand. Fortunately for them it did not come to the fore until quite late and never had to be completely attended to.

Finally, and perhaps most earnestly of all, Paris demanded "direct democracy." She wanted the whole of France to be governed just as she was, by representatives who would do exactly what their constituents told them to do. In effect, she wanted what American progressives wrote into law as "initiative, referendum and recall," the right of quite ordinary citizens to propose bills, pass laws, and fire representatives whenever it pleased them. This was a democratic, not a republican demand. It was, also, historically, the most serious. By fulfilling it, the first modern republic in Europe became the first democratic republic.

In order to meet the demand, however, the democrats had to threaten the rule of law. The few in the Convention who accepted it used it unconstitutionally to purge those who opposed it. This was the famous Girondin Purge of May and June 1793. It was the first of many such purges and other acts which had to be justified as moral since they could not be portrayed as legal, and the Republic, which was able to survive invasion, rebellion, and even civil war, was eventually brought low by them. Democracy is not incompatible with republics. An ideal republic and an ideal democracy would be the same if each citizen were both a voter and a magistrate. In real republics, however, democracy represents dangers which are both practical and theoretical. The best minds among the revolutionaries had not thought these through and were unable to resolve the potential conflict between the rule of law and the sovereignty of the people.

Here we return to Robespierre, for all these measures became the law of France not by any action of the Commune of Paris but by the efforts of the democratic left of the National Convention, the famous "Mountain" party of Robespierre, Danton, Saint-Just, Collot, Marat, and Couthon, to name just a few of the most prominent. With the possible exception of Collot, they were not sans-culottes by any stretch of the imagination. In fact, they all wore the culotte, or what we might call knee-breeches, right through the Revolution. (Robespierre, to be sure, had his made out of republican cotton instead of silk.) They were upper bourgeois of the eighteenth century, addicted to freedom of speech, trade, and enterprise, the right to property and the right to rise. Unlike their fellow bourgeois, however, the members of the Mountain clung so dearly to the democratic faith in the sovereignty of the people that they actually listened to the sans-culottes and toiled to understand and implement their desires. It was in the service of the "people" and often in defiance of their own and other constituents' principles that they instituted the regime known as the Terror.

Robespierre, to take only the best example, was on record at the close of the National Assembly as opposed to a republic, regulated commerce, censorship, arbitrary imprisonment, bills of attainder, capital punishment, and war. Yet as the best-known member of the Committee of Public Safety he put his signature on measures designed to accomplish all these things. Moreover, it seems clear that he was neither a smarmy hypocrite nor a mere political opportunist, though his unbelievably humorless and single-minded exaltation have often driven his detractors to say so. Actually Maximilien François Marie Isidore de Robespierre was more terrifying than any hypocrite could be, for he was a true believer, one of the first genuine democrats in history. A scholarship boy's faith in the "people" had led him, long before the Convention, to oppose the royal veto and the property qualification for voters. Though Arras had elected him to the National Assembly in 1789, it was a proud Paris that sent him to the National Convention in 1792; and Robespierre, from that moment until nearly the end of his career, saw it as his duty to give the people of Paris what it wanted.

Leading the sans-culottes however presented Robespierre and all his colleagues with a serious intellectual problem, all the more serious because it could not be solved by simple hypocrisy: what

philosophy and what history could possibly lend integrity to a democratic republic with policies like the Maximum? We might say medieval communalism, but they could not. The Middle Ages were
anathema to them. Even Enlightenment philosophy was hostile to
what they were doing. Only in the historical world of Plutarch and
Livy and in the utopian dreams of Rousseau was there anything
that might resolve their dilemma. It was thus that the Mountaineers, without fully realizing what was happening, became by degrees more Roman than French.

They began by naming themselves after the extreme democratic
party in Solon's Athens, and their children after Brutus, Gracchus,
Cato, Mucius Scaevola, and Cincinnatus. Then they adopted what
they thought was ancient republican morality. "What is the fundamental principle of popular government?" Robespierre asked the
Convention. The answer:

> It is virtue; I speak of the public virtue which performed so many
> miracles in Greece and Rome, and which should produce much
> more marvelous ones in republican France; of that virtue which is
> nothing else than love of the Fatherland and of its laws.[8]

Machiavelli himself, echoed by the collective wisdom of the
whole eighteenth century, had viewed "virtue," a compound of
manly self-denial, egalitarian honesty, and uncompromising devotion to the polis, as the *sine qua non* for the survival of a republic.
It was obviously congenial to the buttoned-up young man with the
spectacles known to all France and to his own conscience as the
Incorruptible. Mutual loyalty between himself and the people, national virtue, was the key to his belief in his own integrity. Thus
the erstwhile monarchist who had so passionately defended due
process and opposed the death penalty found himself calling for the
death of the king in these words:

> The people do not . . . hand down sentences, they hurl thunder-
> bolts; they do not condemn kings, they annihilate them. . . . In what
> Republic was the necessity to punish the tyrant a matter for liti-
> gation? Was Tarquin summoned before a court? . . . As for me I
> abhor the death penalty. . . . But Louis must die because the [re-
> public] must live.

"Kings," as Saint-Just put it, "cannot reign innocent!"[9] Virtue and
monarchy were incompatible. Thus, on January 21, 1793 (144 years
to the month after the death of Charles I) Louis XVI was beheaded
as the Commune had demanded, in Revolution Square, and the

republican reign of the Commune and the Convention began in earnest.

The first thing necessary was to wipe out the very memory of royalty. Statues of kings were melted down or thrown in the river. Statues of the kings of Israel, high on Notre Dame, were decapitated, and the bodies of the real kings in the crypt of Saint Denis were dug up and thrown in a ditch. On the map, Throne Squares became Nation Squares. Towns and sections renamed themselves Brutus, Republic, Freetown, Pikes, and Social Contract. As in the English Revolution, men too renamed themselves, but this time using Plutarch instead of the Bible. Decks of cards were printed with Philosophers, Virtues, and Republicans replacing Kings, Queens, and Jacks. July and August, named for Caesars, were sacked and a new calendar issued in which months were named for the weather instead of men. (New Year's Day, Year One, of course, was the day of the proclamation of the Republic.) The inch, a measure of the king's thumb, was dropped for the centimeter, a small piece of the measure of the earth. *Monsieur*, meaning my lord, had already gone out of fashion, but now it was against the law to address a citizen as monsieur. On coins and on seals, the king's head and coat of arms was replaced by the head of the lady Marianne, iconographical cousin of Athena and goddess of Liberty, wearing over her unbound hair the floppy red bonnet of the freed Roman slave. Except in America, she had not been on coins since the days of Julius Caesar. Next to her, often, was a great bundle of sticks tied round an ax, instantly recognizable to readers of Livy as the fasces of the Roman Republic, and sometimes a towering Hercules, the sovereign people, protecting children with his arm.

For mottoes, France chose Liberty, Equality, Fraternity; the French Republic, One and Indivisible; Live Free or Die, laconic and Roman all, which usually appeared entwined with the Roman reward for extraordinary acts of patriotism, a crown of oak leaves. For ceremonies France commissioned her greatest artist, now a member of the Convention, Jacques Louis David. He busied himself designing great processions deliberately resembling Roman Triumphs and Panathenaic processions, terminating at statues of Liberty and eternal flames.[10]

In short, the founding of the modern democratic republic was an all but religious act. Born-again classicists were driven to the values of the city-republic of antiquity because nothing else in their experience could explain what they were doing. It was perhaps the last state (as the Jewish and Greek had been the first) where religion, morals, and politics could not safely be distinguished.

Except perhaps on the agenda of the republicans, for they turned to government only after symbol and ceremony had been taken care of. A republic, it turned out, was more than just a state without a king. It had to have laws and orderly ways of making laws. Like any other state, it had to conduct diplomacy, decide long-term policy, and set up an administration. When the king fell, all his appointments lost their legitimacy. At first, no one thought to replace them. The Legislative Assembly, before dissolving, created an Executive Council—a kind of caretaker cabinet—which was meant to hold office until a new constitution went into effect.

Trouble was that, mandate or no, the Convention had very little time to spend working on a constitution. The King of Prussia's army was moving toward Paris by the summer of 1793 and three other kings were readying armies to avenge the execution of their cousin Louis. In addition, large areas of northwestern France were in open revolt and trying to open a port for the army of Louis's brother, the Count of Provence. In the southeast, the great port of Marseille had risen against the government, and up the river Lyon, France's second largest city, had executed her republican governor. In the west, the leaders of Bordeaux and the Gironde region, purged from the Convention by Paris and the Mountain, were fomenting revenge. By December the port of Toulon would revolt, surrendering the entire Mediterranean fleet to the English. The armies of the Republic, inefficiently mobilized and poorly supplied, were being betrayed with numbing regularity by monarchist officers, including three of their best generals, Lafayette, Dumouriez, and Custine.

Very quickly the Convention turned its secondary responsibility to govern France into a paramount mission to preserve the Republic. More slowly, but surely, agencies of awesome power were created, mobilizing every Frenchman in the struggle to save the state. When the Executive Council finally broke over the defection of General Dumouriez in April 1793, the Convention set up an executive of its own, the celebrated Committee of Public Safety to "supervise" the Council, and the Committee of General Security to oversee and appoint the judiciary. Power surged toward them and they rose to the responsibility. Under the "great" committees, France, which had had a particular genius for the centralization since the Middle Ages, slowly dissolved every independent source of political power outside of Paris. The villages, communes, departmental councils, and courts, so laboriously created by the old National Assembly and so completely discredited by the federalist rebellions of Lyon and Bordeaux in 1793, were one by one annihilated.

By December 1793 there were no magistrates left in France not legally subordinate to the National Convention, except the Paris Commune and the Conventioneers themselves. By law even the Commune was in jeopardy, but its hold over the Convention was then so complete it didn't notice. Nor did it notice any danger in the growing compatibility between democracy and centralization of power. Republicanism in France resolved itself into rule by an executive committee of an omnipotent legislature, its tenure fixed by nothing except its own precarious wisdom and the depth of the emergency. The government, as Saint-Just said, "revolutionary until the peace," and the new constitution, approved with hope and fanfare in June, was set aside in October 1793. For the true constitution of the republic we must look, as we have been looking, at the actual practice of the National Convention.[11]

This practice was republican only in its insistence on committee rule and collective responsibility (unless civic virtue can be counted as a republican device). Nevertheless it prevailed, and by prevailing passed on the precedent. It was now possible to label "republic" a state otherwise sternly centralized and modern, governed not by a single dictator but by a committee of strong equals. In its heyday in the Year II, the Committee of Public Safety had twelve members, at least two of which were almost always in the provinces administering the country. Those remaining, nicknamed out of Livy the Decemvirs, were not friends. Some were political enemies. Several just hated each other. Still, all of them put the Committee and the Republic ahead of their differences. Only one, Hérault-Séchelles, was purged by his colleagues (his crimes were corruptibility and the possession of a sense of humor), and two or more of them almost invariably signed each decree. Most members specialized in particular administrative areas like food supplies or the navy, but it was rare for anyone to do anything without bringing it to at least one colleague. The whole Committee, moreover, was subject to reelection every month by the Convention as a whole, which means that if reelection had not been customary, its tenure was shorter than that of the Florentine Priory.

The Convention, however, gave the Committee enormous power; in the end even removing some power from other committees to do so. Also, though it debated fiercely, it generally gave the Committee whatever responsibilities it asked for and made the laws it recommended. Except for one incident in September 1793 it recognized, trusted, and reelected its twelve-man cabinet. Even on that occasion, though it censured the Committee and tried to install a thirteenth member, it backed down when Robespierre, speaking for the Committee, threatened that everyone on it would resign. It was what has since received the name "vote of confidence."

Perhaps, in view of these practices, the Republic of 1793 should be called a war dictatorship or a cabinet dictatorship. It was never, however, a one-man dictatorship. Also, unlike the Roman model, it had no stated term. It is impossible to guess if the Committee would peacefully have laid down its power after the emergency ended, though all its members claimed that was the plan. Within these narrow limits we may call it republican.

In practice, the Committee of Public Safety did its job so well that even counterrevolutionaries have helplessly admired it. Carnot, the member who supervised the great draft of volunteers, found the officers who could train thousands of raw recruits and defeat the royal armies. He promoted eleven generals, seven of whom ended up as Marshals of France under Napoleon. Napoleon was the eighth. Carnot and another member, Prieur, raised musket production to the then fantastic figure of five hundred a day. Saint-Just went out to Alsace at the age of twenty-six and reorganized the Army of the Rhine which then went on to defeat the Prussians at Bitche. Meanwhile the Army of the North began an unbroken string of victories against the Austrians. Within France, Couthon saw to the defeat of Lyon and Collot to its terrible punishment. Saint-André reorganized the navy and he and Prieur of the Marne contained the rebellion in the northwest. Marseilles and Bordeaux surrendered, and Toulon, with the help of a young artillery officer named Bonaparte, was at last recaptured by the Republic.

One may object that these victories, which saved the nation, badly hurt the Republic by insuring the demise of things like regional autonomy and locally controlled militias, but the argument won't hold water. The stubborn fact is that all of the Convention's enemies, internal or external, sooner or later cried "Vive le Roi!" The Republic had no alternative to centralism because there were too few republicans. Only in the Committee and to a more limited extent in the Convention could government by a plenitude of magistrates operate successfully.

Hence the Terror, stigma against which any number of pro-Revolutionary historians have struggled in vain. Thousands executed in Paris until the gutters ran with blood. Summary shootings in Lyon; deliberate mass drownings in Nantes; purges, proscriptions, people's courts, the whole apparatus of what we now call totalitarianism. It is estimated that 16,594 people died in the Terror, 2,627 of them at the hands of the Revolutionary Tribunal in Paris, which was controlled by Robespierre and the Commune. The democratic republic was baptized, it seems, in blood.

In a sense there is no excuse for the Terror. Though it killed few Frenchmen in proportion to the population, they were a precious few, including a poet, a painter, a philosopher, and a scientist of genius: Chénier, Prudhomme, Condorcet, and ("The Republic has no need of scientists!") Lavoisier. Among republicans it made victims of Vergniaud, Madame Roland, Desmoulins, Hébert, Saint-Just, and the great Danton himself, first leader of the Committee of Public Safety. When it ended even Thomas Paine was awaiting execution. Robespierre was its last victim.

Worse possibly than the victims it made were the hypocrites, so many of them that even Robespierre, that single-minded *naïf*, has seemed like a hypocrite to posterity.

Nevertheless, there is a sense in which the Terror, like Robespierre himself, can be understood, if not pardoned. It depends on admitting that the Mountaineers were not hypocrites but men of integrity. All of them and preeminently Robespierre were democrats. Buffeted from every direction by the Revolution, Robespierre had to be very sure of his values. By 1792, he had decided that above all the voice of the people was the voice of God. He was a deputy for Paris. Not only must he serve the demands of the Parisians for bread and for blood, he must trust in the purity, the justice, indeed the divinity of those demands, like an Abraham sacrificing Isaac. Again and again he apostrophized the people as the innocent source of virtue whose only defense was Terror.

Somewhere deep inside, the humanitarian bourgeois must have been shocked by the medieval bloodthirstiness of those demands, but the shock never surfaced. It is not impossible that to the abandoned six-year-old within him the people had become both father and mother—virtue and terror. The insistence of the sans-culottes on direct democracy was a reasonable facsimile of parental omnipotence. When the people disagreed, any means sufficed to maintain a faith in its unity. Thus, when the Paris Commune made its unconstitutional demand in May 1793 for the expulsion of the twenty-two Girondin members, Robespierre could do nothing but fall back, with understandable passion, on the fiction that the people of Paris and the people of France were the same. The Girondins were expelled, and the act wrecked all efforts to wrap the Republic in constitutional legality.

Republics, with their clashing independent internal forces need legality much more than monarchies and tyrannies do. In history their survival has depended on how well they can institutionalize faction. The Romans had done it by creating the Tribunate. The United States had done the same when it adopted the Connecticut Compromise in 1787. Democrats, with their theory still in infancy, could envision only a purge of the less democratic faction, or in the simple language of the sans-culottes, "Death to the enemies of the Revolution!"

Rome lasted almost five centuries. The United States, now a democracy as well, continues to show vigor after two. But the French Republic lasted only seven years. The Terror which saved it in 1793 destroyed it in 1799.

How? It is a melancholy tale and straight out of Polybios. In July 1794 the Convention turned savagely on Robespierre and purged him and his friends exactly as he had purged the Girondins. Democratic theory had given them the means. Republican theory had provided the charge—tyranny. Actually, so far from being a tyrant Robespierre was outvoted in the Committee of Public Safety and later found himself unable to call on the militia of the Paris Commune to overthrow the Convention and save his life. He had nearly twenty-four hours to do it, and the militia, by all accounts, was willing. His biographers seem to agree that like Marius and Sulla he hesitated to overthrow the Republic out of constitutional scruple. Either that, or else his mind could no longer decide, with its former assurance, who was the people. On the morning of July 28, 1794 (the famous Thermidor of the Year II), Robespierre, his jaw broken and bloodied by a pistol wound, was drawn on the tumbril to Revolution Square and guillotined like so many others without even a mockery of a trial.

A collective sigh of relief went up all over France. Virtue and Terror had both died with Robespierre. No one incorruptible enough was left to defend virtue. Terrorists could find no support for further executions. Even democracy was out of fashion. Within a week *Monsieur* had returned to social life, along with gilded carriages and fancy clothes. The Jacobin Club was closed by the police. Suspects were released from jail. Price and wage controls were repealed. That winter there was famine in Paris. Unwilling to submit to repudiation, Paris rose against the Convention, and lost. Then she was deprived first of her militia, nationalized in June 1795; then of her sections; and finally of her Commune. Her republic, which had set the tone for the nation, was at an end.

The national Republic, however, clung stubbornly to life in the midst of all this. Indeed, to the outside world it looked more healthy than ever, and more dangerous. Carnot, the eight future marshals, and the enormous citizen army remained at their posts. Not only did they foil invasion, they drove the armies of the kings out of Belgium, Holland, the German Rhineland, and much of northern Italy. Kings and princes fled. Local republicans sprang into international prominence. Constitutions were reported weekly. It seemed as if all the monarchies of Europe would fall like a well-struck set of ninepins.

Old-style aristocratic republics also fell. The United Provinces not only got rid of their hereditary stadholder but became a unitary democracy to boot. Belgium nearly did the same, but was made part of France instead. General Bonaparte put an end to the thousand-year-old republican constitution of Venice, and the free cities of the Rhineland lost their medieval independence. For this was still a democratic republicanism, impatient with federalism, faction, or any other form of disunity, and disdainful of all things medieval. Old Milan, transformed from a medieval republic to a Renaissance monarchy by the Visconti, now became the keystone of a modern unitary democratic republic with a name out of classical antiquity— the Cisalpine. Genoa and Pisa were formed into the Ligurian Republic. Naples, briefly, returned to a pre-Roman past as the Parthenopean Republic; and Switzerland, in misplaced sympathy, abolished her cantons for a few years and became the Helvetic Republic. Even Rome, for a month or two in 1799, deposed the Pope and became a republic once again.

In the Netherlands the last stadholder, William V of Orange, fled to England, the Estates-General evaporated, the provinces were dissolved, and a constitutional convention created the Batavian Republic. The name Batavian, like Helvetic, comes from an old barbarian tribe, but it was classical just the same, for the words were latin and Roman historians had admired the republican virtue of both the Batavi and the Helvetii. Besides they had both resisted Caesar.

All these republics had Phrygian bonnets, liberty trees, conventions, committee executives, and citizen militias. All worshiped the goddess Liberty and erased from their coinage the baleful busts of kings. In each, leaders went to a good deal of trouble to imitate Brutus, Lykourgos, and Solon in everything from the texts of laws to the styles of address.

Back home in France, the liquidation of Robespierre, the Maximum, and the Terror, combined with the enormous profits of a successful world war, created a regime which, like the Roman Republic in its last century, seemed noble to the world but rotten to its own patriots. Outwardly all seemed well. The Convention had peacefully dissolved itself after writing a new constitution, and the constitution, devised by Siéyès who had been around since 1789, provided many safeguards against monarchy. As in 1793-94, there was a committee executive, a board called the Directory where power was more or less equally divided and disagreements healthily frequent. Its five members were elected by the legislature rather than the voters, like the old Committee of Public Safety (or the English Cabinet). Their terms were five years long, but at least one could be replaced or reelected each year because the terms were staggered.

Legislative power was given, for the first time in the Republic, to two houses instead of one: a Council of Ancients and a Council of Five Hundred, both classical names as might be expected. The last will be remembered as a creation of Solon himself. Members of the two houses were not to be elected by the voters themselves, for democracy might bring back the Terror, but by propertied electors. Overall, it looked a bit like the constitutional monarchy of 1791 minus the king.[12]

Actually, the Constitution of the Year III (1795) quickly became a bit of a sham. Like Cromwell's various systems, it was supported fully only by its authors and foreign enthusiasts. Though everything in it was republican, a very important ingredient was missing; no magistral power had been allotted to the real factions in the France of 1795. Nor could it have been, for a large and fairly coherent group of factions in France supported monarchy.

Though it may come as a surprise, the Terror had nowhere near exterminated the French monarchists. A more moderate regime like the Directory ran into them constantly. Monarchists were strong enough not only to demand that their votes be counted in 1795, but to try to overthrow the Directory when it made a law that two thirds of the legislature had to be former members of the Convention. Royalists were not a bit moderate. Neither were other dissidents, such as Jacobins and sans-culottes, who were no less active and had to be legally restricted. Even the federalists were still around. On the extreme left was a conspiracy led by one Babeuf, who revered Robespierre and had renamed himself Gracchus. Restricting the vote to various levels of property owners was one way of foiling the dissidents, but it was essentially self-defeating.

Then there was the problem of the army. The Directory had no choice but to exclude the vast revolutionary army from politics and maintain the theory that it was a volunteer force under civilian control, for the most obvious lesson in all the classical republican histories was the career of Julius Caesar. They could, of course, have disbanded the army now that France was safe, but everyone was gaining too much from victory for the idea to be considered. Sister-republics seemed worth founding, and the contradiction of a republican empire, despite the fate of Athens and Rome, was missed. It seemed politic to give army veterans the vote whether they owned property or not, which gave great power to the generals; but the Directory assumed it could always give orders to generals. So had the Roman Senate.

Because of the Directory's enemy constituencies, its orders to its generals frequently took the form of sending them to Paris to put down a revolt. In the first months of the regime, Director Barras had to call in General Bonaparte, who had the good fortune to be married to Barras's ex-mistress, to oppose the royalists. Bonaparte obliged with "a whiff," as he put it later, "of grapeshot."[13] When the elections of 1797 produced a monarchist majority in the legislature, Bonaparte again received the call. The general was, however, very busy creating the Cisalpine Republic in Italy (named incidentally for the province the Senate gave Caesar in 58 B.C.) so he sent General Augereau to "maintain order" while Barras and company expelled two directors and purged the legislature.

When the elections of 1798 produced a Jacobin majority and the Directors had to invalidate more than a hundred local elections, Bonaparte was not needed; but it may be guessed that he learned a good deal from all this activity. Understanding, perhaps, what the general had learned, the Directors sent him away from his happy hunting grounds in Italy (where he had created two republics and destroyed a third) and on to Egypt where, one might hope, the desert could swallow him up.

Bonaparte went to Egypt, and there he learned, much as Caesar had, the ways and delights of monarchy. He imitated the pashas. He dreamed of Alexander and Octavian. And much to the dismay of those few leaders still loyal to the Republic, he did not get swallowed up, but returned in triumph to Paris. He no longer had an army, having left it in Egypt, but he hardly needed one. The Republic was by now utterly corrupt financially and by the standards of its own constitution, hopelessly illegitimate. It was not even democratic, whatever it might claim, because on every one of those rare occasions where a majority of Frenchmen had chosen a policy, the regime had thwarted it. People were also getting tired of the republican calendar, especially tired of getting only one *décadi* in ten instead of a Sunday every seven days, and annoyed by the endless festivals of virtue. It was remarkable too, how rich leading republicans had become, and how elegant a pair of sans-culotte trousers could look if executed in beige flannel and given a knife-edge crease.

And so, one day General Bonaparte went to the legislative palace with the army of Paris which he had been given command of the day before, and cleared the halls of the Ancients and the Five Hundred. Going Cromwell one better, he scared the Five Hundred into jumping out of the windows. It was the Eighteenth of Brumaire, Year VIII of the Republic, very soon to be known after a forgotten fashion as November 10, 1799.

It would have been impractical to change everything at once. The first title Bonaparte therefore awarded himself was First Consul. His fellow-conspirators became Second and Third Consuls. Was this deliberate irony, or did they simply not understand how careful the Romans had been to keep their two consuls absolutely equal? Perhaps Siéyès, who wrote this constitution too, was simply collecting antiques. The three houses of the new legislature were given Roman names and Spartan functions. One of them, the Senate, was an excellent copy of Cosimo de Medici's *accoppiatori*. Though all legislators were chosen from lists elected by the people, the Senate made the final choice, and First Consul Bonaparte chose the Senate. In a few years all three houses just stopped meeting.[14]

Of course the Consulate was democratic. The First Consul could consult all Frenchmen by plebiscite (another Roman antiquity) on any question. The first question, in 1799, was whether they approved of the new regime, and 99 percent said yes. The second question, in 1804, was whether they wanted to abolish it and make Consul Bonaparte into the hereditary Emperor of the French. Again 99 percent voted yes. The official count was 3,572,000 to 2,579. The real count was probably the same.

As for the Cisalpine, Ligurian, Parthenopean, and Batavian Republics, they were renamed the Kingdoms of Italy, Naples, and Holland.[15] In 1806, the King of Naples was Joseph Bonaparte, the King of Holland was Louis Bonaparte, and the King of Italy, *ex officio*, was Napoleon.

If the First French Republic had done nothing but expire thus ignobly, we would remember it only as another illustration of the Polybios cycle. But it was much more. Before Napoleon put an end to it, it had revolutionized Europe and become a pattern for subsequent republican experiment all over the world. Most of all, it illustrated the point first made in republican theory by Machiavelli: that if you want to make a republic in a state that has long had monarchy, you must use the methods of tyranny.[16] The destruction of a thousand-year Reich (the French monarchy dated from Clovis and Charlemagne) requires the most narrow and Draconian of measures. It requires both self-education and mass education to an extent that makes a clean sweep of every maxim and symbol of public life. It requires intolerance; it may require blood; and even then it may not succeed. The failure of the Weimar Republic, as this book argues, came from not recognizing this requirement. The almost bloodless success of the Third French Republic, more than ninety years later, came because monarchy had been so thoroughly and lastingly shaken by the First Republic of 1792.

10

Thaddeus Stevens
The Legacy of the American Whigs

O<small>N FEBRUARY</small> 24, 1868, a grim old congressman with an ill-fitting black wig and a clubbed foot limped proudly into the Senate Chamber in Washington leaning on the arm of a younger colleague. "Pale, emaciated, deathlike in appearance [he would be seventy-six in two months and dead in six] but in a stern, vigorous voice and in a bold, lofty manner," he announced to the assembled senators:

> In obedience to the order of the House of Representatives we appear before you in the name of the House of Representatives and of all the people of the United States. We do impeach Andrew Johnson, President of the United States, of high crimes and misdemeanors in office. . . .[1]

The name of the congressman was Thaddeus Stevens. Very few of America's powerful men have been so completely forgotten; but on that day in 1868 he was, even as a dying man, the most powerful politician in America; the acknowledged leader of three successive Congresses so uniquely independent that they had passed two constitutional amendments, overridden fifteen presidential vetoes, and were then preparing for the first and only time in American history to try a president for high crimes and misdemeanors.

196

The Thirty-Eighth Congress of 1863–65 had devised its own cabinet, the Joint Committee on the Conduct of the War, and freed the slaves. The Thirty-Ninth Congress gave southern blacks the vote and guaranteed their civil rights. The Fortieth (1867–69) sent armed troops to govern the South until it might be willing to observe these conditions, and deputed Thaddeus Stevens to carry his unforgiving message on February 24. These three are the most significant and the most republican Congresses to assemble in the United States since the Second Continental Congress met in Philadelphia in 1775. Even the name of the majority party in them, then only recently chosen, was Republican with a capital R.

Neither fact has saved these Congresses from obscurity. On the contrary: Today, only a Capitol buff could give anyone the numbers of those Congresses, and only a scholar the names of their members. One might refer, for example, to the immortal Schuyler Colfax, William Pitt Fessenden, or John Bingham just to hear the puzzled laughter. A flicker of recognition might greet the names of Senator Charles Sumner or Representative Ben Butler. No doubt many Americans will have heard of Rutherford B. Hayes or James A. Garfield, but not because they sat in Congress. Least of all will they have heard of Thaddeus Stevens of Pennsylvania, who has of all of them the most genuine claim to the American memory.

Like his fellow Pennsylvanian, Franklin, Stevens was only a radical congressman, no less disconcertingly old, and equally witty. He was, however, far more sardonic and vindictive than Franklin. When Lincoln, then low in the polls, went to Gettysburg to dedicate the cemetery, Stevens remarked "Let the dead bury the dead."[2] Perhaps it was his seriousness about vengeance that made "Old Thad," unlike Ben, one of the most powerful congressmen in American history. At his death he lay in state where Lincoln had, under the Capitol dome, widely mourned as the architect of Reconstruction. He had been, with a small leadership group, responsible for a program which brought racial equality into the Constitution for the first time, and in the process also restored the constitutional primacy of Congress for a generation.

Georges Clemenceau, then a visiting French journalist but soon to be one of the restorers of republicanism in France, immediately saw in Stevens the outlines of an American Robespierre—a vengeful democratic republican with a distant vision too pure and too dazzling for his countrymen to look long at without blinking.[3]

Who was Thaddeus Stevens? What exactly did he do and why

was he forgotten? Most of all, where did this stange old man come
from? When and where was the vision formed that led what Clemenceau aptly called the Second American Revolution of 1860–68.
These questions all have answers, but the answers are hard to find
in textbooks or American history courses of the past generation;
and I apologize sincerely to graduates of such courses for not being
able to get to them without bringing up the Bank of the United
States and Nullification one more time.

The Thirty-Eighth Congress passed the Thirteenth Amendment in January 1865, no doubt observing that the elections of au-
tumn 1864 had made lame ducks out of many Congressmen who
were opposed to it. The end of the Civil War was in sight that winter, as defeated Confederate armies abandoned Georgia, Tennessee, and northern Virginia. Ratification of the abolition of slavery
would be, everyone knew, a part of the peace settlement which
responsible people in every political camp had already been thinking about for a year or more. The war had been fought to preserve
the Union and it was generally agreed that the peace should have
this as its first object, but there were many views about how to do
this and many more on what other goals ought to be considered in
doing so. The abolition of slavery, for example, a pipe dream in
1860, had risen to the status of war policy in 1862, and a national
goal at last in 1865. It was unlikely to be abandoned, though it would
obviously have to be screwed down in northern slave states like
Kentucky and imposed by bayonets in Mississippi.

Just how much the victors differed about the kind of peace—
"Reconstruction"—they wanted had already become evident in
clashes of 1861 and 1862 between Lincoln, who never believed
either in racial equality or vindictiveness, and the so-called Radical
Republicans (Stevens's group) who wanted to make all men equal
before the law and punish all Confederates as traitors.

Legal theories clashed, too. It was convenient for Lincoln to argue that leaving the Union was unconstitutional and that thus no
state could have actually done it. It was up to the President to exact
professions of loyalty to the constitution from as many southern
leaders as he could and then encourage them to rebuild and operate
their state governments. Stevens and the Radicals wanted a democratic social revolution in the South, which could be managed only
by those few southerners who had stayed loyal to the Union and
by former slaves. The Radicals therefore had to embrace the theory

that the Southern states had indeed left the Union legally and could not get back in without obeying territorial laws imposed on them by Congress. In addition, only Congress had the power to make such laws and the president's role was to execute them.

When the Thirty-Eighth Congress adjourned in March of 1865, the two views were still reconcilable. Lincoln, as always, was on speaking terms with all factions (even Confederates) and his peace policy was not defined. He had come around on abolition. He showed signs of doing the same on negro suffrage. Most of all, he seems, in good republican fashion, to have respected the prerogatives of Congress no less than his own rights as commander-in-chief. He carefully sought Congressional ratification of actions taken under military authority and was the first president ever to appear voluntarily before a Congressional committee.[4] He was assassinated by a man who saw danger in union, not executive usurpation, crying the ironic slogan, "Sic semper tyrannis" of Junius Brutus, a character Booth had, incidentally, played on the stage.[5]

Whatever the irony of the assassination, the first of an American president, it meant that when the Thirty-Ninth Congress met the following December, Lincoln's successor had had a free hand in peace and reconstruction policy for eight months, with no Congress to deal with. Johnson, moreover, had all of Lincoln's reservations about equality with none of his extroverted charm or political wizardry. With Lee's surrender, the executive policy began to stand out, defined at last, and it was stark: pardon for most Confederates, offhand acceptance of abolition, recognition of all Southern state governments, and uncritical acceptance of their newly drafted "Black Codes" designed to keep free blacks in their place.

The Thirty-Ninth, which had been elected to the Savonarolesque tune of the "Battle Hymn of the Republic," was collectively outraged. In that election the people of the North had utterly repudiated the Democratic party, which had called for immediate peace without even abolition. Of 191 Representatives, only 40 were Democrats. In the Senate there were only 10 Democrats out of 52, of which only 5 had been elected in 1864–65 and 3 the Senate simply refused to seat. The preponderance was extraordinary, and, as it turned out, the crucial political fact, for the Thirty-Ninth Congress (with its successor, the Fortieth) was to be the only Congress ever with a two-thirds majority so reliable that it could govern in complete defiance of the President of the United States. Two thirds is the magic fraction by which Congress can override vetoes, proposes constitutional amendments, and *in extremis* impeach the chief executive. As we have seen, the Thirty-Ninth and Fortieth did all three. After a faltering start in 1865, by 1867 Congress came to the point where a bill could become law on the same day, even the same hour it was vetoed, with no debate in either House. In the end only one vote prevented the conviction of President Johnson in 1868 for high crimes and misdemeanors, a vote which ended forever the career of Senator Ross, who cast it.

Eight great measures, together amounting to a full-scale social revolution, had been carried against the executive by the time the Fortieth Congress adjourned in 1869. These were the Fourteenth and Fifteenth Amendments which provided universal civil rights and black male suffrage, two Civil Rights Acts to enforce the amendments, a Freedman's Bureau Act to provide material relief to ex-slaves, and three Military Reconstruction Acts to empower the army to prevent a restoration of the old order. In addition the Tenure-of-Office Act and the Army Act had given Congress so much control over executive appointments that even the commander-in-chief of the army, President Johnson, could do nothing to prevent the acts from being executed. In the process, the men of Congress, in a series of brilliant debates, had established a new theory of the Constitution, created a new democratic definition of the old word "republic," and discredited forever a favorite notion of the Framers that the last and best defense of a federated republic is the independence and sovereignty of the states within the federation.[6]

This unique achievement was, of course, made necessary by the Civil War, America's only civil war, and was in effect, the peace treaty by which the war was brought to a conclusion. The constitutional crisis of 1865–68 was only a reflection of the greater crisis of 1861–65 in which hundreds of thousands fought to give effect to their conflicting versions of what the Constitution devised in 1787 had meant. Moreover, as we can see from the examples of Switzerland, Florence, and the English Commonwealth, civil wars are an endemic disease and perhaps even the distinguishing mark of genuine republics. Where sovereignty, or (which is little less) constituency, is divided on purpose it is not surprising that those in possession of one part will fight those holding another for ultimate power. A firm commitment to peaceful resolution will, as in Rome, preserve the state from civil war, but only so long as this commitment is greater than those which produced the dispute in the first place. Multiplying constituencies may, as it did for a time in Florence, prevent any one group from cohering long enough to make a war, but the danger is always there. Because of this it becomes necessary to understand in constitutional language what the issues of a civil war are and what the treaty means.

For the two parties to the American war in 1861, the issue was easy to frame. All agreed that it had to do with the rights of states within the Union: whether, most importantly, states might secede without being prevented by the federal government, and, more particularly, whether federal measures like the regulation of slavery in territory held by the federation required the assent of those sovereign states whose interests it might injure. States' rights, in short, was the *casus belli* in 1861, and for southern republicans a firm childhood belief that in a federal republic like the United States (which most still referred to in the plural), monarchy could only threaten if the federal government gained effective sovereignty over the state governments.

Northern republicans believed, with equal piety, in the sovereignty of the union over the states. To reconcile this with what had by now become the republican theology, they adopted the view pioneered by the French in 1793 that the essence of a republic was the sovereignty of the whole people. If then, the argument ran, the people were sovereign in the constitution of the Union and not sovereign effectively in the restricted aristocratic republics of Virginia or South Carolina, the safety of the republic must require the United States government to tell the governments of Virginia and South Carolina what to do.

Democracy, in the form of manhood suffrage, had come to many states beginning in the 1820s. It was more or less easy by 1861 to view the aristocratic republic itself as a contradiction in terms. A democratic republic was the only republic. No republic could be said to exist where one class of residents was enslaved by another. Southerners found it more and more difficult to appeal, as they had in 1830, to the experience of the aristocratic slaveholding republics of Athens and Rome. The clause in the Constitution which allowed the federal government to guarantee to the states, "a republican form of government" was now increasingly seen by northerners like Senator Sumner as "a sleeping giant."[7] Hence the Emancipation Proclamation and the Thirteenth Amendment. By 1864–65, when the Thirty-Ninth Congress was being elected, northern republican thinking had embraced democracy to the extent of wondering whether any inequality, civil or political, might be enough to prevent a constitution from being called republican.

Such was the revolution brought about by these Congresses. Why then do Americans know so little about it? More tendentiously, why is it that in the American mind the South seems to have won the Civil War? The French have made a symbol of Robespierre with all his faults, but Americans have enshrined Robert E. Lee. The English, for all their sentimental monarchism, write poems in praise of Milton and Pym, but Americans make movies about the Ku Klux Klan. We seem to know all there is to know about the Civil War (what schoolchild has not heard of Gettysburg) but the nearest most get to understanding the peace is the Emancipation Proclamation. Small wonder we have never heard of Schuyler Colfax, Speaker of the Thirty-Ninth Congress, or Fessenden or Sumner who made drafts of the Civil Rights Acts, or John Bingham who led the fight for the Fourteenth Amendment.

As for Old Thad Stevens, the leader of them all, he rests at Lancaster, Pennsylvania, in a cemetery which he chose himself because it was the only one in town that did not exclude the bodies of blacks. Nearby, by coincidence, is the often-visited mansion and tomb of proslavery President James Buchanan, who met secession with inaction in 1860 and died, like Stevens, in 1868. Residents of Lancaster can show you where Buchanan lies but they'll scratch their heads if you ask for Thaddeus Stevens. The few who know the name will "remember" from history a stiff, bitter, bloody-minded, childless old man, who victimized the prostrate South, harried a noble president from office, and stained the Constitution itself with the muck of partisan politics.

These Lancastrians have read the wrong books—or seen *Gone With the Wind* too often. The books and movies in turn were made because in the late nineteenth century, ten years or so after Stevens' death, Western thinkers abandoned the equality of the races for the sterner Darwinian view that the races were distinct, irreconcilable, and bound to exterminate each other. Reconstruction came just in time. By the Centennial in 1876, the South more or less demanded, as the price of not fighting the Fourteenth and Fifteenth Amendments, that they cease to be effective and that the North make a general apology for the views embodied in them: adopt racism in short, and the North, rather too eagerly, did so. Reconstruction being a great mistake, its authors might be condemned, or what was more effective, forgotten. By the 1880s, a Virginia-born professor of politics at Princeton by the name of Wilson was writing a book called *Congressional Government* in which he condemned the whole Stevens legacy. When he got to the White House he delivered the *coup de grâce* to congressional prerogative and incidentally took to recommending *Birth of a Nation*, the famous pro-Klan movie, as wholesome family viewing.

The remarkable irony in all this is that the earlier generation of southerners who engineered secession were not all racists. Many were much more concerned over the fate of constitutional republicanism than by the fate of slavery. Lee, for example, owned no slaves and fought for Virginia because he thought state sovereignty the only guarantee of republican freedom. Alexander Stephens of Georgia, Vice-President of the Confederacy, wrote after his capture in 1865:

> Depend upon it, there is no difference between Consolidation and Empire; no difference between Centralism and Imperialism. The consummation of either must necessarily end in the overthrow of Liberty and the establishment of Despotism.[8]

—which is the state sovereignty creed in a nutshell.

Now of course all this to-do about despotism might have been just Alexander Stephens's way of making self-interest or even treason sound attractive, just as Thaddeus Stevens's great program may have been merely his way of ensuring that the Republican Party would run the country after the South came back into the Union. It may be, as some say, that all political rhetoric is best reduced to self-interest, but I doubt it. In fact, I think the best way to make sense of both Stev(ph)enses is to understand that each, sometimes with selflessness, believed in republicanism and that their differences were differences in the definition of republic; the northerner arguing that republics had to be democratic and ruled by the legislature, while the southerner held that republics might be aristocratic and must be ruled by the states of the federation.[9] Finally, I would argue that when it came to shackling presidents their views were exactly alike and that they both acted at about the same time to join a party to advance them. They were both, in short, Whigs, members of that national political party that began around 1828 and disappeared as an organization in 1856.

And what, one asks, was the Whig program? Here we embark on a much-vexed question. A small army of professional historians has expressed the most remarkably dissonant set of views on who the Whigs and their opponents the Democrats really were that one is almost driven to a schoolbook to find a straightforward summary of the case. The text, by Morison, is, however, frustrating:

> Who were the Whigs in 1840? The only really accurate answer is, everyone who was not a Democrat. Everyone, that is, except a few rabid abolitionists at one end of the political spectrum, and sullen nullifiers on the other.[10]

Desperately we return to the interpreters. Ulrich Phillips says the Whigs were the upper class of North and South. Charles Sellers says they were the business class of both sections. Louis Hartz grandly concludes they were the *grande bourgeoisie*. Nonsense, says Lee Benson, you can't make a party with just the grande bourgeoisie. There aren't enough of them. Like all American parties the Whigs were just a coalition of ethnicities and localities and Benson has the numbers to prove it.

It may be all true, but the Whigs would never have recognized themselves. The party's leaders at least were more than a coalition of the rich, the outs, and the ethnics. It may even be that they sometimes meant what they said; that is, that the Whigs opposed the Democrats for good reason and that such reason may be found in the speeches made (in a golden age of oratory) by Whig candidates for office in the 1830s and '40s before slavery began to destroy the party. It may even be that the name Whig has a meaning. Why after all did they choose it in 1834 or so? Did it mean to them at all what it had meant to the Scots Covenanters who used it in the English Revolution? Did it have the meaning it had had for the revolutionaries of 1688 or those of 1776? If it did, whiggism must have meant belief in a limited, divided government, a hatred of strong monarchy in any disguise, and a love for the republican values of virtue, simplicity of manner, and equality before the law.

In those comparatively obscure years of 1824–56 about which few retain much besides the national bank, Texas, and the Mexican War, being a Whig would mean being opposed to any growth in the powers of the presidency, and suspicion of the powers of government in general. It would mean being against executive misuse of the veto and executive control of the purse or the sword. It would mean being opposed to foreign war and suspicious of annexing territory. It might mean a mild xenophobia growing out of an understandable but baseless fear that immigrants from monarchical cultures might not understand republicanism.[11] Lastly, it would mean a defense of the Constitution as it stood, wherever it was threatened, except insofar as equality or republicanism might be threatened by its provisions. This would leave room, for example, to be in favor of a national bank, which the Supreme Court had held to be constitutional in 1821, or of restricting but not abolishing slavery, which had been written into the Constitution in 1787.

The facts bear out the hypothesis. These are exactly the policies for which the Whigs claimed they stood, and for which some Whigs sacrificed their careers. They did support the Bank, and they also supported, with due regard for state sovereignty, policies to strengthen the national economy. Beginning as a leadership faction under Henry Clay and John Quincy Adams, they became a true mass party between 1833 and 1840 when they came out against the veto, the spoils system, the removal of Treasury funds from the Bank, and the famous Force Act which authorized President Jackson to send the army into South Carolina to enforce the tariff. Finally, in 1846–48, in a vain but epic struggle, the Whig members of Congress tried to deny President Polk power to prosecute the war against Mexico or to acquire new territory from her.

Most of all, the Whig party in its heyday was opposed to presidential power. Its fear of the executive was deep and lurid. With quixotic disregard for all the maxims of practical politics in America, the Whigs opposed not only presidents of the other party but their own as well. Indeed, their greatest and most successful struggle was with President John Tyler, who was a Whig. The Fates must have liked this joke for they fell in with it immediately, depriving both Whig presidents of their lives before they had completed half their terms. The soul of William Henry Harrison, the first Whig president, fled within a month of his inauguration. (Whigs called him "the Good President.") Two terms later, Zachary Taylor's thread was cut when he took on too much cold milk and fruit on the Fourth of July.

History has it that the end of Taylor's term was the end of the Whig Party. The Whigs nominated their third ex-general in 1852 but lost. The new territory whose acquisition they had opposed so eloquently in 1846 had forced the slavery issue on the country in a form so virulent that Whig constitutionalists could find no position that both Cotton and Conscience factions would support. Some defected to a party (The Know-Nothings) which opposed Catholic immigration. The last Whig convention, a pitifully small affair, nominated Millard Fillmore in 1856. In 1860, the survivors of the older generation of Whigs met in Baltimore, named themselves the Constitutional Unionists, took three states in the general election, and disappeared for good.

The Whigs may have deserved what the Fates dished out to them. They had made it impossible for the party to be led by presidents. Nevertheless, they did not die as easily as the textbooks would have us believe. There were a lot of homeless Whigs in 1856 when the new Republican Party was forming, among them Thaddeus Stevens, who had brought his Anti-Masons into alliance with the Whigs by 1835. Joining the Republicans in Illinois was Abraham Lincoln, who as a freshman Whig Congressman in 1847 had devoted his maiden speech to branding the Mexican War as an act of executive usurpation. Joining in other states were Schuyler Colfax, William Pitt Fessenden, Charles Sumner, and John Bingham, soon to be leaders of the Thirty-Ninth Congress. In fact the list of leaders in the Thirty-Ninth Congress shows a startling consistency. Out of twenty-eight members acknowledged by the relative inactivity of their colleagues as leaders of the Thirty-Ninth, all but six entered politics as Whigs, more than half of them in the years between 1833 and 1846 when the party's power and meaning were in formation. It would be unexpected but not at all unfair to say that the Radical Republicans of 1865 were simply the young Whigs of 1840, running the show at last.[12]

If this is so, it becomes important for us to know what the political climate of 1840 was really like and why men of promise were, in their idealistic youth, attracted to the party of Henry Clay, a party which now seems to have stood only for a national bank and a high tariff. It is time to tell the story of the Jackson, Tyler, and Polk administrations as the Whigs saw them, and preface this with what the Framers thought of presidents.

When bespectacled James Wilson proposed a single executive for the United States on June 1, 1787, the stunned silence went on so long that old Ben Franklin had to rise and break it. The delegates must speak their minds, he said; the issue would not go away. "A foetus of monarchy!" exploded Edmund Randolph when the silence broke. Check him with a committee, said Rutledge, or else don't let him have the power of war and peace. "It will be said," thought Franklin, "that we don't propose to establish Kings. I know it. But there is a natural tendency in mankind to Kingly Government. . . . It gives more of the appearance of equality among Citizens, and that they like." Franklin suggested that there be no salary for executives and that they be impeachable so as to protect them from assassination. Williamson of North Carolina said a single executive "will be an elective king and will feel the spirit of one." He thought it (like Polybios) "pretty certain" that monarchy would come, but asked help to postpone it as long as possible by making the executive ineligible for reelection. Elbridge Gerry said darkly that election by the citizens at large would be the worst method of all, and George Mason of Virginia was so against the idea that he refused to sign the Constitution and went out to lobby for a Bill of Rights.[13] With many misgivings, conservative men who believed in strong government eventually overrode the objections and created the presidency.

More than thirty years were to pass before the Framers' fears were realized, by a man from the democratic state of Tennessee (originally named Franklin). Andrew Jackson took a long time to see the possibilities of the presidential office in the age of democracy. Manhood suffrage was new in the 1820s, just adopted by northern states and still unpopular in the south, and its effect on the presidency was as yet unsuspected. When Jackson was first inaugurated in 1829, there was only one political party and Jackson's few enemies within it dissented on policy and personality, not on the Constitution. Aristocratic eyebrows were raised when Jackson's inaugural guests wiped their boots on the White House carpet, and Vice-President Calhoun was alienated when Jackson defended the wife of his Secretary of War against charges of adultery. Rival Senator Henry Clay was neatly outmaneuvered by vetoes of a pet bill or two; but except for Jackson's wholesale replacement of civil servants with his own supporters, and reliance on a "Kitchen Cabinet" of unappointed advisers, Jacksonian democracy raised no fears of executive tyranny. It was suspicion of central government in any form, not of executives, that led Calhoun into the labyrinth of states' rights and secession; and only Calhoun's southern followers thought that the Force Bill was unconstitutional. All went fairly well, if undecorously, until July 10, 1832.

On that day, Andrew Jackson vetoed the Bank of the United States.

Many still wonder why. True, Jackson saw it as an aristocratic "monster," but it was an enormously useful fiscal tool and had been one since it was first chartered by the first Congress in 1789. Jefferson had opposed it then, but found it very helpful when he was president. Congress had allowed it to lapse in 1811, but thought better of it in 1816, and the Supreme Court had ringingly declared it constitutional in 1821. Nevertheless, as insiders had feared, Jackson vetoed it.

Why not? The veto should not have been regarded as a fearful thing except by those whose fortunes were linked to it. It is hard (as generations of students have found out for themselves) to get very fervent about a bank. Jackson, however, had done something new in handing down this veto, and it was immediately seen as unprecedented. All previous presidents had found it necessary to claim in their infrequent veto messages, that the bill in question was unconstitutional. Jackson had done the same with the "monster." But the Supreme Court had already held the bank to be constitutional, so Jackson wrote:

> To this conclusion I cannot assent. Mere precedent . . . should not be regarded as deciding questions of constitutional power. . . . [The opinion of the Supreme Court] ought not to control the coordinate authorities of this Government. . . . Each public officer who takes an oath to support the Constitution swears that he will support it as he understands it. . . . The authority of the Supreme Court must not, therefore, be permitted to control the Congress or the Executive when acting in their legislative capacities. . . .[14]

To this unprecedented but arguable assertion (the veto won Jackson reelection in 1832) Jackson now added a series of actions which, justified or not, ended by creating a fear of executive tyranny throughout the country and earned him the title "King Andrew I." In 1833, he began to remove the Treasury's deposits from the bank whose lame-duck charter still had four more years to run. This was not easy. The Secretary of the Treasury, Louis McLane, thought it was illegal to do it. Jackson kicked him upstairs to the State Department and moved in William Duane. Duane, however, also refused to remove the deposits on grounds that the House of Representatives had forbidden it. Jackson fired him on September 23 and brought in Roger B. Taney from the Justice Department, who at last did the deed on October 1.

Any resemblance to the "Saturday Night Massacre" is of course anachronistic, as is the sense of apprehension which came over Washington. Jackson was clearly not a crook, but he was no less clearly asserting an executive control over the country's purse which was new in republican America. Ordered by Congress to supply copies of documents relating to the removal, Jackson summarily refused. On December 26 Senator Clay moved in the Senate that the president be censured for action contrary to his oath, and a parade of the finest constitutional scholars in the country strode to the rostrum one by one to condemn removal.

On March 28, 1834, the Clay resolution carried. It was a small thing, really. Senators had voted a censure because they had not the numbers to override a veto. In 1837, a new Senate ordered the censure crossed out of the record. Vindicated by the voters, Jackson had become the first American president to determine that his office, backed by popular election, was equal in power to two-thirds of both Houses of Congress (whose nameless members are most likely aristocrats anyway). So prominent did the presidency become under Jackson that some Americans began to attack presidents physically, as Franklin had feared, hoping perhaps that some of the prestige would rub off on them or that they might have some effect against the great new power of the office. Jackson was assaulted in Alexandria, Virginia on May 6, 1833 and shot at in Washington on January 30, 1835. Like the assassination of the Gracchi, this had never happened before.

It was the veto and the removal which brought Thaddeus Stevens into the anti-Jackson camp. Stevens was then a minor leader of the anti-Jackson party in Pennsylvania, a key legislator whose commitments were somewhat ill-assorted but reliably radical, bourgeois, and democratic. He was something of an abolitionist on the new issue of slavery and a high tariff, a sound currency man when it came to business. His most lasting achievement in state politics was to come in 1835 when, largely because of Stevens' efforts, Pennsylvania established her famous free public school system. Education was dear to him, and any sort of discrimination anathema, values understandable in a poor, brilliant farm boy with a club foot. Stevens' father, a failed Vermont farmer, had deserted his family like Robespierre's had done, when Thaddeus was young. Thanks in part to his mother, who "worked day and night" to educate him, Stevens graduated from Dartmouth in 1814.[15] He had been born in 1792, the Year I of the French Republic and the second year of democracy in Vermont. Since 1815 he had been teaching, lawyering, and manufacturing in Pennsylvania. When Jackson killed the bank it was Stevens who drew up and managed the law which rechartered it as a Pennsylvania corporation.

Younger idealists like Colfax and Fessenden joined the anti-

Jackson effort at about the same time. Like Stevens, they were passionate democrats, but they did not believe that democracy must inevitably promote badly educated Indian-hating generals to the White House there to embrace the veto and grasp at monarchy. They, and others like them, cast about for a presidential candidate who would convincingly espouse the limiting of his own office—and who could win. John Quincy Adams could be trusted but not elected. Defeated by Jackson in 1828, he now sat somewhat dourly in the House of Representatives. Henry Clay had lost to Jackson in 1832 and again in 1836 to Jackson's hand-picked successor. Moreover, Clay was not much less ambitious than his old rival. So was Daniel Webster, and worse, he was less reliable on the veto issue. The last great Jackson opponent, Calhoun, was hopelessly embarked on the route the Confederacy would later follow to limit centralized power, and this route was rapidly becoming unacceptable in the North and West.

It was Thaddeus Stevens and the canny Whig boss of New York, Thurlow Weed, who saw the solution: nominate on Indian-killing general to get the low vote, and make sure of his attitude on the power of the executive branch. In addition, get a southern Clay man to endorse him. Thus, in 1839, was born the ticket of "Tippecanoe and Tyler Too," and General William Henry Harrison, Virginia aristocrat, who had, in his salad days a quarter of a century ago, beaten Tecumseh at the Battle of Tippecanoe, was nominated for president by the Whig Party. The vote for the "Old Lady" (he was sixty-seven) was beautifully managed during the convention at Harrisburg, state capital of Pennsylvania, by Thaddeus Stevens, a leader of the Pennsylvania legislature for five years and a Harrison man for four. Weed swung New York away from General Scott, and together they gathered up the essential southerner, John Tyler of Virginia.

John Tyler, a bony Virginia aristocrat with a nose like a palisade, was said to have wept when Clay lost the nomination, but if he did he rallied quickly. A man of honor approaching the quixotic, he had cast the only vote against the Force Bill in 1833 and resigned from the Senate rather than obey an instruction of the Virginia legislature to cross out Jackson's censure in 1836. Harrison's promise to try to restrict the presidency to one term with a limit on vetoes appealed to Tyler. He accepted the vice-presidential slot and took the southern Whigs with him.

Leaders of the Whigs, determined not to be beaten again by the methods of democracy, entered with gusto into the campaign of 1840 against Jackson's heir Van Buren. Van Buren, the tavern-keeper's son, was successfully branded as an aristocrat, and Harrison, the plantation heir, was made into a log-cabin frontiersman whose favorite drink was simple hard cider. Following good advice, Harrison kept silent during the entire campaign, earning the new nickname "Granny Mum." It was one of the most ridiculous campaigns in American history, which is saying something, but as Stevens and Weed had foreseen it worked perfectly, and Harrison was elected by a landslide. The turnout of eligible voters was 78 percent, a record, so that for once it was impossible to say that the Whigs were merely the party of aristocracy. Clay, his delight somewhat qualified by the fact that he was not president, began to put together the legislative program and Webster to organize the cabinet. For the first time a president had announced it as his policy that he would be a mere "agent of the legislature" as Roger Sherman had advocated in 1787, and Whig legislative leaders were ready to make the most of it.

In an inaugural address famous for its length, Old Tip announced amid repeated references to the threat of Caesars and Cromwells, that his policy would be: (1) to serve only one term and to seek a constitutional amendment requiring this; (2) to use the veto "solely as a conservative power"; and (3) "never to remove a Secretary of the Treasury without communicating all the circumstances to both Houses of Congress" (which is the germ of the Tenure-of-Office Act of 1866 on which Johnson was impeached.)[16] No one can know if Harrison would have carried out his second and third pledges, but he did carry out the first in spades. The inaugural address was too much for Granny Mum and he died of pneumonia within a month of it.

All eyes now turned to John Tyler, who began rather ominously by refusing to be addressed as "Acting President." He also ended immediately Harrison's republican practice of submitting presidential policies to a majority vote of the cabinet. In due time, Henry Clay came up Pennsylvania Avenue to the White House and laid his program before the new president. Congress was in special session with a Whig majority, Tyler had held on to Harrison's cabinet, and Clay was eager to start rechartering the Bank of the United States. Tyler, however, wove suspiciously. He agreed, he said, with some of the points made by the losing side before the Supreme Court in 1821. He did not object as Jackson had to a chartered private bank, but he thought its powers ought not (shades of Calhoun) to infringe state sovereignty. Moreover, he was stubborn about appointing the men Clay recommended to federal office. Foolishly, Clay did not take the hint. While allies framed a bank bill that would suit Tyler's scruples, Clay went ahead with his own bill. It passed resoundingly on August 6, 1841. On August 16, Tyler vetoed it. An unconstitutional threat to state governments, he wrote.

The uproar can be imagined. Clay strode to the White House and the fur flew. At last Tyler told him: "Go you now, then, Mr. Clay, to your end of the avenue, where stands the Capitol, and there perform your duty to the country as you shall think proper. So help me God, I shall do mine at this end of it as I shall think proper!"[17] Weeks passed before cooler heads prevailed and the old Tyler bank bill could be brought out of committee for a second try. Every effort was made to accommodate the Virginian's curious reservations. It passed the Senate on September 3. On September 9 Tyler vetoed it.

Hell hath no fury like that which now struck the Whig Party. They had no two-thirds majority with which to override the president, or the delighted minority party. In two days the entire cabinet (except the ambitious Webster) had resigned. Four days later, the Whig caucus in Congress expelled Tyler from the party. The following spring, a hopeless Clay left the Senate and went home to Kentucky. By the time Tyler had used the veto a fourth time in 1842, a select committee of the House under the chairmanship of John Quincy Adams was calling for a new constitutional amendment to allow Congress to override a veto by a simple instead of a two-thirds majority. It had also, for the first time in American history, officially accused a president of impeachable offenses.

By a comfortable vote of 100–80, the full House accepted the committee report. Before his single term had ended, Tyler had handed down six vetoes, more than any other president, and pocket vetoed four bills, a record exceeded only by Jackson. Eventually one veto was overridden, and this too was a first in American history. As honor had frequently required of Tyler in the past, he became in 1842 a political loner. His loyalists, so few they were called the "Corporal's Guard," could do little for him. Only foreign policy offered a field in which a president had enough freedom of action that he could redeem his reputation under such circumstances. As the Whigs observed him glacially, Tyler and the Corporal's Guard began secretly working on a project which would make for "His Accidency" an everlasting place in American history—the annexation of Texas.

Texas was originally a province of the Republic of Mexico. It had declared its independence of Mexico in 1836 because the largely American population there was incensed at Mexico's continuing effort to abolish slavery. Almost immediately after the Texas declaration there had been talk of annexing her to the United States and almost immediately the northern Whigs, in the person of John Quincy Adams, began to argue against the idea. Tyler, who was a southern slaveowner, was not bound by Adams's antislavery sentiment in his attitude to Texas, nor was he apparently moved by Adams's view that military expansion and aggressive war were a terrible threat to republican government. Besides, Tyler thought he could obtain Texas as peacably as Adams, when Secretary of State, had obtained Florida. In 1843, he let go of Webster who opposed annexation, and appointed a Virginia friend, Abel Upshur, as Secretary of State. Upshur proceeded to negotiate annexation in secret with the Texas government, informing neither the public nor the Senate. The government of the Republic of Mexico, which had never offically recognized the independence of Texas, was told to put up or shut up. The navy was sent without Congressional notice or authorization to patrol the waters of the foreign state of Texas. Indeed, it seems to have been Tyler who discovered the usefulness of executive secret agents, having already sent several to Maine to help change the attitude of that state's press to border negotiations with Canada in 1841.

Upshur's treaty was very nearly complete when the poor man was blown up by a defective cannon named "Peacemaker" while watching a demonstration of new weapons by the Navy Department. Tyler appointed Calhoun to replace him and the treaty was signed. It was too late, however, because in the interval the treaty had leaked, allowing its northern opponents to organize. After a month and a half of debate the Senate rejected it 35–16. Some, like Webster, voted against it because of the political consequences of supporting the annexation of a slave state, but that cannot have been the only reason, since every Whig in the Senate, North and South, save only one from Mississippi, voted against that treaty. Even Clay, the heavy favorite in the 1844 presidential race and the nominee of the Whig Party, put himself on record as opposing the

treaty because he feared an aggressive war with Mexico would result.

The Democrats, however, were delighted to be handed this issue in the era of Manifest Destiny. On a platform of immediate
annexation they felt they could win a popular majority for anybody,
so they nominated the first "dark horse," a loyal but rather obscure
congressman from Jackson's home state of Tennessee named Polk.
True to Democratic expectations, Polk did win (though not by
much: Tyler made a deal with him and dropped out while an abolitionist third party took a key 5,000 votes away from Clay in New
York). The vote gave Tyler, still determined to get credit for Texas,
an excuse to bring up annexation again before the lame-duck Congress in the winter of 1844–45. Unable to ratify a treaty, the Senate
finally agreed to the dubious device of a joint House-Senate resolution, which conferred authority on the president to negotiate the
annexation, by a grudging vote of 27–25. Three days after this
passed, Tyler left the presidency he had so adamantly aggrandized
to Polk who would do worse, and went home with his gay new aristocratic wife. Texas and its consequences remained to destroy the
Whig Party.

If annexation was popular, the Mexican War of which it was the
cause was even more popular. Even now Americans view the defeat
of Mexico and the acquisition of California and the Southwest as
one of the few memorable and positive acts of the 1800s. Not so
the Whigs. With astonishing unanimity, North and South together,
they opposed it. Reduced in numbers by the Tyler fiasco, they could
do little about it, but opposition was for them a matter of principle
no less than political survival. In Lancaster County, Thaddeus Stevens jumped back into politics, campaigning against a "slavehold-
ers' war."[18] Even Calhoun, who had signed the Texas treaty, foresaw
and feared that the slavery issue would rise insoluble from a war
with Mexico. Worse from the Whig point of view was the opportunity war would provide for governments and presidents to ag-
grandize themselves, and for once there was nothing funny about
their fears. Shocked into supporting war by President Polk's report
of an actual battle between the Mexican and American armies,
Congressional Whigs got their first taste of Gulf of Tonkin politics
as they slowly discovered the truth. Polk had deliberately provoked
the Mexican attack by sending an army south of the Texas border

three months before hostilities broke out—that is, when it became clear that Mexico would not sell him California. It was, in the words of one Whig Senator, "as much an act of aggression on our part as is a man's pointing a pistol at another's breast."[19]

The Whigs now faced a narrow dilemma. They had allowed the war to begin; would they vote the men and money for it to continue? If they did not, the country would make them look like traitors. If they did, they would sacrifice the most important principle on which the party had been put together, resistance to executive usurpation. The fourteen antislavery Whigs in the House, led by John Quincy Adams and including Giddings and Delano who would sit in the Thirty-Ninth, found it easy to choose the first alternative. Beginning with the declaration itself and ending with the peace treaty, they voted no on every bill to prosecute the war. The rest, swamped by the great Democratic tide, voted in favor, but grudgingly, seizing every possible parliamentary opportunity to bring the issues to the floor. One senator proposed that the president's power to appoint militia officers be taken away from him. Others subpoenaed executive documents and publicized Polk's refusal to provide them. In distant Concord, Massachusetts, Henry David Thoreau protested by inventing civil disobedience and going to jail. In the Senate, southern Whigs fell in behind Calhoun's strategy of nipping at Polk's heels. Senator Davis of Kentucky moved that the president be charged with usurping the power of Congress by making war on Mexico.[20] Congressman Alexander Stephens of Georgia set the tone for all southern Whigs by charging in the first month of the war that it had been avoidable and unnecessary, that the border claim asserted by Polk was unjustified, and that such an aggressive war would undermine republican virtue. It produces, he said, "downward progress . . . a progress of party—of excitement—of lust for power . . . [and] would soon sweep over all law, all order, and the Constitution itself."[21]

To charges that the Whigs were disloyal, Congressman King provided the reply: "If an earnest desire to save my country from ruin and disgrace be treason, then I am a traitor: if the fear to do wrong makes a man a coward, then I am a coward."[22] Some Whigs even opposed the peace and assorted appropriations to end the war, voting against spending $3 million to buy California, because of the danger they saw in expansion. Whig Senator Thomas Corwin, farmer's son from Ohio, summed up the whole Whig position in a great speech in February 1847 which earned him the title "Black Tom Traitor" from the Democrats:

> I have been oppressed with melancholy forebodings of evil to come, and not unfrequently by a conviction that each step we take in this unjust war, may be the last in our career; that each chapter we write in Mexican blood, may close the volume of our history as a free people. . . .
>
> Sir, if any one could sit down, free from the excitements and biases which belong to public affairs . . . forming his judgement . . . by the suggestions which history teaches. . . . He would speak of a republic, boasting that its rights were secured, and the restricted powers of its functionaries bound up in the chains of a written Constitution [and] a people, in the wantonness of strength or the fancied security of the moment, had torn that written Constitution to pieces, scattered its fragments to the winds, and surrendered themselves to the usurped authority of ONE MAN. . . .
>
> When the makers of that Constitution assigned to Congress alone, the most delicate and important power—to declare war—a power more intimately affecting the interests. . . of the people than any which a government is ever called on to exert—when they withheld this great prerogative from the Executive and confided it to Congress alone, they but consulted in this, as in every other work of their hands, the gathered wisdom of all preceding times. Whether they looked to the stern despotisms of the ancient Asiatic world, or the military yoke of imperial Rome, or the feudal institutions of the middle ages, or the more modern monarchies of Europe, in each and all of these, where the power to wage war was held by one or by a few, it had been used to sacrifice, not to protect the many. . . . After securing this power to Congress, they thought it safe to give the command of the armies in peace and war to the President. . . .
>
> . . . forgetting this old doctrine, that a large standing army in time of peace was always dangerous to human liberty, we have increased that army from six thousand up to about sixteen thousand men . . . the other day we gave ten regiments more; and for not giving it within the quick time demanded by our master, the commander-in-chief, some minion, I know not who, . . feeding upon the fly-blown remnants that fall from the Executive shambles and lie putrefying there, has denounced us as Mexicans . . . traitors to the United States. . . .
>
> It must have occurred to everybody how utterly impotent the Congress of the United States *now* is for any purpose whatever,

but that of yielding to the President every demand which he makes for men and money. . . .

. . . I trust we shall abandon the idea, the heathen, barbarian notion, that our true national glory is to be won, or retained, by military prowess or skill in the art of destroying life. . . .

. . . But the Senator from Michigan says we will be two hundred millions in a few years and we want room. If I were a Mexican I would tell you, "Have you not room in your own country to bury your dead men? . . ."

Why, says the Chairman of this Committee on Foreign Relations, it is the most reasonable thing in the world! We ought to have the Bay of San Francisco. Why? Because it is the best harbor on the Pacific! It has been my fortune . . . to have practiced a good deal in criminal courts in the course of my life, and I never yet heard a thief, arraigned for stealing a horse, plead that it was the best horse that he could find in the country! . . .

What has been the fate of all nations who have acted upon the idea that they must advance? Our young orators cherish this notion with a fervid, but fatally mistaken zeal. They call it by the mysterious name of "destiny." "Our destiny," they say is "onward," and hence they argue, with ready sophistry, the propriety of seizing upon any territory and any people that may lie in the way of our "fated" advance. . . . Recently these progressives . . . have found a god whom these Romans, centuries gone by, baptized "Terminus."

Whoever would know the further fate of this Roman deity . . . will find that Rome thought as you now think, that it was her destiny to conquer provinces and nations, and no doubt she sometimes said as you say, "I will conquer a peace," and where now is she, the Mistress of the World? The spider weaves his web in her palaces, the owl sings his watch-song in her towers. . . .[23]

Once again Minerva's owl takes flight at dusk, but the Whigs simply cannot be dismissed as a joke, or speeches like this as the product of mere political ambition and self-interest. Even less is it possible to assume that sort of effect in the lives of the next generation, some of whom, like Giddings, Cullom, Abraham Lincoln, and Thaddeus Stevens, had already been in Congress. And of course, the Whig predictions of disaster were quite accurate. The conquest of Mexico precipitated the slavery question in a way that could no longer be avoided by appeals to constitutional law. In the next ten years it brought on the Civil War and destroyed the Whig Party.

Whigs who stepped gingerly into the Republican Party in the

1850s had learned several lessons. First, never let presidents have a free hand, especially in wartime. Second, a republican who wishes also to be a democrat and a unionist must pin his hopes in Congress. Third, beware of accidental presidents, presidents who come from Tennessee, and any president named Andrew. Among those who learned was sardonic Thaddeus Stevens, Republican since 1855, partisan of Harrison, opponent of Jackson, Tyler, and Polk, democrat, abolitionist, peacenik, and constitutionalist. Few things could have given him more pleasure than to pronounce the impeachment of Andrew Johnson on February 24, 1868.

11

Léon Gambetta and the *Troisième*
The Parliamentary Republic

WHEN MARX WROTE in 1852 that history repeats itself, the first time as tragedy and the second time as farce, he neglected to tell us how it would play the third time.[1] He might have, for he was at the height of his powers by 1870, long an observer of France, and on September 4 that year a twenty-nine-year-old legislator named Léon Gambetta proclaimed the Third French Republic.

Perhaps the third time farce and tragedy come entwined, like the muses they are. Certainly the Third Republic had more than enough of both. Nevertheless, the history that Marx was talking about, the passage from republic to emperor, did not repeat itself this time, not even in 1940 when, crippled by wars it could not constitutionally control, and an antirepublican right wing which it had labored to exclude from constitutional office, the Third Republic legally put an end to itself.

The Third Republic not only lasted longer than any French regime since the monarchy, and renewed the association with patriotism essential to republican survival; it added something new to the republican tradition: the parliamentary system. Sometimes called responsible cabinet government, it works by having the elected chief of state perform only the ceremonial role, appointing an operating head of government who is responsible not to him but to an elected chamber. What was pioneered *de facto* by the evolving constitutional monarchy in Britain and by that cabinet of 1793 known as the Committee of Public Safety, was named and rationalized in France after 1870 and stands as her great gift to twentieth-century politics. It is used everywhere now, from India to Portugal, and continues in France even under the hostile "presidential" institutions of the Fifth Republic.

From the beginning the Third held an audience. It was an economic and demographic giant, presiding in 1900 over the fourth largest industrial economy in the world. It was a leader in turn-of-the-century Europe, where the only other independent republics were Portugal, Switzerland, and San Marino. Expressing the solidarity of embattled republicans everywhere, it gave America the Statue of Liberty in 1889, stipulating that it face toward monarchical Europe in an allegory of 1776. This was a republic whose rhetoric was obsessively revolutionary and often proletarian; yet it abjured the Terror of the First Republic, and the Blanquists of the Second, repudiated (to Marx's disgust) its lineal predecessor the Paris Commune, and claimed from the first that it was conservative. Indeed the majority of its founders were stymied monarchists, and even the minority who genuinely were republicans had mostly been baptized Jules for Julius Caesar.

To the rest of Europe, and to many of its own citizens, the Third seemed a theater of strife, a perpetual mutiny, a parliamentary version of the primeval chaos. But, as in the Darwinian biology which ruled the minds of its makers, chaos bred life. This republic was as hopelessly contradictory as so many others. It was also, perhaps for that reason, profoundly human and eminently successful. The greatest of its founders, Léon Gambetta, summed it up perfectly when he said in 1876, "I deny the absolute everywhere, and so you can well imagine that I am not going to recognize it in politics."[2]

The man who proclaimed this republic on September 4, 1870 was at the time a very junior legislator from a poor district in Paris, but he had an unsurpassed sense of timing. About noon on the third the news of Napoleon III's defeat and capture by the Prussian army at Sedan reached Paris. That evening the leaderless imperial "legislature" met at the Palais Bourbon. The session was supposed to be secret, on an emergency basis, but in the early morning hours of the fourth, Paris radicals stormed into the hall calling for *la déché-ance*—the abolition of monarchy. It was then that Gambetta made his move. Pushing to the rostrum while others maundered, he turned to the crowd and, without a shred of authority, proclaimed:

> Citizens! Considering that the country is in [a revolution] . . . that we are, and we constitute, the regular power issuing from free universal suffrage—We declare that Louis Napoleon Bonaparte and his dynasty have forever ceased to reign over France.[3]

Hours later, with Jules Simon, he did the same thing at the Hotel de Ville, convened a quick meeting of the moderate republicans, and emerged as one of the chief magistrates of what was now the revolutionary government of France.

Of all the revolutions of Paris, in 1356, 1589, 1789, 1830, and 1848, this was the shortest and the most humane. The bloodshed was all at the front. There was no time to set up the barricades. It seemed as if Gambetta had made the Third Republic with a paragraph of prose, but in fact, the process was just beginning. The new Government of National Defense was succeeded by a National Assembly in February 1871. Civil war arose between this Assembly, pacifist and conservative, and the Paris Commune, chauvinist and Red, which arose from the dustbin of history in March. As in the first revolution, France defeated Paris, but somehow it never established another monarchy. It sat for another four years, doing unprecedented things. Until 1873, France had an executive and a legislature but, legally, no republic. From 1873 to 1876, the same odd arrangement of forces gave France a republic run largely by monarchists. Not until 1876 did republicans control the Republic's legislature. Not until 1877 did they control the ministry. Not until 1879 was the President of the Republic a republican.

In short, the establishment of the Third Republic was not as it seemed on September 4. Like Rome it was not built in a day. Like a stalactite, as historian David Thomson remarks, it was made inch by inch from the top down.[4] And in all this, at nearly every stage in a slow construction, we can see the bright, optimistic, calculating intelligence of the young Gambetta. Having proclaimed the Republic in 1870, he helped rule it in 1871, created the party that legalized it in 1875, led it to victory over its monarchist president in 1877, and trained those who led it through all its crises until the First World War. If any republican can be called the father of the Third Republic it is he.

He was not an unknown in 1870. Gambetta (the name in Italian means "little leg") had made his reputation as a speaker in the cafes of imperial Paris. A rather stocky man of undistinguished height and shape, he had been gifted with an unforgettable face. Under his high forehead, topped with a backswept wave of black hair, were a great Roman nose, prognathous beard, and heavy-lidded dark eyes. A childhood injury had left him with a glass eye and differing profiles. Women adored him and he, a lifelong bachelor, reciprocated with legendary vigor and tenderness. Our two best sources for his life are his letters to female relatives and to his adoring mistress Léonie Léon. When he spoke, he put a large or small audacity in every paragraph, calculated to shock but not quite to raise hackles. One of those who knew him reports that Gambetta was "one of the few orators of our time, perhaps the only one, who could make an audience experience that divine shudder which tightens the throat and makes one's hair stand on end."[5] He could also make them laugh, even in a crisis.

The first time Gambetta shouted, "Vive la République!" he was a boy of eleven, the schoolboy son of a French mother and an Italian father in the small Mediterranean town of Cahors. Far away in Paris romantic nationalist rebels had overthrown the constitutional monarchy of Louis-Philippe and founded the democratic Second Republic. It was 1848, a glorious spring for the republicans of Europe. Monarchs in creaking carriages were hightailing it not only out of Paris, but out of Rome, Vienna, Munich, the Hague, and Palermo. The capitals of Florence, Budapest, and Prague were all invested by the young heirs of 1789 and 1792, constitutionalists and republicans proclaiming liberty. In Paris they also called for equality and fraternity. What they got was promising: a democratically elected National Assembly, a new constitution with a Franklinian one-house legislature, and an executive called a president, each independently elected by manhood suffrage.

But there was a flaw. Observed by young Gambetta in Cahors, it became the unforgettable lesson for a budding politician. On December 10, 1848, the millions of new voters turned out to elect the first president of the Second Republic. Among the campaigners was Louis Napoleon Bonaparte, mustachioed nephew of the Caesar of 1799, feckless leader of a score of conspiracies, former exile, ex-political prisoner. The eleven-year-old Gambetta was all for the liberal Cavaignac and thought Bonaparte's candidacy a tasteless joke; but democracy permanently disappointed him by electing Bonaparte on December 10 by more than four million votes.

Embracing the nephew as it once had the uncle, democracy

continued to be complaisant to Napoleon. The constitution had set the president's term at four years and forbidden reelection. A year before his term would end, on December 2, 1851 (it was the anniversary of Napoleon I's coronation and of his great victory at Austerlitz) Prince-President Bonaparte ordered out the army, rounded up the hundred-odd republicans he could not control, abolished the constitution of 1848, and proclaimed himself president for ten years. There was, inevitably, a plebiscite, and democracy approved by a vote of 7,440,000 to 646,000. When the lucky day rolled around again in 1852, Napoleon proclaimed himself Emperor Napoleon III. This time the plebiscite was 7,824,000 to 253,000. Marx's farce was consummated. The Second French Empire had taken only half the time to replace the Second Republic as the First Empire had to replace the First Republic. The lesson for Gambetta was that plebiscitary democracy was nothing but a tool of monarchy.

The Second Empire managed to make use of day-to-day democracy as well. Every adult male eligible voted every six years for members of the imperial Legislative Body. Of course, as Gambetta easily perceived when he was a republican student in the gaslit Paris of the 1860s, the number of voters did not matter very much. The ballot was not very secret; and, aided by the appointive bureaucracy that penetrated every cranny of the nation armed with draconian press and association laws, the government's "official candidates" nearly always won. The handful of republican legislators who beat these odds, including Gambetta himself in 1869, quickly discovered that not only they but the entire Legislative Body was constitutionally impotent. The Emperor allowed none of the cardinal powers of sovereignty to escape his grasp. He was also a very good politician; too good not to find the policy that appealed to every important constituency, or to do what a majority objected to. Unlike most emperors, Napoleon III also had the gift of avoiding imperialism. He did use a gratuitous military expedition against the Roman Republic in 1849 to help him outflank the French Assembly, but except in Mexico in 1867, he was wary of annexing territory and was content to leave the peoples of the world alone. Napoleon the Little, as Victor Hugo called him, seems in retrospect to have made only one mistake: He lost the Franco-Prussian War.

Or possibly two. Napoleon should have been able to prevent Gambetta's election from Belleville in 1869, but he didn't. The man who was to proclaim the end of the Bonapartes had, sometime in the 1860s, set himself the goal of resurrecting the French republic by using the Empire's democratic weapons against itself. In 1868, he had come out publicly against the *coup d'état* of 1851 while defending a journalist against press censorship. His election in 1869 from radical Belleville took place after he had pledged himself to a program written by the district's electoral committee, a program in which the whole future program of the Third Republic had been set down, a platform of conservative nightmares beginning with universal suffrage and continuing with anticlericalism, civil liberties, universal education, social equality, and an end to standing armies.[6] Most dangerous of all to Napoleon, could he have but seen it, was the fact that Gambetta was not a revolutionary. Accepting the Belleville platform was, like all his political acts before and after, both a call for radical change and an affirmation of peaceful legality. Moderate bourgeois to the core, Gambetta discovered in 1869 how to look like a revolutionary, donning the slightly ill-fitting motley of leftism soon to become the official costume of the Third Republic. This invention, "radicalism," was the key to getting rid and staying rid of kings.

When the Empire collapsed like a tea party in a windstorm on September 4, Gambetta was off the mark earlier than anyone else. Because the revolution was bloodless, he was innocent of the usual consequences of such events. By the sme token, however, he was still nothing but an orator. No one could have foreseen at this point that Gambetta would become the most effective executive in the Provisional Government, indeed the most effective administrator French republics could show since the fall of Robespierre. For two months, Gambetta incarnated the Government of National Defense—a war leader of peerless energy and decisiveness.

Without any confirmation by his colleagues in the new government, Gambetta began by riding over to the Ministry of the Interior in a carriage, occupying the office, and telegraphing to the officers of the whole imperial bureaucracy that he was their new commander. From then on he was completely in charge, so much so that by the end of the government's career it was being called Gambetta's dictatorship. (The actual chief executive, lest the name be entirely forgotten, was a general named Trochu.) His program was clear from that first afternoon: republicanization of the French magistracy, and war to the knife with Prussia so long as war was possible. In other words he would both purge the imperialists and at the same time saddle them with the responsibility for a defeat, while the republicans took credit for any victory.

On September 6, 1870 Gambetta gave the go-ahead to replace the district administrators of Paris and created sixty new National Guard militia battalions in the beseiged city. In the nation at large he made a clean sweep of all eighty-five departmental prefects between September 6 and 14, installing republican officers by the admittedly nonrepublican procedure of appointment. On the sixteenth, he was giving orders to them all to purge the monarchist municipal councils, set up municipal elections, and prepare for a constitutional convention. Only the war got in Gambetta's way. If the Prussians had not halted the process, he might have got his republic by sheer administrative fiat. Indeed, he was still replacing monarchists in the departmental councils and the ministries of finance and education months later, but Bismarck, himself a classic monarchist, complicated everything by refusing to treat with Gambetta's government. By September 25, Bismarck's armies had Paris so completely bottled up that the Minister of the Interior could communicate with the interior only by carrier pigeon. On October 7, Gambetta solved this problem by flying out of Paris and into legend aboard a military hot-air balloon.

By the time Gambetta had picked himself out of the trees at Amiens, however, it was too late to pick up the threads of his policy of republicanizing the French magistracy. Instead, he took over the War Ministry, and threw himself into the task of military defense.

As minister in two departments he was, if anything, even more decisive than he had been with only one. Like his hero, Danton, Gambetta called for mass mobilization in the face of the Prussian advance. He started by reorganizing the ministry, hiring a completely new set of deputy ministers, suspending the rules on pay and promotion, and firing half the general officers in the army. In a decree of October 14, 1870 he promoted a whole new cadre of officers. By November he had an entire new army facing the Prussians around Paris. It was not for lack of energy that the government was beaten, and Gambetta was right about the political gain, even after defeat. The armistice of January 28, 1871 was signed over his objections; and when the rest of the ministers opposed his attempt to exclude monarchists from the elected assembly Bismarck demanded, Gambetta resigned on the issue.

The man's whole performance in office was a *tour de force*, not only because of its clarity and passion, but also because of the genuine restraint and political subtlety that underlay it. If it is true, as Jules Simon said of his colleague in 1869, that "Gambetta and his friends . . . would be more authoritarian than the Empire if they replaced it," it is no less true that the ministry acted "without recurring to intimidation, without violating any law, and without exceeding its powers."[7] The firings were legal and their object was to pave the way for elective replacements, even in municipal posts which had not happened since 1794. Moreover, Gambetta resigned his ministries, without being pressured, at a time when great crowds in Bordeaux were urging him to become "dictator." He wrote:

> When France is free, it will be seen whether we are dictators, and if our greater passion is not to rejoin the commons from which we sprang, this commons, inexhaustible reservoir of all great, all noble thoughts, where each of us must reimmerse himself. It will then be apparent that, if I am possessed of the democratic passion which suffers not foreign invasion, I am also profoundly animated by the republican faith whose horror is dictatorship.[8]

A Solon rather than a Caesar, Gambetta also knew how to make his resignation serve his policy. Just as nothing could have been better for the republic's reputation in the fall of 1870 than Gambetta's energetic prosecution of the war, so nothing could have been more opportune in 1871 than his resignation. The timing of his exhaustion was as good as the timing of his speech on September 4, as good as if he had intended it. Like de Gaulle in 1940, Gambetta was able to avoid completely the onus for the most terrible defeat to date in French history, for the Republic as well as for himself. The founders of the Weimar Republic, as we shall see, would have done well to follow his example. When, after his resignation, the new National Assembly accepted the Prussian demand for Alsace-Lorraine, Gambetta accepted election to the Assembly from an Alsace district so that he might resign a second time, walking out theatrically, with other delegates from the lost provinces, when the transfer was ratified.

Again, one suspects more than luck in the fact that Gambetta, by resigning, took himself out of the picture at precisely the moment when the nation was about to split between city and country, left and right, the Paris Commune and the Versailles National Assembly. After the bloody civil war that succeeded the humiliating peace, only Gambetta was untainted by either. He alone could embody the myth of republican solidarity after the spring of 1871. It is also just possible that Gambetta saw this coming too. Partly as a result of his municipal elections directive of 1870, revolutionary city-republics—communes much like those of the 1790s—had been set up in Lyons, Marseille, and Toulouse in September. Extraordinary effort, soothing diplomacy, and some very careful appointments by Gambetta's Ministry of the Interior neutralized the challenge of these fiercely independent, armed left-wing governments before any blood was spilled. Though Paris had no Commune at that point, Gambetta himself had given the city, in the expanded National Guard, the means to declare and defend its independence, and he may well have reckoned that Paris would act soon in ways even he could neither suppress or mediate peacefully.

In any case, three weeks before Gambetta left office, besieged and starving Paris read its first socialist manifesto, the "red poster" of January 7, 1871. On March 3, after the armistice, the National Guard of Paris illegally elected the "Central Committee," its own Parisian government. On March 18, Parisians led by the Guard attacked a detachment of non-Parisian troops who were attempting to repossess their artillery on Montmartre heights. On that day was born the socialist republic known to history as the Paris Commune.

The Commune on which Gambetta was so studiedly neutral has gone down in half the world's history books as the great nineteenth-century preview of socialist government in the twentieth century. In many ways it deserves the title. One of its members, Pottier, wrote the "Internationale," still the anthem of all socialist movements from Portugal to Vietnam. The name Commune, stripped of medieval associations, did much to distinguish Marx's communism from all other socialisms. The Commune invented the "central committee," gave the red flag its permanent meaning, and pioneered the socialist mobilization of artists and women. Marx himself was in a position to back it immediately from the headquarters of the International Workingmen's Association in London. Its example was studied endlessly until, in 1917, one of those students, Lenin, provided an even better example.

Nevertheless, as Lenin himself pointed out in *State and Revolution* just before he took power, the Commune was much less socialist than the quaking middle classes thought it was. It left both the Bank of France and the Stock Exchange in business as usual. The nearest it came to a general redistribution of property was one week in the middle of April when it confiscated vacant housing, allocated abandoned factories to workers, redeemed property in the pawnshops, limited the working hours of bakers, and created a chain of municipal meat markets. By those standards, New York City was a commune in the 1980s. But then, of course, modern New York would have frightened a nineteenth-century bourgeois as profoundly as Paris did in 1871.

Lenin also recognized that the Commune was a poor excuse for a dictatorship of the proletariat. It was no less a republic than its enemy the National Assembly and not so very different from what Lenin called the "pigsty" of parliamentarism. That was a mistake Lenin did not make. In fact, the Bolshevik dictatorship he created in Russia had the effect, after 1917, of thoroughly obscuring the republican precedent set by the communards. The red flag of the Commune is one of the mementoes in Lenin's tomb, but a Lenin-style party dictatorship was made impossible by the Commune's divisions. Eighty-one members were elected to it in March 1871. All equal in rank and powers, they represented all twenty of the Paris administrative districts. In each of those districts elected councils sat to advise, direct, and if necessary recall them. They represented, moreover, most economic classes, even bourgeois businessmen. Once elected, they divided themselves into ten executive committees and proceeded to govern with energy, despatch, and robust republican argument. When they appealed to the nation at large, the program they offered was well-nigh utopian in its insistence on local autonomy. It would have made France into a confederation of independent municipal communes.

The Commune may have looked to a socialist future, but it was anchored in a Jacobin past. Declaring itself the enemy of capitalism, it left banks alone and reserved its most repressive measures for monarchist catholicism. The Commune was so conscious of its roots in the First Republic of Robespierre that it flew the flag, revived the journals, even sang the songs of 1792, and it dated its acts from the year 79 of the old Revolutionary calendar. In fact, before it was over, it had set up a second Revolutionary Tribunal and a second Committee of Public Safety. Outside of Paris the moderate republicans were hard put to distinguish what they meant by "the Republic" from what Paris meant by it, but they had to do it somehow, since the delegates to the National Assembly, elected on February 8, 1871 were two-thirds of them monarchists and would be only too pleased if they could identify all republicans as enemies of law, order, and property.

And so the civil war began: a monarchist Assembly which had surrendered to the monarch of Germany for the sake of peace and property against a city-republic which would make peace with neither princes nor property. Among the spectators, Otto von Bismarck, who had made the war so as to have his king crowned Emperor in the palace of Louis XIV, and Léon Gambetta, republican, ex-Minister of War, ex-Deputy from Alsace. Both expected to pick up the pieces. For a short time Bismarck did; but so, in the end, did Gambetta. Just as he had refused responsibility for surrender, he now refused responsibility for the bursting of the Assembly's troops into Paris and the machine-gunning of tens of thousands of fellow Frenchmen. At the end of what came to be called Bloody Week, when the last resistance broke at the Père Lachaise cemetery, and scores of communards were lined up against the wall and shot, Gambetta sat in the sun on the Biscay coast of Spain. He gave no speeches, he wrote few letters; the great firebrand was silent for months.

To be fair, he was completely hemmed in. Republicans who believed, as he did, in nationalism and resistance to Germany could not approve the Assembly's action. Republicans who believed, as he did, that France would not accept socialism, could not approve of the Commune. Gambetta's one hope was that the repression of Paris, even one ordered by a government containing republicans, would have the effect of weakening and discouraging the monarchists in the long run. His silence was essential and, once adopted, had to be absolute. This, too, was a political act, as extraordinary and clever a performance as his tenure at the Ministry of War.

It was, moreover, the classic act of a moderate. Gambetta's verve and passion effectively disguised the fact that he really did not like to see people killed—not even foreigners. He had the heart of an extremist, he could certainly sound like one, but he had the analytical coolness of a practical politician, the humor and sense of proportion of a born centrist. He knew what a risk the centrist takes in seeming coward, but he took the risk.[9]

The gamble eventually paid off, but in the meantime Gambetta paid a price for it. At the seashore, taunted by left and right, Gambetta felt frustrated, even sick. His great forward-thrusting black beard drooped. Friends said he aged ten years. No doubt his pleasure was intense when, on June 26, 1871 he crossed the border into France and threw himself into politics again with a key speech. On a platform of republican unity, support of the National Assembly's legitimacy, and opposition to nearly all its policies, Gambetta was elected to three different seats in the by-election of July 9, 1871 and with his usual bravado accepted the one from Paris. That fall he was again at the center of events, representing Belleville, which had been in May one of the most militant districts in the Commune, founding the newspaper *République française*, and leading the republican party.

It was here that comedy took over from tragedy in the drama of the founding of the Republic. How a chamber full of monarchists could write a republican constitution, how a president could lose the power of his office by a single, legal, act, how a tiny republican party could inherit the system designed for a Bourbon restoration, must be described in a different tone entirely. Nevertheless, here too, the central figure is Gambetta, and the extraordinary political skill of the leader of the minority party.

Republican leadership was a most difficult task. The National Assembly elected in February 1871 was, at 768 possible seats, the largest in the world. Multiple elections and the loss of Alsace-Lorraine reduced it somewhat but still only two hundred or so deputies were republicans. The five hundred-odd others all wanted a king. But which king? Only the answer to this question stood in the way of getting one. France's complicated history had left three dynasties on the beach, each with its own pretender, all irreconcilable. The Orléans had helped expel the Bourbons in 1792 and again in 1830. The upstart Bonapartes had replaced the Bourbons in 1803 and 1815, and helped throw out the Orléans in 1848. Unforgivable in a country where historical memories are long. In 1871 each dynasty had a candidate or two and a party in the Assembly. The senior Bourbons, called Legitimists, favored Louis XVI's great-nephew, Henri, Count of Chambord; the Orléanists favored his cousin the Count of Paris and his son the Duke of Aumale; the Bonapartists favored Napolean "Prince Impérial" or his father Napoleon III, now cultivating a garden in England.

The situation would have been pure farce if it had not been for the political seriousness, even sagacity, of all three parties. There were experienced and energetic men in all of them, as well as well-thought-out programs for such things as education, economic development, and administrative reform. Often they could agree on these programs, but the three kings, like King Charles's head, kept coming up. Two choices are a dilemma, but three are uncompromisable. An agreement between them would have made France a monarchy on the day after the February elections or at any time up to 1875 when the Assembly finally wrote a constitution. If they had agreed in 1876 or 1877 they might have made their monarchy (as in 1851) by a presidential coup d'état, but they couldn't and they didn't. As the Spartans with their two kings would have understood, the French believers in one-man rule stood in a relationship to each other that can only and ironically be described as perfectly republican.

The dash of farce was provided by legitimism. Legitimists and Orléanists agreed in 1871, and again in subsequent years, that Henri, the Legitimist candidate could go first and be followed, since he was childless, by the Orléanist candidate. Approached with this idea, the hapless Henri publicly proclaimed, however, that he could not become king unless France abandoned the tricolor flag and returned to the white fleur-de-lys banner of his ancestors. "Long live Henri," wrote a gleeful republican on hearing of this absolutely impossible condition; "He has made himself the George Washington of the French Republic."[10]

Helpless to find a king, the monarchists of the Assembly began to draw together on stopgaps. Henri was expected to die soon and if the Assembly could only outlast him it might then agree on an Orléanist king. On its fourth day, in fact, it had chosen an Orléanist as chief executive, old Adolphe Thiers, partly because it had to have someone to negotiate with the Prussians, and Thiers was there already talking to Bismarck. In its second week, the Assembly had given Thiers the foggy title of "Chief of the Executive Power of the French Republic," insisting however that the last two words did not give the game away, because in return Thiers had promised not to favor any particular form of government, and seemed to acquiesce in their idea of a temporary republic. Thiers however, was a tough old partisan who enjoyed power. A former Prime Minister of King Louis-Philippe, he liked his new job and was vigorous, at eighty, in exercising it, even to the extent of supervising the bloodbath in Paris. When Henri made himself unavailable by his flag declaration, the monarchists changed Thiers' title to "President of the French Republic." For his own part, Thiers could not help warming to such a system: "The republic," he said, "is the system which divides us least." And, he might have added, the regime which gives me most.[11]

Gambetta was resigned to Thiers, who played the game so well. At least Thiers put no obstacles in the way of Gambetta's Republican Union when, beginning with the very first by-elections, the party began its steady climb to a majority. Nor could Gambetta, like some republicans, complain of excessive vigor in the executive. So the former War Minister stuck to the complex task of building a republican party large enough to bring a republic out of this strangely constituted assembly. An excellent campaigner, he spoke everywhere in France, took credit for each new republican deputy, and set his party program with a precise eye on the balance in the Assembly, so as to draw Thiers in his direction.

The program was not very different from the one he had pledged at Belleville in 1869. The first and foremost demand was republican government democratically based on manhood suffrage. (This was the legacy of Robespierre, but Gambetta was too wise to praise him.) Second was a republican army, a national militia based on universal military training. Unlike a professional standing army it would be unusable by tyrants, and it would be no less terrible to the emperors of Germany. Third was universal, free, compulsory primary education. Schools would republicanize the French peasant who had so loved his church and his emperor. To this end, schools would be controlled by the republic itself rather than by the church; and this in turn implied a fourth demand, the separation of the church from the state, which since 1801 had established, protected, and paid it while submitting to its influence. So monarchist had the Catholic Church become that in Catholic countries, from 1848 to as late as 1940, it became almost impossible to be a republican without being anticlerical. Last and very much least for the practical bourgeois politician were radical proposals for an income tax and amnesty for the communards.

The program was radical enough to polarize the Assembly without frightening the monarchists into illegal violence. It pulled Thiers as far to the left as possible. The arrangement worked so well that it looked like collaboration and some whispered that Thiers was grooming Gambetta to succeed him. Nothing, however, suggests that Thiers wanted to resign or indeed that he believed he was ever going to die, so the rumor is probably just a fantasy of those who were unable to appreciate a pair of brilliant political performances. At any rate Gambetta continued to win, or at least take credit for winning, the by-elections; and Thiers, as Gambetta hoped, moved to capitalize on his success. Old Thiers could not accept the program but he could accept the regime, and in a speech in December 1871, startled the Assembly by asking it to give the republic a "sincere trial." It was a signal that he might be abandoning the promise of nonpartisanship he had made in February. Uneasy, the mon-

archists went to Henri, who renounced the tricolor flag a second
time. (Even working kings are apt to be bad at politics. Exiled kings
soar above even ineptitude.) In November 1872, Thiers smiled again
on the republic of which he was, in the absence of a constitution,
still president. "The Republic exists," he said hopefully; "It is the
legal government of the country."[12]

Again the monarchists went to Henri. Again he rebuffed them.
That same winter, Napoleon III had died. In their uneasiness, the
monarchists did the unexpected, they united to pass their third constitutional law, the Rivet Law of March 13, 1873 which further defined the powers of "President of the Republic." By this highly
republican law the monarchist Assembly made it impossible for
Thiers to speak to it without one day's prior notice and removed
his option of responding on the spot to any debate he might provoke. The act made it difficult for him to interfere with the work
of ministers of state and unconstitutional for him to block legislation. By the Rivet Law, essentially, the monarchists took away most
of the powers by which they had hoped the president of the Republic could install a monarchy because they were now afraid Thiers
would use them to install a republic instead. Since its effect was to
create the limited executive of classical republican theory, the move
was no less deeply ironic than its predecessors. It could only benefit
Gambetta, who had nothing to do with it, condemned it as
"puerile," and who, in fact was now calling for the Assembly to
dissolve itself.

In 1873, Thiers was left with only one major political weapon,
his resignation. He had already threatened it several times, aware
that having established his position near the exact center of a deeply
divided Assembly, it was unlikely his resignation would be accepted.
On one occasion he had actually resigned and the Assembly had
sent a committee to his house to urge him to stay on. On May 24,
1873, faced with a vote of censure from the monarchist majority,
Thiers resigned again, but this time, to his dismay, he was not recalled. He was succeeded as president of the Republic by one of
Napoleon III's generals, a convinced Bonapartist named Mac-
Mahon.

Nothing could have been more frustrating to republicans than
the construction of this republic. Until late in 1875, republicans
wrote not one jot of its constitution. Even a congenital optimist like
Gambetta, reassured by scores of by-election victories, was dis-
mayed by the election of a monarchist as president of the Republic.

He feared a coup d'état, and with good reason for several were meditated. MacMahon had made plain how pleased he would be to resign in favor of a king. During the recess of the Assembly in summer, 1873, monarchist committees, overt and covert, scurried around Europe trying to reach a compromise. The Orléanist pretender called on Henri in Austria. Henri himself came to Versailles in secret to see MacMahon about a coup. As usual, however, negotiations broke down. MacMahon was not only ponderous and prestigious, he had a curious, Roman reluctance to break the law. Henri, for his part, still wanted his white flag. The whole thing was a disappointment. When the Assembly met in November it passed another law giving the president a term of seven years. In this way it hoped that even if a republic had to be made, there would still be a monarchist in control of the government after the Deputies went home. Thus, the monarchists still had until 1880 to get a king—if they could only agree on one.

It was not to be. By 1874 Gambetta's party was no longer a faction; it was a juggernaut. It had won 126 out of 158 by-elections for the various kinds of republicans, all of them agreed on no king and universal (male) suffrage as a precondition of future French politics. More to the point, the monarchists, through the novel adventure of obeying laws they had made themselves, and working in close association with the radical republicans, had learned the very republican lesson that public argument and compromise are palatable; neither useless, nor unseemly, nor even unpatriotic. In June, Gambetta was able to defeat a bill that would have limited the suffrage by making the Right laugh at it. By July 23 the vote against the republic on a key bill was only 374 to 333.

It was true that the monarchists still held the initiative. In 1875 they used it at last, and, whether from cynicism or exhaustion or sheer inadvertence, used it to establish the Republic. On January 30 that year, by a vote of 353 to 352 on an amendment offered by an obscure Orléanist lawyer named Henri Wallon, the Third Republic was legally constituted in the following words:

> The President of the Republic is elected by the absolute majority vote of the Senate and Chamber of Deputies, meeting as the National Assembly. He is appointed for seven years and is re-eligible.

With the Wallon Amendment, the monarchists gave up their dream. A cascade of constitutional laws followed. By November 1875, five of them had filled in all the details of the three-part governmental structure outlined in the Amendment. They lasted, with very minor changes, until July 1940, a piecemeal constitution that is still the longest-lived in French history.

As the constitution took shape, Gambetta affected a critical stance and in public made as if to be drawn in the wake of events. Actually he was very pleased. As early as 1873, in a remarkable interview with the *New York Herald,* he had discussed in English constitutional proposals he could not possibly have then made in French. France, he said, had to have a single strong executive. Directories and committees of public safety seemed to have failed. To preserve republicanism, however, he wanted the executive to be elected by the legislature, so that future presidents could not do as Napoleons had done, turn the mandate of universal suffrage into a warrant for democratic monarchy. A second house would help too, he thought, and suggested a partially appointive Senate (this, at a time when the monarchists were calling for a Senate and Gambetta's party was offically opposed to one).

The constitution of 1875 fitted these 1873 specifications quite well and Gambetta on the campaign trail was very quick to defend it, though not of course in these impolitic terms. He even defended the conservative Senate before his old radical constituents in Belleville, predicting with his usual sagacity that a chamber formed of deputies from the municipal and district councils would inevitably educate rural France in the delights of "universal suffrage," and (here he echoed the still-remembered program of the Paris Commune) form a "Grand Council of French Communes."[13] The one thing Gambetta did not get, however, was the strong executive he had wanted in 1873; and once again, with paradoxical logic, it was the monarchists who denied it to him.

The monarchists, it will be remembered, had one last card to play: MacMahon. The president of France was slow-moving and law-abiding, but he was still a monarchist and the constitution of 1875 had given him, despite the chipping of the Rivet Law, great power. Like the president of the United States, he could command the army, appoint all officers and bureaucrats, and negotiate treaties. Unlike the American president, he could make most kinds of treaties on his own hook. Like the queen of England, he could appoint the government and he could, with the Senate's agreement, dissolve the Chamber of Deputies at any time before its four-year term was up. In 1877, MacMahon used both of these latter powers so ineptly that no subsequent French president ever used them again.

What happened was that Gambetta's indefatigable campaigning at last achieved victory. In the elections of 1876, the first under the new constitution, 340 republicans were elected to the Chamber of Deputies, a thumping majority of more than 150. MacMahon, however, could not get on with governments chosen from this majority, in fact, he did his best to find governments elsewhere. When the most left-wing cabinet he could tolerate failed to pass a press censorship law, MacMahon fired it in May 1877 and called on the monarchist Duke de Broglie to be Prime Minister. This was the famous *Seize Mai* (May 16) of popular history. MacMahon's act, which was quite legal, resembled too much the illegal acts of Charles X in 1830 and Louis Napoleon in 1849 not to appear as the prelude to the long-feared monarchist coup. Probably if the monarchists had agreed on their monarch there and then, such a coup would have occurred. As it was, MacMahon went on, still legally, to prorogue the Chamber of Deputies and let his new cabinet purge the bureaucracy.

Though Gambetta had advocated an executive with precisely these powers in 1873, his opposition was instant in 1877. His reaction, characteristically measured, precise, and centrist, was to call a meeting of the republican deputies in Paris and form a united front against the president which held through the entire crisis. There was to be no revolution, no disturbance. Only unconstitutional acts, if any, would be met by unconstitutional resistance. The budget committee, of which he was chairman, refused to appropriate funds until the government changed. Unable to govern, Broglie and MacMahon secured permission from the monarchist Senate to dissolve the Chamber on June 22. In a conscious reenactment of the Oath of the Tennis Court, the three hundred-odd republican deputies met outside the Chamber in the Hôtel des Réservoirs in Versailles, heard Gambetta and others proclaim a unified electoral strategy, and fanned out to the country to win the new elections. "It would be easy," Gambetta had said the year before, "to drape oneself in the toga of the ancient Romans and to die like Cato at Utica. What profit did the Roman Republic derive from Cato's death at Utica? I am fighting to the end while Caesar is alive or to prevent Caesar's return."[14]

The campaign was not over until October 28. In an extraordinary effort, reminiscent of the "democratic" Second Empire, Broglie's bureaucrats censored the press, presented official candidates, stopped meetings, and even arrested Gambetta himself for "insulting the President of the Republic." None of it helped much. Indeed no insult was equal to the aristocratic president's own gracelessness on the campaign trail. Shown a typhoid case in a hospital, he seems to have remarked, "Ah yes, typhoid. I had it myself once. It either kills you or leaves you an idiot." One verse that ran the grounds compared MacMahon to the English general Monck who had restored Charles II, but in French "the place Monck had" sounds like "the position of my ass".[15] The monarchists gained only forty seats by their efforts, and when the new Chamber, the French Long Parliament, met in November, Gambetta's republicans had a still huge majority of 119.

Would MacMahon do as Gambetta had challenged in the campaign, submit or resign? Outside this choice, he could do little that could be construed as constitutional. He could dissolve the Chamber again, or possibly, by dissolving it repeatedly, eliminate it. If he could divide the republicans by artful presidential patronage, he might get a government acceptable to him. He could also, constitutionally, fold the Chamber and Senate together into a National Assembly to revise the constitution, but he needed the Chamber's consent for that and even then he would be faced with a republican majority.

If MacMahon had been a clever politician any of these might have had possibilities. In a realm of illegal action, the cards were all his. He could order the army and the police to collect taxes and move against the Chamber, a move Gambetta so feared that he formed plans for clandestine resistance and a convocation of the Chamber in southeastern France. MacMahon, however, was no better a Napoleon than he was a Bonaparte. He refused to be responsible for illegal or unconstitutional action. Reduced to the original choice of submitting or resigning, MacMahon finally, on December 16, chose the former, asking the republican Dufaure to form a government. In a famous letter drafted by Dufaure, MacMahon explained that the President of the Republic was no longer responsible for the conduct of the government. This meant he accepted for all future Third Republic presidents the nonpartisan back-seat position of the British crown. Of all his goals, MacMahon had achieved only one. He had kept Gambetta, leader of the republican party (and incidentally the current lover of his titled sister-in-law) out of the prime ministership.

Gambetta did not show any disappointment. "How should I be dissatisfied?" he wrote; "It is the first victory gained by the legislative power over the proceedings of personal power, and that without any revolution, riot, or disturbance. That is a new event in our history and all due to Democratic institutions. If you are not satisfied you are very hard to please."[16] So it was, but the strong executive projected by Gambetta was dead. Soured by the struggle, MacMahon resigned a year before his term was up in 1879, when the republicans captured the Senate. Jules Grévy, one of Gambetta's colleagues, was constitutionally elected by the combined Chamber and Senate. Nor was Gambetta any more disappointed at not becoming President of France in 1879 than he had been at not becoming Prime Minister in 1877. Gambetta no longer wanted the office. Inch by inch and willy-nilly, MacMahon and the monarchists had whittled it down to a ceremonial instance.

For seventy years the French presidency remained as they had left it. Of the thirteen holders of the office from 1879 to 1940, no less than four resigned it, one of them because he found himself wandering incoherent one morning at a rural train station dressed in his pajamas. One, Félix Faure, died of a stroke in the arms of his mistress. Only two sought reelection, and of those that did not, three went on to the real post of power, *Président du Conseil,* or Prime Minister. As for Gambetta, rivals whose careers he himself had generously nurtured and for whom he had so often expended his magnificent campaigning energy, kept him out of the prime ministership until the end of his life. In 1881 he finally achieved his prize, held it for only seventy-seven days, and died the following year at the premature age of forty-four.

More than any other republican, Gambetta had been responsible for creating and maintaining the Third Republic. Each of his actions, proclaiming the regime, animating the National Defense, retiring over the treaty and the Commune, campaigning for his Republican Union and managing it in the National Assembly, endorsing the monarchists' constitution, and checkmating MacMahon had brought the Republic closer to fulfillment. His one defeat, on the strength of the executive, actually made the system more republican. With the career of this incorrigible moderate, the paradox of a republic made by monarchists was redeemed. The Third was now fully in the hands of republicans, most of them disciples of Gambetta.

What would they do with it? A great deal, in fact. The whole history of the Third Republic so clearly reflects Gambetta's values that at times one has to think of him as a kind of tutelary saint, watching with his one good eye benignly over the repeated hair-breadth escapes and contingent salvations of his creature. They buried him in the Pantheon, which is the nearest thing to divinization French republicans can offer, and the Belleville program of 1869, though one conservative disciple left it out of Gambetta's collected works, continued to guide republicans of every stripe.

The antirepublican right tried twice to reestablish monarchy, once with Boulanger's coup in 1889, and once, in a dreadful preview of that democratic monarchy called fascism, with the Dreyfus Affair in 1898. Each time republicans put aside what had seemed a life-and-death struggle among themselves to save the arena in which they fought. Two of the greatest of them, Radical Georges Clemenceau and Socialist Jean Jaurès, spent almost their whole careers locked in combat over the meaning of the "social equality" of the Belleville Program, the choice of whether the Republic was to be a capitalist tool or the prize of a workers' revolution. Gambetta, in 1871, had avoided that choice by keeping silent during the Commune. Jaurès and Clemenceau avoided it by never forcing it. "After all, Jaurès," said Clemenceau as the Socialists were bringing down his government in 1909, "you are not God." To which Jaurès replied, "Nor are you the Devil."[17] The man who was not God and the man who was not the Devil were allies only once, but that once was decisive. They saved the Republic from the monarchist enemies of Captain Dreyfus.

Clemenceau, whom Gambetta named mayor of Montmartre during the Commune, was first to make his mark. Until Jaurès was elected to the Chamber in 1893 (an election in which he himself was defeated) he led the fight for republicanism from the left. Entering the Chamber of Deputies in 1876, he took the lead immediately by calling for amnesty for the communards, which an embarrassed Gambetta had found impolitic. Clemenceau had not supported the Commune and liked nothing about it except its contrariness and its nationalism, which he shared. Without a shred of Gambetta's charm or any of his covert genius for compromise, Clemenceau soon came to embody that part of republicanism which Marx called *petit-bourgeois* democracy. Founding the large and long-lived Radical Party, he led that army of small businessmen and local professionals who more and more provided the elite of French republicanism. Individualist to a fault, viciously anticlerical, ultrapatriotic, intolerant of big business and big labor both, they coined the slogan, "No enemies to the left!" and strove manfully with its consequences.

Clemenceau himself, tall and grim-looking with vaguely Asiatic eyes and a huge handlebar mustache, was known as "The Tiger." He had fallen for Thaddeus Stevens at twenty-five and, master like him of short sentences and savage wit, he became like him the great breaker of governments. His work helped prevent the Boulanger coup in 1889, and toppled cabinets in 1881, 1882, 1885, 1887, and 1905. Indeed, he gave himself the credit for the fall of his own ministry in 1909. He was harder still on presidents, undermining an already nugatory office with slogans like "Vote for the stupidest!" Of his own candidate, Pams, in the election of 1913, he said loudly, "It's not a name; it's a noise!"[18] This too was self-defeating, for when he ran for president himself in 1920, he was beaten by the aforementioned lunatic in the pajamas.

Clemenceau's two greatest achievements in government helped solidify in France the precept that although nationalism is entirely republican, imperialism is not. As Prime Minister in 1917, Clemenceau overbore the military professionals, defined defeatism as treason, and diligently earned the title Father of Victory. As leader of the opposition in the 1880s however, he consistently opposed the growth of the French Empire in Africa and Southeast Asia. In 1884, when the second Ferry government moved an army into Tonkin, a faraway place which we now call North Vietnam, Clemenceau accused Ferry of high treason, secret executive action, and risking an interminable land war in Asia. When the vote of confidence came, Clemenceau had brought down another government.

Even Clemenceau's great enemy, Jaurès, could agree with this aspect of his policy. In fact one of the reasons he joined the successful effort to bring down the Clemenceau government in 1909 was because Clemenceau in office was not so pure as Clemenceau in opposition—his government had occupied Morocco. To Clemenceau, the Socialists, who had been trickling into the Chamber since the 1880s, were statists and collectivists. Republicanism is against the Socialist principle, which he called, "the abandonment of individualism . . . the abandonment of the Rights of Man proclaimed in the French Revolution."[19] In equally republican language, Jaurès, who had written a *Socialist History* of that Revolution, accused the Radicals of a new form of monarchism. "Big capital is king," he said in 1894, "the most powerful and the last of kings."[20] Radicals, he argued, refuse to try to dethrone it, and are therefore not republicans but constitutional monarchists.

He was then leader of the United Socialist Party. He had helped to write its program: ceaseless agitation, nonparticipation in "bourgeois governments," preparation for the "proletarian revolution," devotion to the ideas and *praxis* of Marx. One might expect such a man to be sharp, divisive, possibly conspiratorial, like his coleader Jules Guesde. In fact Jaurès was the opposite. Where Clemenceau was realistic, clipped, and unforgiving, Jaurès was idealistic, orotund, and overwhelmingly benign. Like Gambetta he was a southerner. Like Gambetta, too, and unlike Clemenceau, he was a maker of parties, blocs, and coalitions. Whether in the French Socialist Party, the Workers' International, or the Chamber of Deputies itself, Jaurès was the conciliator, the builder of bridges. A professed supporter of violent revolution, Jaurès's rhetoric was polarizing, but his important acts were not. When the Radicals first formed a cabinet in 1895, it was Jaurès who saw to it that the Socialist Deputies did not get in their way.

When the famous *Affaire Dreyfus* broke out in 1897–98, the Socialists were at first neutral. What mattered it to the class struggle if an aristocratic officer corps condemned a bourgeois captain to its secular hell on Devil's Island? Justice, insisted Jaurès's colleague Guesde, was social not individual; this was a family quarrel in the ruling class.

Reluctantly, Jaurès hewed to the party line for the moment. For Clemenceau, however, Dreyfus was the issue of a lifetime. Here was a pure case of individual rights, a defenseless Jew railroaded out of the army by catholics, monarchists, and statists of every stripe. Even Clemenceau's intense nationalism took a back seat to the fight for fairness and truth. *Fiat justitia ruat coelum*—"Let justice be done though the heavens fall." He was then out of office, and full-time editor of the morning paper *L'Aurore*, and on November 1, 1897, he called in an editorial for the case to be reopened, a leader of the hounds in what was to become France's greatest political crisis since the *Seize Mai*. It was Clemenceau who printed, and gave the title to Zola's *J'Accuse* in January 1898.

Chafing under the Socialist ban, Jaurès seized the opportunity to declare for Dreyfus in his paper, the *Petite République*, pennypress descendant of Gambetta's party organ. The Socialists were at

first outraged, and so were Jaurès's old constituents, who voted him
out of office in the 1898 general election, but Jaurès refused to accept the verdict and set out on an eventually successful campaign
to win his party over. He spoke, he wrote articles, finally he carried
his motion at a raucous meeting of the Socialists on October 16,
1898. At the beginning of the following year, he had the satisfaction
of seeing a Socialist join the government, against all the rules, as a
token of solidarity against further coup attempts from the monarchist and antisemitic protofascists on the far right.

Guesde was right, Marx would have greatly disapproved. In a
great industrial country with millions of unprotected workers living
near the margin of subsistence, one Jewish victim on Devil's Island
was of no importance. The point should have been to seize the state
rather than to decentralize and tame it. Was Jaurès, as some suspected, too much a republican and hardly a Marxist at all? Could
a man be a Marxist who was too tolerant to stop his wife from going
to church or his daughter from making her first communion? It may
be, as some historians of socialism have suggested, that this Gam-
bettalike flourish of Jaurès's in the Dreyfus Affair doomed the long-
run revolutionary hopes of French and European socialism, but that
is hypothetical, like a genuine workers' republic. What can be said
for certain is that the alliance personified by Jaurès and Clemenceau between the Socialist and Radical heirs of Gambetta's Republican Union saved the Third Republic from its strongest
enemies. It also gave what we now call Social Democracy an ineradicable stain of republican humanism which, in the persons of
many Willi Brandts and Golda Meirs of our century, it still retains.
"We want revolution," said Jaurès to the International in 1899, "but
we don't want perpetual hatred."[21]

In extremis in 1917, republicans turned to Clemenceau as they
had in 1870 to Gambetta to win the war with Germany. Jaurès, who
had tried to prevent the war through socialist internationalism, was
assassinated by a monarchist in 1914. Clemenceau won his war, but
the cost was very high. First the Republic had to submit temporarily
to one-man rule. To maintain its historic and vital link with nationalism, it sacrificed hundreds of thousands of lives and with them
much of its intelligence and spirit. Subsequent governments acquiesced in nearly every revision Germany demanded in the Treaty
of Versailles. Within France the alliance adumbrated in 1898 between ancient monarchism and modern fascism, reemerged, but

the remedy of a Radical-supported Socialist government in 1936 panicked the bourgeois Frenchman, accomplishing little. As the Thirties wore on, the Senate became more obstructive than even MacMahon might have wished, governments grew more and more fragile, and with them republicanism itself sank into contempt. Prime Ministers began to rule as Clemenceau had in 1918, by executive decree.

When the French defenses broke before the German army in June 1940, the Republic broke as well. On July 10, in the southwestern resort town of Vichy, the Senate and Chamber of Deputies became, as they had been in 1875, a National Assembly. Then, legally and constitutionally, they gave their powers under the 1875 constitution, including the power to write a constitution, to one man, Philippe-Henri Pétain, who with Clemenceau's help had become a hero of the First World War. The face of Liberty, whom the French call Marianne, left the coins of France, together with her 1792 motto, Liberty, Equality, Fraternity. In their place were three new talismans, "French State," "Work, Family, Fatherland," and the profile of an aged Marshal of France in an army hat. The Third Republic had lost its battle with the new industrial economy. Capital had brought back monarchy.

Fascism's revival of monarchy belongs to another chapter and, despite its invention by the Frenchmen Sorel and Maurras, to the history of Germany. Happily it turned out to be temporary everywhere, no less so in France, which is now a republic again (though with a much more powerful presidency). The history of the Third Republic, however, remains unique in the history of republics. During its long, pioneering grapple with the Marxian tides of class war, its continued survival taught that a kingless republic was as viable as a parliamentary monarchy and no less equal to the classic republican task of transforming into politics the serried forces of civil war. Its success in 1918 proved that authoritarian monarchy, as practiced in Germany, Austria, and Russia, was less effective than generations had been brought up to believe. By repeatedly turning potential violence into argument, it proved Gambetta's original theory that it was republics and not monarchies that could best safeguard order and legality. "These party fights in Parliament," said Clemenceau in 1893, "which people tell you are sterile, let me assure you that they are creative. . . . These fights which seem so petty because of our personal pettiness, are grand because of the ideals which are at issue. Never condemn them; they are the life of nations. . . . We have inherited them from the past, we will bequeath them to the future."[22]

The example of the world's first parliamentary republic continues to be instructive, especially in the United States. The constitution of 1875 is a century younger than ours and it may turn out to have been better. In this, as in other matters, the lesson must be Gambetta's: "I deny the absolute everywhere, and so you can well imagine that I am not going to recognize it in politics."[23]

12

Gustav Noske
The Reluctant Republic of Weimar

THE GERMAN REPUBLIC was proclaimed in Berlin at about 2 P.M. on November 9, 1918 by one of the Kaiser's ministers, Philipp Scheidemann. Hearing that the radical socialist Liebknecht was about to proclaim the dictatorship of the proletariat from the balcony of the royal palace down the street, Scheidemann interrupted his lunch to address the crowd at the Reichstag building. When he got back his soup was much cooler, but Scheidemann's party colleague Friedrich Ebert, who had been Prime Minister for the past two hours, was in a flaming rage. "You have no right," he shouted, "to proclaim a republic!"[1]

Of course he didn't. Neither had Gambetta on the night of September 4, 1870; yet Gambetta's republic survived for seventy years, Scheidemann's for only a dozen. Why? The German right had a glib answer. The Republic, they said, was *undeutsch*—un-German—and on this point at least they were indeed right. The fact that West Germany and to a lesser extent East Germany are now republics has little to do with November 9 and is now attributed by most historians to the generation-long chain of catastrophes which began there. Ending with the Allied occupation, these events were so uniquely devastating that the monarchical idea was extirpated from a country which had been the most fertile soil in Europe for monarchy for more than ten centuries.

The German republic proclaimed by Scheidemann on November 9, 1918, the regime that came to be known as Weimar, was as premature, as reluctant, and indeed as doomed as Ebert's outburst made it seem on the day it was born. Its strongest character, Gustav Noske, who filled, like Gambetta, the post of Minister of War, succeeded only in conjuring up the all but demonic forces that destroyed it. When it fell, its replacement, installed under Weimar's own constitution, turned out to be the worst of all monarchies from the standpoint of human rights—a democratic dictatorship. The history of this republic, as has been so often written, is a history of failure. But then what could be more essential to the history of republics than a republican failure in our own century.

Ebert, Scheidemann, and Noske, the nearest we have to founding fathers of Weimar, were leaders of the German Social Democratic Party, the largest socialist party in Europe and favorite of the German-born Karl Marx. The SPD, as it was called by its initials in Germany, represented an enormous working class in one of the newest and greatest of the world's industrial states. On paper, the party was democratic, socialist, and republican. It demanded universal suffrage, it preached (but rarely practiced) class war, and it refused to take office in bourgeois cabinets despite its enormous strength in the German parliament. It hated the military system, attacked imperialism, and called for a defensive militia. It made a show of scorning the monarchy and had declined in 1903 and again in 1909 to allow its leaders to go to an audience with the Kaiser.

Nevertheless, the SPD's leaders, born after 1866 when the Second Reich was set up, had imbibed monarchy with their mother's milk, not to mention their schoolbooks, and were, as events were to show, not socialist revolutionaries at all. For them, as for the French in 1792, the republic was theoretical only. The Germany they grew up in was not only an empire, but a federation of twenty-three separate monarchies. So proud were the Germans of one-man rule that one of the few questions they ever raised about it was whether states like Hesse or Bavaria should or should not give up their dukes and kings in favor of the German emperor. The only real republican force in Germany was the circumstantial one of division into several monarchies, but even here one of the monarchies in the federation, Prussia, was so big it could dominate almost any combination of the others. Both constitutionally and in terms of armies and populations, Prussia was what the men of Rhode Island had feared Virginia might become in 1787.

For young Gustav Noske, growing up in the heart of Prussia, the atmosphere was the most monarchical of all. The honored historians of the day all suspected that the establishment of the Prussian kingdom and the German empire was due to the operations of divine providence. This was a difficult suspicion to get rid of, since at almost every turn for a thousand years the republican forces in European history had been overmastered in Prussia as they had been in most of Germany by those which tended to monarchy. In Noske's schoolbooks, Caesar loomed larger than Brutus, and in German history Switzerland was excluded from the German *Reich* or empire.

So were the city-republics of Italy and Flanders. Of the great city-republics still included only the Hanse remained free, three free cities in a federation of twenty-three monarchies. All the thousands of other medieval communes, including powers like Nürnberg and Augsburg, had been weakened by war and depression and absorbed into neighboring principalities. The Reformation had not strengthened them. In Germany it had meant little more than the making of princes. Even Calvinism, arriving as the personal creed of dynasties like the Hohenzollern instead of as the fighting faith of a revolutionary class, had been monarchist east of the Rhine. The whiggism of barons and parliaments which underlay the English Revolution in Milton's time had failed in every German state except Württemberg, Mecklenburg, and Baden. Neither bureaucracy, nor court, nor estate had ever overruled a king of Prussia. As for the French Revolution, it had come to Germany led by a foreign monarch, Napoleon. On the one hand it was an affront to nascent German patriotism; on the other, a model for modern monarchs. If it destroyed the First Reich, it was only to clear the way for the Second.

Even in 1848, rising in revolution all over Germany, the Germans had not been republicans. They offered the crown of their newly fashioned state to King Friedrich Wilhelm IV of Prussia, who refused it on the spot because it came from commoners instead of princes. In Germany, nothing came from below. From above, on the monarch's own initiative, came everything from the industrial revolution itself to democratic measures in advance of any in Europe, including universal (male) suffrage in 1866 and workers' old age and disability insurance in 1889.

In Noske's boyhood, German history began with Charlemagne's ninth-century conquest of the Saxons, in political terms a replacement of limited tribal monarchy by one far less limited and more rational. Charlemagne in effect rectified the failure of Caesar and his successors to conquer the German tribes in the first century B.C. as they had the Swiss. Until the ninth century one could argue, indeed Tacitus did argue, that the Germans were republicans, but not afterward. Charlemagne was king of both what became France and of what became Germany, but in France the extinction of Charlemagne's line marked a wholesale reduction in the powers of monarchy there. In Germany, a proud professor would be sure to point out, new dynasties revived monarchy under Charlemagne's old titles *rex* (king) and *imperator* (emperor). By the tenth century the Holy Roman Emperor of the German Nation had reconquered the Rome where his titles originated and made himself the first monarch of Christendom, the very type of sacred medieval monarchy. In the Middle Ages nostalgia for the old Roman Empire spawned hopes for a Europe-wide monarchical government to be built, the professors underlined, by German kings. The symbol of the eagle and the title of Caesar, Kaiser in German, had begun even under medieval conditions, to fit the Ottos and Heinrichs of the Saxon and Salian dynasties.

For German schoolboys, the Middle Ages was the era of the First *Reich*, a German word meaning both kingly rule and territorial empire. They were taught to lament that the centrifugal forces associated with its great size had prevented this Reich from carrying through to the twentieth century. They were taught to deplore the machinations of that other great medieval monarch, the pope, and the separatist ambitions of the territorial nobility, which, together with the insolence of the Italian cities and the occasional failure of brilliant dynasties to produce an heir, doomed the First Reich to disintegration after the thirteenth century.

To learn German history in the 1870s and 1880s was to learn that the Renaissance, the Reformation, and the Thirty Years War had been almost unmitigated disasters for the German nation, defeating the unity of the Reich and mocking the motto of its new dynasty of Habsburg (AEIOU, initials in Latin and German of "The Universe is Subject to Austria"). It was to learn how unlucky the

Reich had been to institute the Electoral College by which three bishops and four great princes called *Kurfürsten* gained the right to choose the emperor, how unfortunate it was that the imperial parliament, the *Reichstag,* had made it impossible for emperors to raise an efficient army or get a reliable tax income, and how tragic it had been that France, Spain, Sweden, and despised Poland had reduced a dismembered Reich to servility and starvation in the Thirty Years War.

A Prussian student like Noske would learn that there was only one bright spot in German history between 1300 and 1600, that the disintegration of the old Reich had made opportunities for monarchy within its constituent states. The failure of kaisers made room for kings and queens. The Reformation, they were told, divided Germany, but as each prince adopted Lutheranism he gained a power, later made explicit in the Peace of Augsburg, in 1555, to run the church himself and to force all his subjects to join it. With the conversion of the Kurfürst of Brandenburg, Joachim II of the house of Hohenzollern, to Lutheranism on November 1, 1539, the glorious rise of Prussia was allowed by the professors to begin.

Prussia's was a history so monarchical that even some Germans had no taste for it, thought most of their own state histories showed similar developments. The fact was that none of the "new" and later "absolute" monarchs of the period 1500 to 1789 became so absolute as the kings of Prussia. Bourbons and Stuarts could only dream of the power that was accumulated by the Hohenzollerns. Teachers swelled with pride as they told how the Great Kurfürst Friedrich in the 1640s and 1650s had created an unconstitutional standing army, how he had drafted it among the peasants and quartered it on the now weakened towns. With a patriotic flourish, they would describe how this or that Friedrich had used the army to collect taxes by military execution, defied and swept away local institutions province by province, coopted the local nobility (*junkers* in Prussia) as his salaried colonels and bureaucrats, sentenced persistent opponents to death for treason, and consigned city councils and parliaments to the dustbin of history.

A pious pause would be followed by anecdotes about the energy, efficiency, and modernity of the old Hohenzollerns, Calvinists since 1613, possessed by a sense of duty that would have done credit to Mather and Milton. The brilliant Great Elector, starting with no army and no income, learns in Holland the Machiavellian skills that enable him to first befriend and then defeat the French, the Swedes, the Austrians, and finally his own Estates. The dour Friedrich Wilhelm I, never out of uniform, accumulating tax income from a dozen different unconstitutional sources, takes time out from drilling his grenadiers to smash an inefficient postillion over the head with his cane. The sleepless Friedrich der Grosse, an atheist Calvin, rises at 6 A.M. to write the day's orders to his bureaucrats, a shining example to the world of "enlightened despotism." Even the feckless Friedrich Wilhelm III, defeated by a French revolutionary army, appoints a minister to tell him "Your majesty must do from above what the French have done from below."

How privileged one is, a teacher would say, to live in the great days when a king of Prussia has founded the old Reich again, aided by that flower of the long coopted junker nobility, Otto, Prince Bismarck. Consider the skill, the energy, the courage of this great man, who became the king's chancellor not long before you were born. In 1862 good King Wilhelm I despaired of getting rid of the citizen militia and collecting an army subsidy from the Prussian parliament (parliament and militia both, alas, revived under the impact of the French Revolution). When the king contemplated (God forbid) his abdication on the issue, Bismarck threw himself into the breach, accepted the office of Chancellor, defied the parliament, and collected the tax, just as the Friedrichs and Wilhelms had done before the French Revolution interrupted the course of progress. The army was raised and paid, and everyone knows what the old king did with that army. In three short glorious wars, Prussian arms defeated Denmark, Austria, and at last France, welding the scattered monarchies of Germany into the Second Reich, proclaimed in the palace of the enemy Louis XIV in 1871.[2]

Such was the history Noske learned in youth and that his Social Democratic colleague Landsberg read aloud to his wife in the evenings. The pre-war period in which they achieved their careers only demonstrated how well the history had been learned. In the 1900s the monarchism of Germany was so highly developed and militant that it inspired republicans even in the neutral United States with fear and repugnance. The Kaiser, Wilhelm II, had all the pretensions of his Hohenzollern ancestors, but none of their competence and little of their Calvinist sense of responsibility. He called himself the *Allerhöchster*—All-Highest. A bronze tablet memorialized a bird as the "Fifty-thousandth creature to fall before the All-Highest." He dressed his palace guard in thirty-seven different uniforms including the tricorns of Frederick the Great. He dressed himself in silver helmets surmounted with the black Prussian eagle and long white feathers. His inadequacy, like his famous withered arm, he swathed in the dynastic colors of black, white, and red.

Convinced by the same history Noske had learned in school, he described the Hohenzollerns as stewards of God. Of himself he asserted, "There is only one master in the Reich and that is I, and I shall tolerate no other." After firing Bismarck in 1890 he avoided choosing, as previous second-rate Hohenzollerns had done, a Richelieu of his own, and exercised his nearly absolute power unassisted. One of the more successful things he did with his power, by his own repeated admission, was the selection of his wife's hats. On becoming Kaiser he addressed not the German people, but the army, which swore loyalty to no state or constitution but to the Kaiser alone. "We belong together," he said. To recruits the Supreme War Lord asserted, "When your Kaiser commands you to do so you must shoot at your fathers and mothers."[3]

The first casualty of Wilhelm's personal direction of affairs was the nonaggression pact with Russia. The second was the neutrality of England. Ordering an expansion of "my navy," he acquired the colonial empire Bismarck had viewed with suspicion. It was the Kaiser personally who promised to secure Austria against Russia when she marched an army into Serbia in 1914. When Wilhelm finally did accept a Richelieu (essentially through sheer ineptitude) it was a general of the army, Erich Ludendorff; and Ludendorff, merely by exercising the Kaiser's constitutional powers, became from 1917 to 1918 dictator of the Reich such as even Hitler would not be until months after his appointment as Chancellor. Ludendorff was in charge of wages, prices, food supply, transport, and foreign policy. He in effect hired and fired two Chancellors. Under Article 68 of the imperial constitution, Ludendorff could and did suppress speech, press, and assembly. Even in Russia where it was tempered by incompetence, monarchy never reached such heights.[4]

As a school for republicans the Second Reich had been a disaster. The bourgeois liberals of 1848 and 1862 had long ago been won to monarchy by Bismarck's success in founding it. Even the proletarian Social Democrats had been changed by it. One branch of the party was in fact founded by a monarchist, one Ferdinand Lassalle, who agreed with Bismarck that the state could and should supply the wants of the workers. Lassalle's influence was eventually minimized, but the empire continued to twist the party. From 1878 to 1890, the SPD was under a legal ban based on the unsupported charge that they had had a hand in two assassination attempts on the Kaiser; but the opportunity for heroic resistance was missed when the party dissolved itself two days before the ban went into effect and allowed its exigencies to help make the SPD the most authoritarian party in Germany. When it emerged triumphantly from the ban in 1890, it was, with thirty-five seats in the Reichstag, the most powerful socialist party in Europe and one of the most powerful in the Reich.

In theory it was more Marxist, too, than ever before, but it was no longer either internally or externally republican. As party leader August Bebel wrote to Engels in 1891, "To raise the republic as a goal is not possible under our German conditions."[5] It was too frightening to get German votes, more frightening in fact than the dictatorship of the proletariat. The first postban platform of the SPD, the Erfurt Program of 1891, demanded everything in Marxism except the republic. The SPD was even ambivalent about parliamentarism, anemic though it was in the Reichstag, and considered the use of it little more than a tactic.

Being legal after twelve years had effects on the party which seem in retrospect to have been even worse than those of being banned. Within a decade or so after 1890, the SPD leadership, still proclaiming the revolution of the working class, had in reality ceased to expect it and probably hoped it wouldn't be necessary. The party paper *Vorwärts* had begun to censor radical voices within the party. The party executive had begun to overrule the party congress. Revolutionary theory was adopted, revolutionary tactics, like the general strike, rejected. The party became reformist, or, in the byword of its most famous internal debate, "revisionist."

Gustav Noske, who had worked in a kiddie-car factory since the age of fourteen, had joined this remarkable organization in his twenties through the carpenters' union. By 1900, he had been editor of two of its now legal newspapers in the two centers of old Prussia, Brandenburg and Königsberg. In 1902, in the party's service, he had spent three months in jail for sedition, long enough to read *Das Kapital* at last, and to disdain it. In February 1906, at the age of thirty-seven, he was elected deputy to the Reichstag from the Revisionist center of Chemnitz, and on April 25, 1907 he made a speech, his third as a deputy, which in many ways typifies what socialism had become in the unreconstructedly monarchical state of Germany.

As in 1862, the debate was on the military budget. In the tense era of the Morocco crisis and the naval arms race, harbingers of World War I, the Reichstag was being asked as usual to rubber-stamp the Kaiser's demands for "my" army and navy. The Social Democrats, famous for opposing "militarism" were preparing as usual to vote against them *en bloc*. Proudly, the twenty-eight-year-old Noske rose to protest the patriotism of the Social Democratic Party of Germany. Disarmament he called a bourgeois fantasy: "We have always demanded an armed nation." While opposed to conquest, "We will resist [another nation] with just as decisive action as any of the gentlemen seated on the right. . . ." Noske had called, as historian Carl Schorske neatly put it, "for a freer society in order to produce a stronger state."[6]

The speech was a sensation. Noske's words tended to remove any republican significance from his party's vote against military expenditure, and a "Noske debate" proceeded in the SPD which helped pave the way for the party split of 1917. Defending himself before the SPD Congress in Essen that year, Noske pointed out that nothing he had said contradicted party handbooks and complained of being pushed too far to the left to collect votes. He reaffirmed his long-standing support of Germany's acquisition of colonies, and was delighted when the Congress in the end supported him and silenced the radicals.

It should not be very surprising that on August 4, 1914, ninety-one of the ninety-two Reichstag deputies of the German Social Democratic Party, including Gustav Noske, voted for the military budget that made possible German attacks on France, Belgium, and Russia. Nor is it surprising that the SPD speech on this occasion was given by Hugo Haase, a radical who had spoken against the budget in the party caucus the day before; or that the one successful dissenter, Kunert, managed his feat only by sneaking out of the Reichstag chamber while the votes were being counted.

The Social Democrats had become, as historian Klaus Epstein has written, a tragic case. They could not seriously plan revolution without losing their tactical position, or make one without losing their lives in a vain struggle with superior forces. They could not collaborate with the monarchy for fear of losing their soul; and they could not avoid all the alternatives without losing all of these things. The conditions of existence in a monarchy that really worked, and had worked for centuries, neutralized the largest potentially republican force in Germany. In 1917–18, when the world east of the Rhine began to explode in revolution, the German Social Democrats were all but paralyzed. Beginning with Karl Liebknecht and Rosa Luxemburg, the radicals and revolutionaries had begun splitting with the party in 1915. Some went to jail for plotting strikes in wartime while party leaders Ebert and Scheidemann visited the front and enjoyed officers' hospitality. Noske made strident speeches against Russia both before and after its communist revolution. Meanwhile, because of the monarchy's total control of the press and the army (acquiesced in by the SPD leadership) only a handful knew that Germany was about to be defeated on the Western Front.

The shock when this information was revealed to the public beginning in October 1918 was all the more profound for being completely unprepared for. One immediate result was that the twenty-three monarchs of Germany toppled like tenpins, from Kaiser Wilhelm, King of Prussia, to His (English) Royal Highness Charles Edward, *Herzog* (Duke) of tiny Saxe-Coburg und Gotha. A second result was a naval mutiny at Kiel and a mass refusal by the army to execute any orders to advance. Even Ludendorff had resigned on October 26. The sudden and massive discrediting of all the key elements in the grand apparatus of German monarchy would have seemed to any republican the signal for a total and almost bloodless revolution.

In fact Germany did have a revolution. She also got something called a republic, and a democratic one to boot, led by the SPD. We shall have to return to that revolution, for it is very clear from the history of the Weimar regime that issued from it that something went wrong with that revolution. Something else happened in those turbulent months from October 1918 to August 1919 besides the apparent discrediting of monarchy, some deep failure of the republican forces, or success of the monarchic. Unless the roots were poisoned we cannot account for the difference between Noske's republic and Gambetta's in the flower.

For the difference was profound. Within a year after Germany's first president, Friedrich Ebert, proclaimed the constitution written by the National Assembly at Weimar, a monarchist army had driven the government from its capital. The Kapp Putsch failed, it is true, but the monarchist government installed in Bavaria at the same time lasted for years. By 1925, a major leader of every major republican party had been found guilty of treason or corruption by a German court, including President Ebert himself. Many had been assassinated by monarchists, including Erzberger of the Catholic

Center Party in 1921, Rathenau of the Democrats in 1922, Eisner and Haase of the Independent SPD, and Luxemburg and Liebknecht who had founded the German Communist Party, all in 1919. The murderers by and large faced judges who were as nostalgic for monarchy as they were and most were sentenced to less than a year in prison or allowed to escape punishment completely.

Restoration of the old monarchy was indeed blocked in Weimar Germany, but by the fall of 1930, a kind of government was established which so exactly duplicated the forms of the Hohenzollern Reich that the distinction between restored and new monarchy becomes, for the political scientist, meaningless. Three years later, as we shall see, came democratic dictatorship.

How did this happen? On the surface, right up until 1933, the regime was a federal, democratic, parliamentary republic. There was a national parliament. One democratically elected chamber with fairly equal geographic constituencies made law, and a second chamber with representatives of the seventeen state governments had a suspensive veto. There was a chief of state with the same title and roughly the same duties as the French president, but elected by the more democratic method of universal suffrage (including women). There was a supreme court with the responsibility of judicial review. Under normal circumstances, as in France, a member of the lower chamber would be called by the president to form a cabinet with executive powers. He would do so by setting a program which might attract the support of several political parties, choose leading members of these parties as cabinet ministers, and then present the program to be voted into law by the resulting majority. If this were impossible, the president might dissolve the chamber and call for new elections. It was possible too for the people to pass law by initiative and referendum if the ministry did not do what they wanted. The continued separate existence of no less than seventeen states, all retaining some control over their state police and bureaucracy, and guaranteed a republican form of government by the national constitution, provided an abundance of political opportunity and dispute no less robust than that between the eight to ten major parties in the national legislature. Over all flew the republican flag of 1848—black, red, and gold, rather than the old black, red, and white of Hohenzollern Prussia.[7]

This admirable structure, which was hailed at the time as the most modern and most democratic constitution in the world, was, however, more like a movie set than the skeleton of a building. Close

examination reveals remarkable monarchical features in the struc-
ture itself, and thoroughly monarchical practices in the activity be-
hind it. Even its beginning was faulty, for instead of identifying
Germany (*Deutschland*) as a *Republik* in Article I, it stated that the
Deutsches Reich (German Realm? German Empire?) was a republic.
In the name of the parliament was the same contradiction in terms.
It was, as in 1871, the *Reichstag*. Even the chief executive was
Reichspräsident rather than *Republikspräsident*, and his constitutional position was even more unrepublican than his title. Not only
was his constituency national and democratic, like that of Louis
Napoleon in 1848, his term, at seven years, was longer and he could
be reelected indefinitely. He had no need to stage an illegal coup
like Napoleon's in 1851, because by the constitution's famous Article 48 he was empowered, in times of what he determined to be
"public disturbance," to take "necessary measures." These included the overruling of state laws, the abrogation of all civil liberties, the making of national laws by decree, the execution of law
by the army, and the establishment of exceptional courts and jurisdictions. The fact that such acts required a minister's signature
only completes the picture, for, unbelievably, it had been exactly
the same under the Kaisers.

Properly understood, the *Reichspräsident* of Weimar was nothing but a kaiser in reserve. Like the old emperors, he could do
anything provided the act were countersigned by a chief minister
he himself had appointed. Even without Article 48, his powers were
vast. He appointed and dismissed all officers and bureaucrats, created ministries, held referendums, issued executive orders, signed
treaties, commanded the army and navy, and could even order acts
of war ("defensive," of course) all with nothing but a minister's
countersignature. Let the Reichstag once fail in its control over
ministers and the president would emerge as dictator, for with only
the consent of a minister, the president could dissolve the Reichstag
or prorogue it for weeks; and once Article 48 were invoked he would
have all the powers exercised by the Kaiser (de facto by Ludendorff)
in 1917, the powers described in Article 68 of the imperial constitution under the title "state of siege," or military execution. Under
one extraordinary circumstance, in fact, the ministerial countersignature device would become absolutely meaningless, for if the president died or resigned, it was the chief minister, the Chancellor,
who would succeed him.

Two thin hedges protected parliamentary republican practice

from the overwhelming strength of the kaiser in reserve. One was the power of the Reichstag to impeach the president or the people to recall him. The other was the provision of a veto, by majority vote of the Reichstag, on all presidential decrees under Article 48. Long before Hitler became chancellor, the first hedge had withered and the second had been cut down.

It is almost as if the authors of the Weimar constitution had deliberately planned its demise. More likely they thought of the republic as an experiment, understood it poorly, trusted it not a great deal, and made provision for a monarchy to rescue society in jig time should it become necessary.

Even the constitution of the state of Prussia reflected the kaiser in reserve. Prussia, the largest and most populous state as always, was the only member of the Weimar federation without a chief of state. It was said that this was to reduce Prussia's power in the Reich but this is unlikely since Prussians themselves wrote the Prussian constitution. It seems clear that when the old regime collapsed, Prussia, whose king was *ex officio* German Kaiser and whose prime minister was ex officio German Chancellor, simply left both offices vacant and did without in the interim. To the surprise of many Germans, the Prussian committee executive did quite well. Then, on July 20, 1932, a year or so after presidential government was established in Germany, an Article 48 decree made the Chancellor of the Reich executive of Prussia again, and the bloodless ease with which this was accomplished suggests long preparation of the official mind. Later, a Supreme Court decision had the effect of confirming the decree. The marvel in all this is not that the Weimar regime failed as a republic between 1930 and 1934, but that it ever functioned as a republic in the first place.

That it did is ironically as much a result of the bitter political struggle between rival absolutist factions as it is of the activity of dedicated republicans. As in France in 1871–75, there were many kinds of monarchisms, but German monarchisms, unlike French were all absolutist. Their struggle to gain control of the whole state apparatus, indecisive until 1933, kept the republic alive both in its stormy youth, 1920–25, and in its depression-era decline, 1929–33. The Reichstag reproduced this conflict with remarkable fidelity, from the first general elections of 1920, to the last free ones in 1933. In 1920 parties like the KPD (Communist), DVP (People's), and DNVP (Nationalist), all of which were on record as being in favor of an uncompromised authoritarian state, controlled some 150 out of the 400-odd deputies. Slow republicanization of the DVP in the midtwenties did not reduce the antirepublican numbers, since the process was exactly matched by a decline in their votes and the growth of even more authoritarian parties on the left and right, the KPD and the Nazis. In 1930 the antirepublican deputies numbered some 225. In 1932, they rose to a majority of 340 and parliamentary government became impossible. Since there were still at least three major factions making up this total and no one of them was able to gain complete control immediately, parliamentary politics lingered on until the Enabling Act of March 1933, kept alive, as in the early years, by its worst enemies.

This arch example of the republic as *modus vivendi* shows that the parliamentary republican system should not be blamed for the failure of Weimar. On the contrary, since its rather fortuitous invention by the French, the parliamentary republic has shown that even if it can accomplish nothing else it is the best of all republican systems at domesticating its own enemies. It offers power to the ambitious in doses exactly proportioned to their extraconstitutional strength, and in any but the most extreme and improbable cases, eventually either exposes their irresponsibility or acquires their loyalty. For example, the great leader of the liberal monarchist DVP, a personal friend of the Kaiser named Gustav Stresemann, modified his views enough in 1923 to accept the Chancellorship of the broadest coalition cabinet in the short history of Weimar.

Stresemann's "Great Coalition" stopped the famous inflation, dealt rationally with the French occupation of the Ruhr industrial area, and put down separatist revolts in four states. After it broke up, Stresemann continued his foreign policy as minister in seven successive cabinets, bringing the larger part of his party with him, until he died in 1928. By then he was describing himself as a "republican by reason." Indeed his tenure of power coincides with the period when the Weimar Republic came closest to acceptance, a combination of circumstances which for once allowed patriotism to serve in Germany as it had in Rome to raise the republic above party strife and legitimize it.

Many argue that Weimar fell because of the unique stress put upon it by three forces largely beyond its control: the Treaty of Versailles, the world inflation of the early twenties, and the world depression of the thirties. In actual fact it survived all but the last, and some think that the chance which the last parliamentary coalition under Chancellor Brüning had of beating the depression was a good one. Many of its measures were responsible in part for the Hitler recovery after 1933. No doubt the stress argument has a deeper truth when one adds up all the successive casualties and recognizes that despite appearances many wounds were permanent. Versailles helped discredit the traditional German aristocracy, inflation devastated the lower middle class, and the depression completed a kind of sweep by putting even the German working class on the ropes. Surely even a well-made republic would have been hard put to survive the ruin of so many of its potential supporters. The French republic staggered under the same blows. Nevertheless, two of the three republican parties of Weimar, the Catholic Center and Noske's Social Democrats, survived all three of them without significant reduction of their numbers in the Reichstag. The major monarchist party of the early years, the DNVP, was, however, reduced considerably.

Perhaps the most interesting irony in the history of Weimar is the story of the failure of the DNVP (antidemocratic, antirepublican) and supporters of a Hohenzollern restoration. Hurt by their split over the Dawes reparations payment plan in 1924 and their acceptance of cabinet office in 1925, the DNVP remained in that year the most numerous party in the Reichstag next to the Social Democrats and a power in Germany at large. When Social Democratic president Fritz Ebert died, they ran Karl Jarres, Mayor of Duisburg, for the office and he received nearly a third of the vote in a field of seven candidates.

Supported by the DVP, the DNVP now proceeded to put together an even larger monarchist coalition behind an even stronger candidate, Field Marshal Paul von Hindenburg. Hindenburg seemed a perfect choice for them because he had been Ludendorff's commanding officer in 1917–18 and codictator with him of Germany. Like many German generals (but unlike Ludendorff) he was a member of Europe's most historically loyal aristocracy, the junkers of Prussia who had served the Hohenzollern, often on salary, since the seventeenth century. During the war, in an odd pagan ceremony, thousands of patriotic Germans had driven a nail apiece into a giant wooden statue of Hindenburg on the Königsplatz in Berlin. DNVP leaders confidently expected this man, once elected, to play the role French monarchists had designed for MacMahon in 1871 and to bring the king back as soon as the time was ripe.

When he was elected by a million-vote majority they were jubilant, and republicans like Noske predicted everything from coup to civil war. Their surprise was unpleasant when Hindenburg rapidly demonstrated that, like Washington and Cincinnatus, he had taken seriously his oath to support the republican constitution. Consternation turned to despair when the new president fired the chief of staff of the Army, a fellow nobleman, for inviting the Hohenzollern Crown Prince to take part in army maneuvers in 1926. Supporters of a Hohenzollern restoration, none of whom was getting any younger, dwindled to a rump on the morrow of their greatest electoral success and gave little trouble until a few of them made a private alliance with Hindenburg in the spring of 1932 and tried to put a harness on Adolf Hitler.

When the Weimar Republic fell between 1930 and 1934, it was not supporters of Hohenzollerns or Habsburgs or Wittelsbachs who toppled it (though some were involved), and it was not traditional monarchists who benefited (though several ex-princes were members of the Nazi party). What happened, it seems, is that the "kaiser in reserve" that was the Weimar constitution was seized upon and used with increasing boldness and amplitude by a whole succession of different politicians each seeking one-man rule for his own different reasons. The principal actors were Centrist Chancellor Heinrich Brüning, the aging Hindenburg, the second-rate aristocrat von Papen, the intriguer, General von Schleicher, and finally the *Führer* of the Nazi party, Adolf Hitler. Brüning's contribution was to seek shelter from a divided Reichstag under the constitutional emergency powers of the president. Article 48 decrees had been used several times in the twenties, but not until now by Hindenburg except to repeal the old ones still in force. Brüning went to Hindenburg in July 1930 to ask for one of his depression remedies, a tax on civil servants' salaries, to be passed in this way over SPD opposition. When the Reichstag constitutionally vetoed the decree two days later, Brüning replied with a presidential message dissolving the Reichstag in order, as he told a colleague, "to protect the President's authority."

The dissolution had a shattering effect. New elections gave the Nazi party 107 seats as against 12 in 1928, and the Communists 77 as against 54. In the new Reichstag a narrow majority could still be put together for the republic but not for Brüning's program. There was nothing for it but to continue to rule by decree, and Brüning did so, secure in his personal relationship with Hindenburg and unaware enough of the dangers of monarchy to combine two ministries under himself, and two more, Army and Police, under a general named Groener. He did not reckon with how President von Hindenburg would blossom in his new role as legislator.

Reelected by a large majority in April, the president forced General Groener to resign in May because he had originated a ban on the Nazi Storm Troops. Two weeks later he abruptly dismissed Brüning himself and appointed Franz von Papen, a monarchist ex-cavalry officer of whom he was very fond, together with a cabinet of noblemen to govern the Reich. The DNVP took heart; perhaps Hindenburg would turn out to be a MacMahon after all. Decree rule continued and intensified. (It was Chancellor von Papen who took over the Prussian government.) Increasingly impatient with the constant disagreement that is the soul of republics but original sin to a Prussian general officer, Hindenburg became more and more peremptory as the Reichstag became more and more refractory. Replacing the incapable von Papen with the charming General von Schleicher helped little. In the end it was only by constantly dissolving newly elected Reichstags that Hindenburg, von Papen, and Schleicher could avoid their constitutional veto of decrees. The Weimar system, though not truly republican, was democratic enough in the narrow sense so that it could not be made to yield the aristocratic monarchy that the three squires wanted.

In 1932 there were no less than three general elections, each taking place at the limit of the constitutional interval after dissolution. The Reichstag began to cease to exist. During the second dissolution of that year an ironic note was supplied by the Nazis. Always capable of anything, they were by then the largest party in the Reichstag and holders of the Speaker's chair. On September 12, 1932, when Chancellor von Papen appeared with a dissolution order, Speaker Hermann Göring ignored his request for the floor and instead carried through a vote to veto Hindenburg's last emergency decree. Thus did the Nazis lead the Reichstag in the last republican act of its career.

It remained only to convince Hindenburg that no one else could end the eternal disputes but the man he had scorned as a Bohemian corporal and twice refused to appoint as chancellor. Adolf Hitler had formed what was now the largest party in Germany on the three simple principles of democratic monarchy, or, as the Greeks had called it, tyranny. The first was the *führerprinzip,* a popular version of the old Kaiser ideal according to which every member obeyed Hitler without question and was reciprocally identified with him. The two others were complete unscrupulousness with regard to tactics and complete opportunism with regard to program.

Hitler knew that to get most Germans to call for the first, he had to exercise the second—create total disorder in the streets of orderly Germany. He also had to promise nearly every class and interest precisely what it wanted. The Nazis might sit on the far right, but politically they were, like Bismarck, all over the political map, offering labor peace to businessmen, benefits to workers, uniforms to militarists, and anything to anyone, unless of course he were Jewish. Hindenburg didn't like Jews either, but Hitler's background, manners, and democratic following disgusted him more. Only the combined efforts of his friend von Papen and his son Oskar convinced him in the end that the *Obrigkeitstaat* of his memories could be constitutionally restored by appointing Hitler Chancellor.

He made the appointment on January 30, 1933, doing his best to minimize the damage by surrounding him with a cabinet of aristocratic monarchists, including von Papen himself as Vice-Chancellor and Prime Minister of Prussia. Hitler, however, was too clever for safeguards. Though there were only two Nazis and one sympathizer in the new cabinet, Hitler made sure that they would control, respectively, the army, the national bureaucracy, and the Prussian police. Immediately thereafter he called for new elections, and as the campaign opened staged a fire in the Reichstag in such a way that the left could be blamed. On the very night of the fire orders went out to the Nazi ministers to arrest every Communist in Germany.

The new morning, February 28, 1933, Hitler went to Hindenburg with a new emergency decree suspending all civil liberties in every state in Germany. When the new Reichstag met, it had a Nazi majority of 288. It was presented with only one law, an "enabling act" transferring all its powers of legislation to the cabinet. Since this was a constitutional amendment requiring a two-thirds majority, it would pass only if other parties voted with the Nazis. With one single exception they did, and quite constitutionally the republic came to an end. The kaiser in reserve had become the kaiser in reality by the stunningly minimal device of separating the ministry from the Reichstag. All law in the ensuing Nazi state was to be made either by the president, by the cabinet, or by referendum. The aged Hindenburg continued to issue decrees, written and countersigned by his Chancellor, until he died in 1934 and the offices were combined by referendum. After that lawyers could proclaim, as the Kaiser liked to say, "German law is the will of the Führer."

A few independent powers remained in the Reich: ministerial rivals, the army, the state governments, labor unions and parties. The rivals fell before the Blood Purge of June 30, 1934, a mass murder legalized by presidential decree. The army was brought to heel in 1938 by one of its own traditional means of self-discipline, the discrediting of a few recalcitrant general officers for sexual "conduct unbecoming." The state governments were taken over following the Prussian blueprint in March 1933, their police powers centralized under Heinrich Himmler. Labor unions were integrated into the state by police raids in May 1933 and the Labor Front law of January 1934. As for the parties, Communists were exterminated early and the rest capitulated with the enabling act in March 1933, before being outlawed that summer. Only the Social Democrats (and incidentally the Catholic Church) left a trace worth remembering in defense of the republic's existence and their own.

In 1933, Gustav Noske had been chief executive (*Oberpräsident*) of the Prussian province of Hannover for thirteen years. He had helped the Social Democrats found the Republic, served in two of its first three SPD-led cabinets, and encouraged his party colleagues to serve in many others. He had been a founder and political beneficiary of the party's brilliant and perennial republican ministry in Prussia which had lasted from 1925 until Papen's coup in 1932. His abhorrence of the Nazis was unquestioned, his political perspicacity and energy undiminished. He had scouted von Schleicher for the SPD leaders in January 1933, reporting that Schleicher was serious about blocking Hitler and advising cooperation with the General's curiously left-wing program. Later, when the enabling act came before the Reichstag on March 23, 1933, Noske was proud to see his Social Democrats, ninety-four strong, become the only party in the Reichstag to vote against the bill. When the SPD was outlawed on June 22, Noske, at sixty-five, went into Solon-like retirement in Frankfurt, fortified perhaps with memories of the ban of 1878. He was too old to fight the Nazi dictatorship, but he could and did refuse to endorse or serve it.

A record of courage, and yet, as in 1907, there were voices in the SPD condemning Noske. Even while Hitler tore into the party for causing the mess in Germany, many in the party were blaming

Noske for both the mess and for Hitler. When he reappeared, ghost-like, at the first postwar congress of the SPD at Hannover in 1946, Noske was an embarrassment. When he died there in harness, there was more relief than sorrow.

Why? It was not because of mistakes the party had made in the Reichstag, withdrawing from Stresemann's coalition in 1924 or vainly opposing the conservative policies of Brüning in 1930. Noske could have little to do with them in Hannover anyway. Instead, the charge stemmed from what Noske had done way back in 1918–20 when the republic was being born.

Noske's first unforgivable act was in late October 1918. News of the armistice had blown away monarchy with all of its supports. The army especially, whose leaders had privately admitted defeat, was powerless to make war, either foreign or civil. When the fleet mutinied at Kiel on October 29, soldiers refused orders to put down the sailors, and both called for the republic. Impotent, the High Command called in SPD deputy Gustav Noske to talk to them. Noske arrived on November 4 at the Kiel station wearing a dress suit, a pince-nez mounted between his black beetling eyebrows and handlebar mustache, rather expecting to be murdered in the street. Within hours, however, the sailors had elected him chairman of their revolutionary council, military governor of the port, and governor of the provincial soviet.

It was a small rehearsal for the avalanche of power which was about to fall on the SPD, the only party which, with all its splinters and fringes, Germans knew as opponents of the kaiser-state. At this point Noske did something which was essentially unrepublican. He did not use the leadership the rebels had handed him to help dismantle the Reich. Instead he used it to fulfill the responsibility he had to the existing state, and the mandate the High Command had given him. Before he was through in November, he had quelled the mutiny and returned the German navy to its admirals. Nothing, perhaps, could better illustrate the policy of the SPD in the ensuing German revolution of 1918.

To understand what happened, we need only look at the example of Gambetta, set forty years before. On September 4, 1870, Gambetta was in the same position as Noske. Fundamentally moderate and deeply nationalist, he found the duty to establish a republican government set on his shoulders and carried it with relish against demoralized monarchists at a moment when his country had been defeated at the front. His strategy was to purge the officer corps and continue the war long enough to demonarchize as many important institutions as he could. This is precisely what Noske did not do at Kiel in November, and what the SPD provisional government failed to do in Berlin that winter.

Instead there emerged what a strategist might call the worst case. Wherever the SPD continued the war it confirmed the responsibility of the old army. Wherever it abandoned it, it allowed the army to evade responsibility for defeat. Though the army surrendered, though its commanders forced the Kaiser first to bring socialists into his government and then to abdicate the throne, though Hindenburg himself recommended armistice and Groener the treaty, the generals managed to keep all this secret from the Germans for a generation. Instead it was a civilian who announced the armistice, another civilian who signed it, and a republican assembly with an SPD cabinet which ratified the Treaty of Versailles.

Above all it was the SPD and the republic instead of the army and the monarchy which took the blame for Germany's defeat. In 1873 the German occupation of France ended before the republic could be set up. In 1918 French occupation of Germany did not begin until the republic was in being. It remained until 1930, and the link between the republic and surrender remained with it. At no time during the Weimar period could the SPD escape the charge of treason. The illuminating parallel between the third French and first German republics, both founded in defeat by monarchists and wracked by class struggle and civil war, is so extraordinary that it seems almost tragic that the only Weimar politician who saw it was Adolf Hitler.[8]

Noske certainly did not see it. His next act ignored the lesson of the Paris Commune. In January 1919, two months after the proclamation of the republic, the SPD wartime split had been so magnified by events that there were now three leadership groups and three separate revolutionary strategies competing in the streets of Berlin. Besides Noske's Majority Socialists, who controlled the organs of the old government, there were the Independent Socialists (USPD) of Haase and Cohn, and the *Spartakusbund* of Liebknecht and Luxemburg which became in January the Communist Party of Germany (KPD).

The SPD's strategy, not surprisingly, was conventional: keep the government going, restore order, provide food and shelter, remake Germany in peace through a single democratically elected National Assembly. The KPD, in keeping with Russian policy and their own

Quixotism, wanted to smash the old state and build a new one by leading the revolutionary workers' and soldiers' organizations called *Räte* (in German "councils," in Russian "soviets") which in their energy and localization resembled the Paris sections of the French Revolution. The USPD, in keeping with its middle position, wanted both. Ideally it preferred a government by an assembly representing the existing Räte, a solution which was in many ways the most republican of all, but they strove for peace between the other two factions and were willing to accept almost any government provided that it did not rest on any of the former supports of monarchy.

The old cabinet of the Reich, now led by Ebert, Scheidemann, and the Majority Socialists, was peacefully invested as the Council of People's Commissars by an assembly of the workers' and soldiers' Räte of Berlin one day after Scheidemann proclaimed the republic. With the addition of three USPD members, the Commissars were confirmed by an assembly of Räte representatives from all over Germany in December. This assembly also endorsed the calling of an elected National Assembly in a month. Thus the USPD had its *Räterepublik*, the SPD had its orderly ministry, and both factions had peace.

To the KPD, however, the fact that the Räte, the soviets of Germany, had turned out not to be very revolutionary led to a desperate and premature effort to make the revolution on their own. In Berlin they rose on December 23 and again during Spartacus Week, January 5–12, 1919. Hating the violence but unable to separate the KPD demand of "all power to the soviets" from their own, the USPD representatives resigned from the Council of Commissars and receded from history. The USPD would reappear only briefly to make a series of hopeless but presciently republican pleas in the National Assembly to reduce the powers of the presidency, disenfranchise the dynasties, eliminate Article 48, and replace the single executive with a five-man committee in the manner of the French Directory, a vain protest against the kaiser in reserve. The commissars now signed on three SPD replacements, one of whom was Gustav Noske as Commissar for Defense.

"Someone must be the bloodhound," he said, according to his own memoirs; "I'll take the responsibility."[9] Indeed, he probably relished the role. He was a born Prussian, a believer in order, and a nationalist whose whole career had been shaped and rewarded by monarchy. With formidable energy and no regrets he set out un-

wittingly to become the Thiers of Germany and repress the incipient Commune of Berlin. Almost instinctively he turned to the
army, with whose chiefs Ebert had already been in secret daily communication by telephone since November 8, and which had in fact
asked for Noske's appointment.

By this time what was left of the High Command had begun to
rally and reconstruct the demoralized remnants of Europe's largest
army by calling for volunteers and setting up, under reliable aristocratic officers who had a bit of the common touch, new and essentially private regiments called *Freikorps*. Noske, delighted,
inspected one with Ebert on January 4 outside Berlin. Within weeks
the Free Corps under Noske's direction had broken the KPD rising
in Berlin and lynched Liebknecht and Luxemburg. In February they
reduced Bremen to obedience. By March they had Noske's orders
to shoot on sight at anyone with a weapon, and in another month
they had broken the radicals in Halle, Brunswick, and Dresden. In
May it was the turn of the great cities of Leipzig and Munich; in
July, Hamburg; and in March 1920, Thuringia and Saxony.[10]

Not one but a hundred communes were suppressed; nor did it
even occur to Noske to turn the Free Corps against the French
former enemy—a quixotism which Gambetta would have embraced. He remained as War Minister until long after the Weimar
constitution had gone into effect, doing what he regarded as his
duty, even when his son, a war casualty, committed suicide in his
home. Under Noske's leadership the army succeeded in surviving
on essentially the same conditions as it had existed under the kaisers, limited only later by the 100,000-man provision of the Treaty
of Versailles which it quickly learned to flout.

Not until one of the Free Corps units led the rightist Kapp
Putsch in Berlin and the regular army commander refused to order
his troops to fire on them did Noske begin to realize he had made
a mistake of some sort. In March 1920 he resigned as both deputy
and minister. He was never to hold national office again; but the
military deputies Groener and Schleicher whose careers he rescued,
went on to become leaders in the presidential decree governments
of 1930–33. Both were in fact moderates but, like Noske, they never
understood the meaning and importance of a republic.

Because of Noske's work, order returned to Germany, but it was
the order of the cemetery. His achievement had doomed the republic. He and his party had defeated the KPD without making its
survivors any less totalitarian, and they had decimated and alien-

ated the far more republican USPD. Worst of all they had revived all the institutions of monarchy to do it, including the army and, as became clear after 1930, the constitution itself, written in Weimar not because it had been the home of the author of *Wilhelm Tell*, but because it was the only fairly large town where the Free Corps could guarantee security. Unlike the similarly energetic Gambetta, Noske had accepted responsibility before public opinion both for the nation's defeat and for the repression of the left. The French example hung uselessly, noticed only once and only in part by a little-known party leader on the right, Adolf Hitler, who compared himself to Gambetta during his Munich putsch in 1923.[11]

In the end, the lesson of Weimar for republicans has become the same as the lesson of the French Revolution. To overthrow a thousand-year Reich, republicans may have to be as ruthless as any other revolutionaries, and they must conduct their own reeducation. Republicans must know exactly what they are doing, if only in order to reward their friends and keep their enemies away from the levers of power. They must therefore cleave to republican behavior with an often unpleasant purity and a Calvinist taste for self-examination. They must also recognize the kinship of civil war and one-man rule, and steer clear of both. If it is true that the republic could not have succeeded in Germany until one-man rule was at last irrevocably identified with national disaster in 1945, it is also true that the German republicans' imperfect understanding of what it was they were defending was as responsible as Hitler for the burial of German republicanism in 1933.

13

Five Senators
The Republic
Versus Its Presidents

Senator Sam J. Ervin, of North Carolina, dewlaps quivering, appeared on the television screens of a surprised nation in the spring of 1973. Millions of citizens, brought up on portrait galleries of the presidents, were astonished to discover that the Senate of the United States was more than a menagerie of presidential contenders and that a drawling senator they had never heard of (because he never would and never could run for president) was nevertheless competent, intelligent, and strong.

Had he really come from Morganton, North Carolina, that backwoods, small-town, Dixified sort of America which was so rapidly becoming irrelevant? No, as Senator Baker pointed out, Ervin always neglected to mention that he had graduated from Harvard Law School with honors—and the neglect was deliberate. "If the Senator from Tennessee will yield," said Ervin to the microphone, "I would like to say a word in my own defense on that point. I had a friend introduce me to a North Carolina audience. He said that he understood that I was a graduate of Harvard Law School, but by God, nobody would ever suspect it."[1] To seem like "just a country lawyer" helped a great deal in the struggle with Nixon in 1973, and so did the unspoken Harvard training; but the whole truth was that Ervin had been sprung upon the country neither by Harvard nor by Morganton, but by the Senate of the United States.

Ervin entered the Senate in 1954, late in life and by appointment. Almost immediately he was placed on the select committee of six that brought in the resolution to censure Senator Joseph McCarthy of Wisconsin. Ervin's superb speech on that occasion had been forgotten by 1973, and the whole censure process has been remembered, dimly, as a tardy and incomplete effort by an antique institution to comply with the newly popular demand to put down McCarthyism. No one who reads the speech today, however, could come away without a profound understanding of how the Senate works, and how, twenty years later, it would produce, from its supposed creaky antiquity, the Watergate hearings.[2]

The Senate, said Ervin in 1954, is constitutionally in complete control of its membership, but it rarely censures or expels someone after the people of his state have elected him. There was, as Ervin grinningly noted, no rush to join the censure committee. And, he might have added, the most profound disagreement between Senators is masked by a courtesy that can sometimes descend to the oiliest insincerity. Senators know they must somehow live together or none of what they call "the nation's business" will get done. Roman consuls and tribunes felt the same necessity, unlike the lawmakers of Weimar. Again and again, therefore, Ervin parried in his speech the charge that McCarthy was being attacked for his ideas or for his popularity in Wisconsin. In the end, Ervin's indictment added up to only two charges: first, that McCarthy was irresponsible with the facts, and second, that he refused to return the customary courtesy senators had repeatedly extended to him.

To a senator, discussion of law and policy is the heart of his job. He can carry his policies by convincing fifty other senators, not an impossible task and worth as much concentration as any of the more ordinary devices of power politics. During such discussion each senator must be understood to speak for the values of his constituency about which he must differ with some or all of his colleagues, and for the facts, on which he must always be trustworthy. Rank among senators is supposed to depend, and usually does depend, on the quality of their intelligence, judgment, and preparation. Leadership offices are assigned on the basis of the innocuous union principle of seniority, but influence depends on merit. Only for a hopeless irresponsible like McCarthy may the assumption of the equality of senators be violated. A senator is no one's creature, and has little understanding of the hiring and firing to which other appointive magistrates are subject.

No wonder then, that when Richard Nixon threatened by the accumulation of offices and powers to become the Caesar of the American republic, it was the Senate that most openly and self-assuredly opposed him. No wonder that Sam Ervin, who had shown a knowledge of the Senate's republican habits sufficient to put him on the McCarthy Committee within months of his arrival, should at the end of his career have been put in charge of the Select Committee on Presidential Campaign Practices. If presidents ever do succeed in establishing a monarchy in America, the last institution to stand against them will probably be the Senate.

Such a stand will not be made on the basis of liberalism or conservatism or of any ideology now considered explanatory of political events. Senators differ on these things and will continue to differ profoundly. Their commitment to the republican equality of magistrates, however, is deeper than all these disagreements. So is their intolerance for the arrogance and sycophancy of appointees. Presidents and their minions are simply not very special to them. Since the Reconstruction era, whenever there has been an increase in the power of the executive branch, even or perhaps particularly in wartime, there have been found senators by the score to oppose it, sometimes at the cost of their careers. Perhaps the best way to see where Ervin came from is to consider a succession of his predecessors, four other senators who succeeded each other on the battle line, all of different parties, states, and ideologies: Republican George Hoar of Massachusetts, Progressive Republican George Norris of Nebraska, New Deal Democrat Burton Wheeler of Montana, and conservative Republican Robert Taft of Ohio. Together with Ervin himself, they form a nearly unbroken century of service, from 1878 to 1976.

They were all Kilkenny cats, powerful and outspoken; no two could have been put in the same room without an argument. They were unafraid of power, happy to take responsibility for their own acts and for those of any content to be led by them. They were neither selfless nor unambitious. Two ran for vice-president, one for president, and one (Wheeler) might well have become president had he taken the vice-presidential bait that Roosevelt's agents offered him in early 1940.

Wheeler's refusal, however, epitomizes the antimonarchical principle that in the end unites this mixed bag of senators. He would

not run in 1940 because he disapproved, among other things, of a
third term for presidents and of executive actions which he correctly anticipated would lead the United States into a world war.
Moreover, like the best senators, he was unwilling to keep his disapproval private. All the others made the same kinds of sacrifices.
Hoar broke with his party in the high tide of imperialism to insist
on self-government for the Philippines. Norris would have given the
executive control over public utilities but refused to acquiesce in
"Mr. Wilson's war." Wheeler was an architect of the New Deal, but
when the Supreme Court stood in the New Deal's way, he prevented Roosevelt from "packing" it. Taft's anticommunism was little short of rabid, but he argued that the Korean War was
unconstitutional. There were many like them, but together Hoar,
Norris, Wheeler, Taft, and Ervin form an unbroken chain linking
the 39th and 40th Congresses, which created the unitary democratic republic and impeached Andrew Johnson, to the 93rd, which
undertook to impeach Richard Nixon.

Senator George Frisbie Hoar was a nineteenth-century man,
high collar and all. Though he grew up in Concord, Massachusetts
in the 1830s, surrounded by those endearing radicals Alcott, Fuller,
and Thoreau, he himself was utterly untouched by such native calls
to self-dramatization and he never even grew a beard. He went to
Harvard, where an ancestor had been president of the college in
1672, and on admission to the bar he made his single concession to
the pioneer spirit by moving west—from Concord to Worcester.
The passion of youth, such as it was, brought him into the Free
Soil Party (precursor of the Republican Party) at the age of twenty-
two, and there he remained, as legislator, congressman, and senator,
for fifty-seven years. Over his mantel in Worcester was a Latin motto
which he translated for visitors, "Rest I at home. What need I
more./ Here comfort is, and Mrs. Hoar."[3] No one outside of
Worcester would have remembered this Victorian of Victorians if
he had not committed in his long career two curious breaches of
party discipline which earned him the contemptuous title of "Half-
Breed" from the two warring wings of the Republican Party.

Hoar's first eccentricity was to help manage the impeachment
by the House of Representatives of Grant's Secretary of War, Bel-
knap, in 1876. His second and most memorable act of integrity was
to oppose the acquisition of the Philippine Islands from Spain in
1898. It is in these two actions that Hoar's thirty-five years as a

legislator can be said to carry forward the idea of republicanism at the precise time, 1869–1904, when by its very success it seemed to recede from the nation's consciousness, a time when it was so obvious that the power of the national government was concentrated in the legislature rather than the executive that most Americans forgot how the legislature had acquired its power and why.

In 1883 and 1884, a young graduate student in politics wrote a Ph.D. dissertation analyzing the national government as it had settled itself since the Johnson impeachment. This government was, wrote Thomas Woodrow Wilson, "a scheme of congressional supremacy . . . a government by the Standing Committees of Congress." Sniffing at a presidency "in decline," the ambitious young Wilson was already preparing himself to become the most powerful man in America, Senator from Virginia and Chairman of the Appropriations Committee. Wilson's analysis is quite brilliant, and there is nothing better than its acerbic accuracy from someone seeking to understand the strange world of Gilded Age politics. Presidents like Hayes, Arthur, and Harrison draw smiles even in the gallery at Disneyworld, but it was not they who were weak. It was the office they held that was diminished. Wilson correctly pointed out that the Tenure-of-Office Act (still in force at the time) and the itemized budget were the keys to the subordination of presidents to Congress. With the suspicion of a Southerner born before the Civil War, Wilson wrote disapprovingly of the increase of federal power at the expense of the states; but he missed the republican point that when you weaken one check you must strengthen another. To him the committee system seemed merely a method of diffusing responsibility and wasting time.[4]

By 1900, Wilson had changed his mind. In a preface to the new edition of *Congressional Government,* the newly appointed professor wrote: "It may be, too, that the new leadership of the Executive . . . will have a very far-reaching effect upon our whole method of government."[5]

This was an apt prophecy, for Wilson was both its author and its subject. We know that at this point in his life he had already changed his own goal from senator to president. What light had he seen? The simplest answer is that by 1900 the United States had entered once more on the course of empire, and that nothing prospers the executive more than imperialism. Senator Hoar saw things in those terms, if Wilson didn't, when he stood almost alone of his party in the Senate against acquiring the Spanish Empire.

On January 9, 1899, when he spoke for the first time against the treaty with Spain, Hoar was a dean of the Senate and chairman of its paramount Committee on the Judiciary. He was seventy-two years old, his hair thinning and silver, even the sidewhiskers of his youth long since shaved off. Over parchment-thin eyelids that hung wrinkled and low, he now wore little round wire-rimmed spectacles. A sad cherub perhaps, or an amalgam of wisdom and innocence, Hoar represented both party loyalty and antebellum idealism, neither very fashionable in 1899. For more than twenty years Hoar had sat in the Senate seat where Radical Republican Charles Sumner had been beaten with a cane for attacking slavery. His first speech in the House, almost thirty years before, had been against the readmission of Virginia to the Union. What Virginia had done to her blacks, Hoar told the Senate, the entire country was now about to do to the Filipinos, govern them by executive action without their consent, under an "astonishing and most extravagant construction of the powers of Congress under the Constitution."[6]

To the modern young senators (to be modern in 1899 was to be bearded) who were so avid to plant the American flag wherever they might have a navy to do so, Hoar addressed himself with the apology of an old man:

> After all, I am old-fashioned enough to think that our fathers, who won the Revolution and who framed the Constitution, were the wisest builders of states the world has yet seen. . . . They did not disdain to study ancient history. They knew what caused the downfall of the mighty Roman Republic. They read . . . the history of the freedom, the decay, and the enslavement of Greece. . . . They learned from her the doctrine that while there is little else a democracy cannot accomplish it cannot rule over vassal states or subject peoples without bringing the elements of death into its own constitution. . . .
>
> There are two lessons our fathers learned from the history of Greece which they hoped their children would remember—the danger of disunion . . . and lust of empire. . . . For us the danger of disunion had happily passed by. Our Athenians and our Spartans are bound and welded together again. . . . Our danger today is from the lust of empire. It is a little remarkable that the temptation that besets us now lured and brought to ruin the Athenian people in ancient times.

Senator Hoar rose on his toes, keys jingling, as he quoted Cleon the Athenian against the Athenian Empire. Down he came on his heels as he read from Creasey's *Six Decisive Battles:*

There never has been a republic yet in history that acquired dominion over any other nation that did not rule it selfishly and
oppressively. There is no single exception to this rule. . . . Carthage,
Rome, Venice, Genoa, Florence, Pisa, and republican France all
tyrannized over every province and subject state where they gained
authority.[7]

Hoar lost, the treaty passed by a hair's breadth, and the Philippines were acquired from Spain. There ensued a nasty little guerrilla war with the inhabitants, the Philippine Insurrection, which
until recently missed mention in the history texts. To keep the islands under control, American proconsuls authorized the destruction of food supplies, confiscation of property, killing of civilians,
decimation of prisoners of war, interrogation by water torture, and
a fancy trick learned from the Spanish in Cuba called *campos de
reconcentracion*—concentration camps.

In vain Hoar rose a second time in the Senate, on April 17, 1900,
to condemn these sequels of imperialism. In vain did he raise the
specters of Tyler and Polk, quote Corwin on the spider spinning its
web in the ruins of Rome (cf. above, chapter 10), and accuse his
opponents of "talking in the spirit which destroys republics."[8] History was no longer relevant. The Philippine Insurrection was still
dragging on when Hoar rose to speak a third time on May 22, 1902.

It was his swan song. He had two years to live and little to offer
the younger generation in the Senate. Teddy Roosevelt was president, the same TR who as Assistant Secretary of the Navy had ordered Dewey's fleet to Manila in advance of the declaration of war,
and who had stated repeatedly his belief in an imperial America led
by a strong, independent executive. To an inattentive Senate Hoar
read the suppressed evidence of American atrocities in the Philippines, trying to distinguish between the role of "liberator-republic"
that the United States had played in Cuba and the one of despot
which it was now playing in the Pacific. He defined a republic rather
tepidly as an independent state ruled by the consent of the governed—a limited but democratic view, enough to establish his point.
In the face of unprecedented, wholesale censorship of the news
from the Philippines, Hoar warned prophetically that "if a strong
people try to govern a weak one against its will the home government will get despotic too."[9] Not until 1917, when Woodrow Wilson
had achieved that new ambition of his, would the truth of Hoar's
remark become clear to George Norris, who entered Congress as a
freshman Republican the year Hoar retired.

Norris's restlessness was in perfect contrast to Hoar's rooted-ness. Before 1917, it might have seemed, the two could have had nothing in common but a party. Norris's parents had been married in New York, but by the time George was born in 1861, they were on a farm in Ohio. The son kept moving west. Elected from Ne-braska, he had gone to school in Indiana and taught school in Walla Walla, Washington. The characteristic French-style mustache he grew in Indiana served after his settlement in Nebraska in 1885 to distract attention from his normally unshined shoes and threadbare suits. Perhaps the same reasoning led him to start wearing ten-gallon hats. From any angle, Norris was, unlike Hoar, a risk-taker and a radical.

Radicalism, however, was no greater in Norris than a stubborn loyalty, formed in the Reconstruction period, to the Republican Party. When Nebraska was struck by agricultural depression in the 1890s, the young politician stayed out of the attractive Populist movement, setting the conditions for his long and rather lonely ca-reer as a Republican of the left. Norris was in Congress from 1903 to 1912 and in the Senate from 1913 to 1942—a career still re-nowned for its progressivism. It was Norris who devised TVA, the most famous state socialist measure in American political history. He opposed Coolidge for president in 1924 and Hoover in 1928. In 1932, 1936, and 1940, he supported FDR. The Republican Party did its level best to get rid of him, but Norris refused to give up the struggle until 1936, when he changed his label to Independent.

As a party man, Norris was, indeed, totally unreliable. If Hoar was a "Half-Breed," Norris was a "Son of the Wild Jackass." Never-theless, when it came to republicanism with a small r, Norris was much more consistent than his party. He had a horror of inequality, display, and self-indulgence worthy of Cato himself. He once spoke against the breeding of saddle horses for the cavalry, preferring pon-ies of indeterminate ancestry, and he argued against an early New Deal bill to give money away because the proposal would encourage profligacy. (It was illegal for anyone who got the money to save it.) In political faith, Norris was a democrat like Thaddeus Stevens. Nothing, he thought, should interfere with the direct expression of the will of a majority. In this spirit he fathered Nebraska's unique one-house legislature and the Twentieth Amendment to the United States Constitution which eliminated the so-called "lame duck" ses-sion of Congress. He even tried unsuccessfully to eliminate that vestige of the aristocratic republic, the electoral college, and one of his most famous accomplishments was transferring the powers of the Speaker of the House to the Committee on Rules in 1910.

Democrat or no democrat, however, Norris refused to accept the Jacksonian myth that the most democratic office in the government was the presidency. In fact he was completely unimpressed by the pretensions of the executive branch, and in the area of foreign policy he was deeply suspicious of it. In his thirty-year career in the Senate, Norris's most remarkable apostasy was not in supporting Democrats for president but in opposing a sitting Democratic president when the Republican Party, for once, wanted to support him. The president was Woodrow Wilson, the same man who had written *Congressional Government*. A powerful, progressive executive since 1913, Wilson had infuriated conservatives with his antitrust and income tax legislation. But Norris was delighted with these measures. His opposition would come where right-wing opposition ceased, on the issue of war.

There was little evidence in 1917 to show that the Senator from Nebraska would soon become Wilson's implacable enemy. He had opposed Wilson on military incursions in Mexico (1914) and Nicaragua (1916). In 1916, too, he had briefly espoused the Hoar position in a debate on the reorganization of the colonial government of the Philippines. It was World War I that drove Norris's mistrust of the executive into the open. "The President," he said in 1916, "is leading toward war and Congress is holding back."[10] Norris thought American neutrality could be sustained, that the war was avoidable, and that it only benefited big business anyway. Norris (inaccurately it seems) read the mood of the American people as antiwar. If it were, then Wilson's moves were inexcusable.

Norris was not a pacifist and at no time opposed armaments, or "preparedness" as it was then called. Indeed, with predictable left-wing wisdom, he advocated the nationalization of armor plate and nitrate production, even of the merchant marine. He drew the line instead at expanding the navy and creating a standing army, like an eighteenth-century republican. Norris's ally, Vardaman of Mississippi, called navies and such the known devices of militarism and executive usurpation, but few listened to Vardaman. To keep his own audience, Norris described his position only as a practical way to avoid war. He ridiculed the "naval threat" as thirty-odd Japanese in a rowboat.[11] Still Wilson's initiatives went on. Finally in March 1917, Wilson's proposal to arm American merchant ships reached the floor of the Senate and Norris lost his sense of humor.

Wilson's bill would have allowed American ships carrying goods and passengers into the war zones of the Atlantic to carry guns supplied by the War Department. The theory was that if Germans were going to carry out their threat to sink neutral ships going to belligerent ports, the ships needed to be able to defend themselves. Norris and nine fellow senators saw immediately that if the guns were ever fired, right or wrong, war would begin. In Norris's view the way to avoid war was to prevent American ships from going into war zones in the first place. At the very least, he thought, the president should not be given this power to arm the ships and thus bring on war without a Congressional declaration. The view was a minority one even then. Two world wars have made it look almost quaint. It was here, however, that Norris drew his republican line. The United States must not, in a vast struggle with kaisers, become itself a monarchy. As Cummins of Iowa, one of Norris's nine supporters put it: "I am not in favor of . . . giving the right to declare war to one man . . . . I am opposed to Kaiserizing the United States." On March 4 Norris himself took the floor:

> We ought not to pass this bill because it abdicates our power; it gives the President in effect the right to make war. . . . Do we want to surrender that power? . . . have we any right to do it?[12]

With a delightful flourish, Norris then pulled from his desk a slim textbook on politics by "a leading American authority" and began reading: "'The Framers shrank from placing sovereign power anywhere. They feared it would generate tyranny.'" The book was *Congressional Government*, not an easy place to find arguments against executive power.[13]

President Wilson was neither complimented nor convinced by Norris's selective quoting of his doctoral dissertation, now more than thirty years old. Did he find it embarrassing? Juvenile? As Norris and his nine senators filibustered the armed-ship bill into oblivion, Wilson lashed out at them as a "little band of willful men, representing no opinion but their own [who] had rendered the great government of the United States helpless and contemptible." (Nixon, who admired Wilson, echoed both his tone and phrasing with "pitiful helpless giant.")[14]

Norris became something of a pariah thereafter to both parties, but he seemed as immune to defeat as he was to compromise. He spoke against the declaration of war in April and against the draft law in May. Defying extraordinary odds, he was renominated and

reelected to the Senate at the end of the war, whereupon he opposed the Treaty of Versailles and later helped pass the Neutrality
Acts to prevent future presidents from inviting war prior to a declaration. They worked until FDR found a way around them. In these
later efforts, however, Norris returned to what had previously been
his political theme, the attack on the power of concentrated capital.
More a democrat than a republican, he was never again to be as
eloquent against executive aggrandizement as he had been in March
1917. In 1928 he opposed the Marine landing in Nicaragua, saying
on April 23 that if such unconstitutional executive actions continued, "We shall . . . gradually surrender the functions of the legislature and in the end become a monarchy; not only a monarchy
but an absolute monarchy."[15] The issue, however, soon vanished.

A few years later, as Franklin Roosevelt proceeded to adopt
many elements of his program, Norris's opposition to executive
power ebbed away. When Roosevelt offered his "court-packing" bill
in 1937, Norris let it by without a grumble. In 1941, he was content
to offer amendments rather than oppose the threat to neutrality
represented by the Lend-Lease Act. He did not like fascists. Only
on the draft bill of 1940 did some of his old fire come back ("If we
shall pass the bill we will put this country on a road which means
the ultimate destruction of democracy . . .").[16] But Norris was then
nearly eighty years old and counting his gains instead of his losses.
Fortunately, he had by now a like-minded younger colleague, Burton K. Wheeler of Montana, a Democrat who was as galling to his
own party as Norris had been to the G.O.P., a left-winger who
startled his friends by refusing to carry the train of a left-wing president.

To Wheeler fell the task of providing intelligent and principled
republican opposition to perhaps the most charming, the most
powerful, and the least vulnerable president the United States has
ever had—Franklin Delano Roosevelt. Even now it is hard to say
anything bad about FDR. The good will with which he swayed his
own contemporaries and the inspired political opportunism with
which he wove together nearly every class and interest in America
has made his opponents inconsequential, seemingly ridiculous.
Reasonable critics like Wheeler have been edited out, lost in a hapless welter of anti-Semites, laissez-faire capitalists, and of Franco or
Mussolini. But history never vindicates anything once and for all,
and as the twentieth century wears on, responsible criticism continues to build. The comparison of Roosevelt's NRA to corporatist

fascism is no longer farfetched. The warnings of Herbert Hoover about the chilling effects of federal bureaucracy no longer seem insensitive. Nor, most of all, do the cries of Martin, Barton, and Fish about executive tyranny strike one, in the eighties, as outlandish.

Roosevelt, after all, was the first president to serve more than two terms, the nearest approach America has yet made to a president-for-life. While in office he created the Pentagon, the CIA (OSS), and the Executive Office, the institutions where Watergate was hatched, and he began the replacement of treaties by unratified executive agreements. Twice during his administration the Supreme Court struck down major items in his program because they transferred lawmaking power from Congress to the executive. Finally, it is now clear that as early as 1938 Roosevelt had deliberately and secretly embarked on a foreign policy requiring him to violate the Neutrality Acts.[17] If Lyndon Johnson was surprised by the intense reaction to his attacks on North Vietnam or Richard Nixon by the riots opposing his invasion of Cambodia in 1970, it was because both knew that Roosevelt had done very similar things in 1940 and had eventually been acclaimed for them. It may help prevent future outrages if it can be shown that among those who opposed FDR were some who were as sane and democratically minded as Burton Wheeler.

He was born in a shoe town near Senator Hoar's Worcester, but like Norris, Wheeler was in his own words, a plunger. In 1905, after getting his law degree, he stepped off the platform in Butte, Montana, lost everything he had in a poker game, missed the train to Spokane, and hung out his shingle on the spot. Among his earliest clients were Butte's only optometrist and its best madam, but Wheeler was quick to discover that the real power in Butte was Anaconda Copper. It is typical of Wheeler that he entered politics running against Anaconda. In 1913 Wilson appointed him United States Attorney, but even as an appointee Wheeler was unreliable. He prosecuted violators of the draft law but he was repeatedly and publicly sympathetic to violators of the Espionage Act and radicals ranging as far left as the Wobblies. Montana elected him to the Senate in 1922, and in March 1923 he arrived in Washington, "itching to try out my toga."[18]

Right away he began his career as a maverick by becoming the first senator to smoke on the floor (spittoons had been provided for generations but not ashtrays). On another occasion, when the chairmanship of the Interstate Commerce Committee was going through on a routine "unanimous consent" resolution, Wheeler objected, throwing the Senate into a full month of debate, and eventually winning a purge of the ICC. The next year, Wheeler again defied the Senate's Republican majority. He put through a committee to investigate Attorney-General Harry Daugherty, who had until then survived the Teapot Dome scandals. At Wheeler's direction, the investigators discovered not only that the Justice Department was financially corrupt, but that it was laundering money and spying on senators (*plus ça change*. . .). Daugherty resigned but was spared in two separate trials from being the first United States attorney-general to be convicted of a felony. This distinction Fate had apparently reserved for John Mitchell.

Attacks like these on the executive were, however, fairly cheap. They were aimed at the opposition party and were good politics. Montana loved them. Even Wheeler's growing opposition to American imperialism was popular in the West. No one there complained when he joined Norris in opposing the bullying of Mexico in 1927 or the Nicaraguan intervention in 1928. The real showdown came, just as it had with Norris, when Wheeler raised these issues against a popular president of his own party, one who was above simple corruption and who agreed with Wheeler on domestic reform, one in fact whom Wheeler had been instrumental in nominating in 1932: Franklin D. Roosevelt.

On February 5, 1937, Wheeler says in his autobiography, he learned of Roosevelt's bill to add to the Supreme Court one new Justice for every member (six at the time) who did not choose to retire at seventy. FDR, who had just been reelected by a landslide, wanted to reverse the series of court decisions which had held so much of the New Deal to be unconstitutional, and he thought he had found a constitutional way to do it. The Constitution was silent, it is true, on the size of the Court, but Wheeler decided instantly that FDR's move was an "anti-Constitution grab for power."[19] He had a sober discussion with his wife about what they would do when he lost his Senate seat and the next morning issued a public attack on the bill. Within days he had accepted an offer by eighteen other senators, mostly right wing, to lead the opposition on the floor. Wheeler agreed with these anti-New Dealers on almost nothing. Fellow progressives like Norris either shied away or backed the president. Moreover Wheeler, who really liked Roosevelt, was subjected to constant carrot-and-stick treatment from the White House. One day the treasurer of the Democratic National Com-

mittee called to say the president thought Wheeler and his group
were prima donnas. "Of course we're prima donnas," retorted
Wheeler; "that's the reason we're here. He wants to be the only
prima donna but we're going to show him there are three branches
of government."[20]

As a leader Wheeler was brilliant and indefatigable. His Senate
steering committee met every day in secret. Outside supporters
were lined up against pressures such as he had "never seen," including a speech in which FDR claimed that the one third of a
nation could not be better housed or fed without a packed court.
Replying, Wheeler said, "Create now a political Court to echo the
ideas of the executive and you have created a weapon . . . which
in the hands of another president could well be the instrument of
destruction."[21] Finally, in a spectacular coup, Wheeler got his friend
Justice Brandeis to enlist Chief Justice Hughes. Hughes wrote an
unprecedented letter opposing the bill and the next day Wheeler
read it into the record of the Judiciary Committee. When Vice-President Garner learned of the letter he told Roosevelt, "We're licked."
They were, by fifty votes, and Roosevelt had lost a major bill in
Congress for the first time.

In 1938 Wheeler did it again, though not quite as successfully.
This time it was a bill to reorganize the executive branch, not a bad
project by itself, but the means was to be an executive order which
Congress could not override except by a two-thirds majority.
Wheeler was incensed in a world ridden by dictatorship at what he
called a Congressional declaration of its own incompetence to leg-
islate. Once again he found himself leading conservative senators
in opposition to FDR. As the debate came to a head, Wheeler introduced an amendment which cut the executive order feature from
the bill. It did not pass, but it changed the character of the debate
from institutional to constitutional. Wheeler was fearless and clear
as usual. The unamended bill, he said on March 8, would "turn over
dictatorial powers to the president." Wilson and Hoover had asked
the same power, retorted the bill's manager; "Did Hoover want to
be a dictator? Did he look like a dictator?"

"He did to me," said Wheeler.

Above the laughter, his opponent replied, "Yet the Senator believes that when this power is asked by the President of the United
States he wants to be a dictator?"

"I did not say that at all," replied Wheeler, "I do not believe the
president wants to be a dictator . . . but when Congress abdicates"
it makes him into one.

Three days after the Senate finally passed the bill, Franklin Roosevelt called a late-night press conference to announce "I have no inclination to be a dictator," the nearest that healthy personality ever came to denying he was a crook, but the Congress had had enough and the bill was defeated a week later in the House.[22]

Twice Wheeler had been instrumental in reining in the most powerful executive in American history. The third time, however, he failed utterly, not only on the immediate issue, which was World War II, but in the long view as well. History has long since exonerated Roosevelt in the name of national survival and dumped Wheeler forever into a file marked "Midwestern Isolationist." For what it is worth, however, Wheeler's suspicion that from 1937 to 1941 "FDR . . . never tried to keep us out of the war—while deliberately misleading the people into thinking that he was,"[23] has now been completely borne out by the facts. To take only one example, when Roosevelt declared, two days after war broke out in Europe in September 1939, that, "This nation will remain a neutral nation," he had already secretly planned joint naval action against Hitler with the British ambassador a year before and with the king of England himself in June. Joint naval staff talks had been going on secretly in Washington since May. When Roosevelt said, in that same Fireside Chat, that, "Your government has no information which it withholds or has any thought of withholding from you," he was being at the very least disingenuous. When he continued, "It is honest for me to be honest with the people of the United States," he was protesting too much.[24]

Of course. He had to. The American people had been deeply shocked by the unrighteousness and meaninglessness of the First World War and even those who, like Wheeler, thought fascism an unmitigated evil were afraid war might be a worse one because it fostered tyranny at home. Roosevelt could not tell them the truth. In fact, he ran for the unprecedented third term in 1940 largely because he was sure that only he could lead the country into war with the Axis. On September 3, by executive order, he gave fifty destroyers to England. Then, in the last two weeks of the campaign, pressed by the Republican candidate's peace declarations, he repeatedly promised that there was no secret diplomacy and would be no foreign wars. A month after these pledges FDR, now safely reelected, was asking Congress to authorize giving vast quantities of arms to Britain—the Lend-Lease Act.

Wheeler, who had opposed ending the arms embargo in 1939, the peacetime draft, and the destroyer deal in 1940, and who had used all his power in the Democratic convention to get a peace plank in the platform, dug in on Lend-Lease for what was to be his last stand. He correctly perceived that if Roosevelt were allowed to continue his resolute movement toward the armed defense of England there would not only be war, which was bad enough, but a de facto takeover by the president of the most precious power of any republican legislature—the power to authorize war. Wheeler saw too what Roosevelt was unwilling and others unable to make clear, that Lend-Lease, though technically not a violation of neutrality, was the crucial link in the chain of presidential decisions leading from neutrality to belligerency. If Roosevelt were to be stopped at all he would have to be stopped here.

Wheeler's stand made him, of course, a bedfellow of Nazis and German sympathizers everywhere. He knew it and he hated it. The antisemites in the antiwar movement were, he wrote, "Hard as maggots to shake off."[25] He knew as a good politician that it would be almost impossible for any but senators and a few thinkers to understand why he thought it was antifascist to be antiwar. He suspected too, as he had in the Court fight, that regardless of his reelection in 1940, his career was at an end win or lose. Nevertheless, Wheeler was no less a plunger at sixty than he had been at twenty-three.

He opened on January 11, 1941, with the most intemperate and most famous remark he ever made, calling Lend-Lease "the administration's Triple-A foreign policy; it will plough under every fourth American boy." Stung, Roosevelt called this "the most untruthful, the most dastardly, the most unpatriotic thing that has been said in public life in my generation."[26] Even Wheeler came to regret the Triple-A statement. When he rose to address the Senate on February 28 he was a bit less pungent and better prepared. "It is a bill," he said, "which would . . . invite the Chief Executive to plunge the country into war, and create a dictatorship. It's title should be [here he was referring to the act that put an end to Weimar] the 'American Enabling Act of 1941'." In support of this view, Wheeler came armed with an enormous dossier of court decisions, legal scholarship, and speeches of bygone republicans. He quoted Abraham Lincoln on the Mexican War, other old Whigs, and contemporary students of constitutional history. He attacked pro-war conservatives for invoking the Constitution against welfare and not against Lend-Lease. Demonstrators were on the steps of the Capitol as Wheeler called on the executive to clear the police out of the building. When we stop Americans from telling their senators what they want, "we put ourselves on the same plane with the royalists of Europe who produced the present holocaust."

In sum (it took him two days to make his speech) Wheeler said:

> I ask Congress not to give away the powers it should exercise under the Constitution . . . to lightly toss away its duty and prerogative and give them to the President. If the American taxpayers want to help England . . . then we can do that within the framework of the Constitution. But no reason exists—and never will exist in a democratic republic—to delegate our powers to the President of the United States, as is proposed to be done under this measure.[27]

Lend-Lease passed the Senate 60–31 on March 8. Wheeler had lost and knew it, but he went on vainly opposing Roosevelt's policy. He even leaked the massive army deployment plan to the isolationist *Chicago Tribune* in September 1941. The reason this created no Pentagon Papers affair is because the *Tribune* did not publish it until December 4, 1941. Three days later, told of the Pearl Harbor attack by a reporter, Wheeler exclaimed "Let's lick 'em!" and plunged into war work. As usual he was sincere, but that was no longer enough for Montana. He lost his seat by a landslide in 1946. Many years later Wheeler told his ghostwriter he had "stopped the trend toward autocratic presidential power but the Second World War gave it new momentum. I greatly fear this trend." An odd thing to say in the year of Kennedy's inauguration. No doubt his ghostwriter understood; the senator was an old man, retired, a bit behind in his ideas, colorful and controversial in his time; let him say what he wants.[28]

Wheeler's successor died long before Wheeler did. Robert A. Taft of Ohio succumbed to cancer in 1953, less than a year after his unsuccessful attempt to take the Republican nomination from General Eisenhower. The son of a republican president and, like Hoar, a staid party man, Taft was known as "Mr. Republican" almost from the moment he entered the Senate in 1939. It was a lot easier for the Republican Taft than it was for a Democrat like Wheeler to oppose Lend-Lease. In fact his opposition was somewhat obscured by its obviousness. He had always distrusted Roosevelt and he hated the New Deal as became a member of what was now the party of property. Few listened to the reasons Taft kept giving for his opposition to the Democratic program. They were lower-case, not upper-case republican, and already nearly obsolete in American political discourse. The administration, he said repeatedly in the 1936 campaign, substituted "an autocracy of men for a government of law." Moreover, said Taft, the growing power of the central government and of the executive within it was dangerous whether legal or not.

> History shows that once power is granted it is impossible for people to get it back. In Greece republics gave way to tyrannies. The Roman Republic became an Empire. Medieval republics became monarchies. If we extend Federal power indefinitely, if we concentrate power over the courts and congress in the executive, it will not be long before we have an American Fascism.[29]

Few heard that message. What they did hear and would always hear from the son of William Howard Taft was partisan opposition to Democratic policies. Even when Taft reached the Senate in 1939, quickly making his reputation as a superb and thoughtful leader, the partisan politician was always his most obvious role. When he attacked Secretary of War-Designate Stimson in the Military Affairs Committee in July 1940, it was assumed that he did it out of rancor that a Republican should serve in a Democratic cabinet. Actually Taft was trying to get Stimson to admit he supported intervention to aid England in World War II (and he came within an ace of doing so). Similarly, when Taft joined Wheeler in opposing the destroyer deal and the draft, no one really heard him over the partisan din denouncing standing armies and the "garrison state." Nor did they understand why he said that war was "worse than a German victory."[30]

Even in the Senate only Taft could see clearly that it was the republic, not the democracy, of the United States that insured it against fascism. "That government," he said on August 14, 1940, "might be denominated a democracy which every four years elected a man who had absolute power to run everything as he chose. That is literally a democracy, because it is the rule of the people."[31] But it is not a republic. When Taft successfully led the attack on a federal ballot for soldiers in 1944, it sounded as if he were merely trying to take votes from Roosevelt; not that he was defending the Constitution's elections' clause or that he feared military control over civilians. Even after the war, when Taft took off after Truman, it could easily be assumed, and was, that Mr. Republican was at it again.

Taft did not come out of such duels with his principles entirely uncompromised either. His continued endorsement of McCarthy was considered even in 1950 to be an easing of principle for political advantage. Clearly it was, but historians have shown us a certain depth under the crassness. Red-baiting was a Truman policy before it was turned against him by the Republicans in Congress. The administration fostered it in order to win adoption of the massive interventionist program of 1947–49. Every piece of that program Taft opposed, from the Truman Doctrine (a "policy of dividing the world into zones of political influence"), to the Marshall Plan ("we throw our dollars around and try to run the show"), and NATO ("a twenty-year warrant for the executive to take us into war at his discretion").[32]

Fear of communism put it through. It is ironic that McCarthyism developed, tactically, as a sustained attack on the executive branch (for not fighting communism hard enough). The stupidity and scurrilousness of McCarthyism have obscured and vitiated the fact that the first assertion of "executive privilege" since the nineteenth century was not made by Nixon but by Truman and Eisenhower against the Congressional investigative power and the McCarthy senatorial committees.

In short, Taft's partisanship was based, as was no other contemporary senator's, on a philosophic consistency best called republican. His philosophy was never easy to understand. Labor, for example, hated him for the Taft-Hartley Act of 1947, forgot he had acted instantly in labor's behalf when Truman asked authority to draft strikers in 1946, and were baffled when Taft tried to explain both acts on the basis of the same constitutional republicanism. Similar confusion would blight Sam Ervin's career. Principle, however, gives the only angle from which one can view Taft's astonishing performance of June 28, 1950.

It was three days after the war broke out in Korea. President Truman, taking advantage of a Russian boycott of the Security Council meeting at Lake Success, Long Island, had secured a United Nations resolution calling for military sanctions against the aggressor North Korea. He had immediately authorized Japanese proconsul MacArthur to send American ground troops to South Korea under the resolution. Caught by surprise, Taft rose in the Senate. Peering like an old cat through the thick glasses that had kept him personally out of war, he began by agreeing that North Korea had committed aggression and that it had probably been instigated to do so by Russia. If Truman requested a Congressional joint resolution authorizing the sending of troops, Taft said, he "would vote for it." But Truman had not made that request, any more than Roosevelt had when he occupied Iceland in 1941. The action was therefore unconstitutional.

> . . . It seems to me . . . a complete usurpation by the president of authority to use the Armed Forces of this country. If the incident is permitted to go by without protest, at least from this body, we would have finally terminated for all time the right of Congress to declare war, which is granted to Congress alone by the Constitution of the United States.[33]

It was the first time Taft had said that, but not the last. He was to repeat the charge again and again in 1950 and 1951, which, one should remember, was the high tide of McCarthyism. One day historians may be forced to consider the notion that McCarthyism was a hatred, not so much of the left as of appointive centralized government, a last sulfurous flame from the dying republican fire.

In 1954, with the aid of Sam Ervin, the Senate purged itself of McCarthy. Meanwhile the voters themselves had purged, one by one, the senators who expressed their republicanism as "isolationism." McCarthy's legacy was a cold war Congress. For the ten years after Taft's sudden death in 1953 there would be no one in the Senate to question the view that the United States should rule the "free world" or that it was the president's job to direct the empire. Certainly no such question ever passed the eloquent lips of Sam Ervin. He had won a medal in World War I, his patriotism was simple, and his support of American intervention from Lebanon in 1958 to Vietnam in 1964 was thorough and straightforward. Until Watergate, his career would have seemed unexceptionable. Even in his long, vain opposition to civil rights legislation, beginning with an attack on *Brown v. Board of Education* in 1954, he was comfortably flanked by like-minded fellow Democrats. Only one curious note appears in that career to belie the simplicity of Ervin's partisanship and patriotism—and incidentally to illuminate his stand on civil rights. This note is his defense of civil liberties.

In 1967, Ervin, as Chairman of the Senate Government Operations Subcommittee, introduced and successfully piloted into law an act to prevent, among other things, gross and intrusive psychological testing of federal employees. In 1968, he tried to amend the chillingly named Omnibus Crime Control and Safe Streets Act which he had been unable to modify in committee. Finally, in 1970,

having learned computer language to prepare himself, he attacked
federal data banks, army surveillance of civilians, the Narcotics
Control Bill, and the District of Columbia Crime Control Act as
violations in spirit of the Bill of Rights. The speeches he made then
make clear that Ervin's political philosophy was a republicanism of
the most archaic sort, one Ervin himself would call Jeffersonian but
which is more simply described as Whig.[34]

In Ervin's view, governments, especially central governments,
were mean, awkward, blunt instruments needing constantly to be
trimmed and thwarted. He revered the eighteenth-century Whigs
he had studied as a history major in college and worshiped as they
had the common law doctrines he had learned at Harvard Law
School. His opposition to civil rights, it turns out, came from the
same shelf as his opposition to the no-knock provisions of the Narcotics Control Act. Ervin was not a Claghorn. Never did he echo
the racism of his constituents and seldom their discredited doctrine
of states' rights. Instead, he examined each successive federal Civil
Rights Bill with one peevish eye on the common law and the Constitution, reporting at last to the Senate that all of them were
"monsters." When the climactic Voting Rights Act of 1965 came
to the floor, Ervin gave possibly his greatest speech, an erudite and
nearly unassailable proof that it was in effect an ex post facto law;
that is, it defined and punished as crimes things people had already
done at a time when they were not crimes.[35]

Unable to stop this or any other civil-rights act after 1963, Ervin
decided to fight tongue-in-cheek. He proposed that Indians be covered by the Open Housing Act of 1968. Because this one passed,
Ervin became the father of civil rights for Indians. In 1973, Ervin
was conscious of failure. Many of his old allies had died or retired
and he was rapidly becoming the last southern Whig in the Senate.
His colleagues deferred to his constitutional knowledge, laughed ap-
preciatively at his favorite expressions ("clear as the noonday sun,"
"the last lingering note of Gabriel's horn"), but they had voted him
down on everything except the anomalous Federal Employee Rights
Act.[36] He was ready to announce his retirement when the Senate
majority leader, Mike Mansfield called him in Morganton, North
Carolina to cook up the Senate Select Committee on Presidential
Campaign Practices. In fact his imminent retirement was one of
the reasons Mansfield chose him, so that the charge of partisanship
or ambition could not be laid to a committee which both knew
might destroy the administration.

And so Sam Ervin, like George Hoar, came to the climax of his career at the very end of it, at the age of seventy-eight, in a way he had never foreseen. He was to attack and bring down a president with whose conservatism he agreed and of whose interventionism he had approved right down to the invasion of Cambodia.

Ervin never did see the connection between the foreign policy discretion he liked and the domestic tyranny he detested, but on the narrow ground he was, by general agreement, magnificent. At the time he admitted to Senator Baker that he had been to Harvard Law School, for example, Ervin was examining John Ehrlichman. The former chief of the "Domestic Council" in the Executive Office had authorized the burglarizing of the office of a psychiatrist named Fielding by members of the White House staff. As Ehrlichman explained it, the object was to compile a psychiatric profile on Daniel Ellsberg as a possible conspirator and spy, and he thought that this was not only justified by necessity but also within the foreign policy discretion of the president—the "national security" power as he repeatedly put it. "The foreign intelligence activities," drawled Ervin, "had nothing to do with the opinion of Ellsberg's psychiatrist about his emotional or psychological state."

"How do you know that, Mr. Chairman?" replied Ehrlichman.

"Because I can understand the English language," thundered Ervin, "It's my mother tongue!"[37]

Did Ehrlichman speak English? Perhaps, but not English common law. The next day, Ervin found himself in a great debate with Ehrlichman and his lawyer on the meaning of the same Omnibus Crime Control and Safe Streets Act he had helped write and tried to amend in 1968. Section 2511 featured the ominous clause

> Nothing contained in this chapter . . . shall limit the constitutional power of the President to take such measures as he deems necessary to protect the Nation against actual or potential attack . . . to obtain . . . intelligence . . . deemed essential . . . or to protect national security information against foreign intelligence activities.

But the key word, said Ervin, was *constitutional*. Some members of the drafting committee thought the president had powers, "that would make an eastern potentate turn green with envy," Ervin snorted, but "I do not believe the president has any power at all except such as the Constitution expressly gives him or such as are necessarily inferred from the expression of those powers." The burglary, he repeated, was "domestic subversion," not foreign intelligence, in violation of both law and the Fourth Amendment. A rapt public agreed with him. So did the House Committee on Impeachment which put the burglary in an article against Nixon. Ehrlichman did not agree, however, and neither it seems did Senator Baker. It will be quite a while before we know whether the next generation agrees with the old Senator or the young executive appointee.[38]

Watergate and Nixon's near impeachment are past. Already memory, shortest of all for pain, has obscured the "imperial presidency" and the creed that made it possible. The central government and its ascendant executive, from Roosevelt to Nixon, had by 1973 exercised every power, with the possible exception of taxation, which generations of whigs and republicans had studied to deny them. It had had an imperial navy since Theodore Roosevelt, a state police since Wilson, a standing army, a praetorian secret service, and a clandestine diplomacy since FDR. All these presidents had made war without a Congressional declaration, turned administrative regulations into law, and executive agreements into treaties of alliance. From Roosevelt to Nixon palaces had been built for them (Camp David, San Clemente). Since 1909 their faces had replaced Liberty on every coin. Under Nixon even the spending power was in the process of being taken away from Congress. The executive had in the ill- remembered words of Thomas Jefferson

> . . . refused his assent to laws, the most wholesome and necessary for the public good . . . made judges dependent on his will alone . . . erected a multitude of new offices, and sent hither swarms of officers to harrass our people and eat out their substance . . . kept among us, in times of peace, standing armies without the consent of our legislatures . . . affected to render the military independent of and superior to the civil power . . . quarter[ed] large bodies of armed troops among us . . . tak[en] away our charters, abolishing our most valuable laws, and alter[ed] fundamentally the forms of our governments . . . declar[ed] themselves invested with the power to legislate for us in all cases whatsoever . . . excited domestic insurrections amongst us. . . .
>
> A prince, whose character is thus marked by every act which may define a tyrant, is unfit to be the ruler of a free people. . . .[39]

These days it is clear only that senators, by the very nature of their office, are the most likely officers of this republic to question the secular trend—to understand that the people is sovereign here, not the government; to believe that no one magistrate acts for that sovereign, not even the president of the United States. As R.M.N.

boarded the "executive helicopter" and soared off into exile on August 9, 1974, it was also clear that, after three-quarters of a century, the Senate had at last beaten the odds and, with the aid of a handful of other institutions and circumstances, checkmated the imperial presidency. Whether the victory will be only temporary, like the one in 1868, will not be known for a long time.

14

Conclusion
Squaring the Circles of Polybios

THE SMOOTH BENIGNITY of the present Republican president, Ronald Reagan, makes it doubly hard (and thus perhaps more necessary) to recall the extraordinary behavior of his predecessor. When Richard Nixon was reelected in 1972, the American people were endorsing, by the largest margin in history, a president who had secretly bombed, and publicly and unilaterally invaded, two independent nations, ordered illegal intelligence operations against United States citizens, and financed a whole series of essentially private policies with the equivalent of private taxation—campaign funds offered by corporations to influence executive action. Publicly, Nixon had claimed the right, untrammeled by Senate consent, to appoint Supreme Court Justices, to limit his execution of Acts of Congress, to carry out acts of war without legislative declaration or consent, and to subject any citizen to presidential surveillance in the name of national security. He had not by any means been the first to try most of these, but he was the first to assert that there was nothing wrong with them. There was even an air of assured custom about his actions.

It was not yet known in November 1972 that Nixon had ordered his appointees to obstruct justice, tap telephones, open mail, and steal the papers of ideological enemies; or that he had endorsed all these regal usurpations as an integrated program (the Huston Plan) as early as June 1970. The 1969 orders to bomb Cambodia and Laos, too, were not yet officially acknowledged, but everything else was public. Even the charge that Nixon men were involved in the burglary at Watergate was known before the election. The public reaction to all this stunned believers in the democratic presidency and confirmed everything that Aristotle, Cicero, and even James Madison had written about the threat posed by democracy to republican institutions.

It is not easy nowadays to recapture the mood of the winter following that election, when the United States was, in the words of the defeated Democratic candidate, "closer to one-man rule than at any other time in history."[1] With difficulty it may be recalled that before the tapes were transcribed, before John Dean testified, before even Judge Sirica sentenced the Watergate burglars, there was nothing to the affair except a few hard-to-confirm stories in the Washington *Post*. Still secret at inauguration on January 20 was Nixon's "exciting prospect" for his second administration: complete control of the government, destruction of his "enemies," use of the Justice Department and the Internal Revenue Service against opposition both political and constitutional, and use of "the Bureau," meaning the FBI (Director Hoover, who had torpedoed the Huston Plan, would torpedo no more, having died in May 1972).

Everyone heard in January, however, that Nixon had fired 2,000 appointees in the executive branch, including the entire Cabinet, a week or two after election, and that he was also in the process of installing loyal members of his personal staff in Cabinet undersecretaryships. For many of them, this would be their first rude encounter with the constitutional requirement of Senate confirmation, but that turned out to be fairly easy to smooth out. Reliable Pat Gray went up for confirmation as FBI Director. Roy Ash got busy organizing a "super-cabinet" in which nobody would need to be confirmed. A purge of the CIA was begun. At the Office of Economic Opportunity that January, an unconfirmed Acting Director set about dismantling the agency. The name of John Dean was heard, a staff member who refused to testify at Gray's hearing on the grounds of something called "executive privilege."

By April, Attorney-General Kleindienst was explaining that executive privilege protected *any* member of the executive branch from the grim necessity of talking to Congress or a court. If Congress didn't like that they might as well "impeach" Nixon. Nor could a staggering Congress outflank the president by legislation. In the month before the election Nixon had pocket-vetoed no less than eleven separate spending bills, announcing just after the election and again in March that he would veto any spending bill he thought excessive, and that if Congress overrode him he would simply "impound" or refuse to spend the funds, just as he had already done with the appropriations for environmental protection.

The press, too, was on notice to approve the president. In December 1972, an unconfirmed Nixon appointee named Clay Whitehead had threatened local television stations with Federal Trade Commission action if they continued to broadcast the "elitist gossip" of the network news. On the war front, the Gulf of Tonkin Resolution had been repealed for more than a year, yet the previous May had seen the mining of Haiphong. In the month after election, the "Christmas bombing" fell, unannounced and unexplained, on Hanoi, and in January the bombing of Cambodia was resumed in defiance of a Senate resolution.[2]

It would be hard to imagine a more comprehensive list of unrepublican acts in a republican regime. One would have to go back to a Bonaparte, or down to a Ferdinand Marcos, to find anything more concerted. Ten years later it is still not clear whether the eventual reaction, half an impeachment mounted by a more or less elite minority and followed by a voluntary resignation, has been effective in preventing a repeat performance. Ten years later the average American citizen still seems to consider the Nixon resignation to have been the result of narrow violations of criminal law, and would doubtless find it peculiar and impossible to try to fit his policies into some such combative category as "crimes against the republic."

That the American people should have reacted to Nixon with such stubborn and overwhelming approval must be laid, in my view, to ignorance. A history is missing in the United States. A body of knowledge thought by people like Adams and Jefferson to be indispensable to the exercise of citizenship has been relegated to society's back burner, scholarship. Surely republicanism is a most complex and demanding tradition, and Americans are famous as a people for their neglect of tradition and for their insistence on simplicity. Nevertheless, it takes some effort, even in a country that Philip Rahv renamed Amnesia, to forget republican history.

Republics before this century would not have allowed such ignorance, and might not have survived it.[3] It was, however, easier for them to set that kind of store by republican education at a time when history was still a branch of literature, one which aimed deliberately at "moral example," and when the Western mind was more disposed than it is now to see continuity in history rather than quantized change. Florence found it easy to learn from Rome because most Florentines seem to have thought that the city was a surviving branch of the old Roman Republic, founded before Caesar.

How much republican citizens knew is rather a marvel before the age of widespread literacy, and remarkable even afterward. Solon's political techniques, his ingenious balancing of "Coast," "Plain," and "Mountain," his exemplary resignation, were known through the once ubiquitous schoolboy text, Plutarch's *Lives*, to every literate republican from the Renaissance to the end of the nineteenth century. Together with Aristotle's *Politics* and Thucydides' terrible elegy for Athenian imperialism (*The Peloponnesian War*), Plutarch was the transmission belt for Greek republicanism and an ever present text for partisans from Machiavelli to Senator Hoar. It was there that Robespierre and his colleagues found their party name *Montagne,* there that Abbe Siéyès found names for all his constitutional assemblies, and likely that it was in Plutarch's report of Solon's class legislation that John Adams first got the idea of dividing the citizens of Massachusetts into thousand-, three hundred-, one hundred-, and sixty-pound men according to personal wealth.

Livy's *Ab Urbe Condita,* which, with Sallust, Cicero, and Tacitus, was to be found at the desks of most of these same schoolchildren, served to remind many generations of republicans of the indispensable example of Rome. Livy's book taught Machiavelli and provided the platform for his *Discorsi.* Milton reflected him on nearly every page, as did his radical Whig successors from Algernon Sidney to John Adams. The French Revolution, too, with its constant appeals to Brutus and the Gracchi, its ultimately futile warnings of a Caesar, is inconceivable without the Roman Republic.

The relative eclipse of Solon's Athens and Brutus's Rome is not made up for by the memory of Samuel's Israel, kept greener by the odd combination of deassimilated Judaism and evangelical Protestant Christianity. When the Prime Minister of Israel, Menachem Begin, was hailed as *melech* (king) in 1981, far too few eyebrows were raised. Yet *I Samuel* 8, a troublesome text even for the medieval monarchists, had been essential to the radical arguments of Knox, Ponet, and Goodman, and Mornay, to Calvin himself, to Milton, and even to secular Calvinists like John Adams, Rousseau, Thaddeus Stevens, and Sam Ervin. One looks in vain for the likes of Baruch Korff and Billy Graham to cite Samuel in order to ease a renunciation of Nixonism.

It is true that patriarchal tribalism, the ultimate source of the republicanism of Samuel, Solon, and Brutus together, is declining in all parts of the modern world. Regionalism and localized nationalism, however, stubbornly refuse to die even in the most advanced countries. Movements like those of the Québecois or Catalan separatists provide the same example, weak in theory but strong in practice, that Switzerland offered the West in the Middle Ages. Municipal republicanism is also alive and well, in San Francisco no less than in San Marino, surprisingly similar in its practice and influence to Florence, Geneva, and Antwerp four or five centuries ago. Nor has communism entirely emptied the word *commune* of its medieval meaning. Neighborhood and block politics in Brooklyn are not so very different from that of the *sections* of revolutionary Paris or the militia districts of medieval Florence.

Still, the fabric is thin. Though Paris is exhilaratingly aware of its own rebellious history and Switzerland still celebrates William Tell, other communities in the West know little of them. Like some wines, these traditions do not travel well. Similarly, the Dutch Republic, having become a conventional constitutional monarchy in 1815, no longer inspires twentieth-century republicans as it once did the English or American Commonwealthsmen. It is hard to predict whether any republican history can be revived or made useful at this late date, when a full explanation even of the standard "checks and balances" demands more attention than most can muster. Can a 1980s activist, anxious to save the oceans or to learn industry from Japan, be persuaded to sit still for a lesson from fifteenth-century Florence?

Perhaps, if the history can be boiled down in the manner of ancient political science, he can be. For a dozen republics, we can substitute the general model, the habits and biases of republicans or, at the very least, their characteristic values.

The essential republican principle is that no one person shall rule the community, that everyone shall have a part in the public's business. The fundamental bias is toward plurality, balance, and competition. The public's business must be one and known to all, but those who conduct it must be many. To achieve this difficult goal, the republican leans on four essential political techniques and four essential moral virtues. The virtues are sobriety, service, independence, and ambition. The techniques are, in alphabetical order: minimizing appointment, multiplying constituencies, rotation in office, and separation of powers. Each is to some extent dependent on the others and the history of republics offered in this book shows that no republic can long exist without practicing, to some degree, all eight of them.

The first technique is to control appointment. In a republic, whether democratic or aristocratic, the important magistrates may hold office by almost any title, even heredity, but they may not hold office by appointment. The appointee is of necessity the servant of his employer, his *creature*, as the eighteenth-century Whigs so aptly put it. Like the centurion's servant in the Gospel, he comes and goes at the will of his superior. He can only represent the republic indirectly, or, in extreme cases, by resigning in protest. The more appointees there are in a government, the greater the power of the appointing officer. Appointees closest to a particularly powerful appointer can end by taking over. It took only a few centuries for the English king's valet ("Chamberlain") and private secretary ("Chancellor") to become the heads of government. In only one century, the Frankish king's butlers ("major domo") became the kings of France.

Even tenuring appointees does not entirely limit the power of the appointer. As long as he retains any power over their salary, their perquisites, their own subordinates, or even the policy they are to execute, they remain to that extent his creatures. In the United States, cabinet members may complain to the president, or limit their duty to carrying out existing law, or claim a duty to Congress which creates their offices, confirms, and interrogates them, but as long as the president hires and fires them, they belong largely to him. If there is only one who hires in the state, the appointee who resigns will have no place to go.

It may not be necessary in a republic to tenure all mailmen, or indeed, as in Florence, to elect them, but it is necessary to limit their numbers. It is also necessary for a republic to spread out the power to appoint them among many magistrates who are themselves independently chosen by any means other than appointment. Any means. Republics in the past have used drawn lots

(Athens, Florence), cooptation (Rome), and even heredity (Athens, Venice) in addition to the more ordinary and democratic means of election by some constituency of voting citizens. Each has its drawbacks, but none threaten the republic's balance as appointment does. In the back of the republican mind is the unacceptable vision of a state in which nearly every citizen owes his livelihood to a magistrate, perhaps where all owe it to only one magistrate, and freedom, in its most practical sense, simply ceases to exist.

Similar reasoning lies behind the republican's faith in multiple constituencies. For the democrat the idea of having some people choose one magistrate and others another is tolerable at best. In America the democrat argues that giving two representatives to each county in a southern state senate is the same as giving the vote to cows. Each year he argues for the abolition of the electoral college on the grounds that the whole nation should be a single constituency for the election of presidents. Not so, says the republican. Multiply and subdivide constituencies and you give more power to each citizen. More importantly, you carry the inevitable clash of politics up from the level of the individual citizen and force the magistrates themselves to fight it out. Each has his own "power base" largely impregnable to the products of other such bases. Each is independent of all other magistrates and answerable only to a part of the people itself. Each is therefore free to argue policy in public with all the other magistrates.

The argument moreover reflects the true state of the electorate—willful, divided, opinionated, but responsible. A single national constituency allows magistrates falsely to embody the will of the people and gives the impression that that will is coherent and docile. It also brings monarchy closer, since when all magistrates are products of the same constituency, any hint of a hierarchical relationship among them tends to enlarge, embed, and perpetuate itself, making the most able, the most willful, or the most representative among them the ruler of the rest.

Again, the republican does not care so much how the constituencies are divided, so long as it is done. Neighborhoods elected magistrates in Florence, counties and towns in England, districts of 30,000 citizens in America. In ancient Athens and Rome it was tribes—extended families. Some European states have in the past represented regions or social classes. Republican theorists like Harrington and Saint-Simon have suggested having magistrates represent categories of property or professions, hewers of wood and drawers of water. For a republican none of this is impossible. In fact, the more fellow feeling a grouping had, the more desirable it would be to make it a constituency. The unofficial magistracy of parties is not unwelcome. Modern pressure from urbanites and suburbanites, from rich or poor, or from ethnic minorities to have magistrates of their own gives a republican no particular trouble, though it has in the past given democrats fits and bureaucrats heart failure.

No pattern in republican history is older, and no device has been more reliable in keeping monarchy at bay. For a single constituency to elect all magistrates means that one day there will be only one magistrate, and an elected king or queen is no better than a hereditary one.

Even if she were to be elected every year. Because the third cardinal principle of the republican is that no magistrate may be allowed to stay in office too long. Five, six, ten years in office, and she becomes, just as bureaucrats do, "entrenched." According to the theory, no magistracy is without power and few are without patronage—such is the definition of political office. Allow the same person to hold one for too long and that person becomes more powerful than the other magistrates, even those more able, or those with "higher" offices. Presidents with four- to eight-year terms may defer even to their own appointees, a J. Edgar Hoover, for example, who had been there forever. If he had been, shudders the republican, elected for forty years instead of appointed, he might have made himself a monarch.

Even at the risk of governmental inefficiency, magistrates must go. Even the best must go, on principle. How long each should stay is a practical matter on which republicans have differed since republics began, but in general, the higher their office the sooner they must go.[4] Florence gave its highest officers, the Priors, only three months on the job—nonrenewable—but this may be the outside limit. Florence's lower officers, the *accoppiatori* who did have reelection privileges, became Florence's de facto rulers. French presidents may hold their job for seven years and be reelected for another seven, but that is the limit, and until 1958, the office was largely ceremonial.[5] A couple of hundred equally powerful legislators or judges may hold office for life, but when a republican hears of someone made consul or president or dictator for life, even by majority vote, like Julius Caesar or Papa Doc, he knows another republic has perished.

A second advantage to rotation in office is the spread of political responsibility and experience. In general, argues the republican, the more citizens there are in a state who have actually held office, the more likely people are to respect the magistrates and aid them in carrying out their responsibilities. Conversely, magistrates are more likely to respect the citizens subject to their authority when they know some will one day be ordering them. Both will be that much more loyal to the republic itself to the extent they have served it. Each office, too, is a training ground for others and in the republican view, no state can have too many citizens qualified for public office. Short tenures also deprofessionalize public service. They reduce its mystery, make it more accessible, help prevent the desperate resort (for a republican) to the filling of vacant offices by appointment. They lead to the proud boast of so many republicans, from Cincinnatus to John Adams, that upon leaving office they had not lowered but raised their dignity. While the people are sovereign, the highest title in the state must be, simply, "citizen."

Third, short tenures increase the representative character of magistracies. Just as the power to hire and fire makes creatures of appointees, so the constituency's regular opportunity to elect or retire makes public servants of ambitious politicians. Here is one republican tenet that has never been forgotten, for democrats have taken it up.

Fourth and last, rotation in office not only gives the public control of gifted officers—it attracts such people to office in the first place. The shorter the term, the more often an office is open. Ambition is satisfied and the public the more brilliantly served. It is often asked why there were so many talented young politicians available to make the Revolution in America in 1775, and one of the answers must be the number and variety of local offices there, combined with the shortness of tenure for each—usually one year. It has even been suggested that the Founding Fathers made their revolution largely because the top of the colonial magistracy was different in tenure from the bottom. The terms of governors and governors' councils were so long that the ambition of younger men was thwarted. Hence, Adams expelled Hutchinson in Massachusetts, and Patrick Henry Lord Dunmore in Virginia, for the same reason that Sulla had made war on Marius. Under present conditions, each American generation can share at most only seven presidencies. With one thousandth our population or less, ancient Rome could guarantee its most gifted citizens sixty consulships in the same thirty years. Under such conditions it is no wonder perhaps that so many brilliant Americans become artists—or that so few Romans did.

Perhaps the most recognizable of the four republican tenets in America is the fourth, separation of powers. In the mind of the republican it is not enough to multiply offices, one must also divide power itself. The magistrate who somehow gains control of more than one of the great powers of sovereignty may become monarch in fact, no matter how many other magistracies continue to exist. Since the ancient writers Polybios and Aristotle, much of republican thought has in fact been devoted to identifying those powers and defining them. For the past two centuries the consensus has been that there are essentially three of them: law, money, and war. These three have been recognized as the cardinal powers of sovereignty by legal scholars in both monarchies and republics, but it is in republics that identification and analysis become essential.

A republic's survival depends absolutely on keeping a grip on these powers, and the republic, it will be remembered, is an abstraction with no hands to grip with. For the republic to hold power, therefore, it must divide it among several real hands. The irreducible minimum of magistrates in a republic must then be three, at least one for each power. Yet the powers are interdependent, no one may make law or war without money, or tax without either law or force. The relations of the powers must be intimate and the magistracies in charge of each must balance perfectly and communicate efficiently. Thus Florence had one committee for war, another for taxes, but it allowed both to write law which still other committees had to ratify. In our own tradition, derived from England, the three prime powers are all given primarily to the legislature, which is divided into two houses, each with its complement of independent magistrates.

Further subdivision of the three powers has provided other ways to parcel them out among magistrates so as to achieve the ideal division and harmony. Thus the law power may be divided into lawmaking, enforcement, and interpretation, leading to the familiar American official triumvirate: Congress, President, and Supreme Court. Similarly, the war power, subdivided into declaration, support of armies, and command, leads to an equally familiar pair of magistracies, Congress holding the first two powers and the president the third. In the matter of money, however, a similar tripartite division into taxing, spending, and coinage points out that in American republican theory the legislature is absolutely paramount. It controls all three. In money matters, the president, even armed with a veto, is at Congress's orders. This is because in nearly all republican thought the money power is the most important and must therefore at all costs be kept out of the hands of any one magistrate. Republican history is full of elegies for states to whom monarchy came when one magistrate gained control of taxation. Coinage, too, is important. The single coiner puts his face on coins, legislatures that of liberty; and each symbolizes the power to inflate and deflate. Even in democratic thought the idea of a majority of the people somehow losing its direct control of the purse is galvanizing and apocalyptic. After *vox populi vox dei*, "No taxation without representation!" is the republican slogan most quoted by democrats.

Still other divisions are possible. The war power gives rise to one of the republican's greatest fears, a standing army, the "monopoly of violence" in the flesh. War above all requires unified rapid action and republics cannot always remain at peace. Is it necessary, therefore, to have a military force in being, obedient to orders and commanded by one magistrate? How can the law and money powers be made safe or separate from such a force? One answer has been a confederated local militia like the force that won American independence. The Second Amendment to the Constitution was, in fact, written to perpetuate such a militia basis for the war power. Unprofessional, militias rise as if from the earth in emergencies and return to peacetime occupations the minute the war is over. Commanders may not even be able to get them to cross state borders, much less violate a republican constitution. The Minuteman idea is ancient and wholly republican, originating with the hoplite infantry of ancient Greece, the tribal levies of Israel, and the cantonal pikemen of Switzerland which Machiavelli vainly tried to adapt for Florence.[6]

No less to be feared than a standing army is a standing navy. Since the Athenians took over Delos, a navy has been the classic instrument of colonialism, its existence practically a guarantee that the republic will exceed its boundaries and the war powers concentrate in the hands of whatever official commands it. If a republic gets an empire, Rome showed, it will get an emperor too. Thus American republicans in 1807 tried to build ships which could not sail much more than ten miles from shore, perhaps to atone for their party's responsibility in America's first executive police action—a naval attack on Libya in 1802.

Finally the war power leads the republican to consider very carefully the provision of bodyguards to magistrates. In the past these have proved to be as dangerous to liberty as full-scale armies. One of them overthrew the Athenian republic in the 580s B.C. Roman law allowed no armed troops of any kind in the city. As the republic fell, the law was broken, creating the Praetorian Guard. Even the smallest of armed forces must owe its loyalty to the republic. Once it gives that loyalty to an individual magistrate, the choice is either monarchy or civil war.

These four tenets by no means exhaust republican thinking. Rich though this tradition is in political technology, it is even richer in what might be called moral philosophy. Anyone who reads in the literature of republicanism will be immediately struck by the extraordinary number of references to morality. Ancient republicans like Livy dwell on the god-given ethics which preserve the public thing. As the religious sanctions on government decline after the Middle Ages, writers like Machiavelli and Milton fill their books with the mores requires of citizens of a successful republic. In the eighteenth century, Montesquieu elevates the Livyan word "virtue" to talismanic heights. Republics, he writes, require virtue as a foundation as monarchies depend on honor.[7] Virtue is the epitome of republican morality, its meaning much the same as it had been for Livy, a combination of sobriety, service, independence, and ambition. If all citizens do not behave according to these four maxims, republics will succumb to the twin evils that stalk them all, monarchy and civil war.

The *sine qua non* of republican survival, republicans insist, is sobriety. The ideal republic must be one in which everything is frugal. Dress, meals, work, amusements, ceremonies, and even sex must take place without indulgence and contribute to a general atmosphere of restraint. The republican, even in Athens, must be as Spartan as possible. Old-fashioned republicans like Cato in Rome deplore intricate hairdos, fringes on the toga, Lucullan banquets, specialized artisanry, the scale of entertainment in the Colisea and Circuses, toplofty military triumphs, sexual excess, serial marriage, and overindulgence of every kind. Though cities are typically republican, the urban republicans of Athens, Florence, and even Boston, Massachusetts are seized regularly with foreboding at urban displays of luxury and often dream as feverishly as Thomas Jefferson did of the destruction of cities. A farmer, they think, is naturally frugal and therefore naturally republican. Cincinnatus, who wiped the sweat from his brow, left his plow to become dictator of Rome, and then returned to his farm, is the type of the republican magistrate. George Washington consciously copies him. Recalling him, republicans Franklin and Rousseau wear coonskin and homespun to shame the monarchical luxury of eighteenth-century Paris. In the same city, John Adams deplores the morals of the women, and Franklin's hypocrisy in taking advantage of them.

It is a maxim of monarchies that "the king should live of his own," while displaying the preeminent wealth that goes with his position. A king should be lavish like Louis XIV, not miserly like Henry VII. Gifts of foreign states are given to him personally. He is too rich to be corrupted by them. The maxim of republics is the contrary. A magistrate must live on his salary, display little, move among the populace like the citizen he is, temporarily called upon to serve fellow citizens. He should accept gifts from no one, but if pressed he accepts in the name of the republic. He shall have no palaces, whether at Hyannisport or San Clemente. He must be tight with his own money and a positive skinflint with the public's money. Among private citizens differences of wealth are suspect, private fortunes (like Cosimo de Medici's) are dangerous. Even more than the democrat, the republican favors equality. So fundamental is sobriety to the republican style that it is possible to argue that the Puritanism of Geneva and Boston came from political faith as much as it did from religious faith.

The second moral idea behind republics, service, is closely linked to the first. Possessed by frugality and self-restraint, the citizen is better equipped to serve the republic in any one of its multiplicity of public offices. If her own affairs are simple, she will have time to manage the affairs of the public. If her wants are minimal, she will not be seeking office in order to satisfy them. If she likes her life-style to be undistinguished, she will be unlikely to seek office merely to distinguish herself, and she will be as prepared to obey as she is qualified to command.

Such a citizen will put the republic first and himself second. He may be capable of slightly chilling prodigies like Brutus' execution of his traitorous sons or Scaevola's deliberate burning of his right hand. At the very least he will keep his hands out of the public till and resist the temptation to use his private or official power against res publica. The common weal, the public rather than the private happiness, will be his goal. The service of all will replace mere loyalty to individuals. Such anyway is the dream. Utopians of the past,

like Livy, place it in some dim golden age, the beginnings of Rome.
Utopians of the future, like Rousseau and Saint-Just, place it just
around the corner. It is a powerful dream, no less powerful for being
secular, and at the minimal level of simple honest administration,
it seems not entirely unattainable.

Less utopian than the idea of service, at least to Americans, is
the ideal of independence. The citizen of a republic, according to
republican tradition, must be ornery. The magistrate must command her strictly according to the law or risk the most ulcerous and
determined resistance. The object is to erect a universal check
against the usurpation of any authority the republic has not spe-
cifically granted. Independence also implies that a citizen must have
her own power base, not a constituency this time but a family and
a livelihood, which gives her leeway to oppose a usurping magistrate. With reasoning similiar to that which underlies the effort to
minimize appointive office, the republican argues that employers
are better citizens than employees, the landed better than the landless. In the Jeffersonian vision, in fact, the independent "yeoman
farmer" is of all possible citizens of a republic the most reliable.

Independence is no less a virtue in magistrates. An officer cannot do his duty under the law if he owes greater duties to other
citizens or other magistrates. The republican rejoices when a legislator defies the executive despite the threat of reduced patronage.
Without fear or favor was the motto of the Roman tribune. Modern
journalists now claim the phrase but few find it possible to live up
to it.

Last and most paradoxical of the ingredients of republican virtue is ambition. Ambition cuts both ways. It is the badge of great
magistrates and without it the republic would be deprived of its
ablest potential servants. Too much of it, however, may easily lead
a Caesar to monarchy or a Marius and Sulla to civil war and the
breakdown of law and order. The republic must be able to call up
a Jaurès and a Clemenceau from their provinces. Given a Webster,
a Clay, and a Calhoun, it must use all three. It must legitimize the
mightiest ambitions and find the best place for their exercise. Somehow, however, it must also keep them in harness, prevent one from
eliminating the other, and provide for what is called at American
presidential inaugurations an orderly transition between them.

Much more than democrats or monarchists, republicans have
recognized that power is sweet, and that power corrupts. Delight
with power and suspicion of it contend on every page of the records

of the American Constitutional Convention of 1787. Republics have too many offices in their gift to discourage the wish for power. For some republicans, Machiavelli for one, it is better to have a strong monarchy than a gang of unambitious and incompetent magistrates. For a republican, the encouragement of politicians and suspicion of them must go hand in hand, with irony perhaps as a Paraclete. Purely personal, empty ambition is easy to spot and easy to use or thwart, but even the ambition to serve the republic may unconsciously mask, as it did in Cromwell, a will to absolute power. This republic, too, as we have seen, was brought perilously close to monarchy in the winter of 1972–73, and one man's ambition was a major cause. No doubt another was America's growing ignorance of republicanism and perhaps the American citizen's neglect of the republican virtues. Whatever the cause, the escape was by a hair's breadth.

For a republic is a rather delicate thing. The balance is critical and sometimes very easy to upset. Our own, at two hundred years, is older than most. More than two thousand years ago the historian Polybios wrote a history of the world that Rome had recently conquered. Believing it to be the chief cause of Rome's success, he devoted a whole book—Book Six—to an analysis of Rome's "complicated" republican constitution. It was, he claimed, at the peak of a predictable cycle, familiar from the history of a thousand other states. Monarchy, he wrote, always gives way, as it had in Rome, to tyranny, tyranny to an aristocratic republic, an aristocratic republic to a more democratic one.

Now at her constitutional acme, Rome had conquered the world. Because the constitution of Rome contained elements of previous systems, it was exceptionally stable. But the cycle was bound to continue. A democratic republic, according to Polybios, inevitably gives rise to mob rule and mob rule (ochlocracy) gives way to monarchy again. It is inevitable, wrote this dour Greek a century before Julius Caesar, that the Roman Republic will fall and monarchy return. Either the techniques of balance or republican virtue itself will fail, as they had everywhere else in the ancient world.[8] Officials will become corrupt, ambition overweening, luxury uncontrollable. The increasing dependence of the people on the magistrates will raise their demands and lower their level of responsibility.

Because this is not a bad description of what happened in Rome in the next century, Polybios' book has left the republican tradition with a stubborn and ominous problem. How can a republic be permanent? One of the founding problems of political science, referred to by Benjamin Franklin at the conclusion of the Constitutional Convention ("A republic, if you can keep it"), it has often been neglected but it has never been satisfactorily solved. Perhaps no solution exists, but hypotheses, at least, ought at this point to be easier to imagine.

The republican tradition offers two kinds of precautions to restore a faltering republic. One is the restoration of virtue, a prophetic renewal as suggested by the careers of Samuel, Cato, Savonarola, Calvin, Rousseau, and Robespierre, and by the despair of Machiavelli. To revive the four republican virtues of service, ambition, independence, and sobriety might not be the impossible task that Machiavelli said it was in the *Discourses*, but our examples seem to demonstrate that only religion can accomplish it. Moreover, there is little doubt that it would require leaders of precisely the same stripe as Cato or Robespierre, and the ayatollahs of Iran.

The obstacles are enormous, and so is the cost. To the Calvinists the price of victory was moral totalitarianism. For Cato, Savonarola, and Robespierre there was no victory to be had. Not only could none of them change his people's values permanently, each was repudiated by them and driven to his death. Even had they lived, to quote Machiavelli, "One man cannot live long enough to have time to bring a people back to good habits."[9]

American republicans must hope then, either that republican theory is wrong when it asserts that a republic cannot be maintained without virtue—or else that the observers are wrong when they say, as they do so often, that virtue in America is declining. After all, this country's wealth has been the highest in the West for three centuries, and "moral decline" has been criticized here at least since 1790, when John Adams's son-in-law wrote:

> Our free-born ancestors such arts despis'd
> Genuine sincerity alone they priz'd;
> Their minds with honest emulation fir'd,
> To solid good—not ornament—aspir'd;
> Or, if ambition rous'd a bolder flame,
> Stern virtue throve where indolence was shame.[10]

The reader will not need to be told by now that this writer is inclined to stand with Solon and Benjamin Franklin on the side of praxis or techniques as opposed to prophesy. In any era, I think, it is easier, more definable, far more productive, and far less dangerous to tinker with a constitution than it is to revive a faith. Eschewing the call to moral renewal, I think it more appropriate to end a history of republics with an application of the tinker's kit: separation of powers, rotation in office, multiplying constituencies, and minimizing appointments, all of which find ingenious use in that most recent of the tinker's inventions, the parliamentary republic.

The parliamentary republic is not a deliberate invention. It was stumbled on by the British in the eighteenth century and only defined as an institution by the French in 1875. In both cases, the principal architects were inadvertent monarchists. It has not been tried in the United States, largely because the Framers of the Constitution were unable to see the seeds of the future in the British system they so much admired, and because the radical Republicans of 1865–68 would not or could not have considered what had not been called a republican regime since the time of John Adams.

In a nutshell, the parliamentary republic consists of nothing more than a cabinet of executives elected and maintained in power by a majority of the legislature, with a chief of state if necessary to appoint them formally. Unorthodox in the United States, the system is of course normal in most of the functioning republics elsewhere in the world, smaller nations where our constitution is as exotic as baseball. Western countries like Chile, Canada, Brazil, Austria, Finland, Ireland, and Israel (in chronological order) have adopted it without strain. Non-Western countries like Turkey, India, and Congo seem to flourish under it. Disguised as constitutional monarchy, it is the rule in England, Benelux, Scandinavia, and Spain. By 1945 it was familiar enough to be imposed by the Americans themselves in Italy, Germany, and Japan. It is not hard to envision it here. Congress would be elected as usual, but instead of an at-large election for president, there would be an election of the entire cabinet by the Senate or by a joint session of Congress. The cabinet would be subject to recall by the same body if it lost a major bill and new elections would then be held. The principle of rotation in office would be maintained through the normal two- and six-year terms of legislators.

It sounds quite odd, but in fact such a system could be imposed without even amending the Constitution. Half the object—recall—could be accomplished by regular and successful impeachment of executive officers, including presidents. It would be traumatic indeed, but perfectly constitutional. Similarly, the other half—election—could be instituted if Congress, in exercising its duty to count the votes of the Electoral College, would simply declare every presidential election a tie and proceed to the constitutional system, unused since 1825 and 1876, of putting the choice to itself or its agents. It is, of course, easier to amend the Constitution than to go through these novelties. Though the cumulative effect of amendments since 1868 has been in many ways unrepublican, and republicans ought not to hope for too much from that quarter, amendment does offer the opportunity to preserve the useful and popular features of the at-large presidential election. In the words of Machiavelli:

> . . . If the number, authority, and duration of the term of service of the magistrates be changed, the titles at least ought to be preserved. This, as I have said, should be observed by whoever desires to convert an absolute government either into a republic or a monarchy; but . . . he who wishes to establish an absolute power . . . a tyranny, must change everything. . . .[11]

A model amendment along these lines would redefine the office of president so that its duties would be limited to presiding at state dinners, opening stadiums, entertaining the press, and throwing out the first ball of the baseball season, etc. Its one genuinely political duty would be to appoint formally as Secretary of State the politician most able to command a congressional majority for his or her policies, and to call for new congressional elections when this was not possible. All executive powers under Article II of the old Constitution would be confided to the Secretary of State, except for the veto, which would cease, and the pardon, which would stay with the President (we might now risk a capital letter on him or her). The Secretaryship of State, simultaneously with all other major executive offices, would be filled by majority vote of both houses of Congress.

The suggestion is not a frivolous one. One of its more important immediate results would be to make Congress fully responsible to the electorate for the success or failure of government policy. Any congressman or -woman who voted for the three or four major policies of a Cabinet would be counted, for better or worse, in the government party. He or she would be reelected largely on the question of whether that government was working or not. Nor could he or she charge the President with vetoing its policy or refusing to back it. The responsibility would be inescapable, not only for the legislator, but for the constituency as well.

The more important result, at least for republicans, would be to reduce by a dozen or more the number of appointed officials with high executive responsibility. At the same time, the remaining appointees would be greatly reduced in status and far less likely to entertain the immodest notion that the power they exercised was political instead of merely administrative.

As solutions go, this one is unsettling. Still, "We shall never find any course entirely free from objections," as Machiavelli pointed out, and this seems to be one of the rare ones that would cause fewer problems than it solves.[12] The parliamentary republic has, in historic practice, only one besetting flaw, and that is its tendency to be immobilized by fragmentation of the legislature, or to limp along for years under coalition cabinets. While the weakness of a monarch can be kept private most of the time, the weakness or division of a republican legislature must be public. Public indecision, in turn, weakens the respect in which the whole system is held. The longer it continues while decision is wanted, the more there emerges a desire for authoritarian rule—usually in the form of the kind of monarchy now called dictatorship. To this cause, at least in part, one may attribute the brief eclipse of the French Republic from 1940 to 1944, the failure of the Spanish Republic in 1936, and the demise of innumerable republics in the Third World since their independence.

But this is a flaw that also appears to some extent in the presidential republic. In the form of an inability of the executive and the legislature to cooperate, indecision has been the normal condition of government in the United States for more than a generation, and its effect, though slow and incremental, has been the same. The electorate attributes more and more power to that "fetus of monarchy," the executive branch. Adopting a parliamentary republic would be more likely, in our case, to remove the flaw than enlarge it.

The parliamentary republic, however, may never come to the United States. Even when offered in the tinkering spirit of the Framers, large solutions run afoul of a doubtless healthy constitutional conservatism. Smaller adjustments are more palatable, and republicans are full of them.

In the area of economic policy, for example, the republican offers a roll call of suggestions, all aimed at decentralizing the power of the purse, which begins with increasing local taxes and ends with reducing federal ones. In the area of diplomacy, the republican favors tight limits on even the most benevolent imperialism, lest the United States go the way of Rome and Athens. In the area of military service, the republican is in favor of anything approaching the Swiss policy (also found in Israel) of universal military training on the one hand, and a vanishing standing army on the other. A good republican tinker can even insist on plural control of nuclear weapons.

Of all the world's nuclear powers, so far as is known, only the United States and France (which made the error of imitating the American presidency in its 1958 constitution) place complete power to use atom bombs in the hands of a single person. An almost perversely democratic argument has it that since there are over five hundred elected magistrates in Congress, and since missiles take less than an hour to complete their trajectories, there is no time to consult the Congress on such an issue. Thus we have arranged it that the most fateful and final decision which could ever be made in our politics will be made by one man or woman, acting alone.

Why do we tolerate this? There would be nothing absurd about an act of Congress which required the president to consult (as indeed he usually has on great issues) with an inner cabinet made up of holders of certain statutory offices. The British Prime Minister is already subject to such a system. Moreover, a thoroughgoing republican would want something even more drastic. To republicans cabinet or subcabinet officials are appointees, potential creatures, who must be prevented from making policy. It is Congress that has the right to declare war, though it illegally alienated that right with the War Powers Act of 1973. The republican therefore proposes a statute requiring that before the president orders a missile launched, or pushes a single button, he or she must send a war message to Congress via the same command and control technology which allows him or her to issue these appalling orders in the first place. By law it would then be up to each member of Congress to vote for peace or war within the time limit prescribed by circumstances.

Under the existing (and draconian) rules of the House of Representatives, even a minute or two of debate would be possible. The technology to make this possible has been available for years, and only the persistence of conspiratorial habits learned in the Manhattan Project has prevented it from being adopted by the legislative branch. Giving each Congressman his own black briefcase, even if it contained only an audio transceiver, might well raise the general sense of responsibility of the whole Congress. Simply introducing the idea as a bill would provide the best possible excuse for a much-needed national debate on nuclear armaments. Best of all, the War Powers Act could be pruned and possibly uprooted, while the "imperial presidency" that has threatened the Constitution since this century began would lose the most cogent reason for its existence, military necessity.[13]

Given the choice, however, a republican would prefer to tinker, not with nuclear command but with symbolism and mythology. He believes, as someone once wrote, that if one can but tell the stories of a people, one cares not who makes its laws.[14] The stories are now being told by thousands of unwitting monarchists. American history itself has resolved, at the elementary level, into a chronicle of presidential character, conveniently divided into thirty-nine presidential administrations. Presidents have their own flags, their own planes, their own "retreats" around the country. "Hail to the Chief" is heard more often than "The Star-Spangled Banner." The most trivial events of a presidential election get more attention than the passage and publication of laws. Children are taught virtue through the contemplation of Washington, Jefferson, Jackson, Lincoln, and Roosevelt (first names unnecessary, except for the Roosevelts) and are not even taught the last names of John Milton, Roger Sherman, Thaddeus Stevens, or George Norris. Ben Franklin hangs on grimly, despite the fact that no one celebrates his birthday, and despite being dropped off the half-dollar in favor of a president whose most lasting accomplishment was to fall before an assassin's bullet in the age of television.

Whose birthday *should* we celebrate? Whose head *should* be on the coins? Better consult the national special-interest groups than current presidential mythology. Better Martin Luther King than Washington for a holiday in these times; better Susan B. Anthony than President Eisenhower on a dollar. At least Ms. Anthony is female.

Feminism? Not exactly. In the lower recesses of the Louvre there is a monumental head of the goddess Athena "which yet survives," a kind of republican Ozymandias. A high, crested helmet surmounts eyes whose pupils are not incised, so that her stare is at once fearless and pensive. The expression seems appropriate for a goddess acquainted with both power and oblivion.

Imagining the head as a focus of worship requires a stretch of the imagination. Athena was neither an ordinary woman nor an ordinary goddess. Her mother, Wisdom, was consumed by Zeus while pregnant; and Athena came into the world fully grown and fully armed through her father's forehead. Understandably, she was seldom a dutiful daughter. The supreme intelligence of her mother, the wrath of her father, and the weapons she always carried must have made her formidable to her worshipers. Still, the most marvelous republic of the ancient world deserved no less for a patron. The olive would have been wasted on Sparta, and the Parthenon would have been ill-fitted for Demeter or Aphrodite.

It is something of a defeat for gray-eyed Athena to be in the basement of the museum while Aphrodite stands in the central court, but there are compensations. Upstairs, in the coin collection, you can see Athena on the tetradrachma issued by Athens after she defeated the Persian Empire. If you look at the French coin you paid with to get into the Louvre, you will see that Marianne, symbol of the Republic, has the same sharp nose and chiseled features. She has only exchanged a horsetail helmet for a liberty cap. Pick up a Swiss franc or an old silver dollar and you will see the same steady gaze. She is Liberty. The calm head in the basement is only the eldest of an inconographic sisterhood, and the American visitor is struck by the fact that the goddess who surveyed the city of Athens from the Akropolis must have looked very much like the colossus given by France to watch over the Port of New York.[15]

The first job for republicans may be just to make Liberty visible.

BIBLIOGRAPHICAL
ESSAYS AND NOTES

*I*N THIS SECTION the reader will find footnotes for each chapter, preceded by an abbreviated bibliographical essay which tries to evaluate and acknowledge the major sources for each chapter. It is designed so that a learned or skeptical reader can follow my trail easily; but it is also designed for students. Since this is the first book on the entire republican tradition in a very long time, it must perform the service of a compendium for those who wish to become acquainted with the woods without wasting too much time on any one tree.

Chapter 1: Introduction

BIBLIOGRAPHICAL ESSAY

The last major survey of the republican tradition in the West seems to have been published more than two generations ago, H. A. L. Fisher's *The Republican Tradition in Europe* (New York: G. P. Putnam's Sons, 1911). At the time, Europe's only *de jure* republics were France, Switzerland, and Portugal, and the book is understandably tepid. A decade ago Olivier Lutaud traced, with more excitement, the tyrannicide idea from the sixteenth to the nineteenth century in *Des Révolutions d'Angleterre à la Révolution Française* (The Hague: Nijhoff, 1973). Its predecessors, like John Adams's *Defence of the Constitutions of America* (1787–1788) in *Works of John Adams, Second President of the United States*, ed. C. F. Adams, 10 vols. (Boston: Little, Brown & Co., 1850–1856), are often too partisan. Indeed Adams's *Defence* and Machiavelli's *Discourses on Livy* have become part of the history they describe and are discussed in chapters 5 and 8 below.

There are other nonspecialized works on the subject. Amaury de Riencourt, a Genevan, wrote two books comparing the United States in this century to the Roman Republic of the second century B.C. (*The Coming Caesars*, New York: Coward, McCann, 1957, and *The American Empire*, New York: The Dial Press, 1968). You can find a republican focus in other significant publications, too, from Johnny Hart's cartoons (*The King Is a Fink*, New York: Fawcett, 1969) to the Claudius novels of Robert Graves (*I, Claudius* [1934], New York: Random House, 1961) and the Dune science fiction of Frank Herbert (*Dune*, New York: Ace Books, 1964), not to mention George Lucas's *Star Wars* film trilogy.

Nor have historians neglected the idea. There is a marvelous, long reflective dialogue by Charles Beard, one of America's great historians (*The Republic*, New York: Viking, 1943) and more recent books by M. E. Bradford (*A Better Guide Than Reason*, La Salle, Ill.: Sherwood, Sugden & Co., 1979), Arthur Schlesinger (*The Imperial Presidency*, New York: Popular Library, 1974), and George Reedy (*The Twilight of the Presidency*, New York: New American Library, 1970) are, fortunately, still in print. It is also necessary to add, since *The End of Kings* amounts to a Whig interpretation of history, that it was written with full awareness of all the pitfalls so wittily pointed out fifty years ago by Herbert Butterfield in his classic *The Whig Interpretation of History* (1931) New York: Norton, 1965.

NOTES

1. George Will, "When Government Fails," in *Newsweek*, May 11, 1981, p. 100. Possibly, in the era of Ronald Reagan, Will meant to distinguish between a Republican essence, represented by the Party, and a less parochial small-r essence which is completely different. If so, it is high time, because apart from a tepid endorsement of state and local autonomy, there is at present nothing republican about the Republican Party.

2. J. A. O. Larsen's *Representative Government in Greek and Roman History* (Berkeley, Cal.: University of California Press, 1955) presents the best available evidence for representative government in antiquity. He would have liked to find more of it, but, except for leagues and confederations of city-states, there was not much to find.

3. John Toland, *Life of James Harrington,* in Toland, ed. *The Oceana and other Works of James Harrington, Esq.* (London: Printed for A. Millar. 1737), p. xxxiv.

4. Noah Webster, *Dictionary* (1828) (New York: Johnson Reprint, 1970), articles "Republic" and "Republican."

5. Edmund Burke, *Address to the Electors of Bristol* (1774), in P. Stanlis, ed., *Selected Writings and Speeches* (Garden City, N.Y., Doubleday Anchor, 1963), p. 187.

6. James Madison, "Federalist" 10, in C. Rossiter, ed., *The Federalist Papers* (1787) (New York: New American Library, 1961), p. 78.

7. Madison, "Federalist" 10, *ibid.,* p. 79.

8. Madison, "Federalist" 10, *ibid.,* p. 82.

9. Madison, "Federalist" 14, *ibid.,* p. 100.

10. Madison, "Federalist" 39, *ibid.,* p. 241.

11. Madison, "Federalist" 43, *ibid.,* p. 274.

12. Alexander Hamilton, "Federalist" 22, *ibid.,* p. 146. Similar ideas are to be found in Hamilton's numbers 71, 77, 78, and 84, *ibid.,* pp. 433, 464, 467, and 513.

13. Madison, "Federalist" 52, 63, *ibid.,* pp. 327, 385. Scholars are unsure whether number 63 is by Hamilton or Madison, but this very uncertainty tends to prove the point made here.

14. John Adams to Roger Sherman (1789) in Adams, *Works* (Boston, Little, Brown & Co., 1851–1856), vol. 6, p. 428. Samuel Johnson, *Dictionary* (1755) (London: W. Strahan, 1765), articles "Republic" and "Republican."

15. David De Leon, *The American as Anarchist* (Baltimore: Johns Hopkins University Press, 1979).

Chapter 2: Samuel and Solon

BIBLIOGRAPHICAL ESSAY

Because the word "republic" is Latin, neither the Hebraists nor the Hellenists in the historical profession have used the term since about the middle of the last century. Many, however, have applied the concept without using the word, and the scholarly reader will recognize how much this chapter owes to them. Among the Hebraists, Martin Noth is perhaps the most important. In his *System der Zwölf Stämme Israels* (1930), Darmstadt: Wissenschaftliche Buchgesellschaft, 1966, Noth was first to suggest that Israel's government before Samuel was analogous to the Amphictyonic League of Greek cities. In *History of Israel* (London: A. & C. Black, 1960) Noth condenses his theory, of which scholarly criticism later blurred the details but confirmed the outline. In various forms, it can now be found in historical works of all scholarly traditions, including the encyclopedic Jewish *World History of the Jewish People* (New Brunswick, N.J., Rutgers University Press, 1971, vol. 3, *passim*), and the Christian, John McKenzie's *World of the Judges* (Englewood Cliffs, N.J.: Prentice-Hall, 1966). Further detail on nomadism and politics may be found in T. J. Meek's *Hebrew Origins* (New York: Harper, 1960) and R. De Vaux's *Ancient Israel* (tr. J. McHugh, New York: McGraw-Hill, 1961). Much of this history can be very conveniently located in what are known as commentaries on individual books of the Bible. For *Samuel*, I have used S. Goldman (London: Soncino Press, 1951) and for *Judges*, J. Martin (New York: Cambridge University Press, 1975).

For the Hellenists, the outline of scholarship seems less clear, though Robert Drews's *Basileus* (New Haven, Conn.: Yale University Press, 1983) neatly sums up the evidence on archaic monarchy. What the Greeks themselves surmised may be found in J. L. Myres's classic *Who Were the Greeks?* (Berkeley, Cal.: University of California Press, 1930) but that is a very long way from what the historians are thinking nowadays. The best summary of the very live question of Greek prehistory is Emily Vermeule's *Greece in the Bronze Age* (Chicago: University of Chicago Press, 1964), to which one should add the tendentious and brilliant opponents: M. I. Finley (*The World of Odysseus*, New York: Viking, 1954), Denys Page (*History and the Homeric Iliad*, Berkeley, Cal.: University of California Press, 1959), and George Thomson (*Studies in Ancient Greek Society*, New York: Citadel, 1961). They disagree on many things, including whether the Trojan War really happened, but they are unanimous in calling on anthropology to bring together the two irreducible and often contradictory kinds of artifacts they work with, potsherds and Iliads.

For Greek republicanism after 800 B.C., I have used Victor Ehrenberg's *The Greek State* (London: Blackwell, 1960) and A. Andrewes's *The Greek Tyrants* (New York: Harper, 1956). Lest the reader make the mistake of thinking their clarity indicates scholarly certainty or consensus, he should take up the massive *History of the Greek City-States* by Raphael Sealey (Berkeley, Cal.: University of California Press, 1976), which records most of the controversies. Solon himself has had biographers since Plutarch, notably W. J. Woodhouse (*Solon the Liberator*, London: Oxford University Press, 1938).

As far as I know, no one has yet tried to compare, on a historical basis as well as an anthropological one, the ancient polities of Israel and Hellas. A remarkable book by Cyrus Gordon (*The Common Background of Greek and Hebrew Civilizations*, New York: Norton, 1965) argues, on literary evidence, that the similarities will eventually turn out to be as great as the differences.

If it is true, as Gordon suggests, that the first written language on Crete was not Greek but West Semitic, it will be even more necessary to think of the Greek incursion into the civilized eastern Mediterranean as analogous to that of Israel in the Exodus. Meanwhile, the reader may ponder the growing list of ethnographies of herding nomads. Comparative anthropologists Ronald Cohen and Alice Schlegel found most of them to be, in our sense, republican ("The Tribe as a Socio-Political Unit," in *Essays on the Problem of Tribe*, Seattle, Wash.: University of Washington Press, 1968). Writes Elizabeth Thomas of the cow-herding Dodoth of northern Uganda: "...there are no chiefs or kings in Dodoth, or persons born to rule. The government of the country is traditionally in the hands of elders, whose control has a religious basis, being achieved through intercession with God" (*Warrior Herdsmen*, New York: Random House, 1965, p. 57).

NOTES

1. Plato, *Timaeus*, ed. H. D. P. Lee (Baltimore, Md.: Penguin Books, 1965), pp. 34, 35.

2. Judges 5:19–21, *New English Bible*.

3. Judges 9, *Revised Standard Version*.

4. Judges 9, *New English Bible*.

5. Shakespeare, *Henry IV*, Part 2, act 3, sc. 1.

6. I Samuel 8, *Revised Standard Version*.

7. For the original meaning of basileus as feudal lord see R. Drews, *Basileus* (New Haven, Conn.: Yale University Press, 1983), and J. Chadwick, *The Mycenaean World* (London: Cambridge University Press, 1976).

8. Homer, *Iliad* 1, trs. A. H. Chase and W. G. Perry (New York: Bantam Books, 1972).

9. Aristotle, *Politics* V:10, ed. T. A. Sinclair (Baltimore, Md.: Penguin Books, 1962), p. 217.

10. Gelo, quoted by Herodotos in *Histories* 7:157, ed. A. de Sélincourt (Baltimore, Md.: Penguin Books, 1954), p. 469. The reader will not, I hope, be disconcerted by the return to Greek from the old Roman transliterations of some names like Herodotos, Polybios, and Lykourgos. The direction is a good one, I think, because to go the other way leads to the now quaint early humanist citation of Homer as Homerus and the misleading (see below, note 22) mistitling of Plato's *Politeia* as *Republic*.

11. Theognis, in *Works of Hesiod, Callimachus,* and *Theognis* (London: H. G. Bohn, 1856), quoted by Will Durant, *The Life of Greece* (New York: Simon and Schuster, 1939), p. 445.

12. Plutarch, "Solon" 14, tr. I. Scott-Kilvert, in *The Rise and Fall of Athens* (Baltimore, Md.: Penguin Books, 1962), pp. 55–56.

13. Plutarch, "Solon" 16, *ibid.*, p. 59.

14. Plutarch, "Solon" 25, *ibid.*, p. 68.

15. Plutarch, "Solon" 16, *ibid.*, p. 59.

16. Plutarch, "Solon" 20, *ibid.*, p. 62.

17. Plutarch, "Solon" 15, *ibid.*, p. 57.

18. Plutarch, "Solon" 27, *ibid.*, p. 71.

19. Plutarch, "Solon" 30, *ibid.*, p. 73.

20. Plutarch, "Solon" 30, *ibid.*, p. 74.

21. Plutarch, "Solon" 31, *ibid.*, p. 75.

22. Socrates, it seems to me, was a republican of a profoundly aristocratic stripe, a reactionary in his own time, and so despairing of self-government in 400 B.C. that (as I. F. Stone argued in his lectures at the 92nd Street YMCA in November 1982) he deliberately antagonized the *heliaia* and invited his execution by more democratically minded fellow-citizens. It should be noted that Plato's *Republic* represents aristocratic republicanism in a most thoroughgoing and unattractive way through Socrates's own mouth. It should be remembered that the book goes under a Roman title, and that in the original it was *Politeia*, or "How things work in a city-state."

Chapter 3: From Brutus to Brutus

BIBLIOGRAPHICAL ESSAY

The fraternity of Roman historians, in whose hall I serve here, is more aware than any other of the meaning and roots of the word "republic." It is natural that they should know a Latin word, but curious that they have not gotten the word out. Some, of course, are not republicans. The nineteenth-century dean of the fraternity was Theodor Mommsen (d. 1903), who, though active in the politics of his time, was too much of a German patriot to pursue the analogy of Kaiser and Caesar to its conclusion. Of the great leaders of the fraternity since Mommsen, only Ronald Syme, an Oxford don from New Zealand who was born in the year Mommsen died, has written authoritatively on the decline and fall of the Republic as if it were, on the whole, regrettable. Syme's book is a scholarly monument called *The Roman Revolution* (Oxford: Clarendon Press, 1939), and like everyone else who takes up this topic I have begun with it. To Syme's mastery of the facts, to his clear-eyed recognition that the Roman Republic was closed and undemocratic, and to his damning reconstruction (done when Rome itself had fallen to the likes of Mosca and Mussolini) of the careers of Caesar and Augustus, one should add the works of his students and others: Lily Taylor (*Party Politics in Rome in the Age of Caesar,* Berkeley, Cal.: University of California Press, 1949), Hartvig Frisch (*Cicero's Fight for the Republic,* Copenhagen: Gyldendal, 1946), H. H. Scullard (*From the Gracchi to Nero,* New York: Praeger, 1959), John Dickinson (*Death of a Republic,* New York: Macmillan, 1963), and Arthur Kaplan (*Catiline,* New York: Exposition Press, 1968).

On the Roman constitution itself, the outstanding book is quite old, and American (G. W. Botsford, *The Roman Assemblies,* New York: Macmillan, 1909). To it one should add an even earlier work, Thomas Taylor's *A Constitutional and Political History of Rome* (London: Methuen, 1899), and Lily R. Taylor's newer *Roman Voting Assemblies* (Ann Arbor: University of Michigan Press, 1966).

I have been unable to find a work on what the Romans meant by the phrase *res publica;* but there is one on *libertas* by C. Wirszubski (*Libertas as a Political Idea at Rome,* London: Cambridge University Press, 1961), a chapter on *imperium* in R. Koebner's *Empire* (New York: Grosset and Dunlap, 1965), and chapters on several key concepts in F. Adcock's *Roman Political Ideas and Practice* (Ann Arbor: University of Michigan Press, 1959) and K. von Fritz's *The Theory of the Mixed Constitution in Antiquity* (New York: Columbia University Press, 1954).

For the story one must go to the Romans themselves, or their Greek subjects and tutors. Plutarch's biography of Brutus is only one of his Roman *Lives.* He also wrote lives of both Gracchi, both Catos, Scipio, Marius, Sulla, Crassus, Cicero, Pompey, Antony, and Caesar himself. For Caesar and his successor monarchs there is Suetonius's lively *Twelve Caesars* and Tacitus's grim *Annals.* For Cicero there is the absolutely unparalleled record of his own letters. For the period after the Gracchi there is the accusatory Sallust. Finally, for the early history of the Republic, there is Livy. A great writer but a conscienceless historian, Livy must be constantly supplemented by modern works like the patient *Commentary on Livy* of R. M. Ogilvie (New York: Oxford University Press, 1965). My own quotations are from the wonderful Penguin editions of these classics.

NOTES

1. Livy, "Ab Urbe Condita" I:57, in *Early History of Rome,* tr. A. De Sélincourt (Baltimore, Md.: Penguin Books, 1960), p. 81.
2. Livy, "Ab Urbe Condita" I:58, *ibid.,* p. 82.
3. Livy, "Ab Urbe Condita" I:59, *ibid.,* p. 83.
4. Livy's date, 509–510 B.C., is believed to be two years off by modern historians.
5. Livy, "Ab Urbe Condita" III:26, *ibid.,* p. 197.

6. Livy, "Ab Urbe Condita" II:55, *ibid.*, p. 153.

7. Polybios, *Histories* V:33, tr. W. R. Paton (Cambridge, Mass.: Harvard University Press, 1922), vol. 3, pp. 80–81.

8. Polybios, *Histories* VI:2ff., *ibid.*, pp. 268–269.

9. Plutarch, "Cato the Elder" 27, in *Makers of Rome*, tr. I. Scott-Kilvert (Baltimore, Md.: Penguin Books, 1965), p. 150.

10. Plutarch, "Cato the Elder" 8, *ibid.*, p. 127.

11. Plutarch, "Marius," in *The Fall of the Roman Republic*, tr. R. Warner (Baltimore, Md.: Penguin Books, 1958), p. 245.

12. Suetonius, *Twelve Caesars* I:77, tr. R. Graves (Baltimore, Md.: Penguin Books, 1957), p. 42.

13. Plutarch, "Caesar," in *The Fall of the Roman Republic*, p. 245.

14. Plutarch, "Caesar," *ibid.*, p. 220.

15. Plutarch, "Brutus" 4, in *Makers of Rome*, p. 226.

16. R. Syme, in his *The Roman Revolution* (Oxford: Clarendon Press, 1939), chap. 4, doesn't think that Caesar planned monarchy, but he uses a definition of monarchy that includes hereditary succession. Despite Syme's vast authority, I think it is obvious that Caesar planned monarchy, certainly in the sense that the Romans feared monarchy.

17. For a different view on the coins see H. H. Scullard, *From the Gracchi to Nero* (New York: Praeger, 1961), p. 154, and note 26, p. 410.

18. Shakespeare, *Julius Caesar*, act 1, sc. 2, line 235.

19. Plutarch, "Brutus" 10, in *Makers of Rome*, p. 231.

20. Plutarch, "Brutus" 47, *ibid.*, p. 265.

21. Plutarch, "Brutus" 52, *ibid.*, p. 269.

Chapter 4: William Tell

BIBLIOGRAPHICAL ESSAY

Of course, there is really no alternative to a republican history of Switzerland. There is no Habsburg version (it would have been too embarrassing, and, in an illiterate age, pointless) and no émigré or irredentist version. Whether one reads it in French or German (or, less frequently, in English or Italian), Swiss historiography is in itself a model of Swiss pluralism, strongly consensual, and tensely tolerant on all those linguistic, geographic, and religious grounds. By far the most charming introduction to it is J. Christopher Hérold's old book, *The Swiss Without Halos* (New York: Columbia University Press, 1948). For Swiss with halos intact, in English, there is an ambitious political science monograph by Benjamin R. Barber (*The Death of Communal Liberty*, Princeton, N.J.: Princeton

University Press, 1974), basically a history of the canton of Graubünden (Grisons). Perhaps the newest general history is the collaborative *Handbuch der Schweizer Geschichte,* vol. 1 (Zürich: Verlag Berichthaus, 1972), and in English the most handy is the *Short History of Switzerland* by E. Bonjour, H. S. Offler, and G. R. Potter (Oxford: Clarendon Press, 1952). My account is largely from these general histories.

For Switzerland's early history, it is important to maintain the contrast with the rest of medieval Europe, from the Empire (cf. Boyd Hill, ed., *Rise of the First Reich,* New York: Wiley, 1969, and *Medieval Monarchy in Action,* New York: Barnes and Noble, 1972) to neighboring republics (W. F. Butler, *The Lombard Communes* [1906], Westport, Conn.: Greenwood Press, 1969). All were enmeshed in the same institutions then but are now treated as precursors of other polities called "nations" which were undreamed of in the Middle Ages. Indeed, from the thirteenth century onward the reciprocal influence of the Swiss forest-communes and the city-republics of both Germany and northern Italy is so continuous that their stories could be told in a single chapter. Nevertheless, the Swiss republic was at its origin rural, and the Italian republics were not only urban but humanist, a crucial difference, as is pointed out in Chapter 5.

For Schiller's 1804 incarnation of the myth of *Wilhelm Tell* I am obliged to Josef Schmidt's useful little companion in the Reclam *Erläuterung und Dokumente* series (Stuttgart, 1970). The most recent fictional version of the myth was written by the major Swiss modern, Max Frisch, for use in grade schools (*Wilhelm Tell,* Frankfurt am Main: Suhrkamp, 1971).

NOTES

1. Max Beerbohm, "*Porro Unum . . . ,*" in *Yet Again* (1909), in *Works,* vol. 3 (London: Heinemann, 1922), p. 40.

2. Julius Caesar, *Dé Bello Gallico* (*The Conquest of Gaul*), tr. S. A. Handford (Baltimore, Md.: Penguin Books, 1980). And for an analysis of Rhine barbarians by the last republican historian of Rome, see Tacitus, *Germania* in *On Britain and Germany,* tr. H. Mattingly (Baltimore, Md.: Penguin Books, 1948), chaps. 7, 11.

3. Niccolò Machiavelli, *Discourses on the First Ten Books of Livy* (1513), Book 1, chap. 13; Book 2, chaps. 4, 12, 19, 22, in Machiavelli, *The Prince and Discourses,* tr. L. Ricci and E. Vincent (New York: The Modern Library, 1950).

4. Francesco Vettori to Machiavelli (1513), quoted in E.T. Rimli, A. Mojonnier, and E. A. Gessler, *Histoire de la Confédération* (Zürich: Editions Stauffacher, 1967), p. 231.

5. Friedrich Schiller, *Wilhelm Tell,* act 4, sc. 3, in *Schiller's Dramatic Works,* tr. Theodore Martin (London: C. Bell, 1910), p. 403. Martin's 1894 verse translation is far superior to Mainland's line by line version: *William Tell* (Chicago: University of Chicago Press, 1972).

6. Schiller, *Wilhelm Tell*, act 1, sc. 3, tr. Martin, p. 329.

7. Schiller, *Wilhelm Tell*, act 1, sc. 3, tr. Martin, p. 328.

8. Schiller, *Wilhelm Tell*, act 3, sc. 3, tr. Martin, p. 377.

Chapter 5: Niccolò Machiavelli

BIBLIOGRAPHICAL ESSAY

What Ronald Syme has been to ancient Roman historiography, his contemporary Hans Baron has been to the Florentine. Baron's zeal to date the humanist manuscripts of the likes of Bruni and Salutati eventually coalesced into an overall thesis (new when he first proposed it in the 1930s) that the Florentine humanism of 1400 was "civic"—that is, republican. A refugee from Weimar Germany, Baron published his magnum opus, *Crisis of the Early Italian Renaissance* in America in 1955 (Princeton, N.J.: Princeton University Press, 1966). Forentine history has since been rewritten by his English-speaking disciples, notably Gene Brucker (*The Civic World of Early Renaissance Florence*, Princeton, N.J.: Princeton University Press, 1977), Donald Weinstein (*Savonarola and Florence*, Princeton, N.J.: Princeton University Press, 1970), Felix Gilbert (*Machiavelli and Guicciardini*, Princeton, N.J.: Princeton University Press, 1965), Martin Becker (*Florence in Transition*, 2 vols., Baltimore, Md.: Johns Hopkins University Press, 1967–1968), George Holmes (*The Florentine Enlightenment*, New York: Pegasus, 1969), and Nicolai Rubinstein (*Florentine Studies*, Evanston, Ill.: Northwestern University Press, 1968).

Articles by Jerrold Seigel (*Past and Present*, July 1966) and David Robey (*Past and Present*, February 1973) correct, but do not undermine, Baron's extraordinary edifice. In William Bouwsma's *Venice and the Defense of Republican Liberty* (Berkeley, Cal.: University of California Press, 1968), the Baron thesis is extended to sixteenth-century Venice. In Lauro Martines's masterly *Power and Imagination* (New York: Knopf, 1979), it has provided a foundation for the whole history of Renaissance Italy. In J. G. A. Pocock's convoluted *Machiavellian Moment* (Princeton, N.J.: Princeton University Press, 1975), Baron's Florence is so reconstructed as to provide a frame for the English Commonwealth and the American Revolution. Not since Machiavelli's fellow-citizens, Verrazano and Vespucci, helped to discover it, has the link between America and Florence seemed more clear.

As Baron himself saw (*English Historical Review*, July 1961), his thesis was a key to the long debate on Machiavelli, several centuries of which are conveniently condensed in De Lamar Jensen's Heath Pamphlet, *Machiavelli, Cynic, Patriot, or Political Scientist* (Lexington, Mass.: D. C. Heath & Co., 1960). One should add to it the extraordinary *New York Review of Books* essay by Isaiah Berlin (in *Against the Current*, New York: Viking,

1980), Leo Strauss's *Thoughts on Machiavelli* (New York: Free Press, 1958), Robert Ridolfi's 1954 biography (tr. C. Grayson, Chicago: University of Chicago Press, 1963), and the books by Gilbert and Pocock noted above. I have taken my own look at the unquiet ghost of Old Nick from a viewpoint near that of Federico Chabod (*Machiavelli and the Renaissance,* tr. D. Moore, Cambridge, Mass.: Harvard University Press, 1958).

NOTES

1. Hans Baron, *Crisis of the Early Italian Renaissance* (Princeton, N.J.: Princeton Univesity Press, 1966), p. 43. Baron is quoting a Medici rival, Maso degli Albizzi, from the Florentine council's notes.

2. Leonardo Bruni, "Panegyric to the City of Florence" ("Laudatio Fiorentinae Urbis" [1403–1404]), tr. R. Witt in B. Kohl and R. Witt, eds. *The Earthly Republic* (Philadelphia: University of Pennsylvania Press, 1978), pp. 173–174.

3. Francesco Petrarca to Cicero (1345) from *Letters* 24:3, in M. Bishop, tr., *Letters from Petrarch* (Bloomington, Ind.: Indiana University Press), 1966, p. 206.

4. Coluccio Salutati, "De Tyranno" (1400), in E. Emerton, ed., *Humanism and Tyranny* (1925) (Gloucester, Mass.: Peter Smith, 1964), pp. 78–93.

5. Bruni, "Panegyric," in *The Earthly Republic,* pp. 153–154.

6. For Salutati's reasoning, see H. Baron, *Humanistic and Political Literature in Florence and Venice* (Cambridge, Mass.: Harvard University Press), p. 151.

7. Bruni, "Panegyric," in *The Earthly Republic,* p. 151.

8. Harold Acton, *The Pazzi Conspiracy* (London: Thames and Hudson, 1979), p. 72. See also the contemporary account of Angelo Poliziano, one of the first humanists to sign on as a creature of the Medici. In this version one hears "Palle!" for the Medici, but the cry "Popolo e libertà!" is missing. Poliziano and others are published in R. Watkins, tr., *Humanism and Liberty* (Columbia, S. C.: University of South Carolina Press, 1978).

9. Francesco Guicciardini, *History of Florence* (1508–1509), chap. 9, tr. M. Domandi (New York: Harper, 1970), p. 70.

10. Ferdinand Schevill, *History of Florence* (New York: Harcourt, 1936), p. 438.

11. Girolamo Savonarola, *On the Constitution . . . (Trattato circa el regimento e governo della città de Firenze* [1498]) can be found with other humanist texts in R. Watkins, ed., *Humanism and Liberty* (Columbia, S. C.: University of South Carolina Press), 1978.

12. Niccolò Machiavelli, *Discourses on Livy* (ca. 1513), Book 2, chap. 2, in L. Ricci and E. Vincent, tr., *The Prince and the Discourses* (New York: The Modern Library, 1950), p. 282.

13. Garrett Mattingly, "Machiavelli's Prince, Political Science or Political Satire?" in *American Scholar*, vol. 27, 1958.

14. Machiavelli, *Discourses*, Book 3, chap. 3, Modern Library ed., p. 405.

15. Machiavelli to Francesco Vettori (April 16, 1527), quoted by F. Gilbert, *Machiavelli and Guicciardini* (Princeton, N. J.: Princeton University Press, 1965), p. 242.

16. Machiavelli, *Discourses*, Book 1, chap. 49, Modern Library ed., pp. 239–240. Of all the commentators on Machiavelli it seems to me that Federico Chabod (see above, bibliographical essay) best sees this despair in him.

Chapter 6: *John Calvin*

BIBLIOGRAPHICAL ESSAY

Tracing the republic over this two-century Möbius fold into modern history is delicate. The best attempt so far, J. G. A. Pocock's *The Machiavellian Moment* (Princeton, N. J.: Princeton University Press, 1975), tries to get from the Italian Renaissance to the Puritan Commonwealth by way of Venice, as if Calvin were not really in the picture. Michael Walzer's *Revolution of the Saints* (New York: Atheneum, 1968) begins with Calvin but tends to read all Reformed republicanism as revolutionary resistance. My own path depends on a definition of "republic" which was not that of the conciliarists themselves in the fourteenth century, or even of Jean Bodin *(Six Livres de la République* [1576], tr. and abridged M. J. Tooley, Oxford: Basil Blackwell, n. d.) in the sixteenth. It must also reckon with the fact that not all Calvinists were republicans (the Prussian kings certainly weren't), and that Calvin himself was a political republican only by bare preference. Nineteenth-century historians further confuse the picture by uncritically comparing sixteenth-century Calvinists with eighteenth-century Whigs and nineteenth-century Liberals.

Nevertheless, I can claim some predecessors, particularly Francis Oakley. Article by article (his latest was in *Archiv für Reformationsgeschichte,* 1977) Oakley has been digging up the Scottish and French "...Road from Constance to 1688" (*Journal of British Studies,* 1962). He and Brian Tierney, Hubert Jedin, E. F. Jacob, Walter Ullman, and Michael Wilks form a small band of specialists in pre-Reformation church history who build more and more on the foundations laid by a past master, John N. Figgis. Around 1900 Figgis first defined conciliarism as an early form of whiggery.

For the other end of the Reformation, materials are divided, like the Council of Constance itself, into nations. For French politics and thought, I drew on Pierre Mesnard (*L'essor de la philosophie politique au XVIe siècle* [1938], Paris: Vrin, 1969), Roland Mousnier's *The Assassination of Henri IV*, tr. J. Spencer (London: Faber, 1973), W. F. Church's *Constitutionalism and Resistance in Sixteenth Century France* (Cambridge, Mass.: Harvard University Press, 1941), Howell A. Lloyd's *The State, France, and the Sixteenth Century* (London: Allen & Unwin, 1983), J. R. Major's meticulous works on the Estates, and George Huppert's *The Idea of Perfect History* (Urbana, Ill.: University of Illinois Press, 1970). Nannerl Keohane's magisterial *Philosophy and the State in France* (Princeton, N.J.: Princeton University Press, 1980) helps explain why rebellion went out of fashion in the seventeenth century in Calvin's France.

For the Scots the indispensables are W. Croft Dickinson's general history (Vol. 1, New York: T. J. Nelson, 1961), David Stevenson's *The Scottish Revolution* (New York: St. Martin's, 1973), and Gordon Donaldson's *The Scottish Reformation* (London: Cambridge University Press, 1960). Recently Paul Saenger has taken a look at Burgundy, which included the Netherlands in the fifteenth century (*The Earliest French Resistance Theories*, University Microfilms, 1979). For Dutch politics and thought, one must begin, unless one reads Dutch, with Geoffrey Parker's *The Dutch Revolt* (Ithaca, N. Y.: Cornell University Press, 1977).

The scholars who can see Europe whole around 1600 are few. Essential are Quentin Skinner (*The Foundations of Modern Political Thought*, 2 vols., London: Cambridge University Press, 1978), N. M. Sutherland (*The Massacre of Saint Bartholomew*, New York: Barnes and Noble, 1973), H. G. Koenigsberger (*Estates and Revolutions*, Ithaca, N. Y.: Cornell University Press, 1971), Garrett Mattingly (*The Armada*, Boston: Houghton Mifflin, 1959), Emile Léonard (*A History of Protestantism*, tr. J. Reid, 2 vols., London: Nelson, 1965–1967), and J. W. Allen (*A History of Political Thought in the Sixteenth Century* [1928], New York: Barnes and Noble, 1960). Tiny Geneva must be seen from the view point of an entire Europe, as the well-known work of Robert M. Kingdon demonstrates. Even the most useful histories of Geneva's intramural politics, by E. William Monter, take on this global perspective eventually.

As for Calvin himself, the entire Western world claims him but seldom studies him. The best biography, in the French of Emile Doumergue, is now fifty years old. The must-touted revival of his theology has not survived the German of Karl Barth. The best survey in English (John T. McNeill, *History and Character of Calvinism*, New York: Oxford University Press, 1954) is more than thirty years old. It seems to have taken a century of debate to determine the rather obvious fact that Calvin was not a democrat, yet none of the debaters saw fit to apply the term republican (cf. R. Kingdon and R. Linder, eds., *Calvin and Calvinism, Sources of Democracy?*, Lexington, Mass.: Heath Pamphlet, 1970). It is no surprise that Hans Baron once took a sidelong glance at Calvin (*Historische Zeitschrift*, Munich, May 1924) but the best of all that is new and reliable is W. Fred Graham's study, *The Constructive Revolutionary* (Atlanta: Ga.: Knox Press, 1971).

NOTES

1. "me tournoyer," wrote Calvin, as a knight would a horse. This and almost all Calvin's autobiographical remarks are found in his "Preface" to *Commentary on Psalms* (1557), in *Opera Omnia* (part of the multivolume *Corpus Reformatorum*), eds. G. Baum, E. Cunitz, and E. Reuss (Brunswick: C. Schwetschke, 1863–1900), vol. 31, column 24.

2. *Ibid.*, also *Calvin*, ed. J. Dillenberger (Garden City, N. Y.: Doubleday Anchor), p. 28.

3. Calvin, "Articles of Organization." For this and other ecclesiological documents the most convenient source is Calvin, *Theological Treatises*, ed. J. K. S. Reid (Philadelphia: Westminster Press), 1954.

4. John Knox to Mrs. Locke (1555), in W. S. Reid, *Trumpeter of God, The Life of John Knox* (New York: Scribner, 1974), p. 240.

5. Calvin, *Institutes of the Christian Religion* (1536), Chapter 6:54. To the many editions and recastings of the *Institutes* in French and Latin there are few guides. The best in English is the annotated translation of the *Institutio* of 1536 by Ford L. Battles (Atlanta, Ga.: John Knox Press, 1975). The standard French edition of the *Institution chrétienne* follows the 1541 text with notes to those of 1536 and 1539 (4 vols., ed. J. Pannier) (Paris: Les Belles Lettres, 1961).

6. Christopher Goodman, "How Superior Powers Ought to be Obeyed" (1558), in E. Morgan, ed., *Puritan Political Ideas* (Indianapolis: Bobbs-Merrill, 1965). John Ponet (Poynet), "A Short Treatise of Politique Power" (1556), in W. S. Hudson, *John Ponet* (Chicago: University of Chicago Press, 1942). John Major (Mair), "Disputatio de auctoritate concilii...," in J. Dupin, ed., *Joanni Gersonii Opera Omnia*, 5 vols. (Antwerp: Dupin, 1706). George Buchanan, "De Jure Regni Apud Scotos" (1567–1579), tr. J. Aikman (Edinburgh: T. Ireland, Jr., 1829).

7. Calvin, *Institutes* (1536), chap. 6:55, and *Institutes* (1560), Bk. 4, chap. 20:31; *Institution* (1541), chap. 16 (Paris, 1961), vol. 4, p. 239.

8. Calvin, *Institutes* (1559), Bk. 4, chap. 20:8; *Institution* (1541), chap. 16 (Paris, 1961), vol. 4, p. 233.

9. Calvin, "Adresse au Petit Conseil," in *Opera Omnia, Corpus Reformatorum*, vol. 9, p. 887; Calvin, "Adresse aux ministres," *ibid.*, p. 891.

10. Theodore de Bèze, "De Jure Magistratum..." (1574); François Hotman, "Franco-Gallia" (1573); and S. Junius Brutus (Philippe du Plessis-Mornay), "Vindiciae contra Tyrannos" (1576), can be found, abridged,

in J. H. Franklin, ed., *Constitutionalism and Resistance, Three Treatises* (New York: Pegasus, 1969). The most eloquent protest against monarchy in this period was printed by the Huguenots as one of their own from 1574 onward, but it is by a non-Calvinist, Montaigne's friend Etienne de la Boétie: *Discours de la servitude volontaire, ou Contr'un* (ca. 1555) (Paris: Editions sociales, 1971).

11. For a translation of the declaration, see Herbert Rowen, ed., *The Low Countries in Early Modern Times* (New York: Harper, 1972), pp. 102–104.

12. Rowen, ed., *Low Countries*, p. 92.

Chapter 7: John Milton

BIBLIOGRAPHICAL ESSAY

Scholarship on the English Revolution is one of the great monuments of the historical discipline in this century. It has even produced great narrative in the works of C. V. Wedgewood and Samuel R. Gardiner. All students, too, recognize the importance of ideas, no matter how deep they may go into reconstructive sociology or prebourgeois economics; and republicanism is one of those ideas, no matter how unfortunately its historiography is divided between those who see it as coming out of humanism (Zera Fink, *The Classical Republicans*, Evanston, Ill.: Northwestern University Press, 1945) and those who see it as a product of Calvinism (Christopher Hill, "Discipline, Monarchical, Aristocratical and Democratical," in *Society and Puritanism*, London: Panther Books, 1969). Perez Zagorin devotes more than one chapter to varieties of republicanism (*History of Political Thought in the English Revolution*, London: Routledge & Kegan Paul, 1954), but a full reconstruction of the republican synthesis in this era still requires some pretty wide wandering. Specialists will observe that my most faithful guides have been Michael Walzer (*Revolution of the Saints*, Cambridge, Mass.: Harvard University Press, 1965), J. G. A. Pocock (*The Ancient Constitution and the Feudal Law*, New York: Cambridge University Press, 1957), Edmund S. Morgan (*Puritan Political Ideas*, Indianapolis: Bobbs-Merrill, 1965), and Christopher Hill, any one of whose many books on the subject could serve as an introduction to political Puritanism.

In America, Puritans raised their city on a hill, but Americans are rarely told how republican that city was. The incomparable Perry Miller regrettably set a course away from church government and toward theology (*Errand into the Wilderness*, Cambridge, Mass.: Harvard University Press, 1956). Alan Simpson followed (*Puritanism in Old and New England*, Chicago: University of Chicago Press, 1955). Darrett Rutman (*American Puritanism*, New York: Norton, 1970) distinguished between what was

Puritan and what was merely English about New England, but scanted what was radically English about Puritan politics. Larzer Ziff (*Puritanism in America*, New York: Viking, 1973) sets a different course from Miller's and Sumner Chilton Powell shows, in *Puritan Village* (New York: Anchor, 1965), what the Puritan utopia looked like at grass roots, incidentally reminding us that even in the seventeenth century the peasant commune is associated with the republican tradition, as it had been in medieval Switzerland.

The major republicans of the period, from trimmers to regicides, all have biographers and editors. For Edward Coke there is Catherine Drinker Bowen (Boston: Little, Brown, 1957); for Marchamont Nedham, Philip Knachel (Charlottesville, Va.: University of Virginia Press, 1969); for Parker and Robinson, Wilbur Jordan (Chicago: University of Chicago Press, 1942); and for Henry Marten, Ivor Waters (Chepstowe, England: Chepstowe Society, 1973). For the Levellers there is H. N. Brailsford (Stanford, Cal.: Stanford University Press, 1961); for the Radicals, Christopher Hill (*The World Turned Upside Down*, New York: Viking, 1973); and for the Diggers, G. H. Sabine (Ithaca, N. Y.: Cornell University Press, 1941). For James Harrington there are J. G. A. Pocock (London: Cambridge University Press, 1977) and Charles Blitzer (*An Immortal Commonwealth*, New Haven, Conn.: Yale University Press, 1960). For Henry Vane there is Margaret Judson (Philadelphia: University of Pennsylvania Press, 1969); for Andrew Marvell, John Wallace (London: Cambridge University Press, 1968); for Cromwell a mighty host headed by Christopher Hill (New York: Harper, 1972) and Antonia Fraser (New York: Dell, 1975); and for Milton, an entire industry.

Milton, of course, deserves it. His poetry transcends all biographers and even his erudition is greater than that of his annotators. Alas, this leads to specialized scholarship, which in turn leads, at the very least, to a separation of the poet from the politician. My own Milton is far less a poet than he should be, rather like the Milton of Don M. Wolfe (New York: T. Nelson, 1941), Arthur Barker (Toronto: University of Toronto Press, 1942), Charles Sensabaugh (Stanford, Cal.: Stanford University Press, 1952, and Princeton, N.J.: Princeton University Press, 1964), and of course Christopher Hill, whose *Milton and the English Revolution* (New York: Viking, 1978) appeared after this chapter was written but soon enough to give me the opportunity to argue in footnotes with a master.

NOTES

1. James I, *The Trewe Lawe of Free Monarchie* (1598), in *Political Works*, ed. C. H. McIlwain (Cambridge, Mass.: Harvard University Press, 1918).

2. Shakespeare, *Richard II*, act 3, sc. 2. The play was printed in the same year as James's *Trewe Lawe*, was deliberately revived as propaganda for

the Essex rebellion in 1601, and was still delivering its political message when the Royal Shakespeare Company brought a new production to the United States in 1974, the year of Richard Nixon's resignation.

3. One can find the Tudor idea of commonwealth in Thomas Elyot, *Boke named the Gouernor* (New York: Burt Franklin, 1967), Bk. 1, chaps. 1 and 2, and in another book that seems at first to be a monarchical tract, Thomas Smith's *De Republica Anglorum* (1565) (London: Cambridge University Press, 1906). For Henry's clocks, see Lacey B. Smith, *Henry VIII* (London: Panther Books, 1971), p. 23.

4. John Milton, "Defensio Secunda" (1654), in Milton, *Complete Prose Works* (New Haven, Conn.: Yale University Press, 1953ff.), vol. 4, p. 614. Like Calvin, Milton embedded his autobiography in the opening of a scholarly work, his long defense of the English republic against the attacks of Salmasius.

5. *Ibid.*, p. 619. Milton "cherished" Florence (*Complete Prose Works*, vol. 1, p. 328) and he enjoyed Rome. He turned back before he could visit Athens, but he returned to England via Florence and Geneva: a complete republican tour, except for Greece and Israel.

6. Milton, "Eikonoklastes" (1649), in *Complete Prose Works* (Yale), vol. 3, p. 344.

7. Milton's praise of the tyrannicide Brutus in *Prolusion VI* may be an echo of these events. It is usually dated to 1628. *Complete Prose Works* (Yale), vol. 1, p. 267.

8. Milton to Gil, in *Complete Prose Works* (Yale), vol. 1, pp. 316–317. In the view of Christopher Hill, there is much political and religious radicalism in the young Milton which his surviving works veil or exclude. That Milton in this letter praises Gil's ode in praise of a Dutch defeat of Spain is probably political; but one shouldn't go too far. Sometimes Hill teases more out of Milton's plain texts than a Familist from his Bible.

9. C. V. Wedgewood, *The King's Peace* (London: Fontana, 1966), chap. 1.

10. Milton, "Lycidas," line 110ff., in J. T. Shawcross, ed., *The Complete Poetry of John Milton* (Garden City, N. Y.: Anchor Press, 1970).

11. Milton, "Commonplace Book" (1637ff.), in *Complete Prose Works* (Yale), vol. 1, p. 267. This is Milton's record of his own reading. Readers of this book will recognize a great deal of it.

12. The name "Committee of Safety" appears again in the revolutionary republics of Massachusetts in 1775 and of France in 1793, to mention only two. The Committee of Both Kingdoms is echoed by the titles of the Joint Committees on Reconstruction and on the Conduct of the War in Civil War congresses. "Convention," used by Parliament at the Restoration in 1660, was borrowed by the United States in 1787 and by

France in 1792, under the meaning of legitimate legislature held without a king's mandate and holding sovereign power.

13. "Charge Against Charles Stuart" (January 20, 1649), in C. Blitzer, ed., *The Commonwealth of England* (New York: Dutton, 1963), p. 85.

14. "Act Abolishing the Office of King" (March 17, 1649), *ibid.*, p. 132.

15. Milton, "Commonplace Book" (1637ff.), in *Complete Prose Works* (Yale), vol. 1, pp. 414, 421, 477. Felix Raab, *The English Face of Machiavelli* (Toronto: Toronto University Press, 1964), is the indispensable work on Machiavelli's influence in England.

16. Milton, "The Tenure of Kings and Magistrates" (1649), in *Complete Prose Works* (Yale), vol. 3, pp. 206, 237.

17. Milton, "Eikonoklastes" (1649), *ibid.*, pp. 343, 393.

18. *Ibid.*, p. 581.

19. Antonia Fraser, *Cromwell* (New York: Dell, 1975), p. 487.

20. *Ibid.*, p. 581.

21. James Harrington, "The Commonwealth of Oceana" (1656), in *Political Works* ed. J. G. A. Pocock (London: Cambridge University Press, 1977). For the Harringtonians and their inventive terminology, see works in bibliography above by C. Blitzer, Z. Fink, and P. Zagorin.

22. Milton, "The Readie and Easie Way to Establish a Free Commonwealth" (1660), in *Prose Works* (New York: Columbia University Press, 1900), vol. 6, pp. 136–138.

23. *Ibid.*

24. *Ibid.*, p. 148.

Chapter 8: John Adams and Benjamin Franklin

BIBLIOGRAPHICAL ESSAY

The growth of temporal and cultural provincialism among American historians in this century has had some advantages, but losing touch with the European republican tradition is not one of them. By the 1940s it had become almost impossible to see the political meaning of America in any terms but the democratic. Constitutionalism, even the Bill of Rights, had come to be seen as products of democracy, that is, majority rule.

Clinton Rossiter's *Seedtime of the Republic* (New York: Harcourt, Brace, 1953) tried to reintroduce the term republican, but failed to reorient the profession's view of the American Revolution. Finally in 1959, a lady named Caroline Robbins revealed to Americanists the forgotten world of *The Eighteenth Century Commonwealthman* (Cambridge, Mass.: Harvard

University Press, 1959), the English "High Whig" or republican left, to whom John Locke was merely a conservative fellow-traveler, and whose line was continuous from Milton and Harrington through Sidney, Hoadley, Molesworth, Moyle, Trenchard, Gordon, and Wilkes, to John Adams and Benjamin Franklin. In 1959, it seemed strange that the single greatest influence on the political thought of the Framers should be these comparative unknowns; yet who else would John Winthrop's disciples have read but John Milton's?

Historians who followed Robbins into the world of Dissenters and Commonwealthsmen have since become the acknowledged lawgivers in the field of American Revolution studies. Bernard Bailyn (*The Intellectual Origins of the American Revolution*, Cambridge, Mass.: Harvard University Press, 1971) and Gordon Wood (*The Creation of the American Republic 1776–1787*, Chapel Hill: University of North Carolina Press, 1969) have been awarded Bancroft Prizes by the profession. The English scholar J. R. Pole (*Political Representation in England and the Origins of the American Revolution* [1966], Berkeley, Cal.: University of California Press, 1971) contributed a rigorous analysis of one of the major High Whig principles. Now these have an army of companions (Trevor Colbourn, R. W. Shoemaker, Drew McCoy, Lois Schwoerer, Joyce Appleby, John P. Reid, and even a German scholar, Willi Paul Adams). Recent summaries of the literature by Isaac Kramnick ("Republican Revisionism Revisited," in *American Historical Review*, December 1982) and Linda Kerber ("The Republican Synthesis Revisited," paper delivered at the Annual Meeting of the American Historical Association, December 1982) show that the effort is making an honest woman of the Republic again, at least in academe.

I add little here to their achievement, except an energetic attempt to get the word out, and the insistence that "democratic republican" is not a solecism. It seems astonishing to me that the Madison definition of republic is still current, that the United States is still defined as a democracy long before the Jacksonian period, that many of Franklin's works remain unpublished, that Adams's *Defence of the Constitutions of America* has not been reprinted since 1851, or that the publication, at last, of Madison's *Notes* in a one-volume paperback has not yet made the work a basic text for Americans. All the sources for Adams and Franklin are in unadmirable disorder, as a glance at the footnotes will demonstrate.

For the predecessors of the Framers, editions are beginning to appear. Caroline Robbins has edited Henry Neville (*Plato Redivivus*, 1681) and Walter Moyle (*Essay Upon the Constitution of the Roman Government*, 1699) in *Two Republican Tracts* (London: Cambridge University Press, 1969). D. L. Jacobson's *The English Libertarian Heritage* (Indianapolis, Inc.: Bobbs-Merrill, 1965) is actually an edition of John Trenchard and Thomas Gordon, *The Independent Whig* and *Cato's Letters* (ca. 1730). Sidney's *Discourses on Government* was at last reprinted in 1979 (ed. J. P. Mayer,

New York: Arno, 1979) but Robert Molesworth's "Preface" to *Franco-Gallia* has not been issued since 1775. No wonder Garry Wills (*Inventing America*, Garden City, N. Y.: Doubleday, 1978) attributes the Declaration of Independence to Scottish Presbyterians.

NOTES

1. John Adams, "Thoughts on Government" (1775), in *The Adams Papers*, Series 3 (Cambridge, Mass.: Harvard University Press, 1977), vol. 4, p. 87. For more on Algernon Sidney, see Adams, *Legal Papers* (Cambridge, Mass.: Harvard University Press, 1965), vol. 3, p. 270, (*Rex v. Wemms*, 1770), and *Papers*, Series 3, vol. 2, p. 100 (Adams to J. Warren, June 25, 1774).

2. John Adams, "Autobiography," in *Diary and Autobiography* (Cambridge, Mass.: Harvard University Press, 1961), vol. 3, p. 418. Franklin's theory of colds had been long in incubation by 1776: Benjamin Franklin, *Papers* (New Haven, Conn.: Yale University Press, 1976ff.), vol. 20, pp. 529ff.

3. Adams, "Autobiography," in *Diary and Autobiography*, vol. 3, pp. 275–276; Adams to William Tudor (March 29, 1817). For Adams's discovery of Machiavelli and Milton, see Adams, "Diary," in *Diary and Autobiography*, vol. 1, p. 179 (December 8, 1760, and April 29, 1756).

4. Adams's views are easier to document than the ever-discreet Franklin's. For the evidence, see Franklin, *Papers* (Yale), vol. 12, pp. 206, 244, 253; vol. 13, pp. 135ff.; vol. 15, p. 75; vol. 17, pp. 160ff.; vol. 20, p. 394; and Franklin to Galloway (February 25, 1775), in Franklin, *Writings*, ed. A. H. Smyth (New York: Macmillan, 1907), vol. 6, p. 312. See also V. W. Crane, *Benjamin Franklin's Letters to the Press* (Chapel Hill, N.C.: Univesity of North Carolina Press, 1950), pp. 132–134, 268–276.

5. John Adams, "Diary" (December 17, 1773), in *Diary and Autobiography*, vol. 2, p. 85. Adams to J. Warren (December 17, 1773), in *Papers*, series 3, vol. 2, p. 1.

6. Phillips Russel, *The First Civilized American* (New York: Brentano's, 1926), was written for the Sesquicentennial. Catherine Drinker Bowen, *The Most Dangerous Man in America* (Boston: Little, Brown, 1974), was planned for the Bicentennial.

7. Benjamin Franklin to Jonathan Williams (September 28, 1774), in T. Fleming, ed., Benjamin Franklin, *A Biography in His Own Words* (New York: Newsweek Books, 1972).

8. John Adams, "Novanglus" (1774), in *Papers*, series 3, vol. 2, 1977. Adams's earliest response to his meeting with Franklin is his reserved recommendation of him to his wife: John Adams to Abigail Adams, July

23, 1775, in *Adams Family Correspondence* (Cambridge, Mass.: Harvard University Press, 1963), vol. 1, pp. 252–253.

9. Benjamin Franklin, "Edict of the King of Prussia" (September 22, 1774), in *Papers* (Yale), vol. 20, p. 413.

10. John Adams, "Thoughts on Government" (1776), in *Papers*, series 3, vol. 4, p. 87.

11. Franklin's democratic views are oddly obscured in the literature. For this view of him, see Bernard Knollenberg, "Benjamin Franklin, Philosophical Revolutionist," in *Meet Dr. Franklin* (Philadelphia: American Philosophical Society, 1943). For some of the evidence, see Franklin, *Writings* (New York: Macmillan, 1907), vol. 10, pp. 54–60; Letter to Thomas Paine, in *Works* (New York: Putnam's, 1888), vol. 9, p. 266; and Madison, *Notes of Proceedings at the Federal Convention* (1787), ed. A. Koch (New York: Norton, 1969), pp. 404, 426.

12. John Adams, "Defence of the Constitutions of America" (1786–1787), vol. 1, chap. 4, and vol. 3, in *Works of John Adams*, ed. C. F. Adams (Boston: Little, Brown, 1851), vol. 4, pp. 389–390; vol. 6, pp. 210–211; vol. 9, p. 623.

13. J. Paul Selsam, *The Pennsylvania Constitution of 1776* (1936) (New York: Octagon, 1971), chap. 4 *passim*, pp. 185–186. Richard A. Ryerson, *"The Revolution Is Now Begun"* (Philadelphia: University of Pennsylvania Press, 1978), chap. 9. See also Franklin, *Papers* (Yale), vol. 22, pp. 513–515, and Samuel B. Harding, "Party Struggles over the First Pennsylvania Constitution," in *Annual Report* of the American Historical Association, Washington, D. C., 1894.

14. John Adams, "Report to the Committee on the Constitution of Massachusetts" (September 1, 1779), in *Works* (1851), vol. 4, pp. 219ff. See also Robert Taylor's edition of state documents, *Massachusetts: Colony to Commonwealth* (New York: Norton, 1972).

15. Pennsylvania Constitution of 1776, in J. H. Fertig, ed., *Constitutions of Pennsylvania*, Harrisburg, Pennsylvania, Legislative Reference Bureau, 1926.

16. John Adams, "Defence," vol. 3 (1787), in *Works* (1851), vol. 6, p. 10. Letter to Joseph Hawley (August 25, 1776) and letter to Francis Dana (August 16, 1776), in *Works*, vol. 9, pp. 435, 429–430. On Franklin's sleepiness at meetings, see Adams to Warren in Adams, *Correspondence*, series 4, Boston (1878), p. 431.

17. Adams, "Autobiography" (June 2, 1778), in *Diary and Autobiography* (1961), vol. 4, p. 90.

18. Adams, "Thoughts on Government" (1776), in *Papers*, series 3 (1977), vol. 4, p. 90.

19. Adams, Letter (September 22, 1787), in *Works* (1851), vol. 8, pp. 451–452.
20. Madison, *Notes of Proceedings at the Federal Convention* (1787), ed. A. Koch (New York: Norton, 1969), p. xv.
21. Adams, "Defence of the Constitutions of America" (1786–1787), in *Works* (1851), vol. 4, p. 401.
22. Franklin to Charles Carroll (May 25, 1789), in *Works* (1888), vol. 10, pp. 84–85 (Franklin's emphasis).
23. Adams to Richard Price (April 19, 1790), in *Works* (1851), vol. 9, p. 564. See also Adams to Cotton Tufts (June 28, 1789), James Lovell (June 4, 1789), and William Tudor (June 28, 1789), cited from the Adams microfilms by John Howe, *The Changing Political Thought of John Adams* (Princeton, N. J.: Princeton University Press, 1966), pp. 153–154.
24. Franklin, "Address," in Convention (September 17, 1787), in Madison, *Notes,* ed. A. Koch (1969), p. 654.
25. James Madison's definition is treated above (Chapter 1) and is found in *Federalist* 10 (1787) (New York: New American Library, 1961), p. 81. Adams's is in "Defence" (1786), in *Works* (1851), vol. 4, pp. 296, 558.
26. John Adams to Roger Sherman (July 17, 1789), in *Works* (1851), vol. 6, p. 428 (my emphasis). The original definition in "Defence" (*ibid.,* p. 206) is attributed to "Johnston." This must be Samuel Johnson, who used the same definition in the *English Dictionary* of 1755, supporting it with a quotation from his fellow-essayist, Addison. Montesquieu used a similar definition in distinguishing aristocratic from democratic republics in the *Esprit des Lois* of 1748: Montesquieu, *Oeuvres complètes* (Paris: Seuil, 1964), p. 532.

Chapter 9: Maximilien Robespierre

BIBLIOGRAPHICAL ESSAY

If the French have never forgotten what a republic is, perhaps it is because the French Revolution, unlike the American, has never ended in the historiographical sense. Left and right in France still argue passionately whether or not it was a good thing, and so do the very best French historians. The great republican scholars have succeeded each other regularly in the chair of Revolution studies established by the City of Paris (Alphonse Aulard, Albert Mathiez, Georges Lefebvre, Albert Soboul). On the right is a dynasty that runs from Hippolyte Taine to Pierre Gaxotte, not excluding François Furet and Denis Richet. Recent summaries by Denis Woronoff (*La République bourgeoise, 1794–1799*, Paris: Seuil, 1972), Marc

Bouloiseau (*La République jacobine, 1792–l'An II*, Paris: Seuil, 1972), and Michel Vovelle (*La Chute de la monarchie, 1787–1792*, Paris: Seuil, 1972) can give an introduction to this controversy. Jean Massin's *Almanach de la Révolution* (Paris: Club français du Livre, 1963) can help sort out the dates, provides superb iconography, and is republican to the core.

Revolution specialists will not fail to notice here the Paris of Marxist republican Albert Soboul (*Les sans-culottes de l'An II*, Paris: Seuil, 1958). Also clear is the sort of halfway left-wing view characteristic of British and American students of the Revolution: Norman Hampson, J. M. Thompson, Alfred Cobban, and particularly Robert R. Palmer, whose *Twelve Who Ruled* (Princeton, N. J.: Princeton University Press, 1941) is not only an excellent collective biography but the essential work on the Republic as a functioning government. Palmer's monumental *Age of the Democratic Revolution* (Princeton, N. J.: Princeton University Press, 1959, 1964) documents the powerful world-wide effect of the revolutionary republic (a better title for it might well be the "Age of the Republican Revolution") which made Shelley, Beethoven, Schiller, and briefly even Hegel into republicans; not to mention William Blake, for whom republic became a mythic vision (David Erdman, *Blake, Prophet Against Empire,* Princeton, N. J.: Princeton University Press, 1954). This same study by Palmer contains in addition an essay on Robespierre which is the newest and most reliable thing written on the Incorruptible by an American.

Of course, Robespierre is not an easy man for biographers to love. Albert Mathiez was devoted to him, indeed, to the point of self-identification, but he never completed the biography he had planned. The two most detailed biographies are by Gérard Walter (2 vols., Paris: Gallimard, 1946) and J. M. Thompson (2 vols., New York: Appleton-Century, 1936), and the most psychologically definitive is by Max Gallo (Paris: Livre de poche, 1968), but the best introductions to the controversies that rage around Robespierre's motives, and to the savage attacks of both left and right, are George Rudé's *Robespierre: Portrait of a Revolutionary Democrat* (New York: Viking, 1975) and Norman Hampson's fascinating dialogue, *The Life and Opinions of Maximilien Robespierre* (London: Duckworth, 1974).

NOTES

1. Pierre-Paul Vergniaud (Girondin leader), "Speech" (March 1793), in Claude G. Bowers, *Vergniaud* (New York: Macmillan, 1950), p. 340.

2. "green veins" Madame de Stael, "Considérations" (1818), vol. 2, p. 130, in J. M. Thompson, *Robespierre* (New York: Appleton-Century, 1936), vol. 1, p. 52. "No balls" Danton quoted in the memoirs of Honoré Riouffe in H. Christophe, *Danton*, tr. P. Green (London: Barker, 1967), p. 429. "Never smiled" Fréron quoted in Thompson, *Robespierre*, vol. 1, p. 9.

3. H. Fleischmann, *Charlotte Robespierre et ses Mémoires* (Paris: A. Michel, 1909), pp. 290–292.

4. For the republicanism of Rousseau, which, unlike that of his fellow-citizen Calvin, is undisputed, see his "Du contrat social" (1762), in *Oeuvres complètes* (Paris: Pléiade, 1964), vol. 3, pp. 361–362, 379–380. *République* for Rousseau was a government of laws (*ibid.*, p. 382). Machiavelli's *Prince* he thought "a book for republicans" (*ibid.*, p. 409). For passages quoted by Adams in *Defence of the Constitutions of America*, see *ibid.*, pp. 402, 404, 406. Enlightenment republicans before Rousseau are connected with both English Commonwealthmen and Dutch and French radicals by M. Jacob in *The Radical Enlightenment* (London: Allen & Unwin, 1981).

5. Fréron quoted in J. M. Thompson, *Robespierre*, vol. 1, p. 9.

6. For Jefferson's dinners, see T. Jefferson, Autobiography (New York: G. P. Putnam, n. d.), p. 113, and "Letters" (June 3 and September 19, 1789), quoted in C. D. Hazen, *Contemporary American Opinion of the French Revolution* (1897) (Gloucester, Mass.: Peter Smith, 1964), pp. 42–44, 50.

7. The feminine pronoun here stands for *la Commune de Paris*, as it will later for *la République*. In English, use of the feminine personification is a bit antique and nautical, but I think the attempt to recapture it for republican thought may be worth making, as I explain in Chapter 14 below.

8. Maximilien Robespierre, "Discours sur les Principes de morale . . ." (February 5, 1794), in *Discours et rapports a la Convention* (Paris: Editions 10/18, 1965), p. 214.

9. Robespierre, "Discours sur le jugement de Louis" (December 3, 1792), in *Discours et rapports*, p. 69. Saint-Just, "Discours sur le jugement de Louis" (November 13, 1792), in *Oeuvres choisies* (Paris: Idées/Gallimard, 1968), p. 80. See also A. Soboul, ed., *Le Procès de Louis XVI* (Paris: Julliard, 1966).

10. For discussions of republican iconography, see Marvin Trachtenberg, *The Statue of Liberty* (New York, Viking, 1976); Lynn Hunt, "Hercules and the Radical Image in the French Revolution," forthcoming in *Representations*; Maurice Agulhon, *Marianne into Battle*, tr. A. Lloyd (London: Cambridge University Press, 1981); E. Wynne-Tyson, *Mithras: The Fellow in the Cap* (New York: Frohnhoefer's, 1972); Winifred Schleiner, "The Infant Hercules: Franklin's Design for a Medal Commemorating American Liberty," in *Eighteenth Century Studies*, Spring 1976, p. 235; G. Hunt, *The History of the Seal of the United States* (Washington, D. C.: Dept. of State, 1909); and the classic handbook for artists, C. Ripa, *Iconologia* (1593), 5 vols. (Perugia: P. Costantini, 1764–1767).

11. The Constitution of 1793, which never went into effect, can be found in *Constitutions de la France depuis 1789* (Paris: Garnier-Flammarion, 1970). The report of the Committee on Public Safety is in Saint-Just, *Oeuvres choisies*, pp. 168ff. (quotation from p. 181). See A. Ollivier, *Saint-Just* (Paris: Livre de Poche, 1954), pp. 291–297.

12. The Constitution of 1795 is in *Constitutions de la France depuis 1789* (Paris: Garnier-Flammarion, 1970).

13. Felix Markham, *Napoleon* (1963) (New York: New American Library, 1966). The best biography in English. Napoleon, ironically, came from a family of Corsican aristocrats who had come there from renaissance Florence and had helped lead Paoli's republican independence movement on Corsica in 1761–1768.

14. The Constitution of the Consulate is in *Constitutions de la France depuis 1789* (Paris: Garnier-Flammarion, 1970).

15. Simon Schama, *Patriots and Liberators* (New York: Knopf, 1977), is the definitive study of the fall of the Dutch republic.

16. Niccolò Machiavelli, *Discourses on Livy* (1513), Bk. 1, chaps. 16, 17, 18, in *The Prince and Discourses*, tr. L. Ricci and E. Vincent (New York: The Modern Library, 1950).

Chapter 10: Thaddeus Stevens

BIBLIOGRAPHICAL ESSAY

Historians of the Jacksonian period in American history have always been hardy and contentious. Arthur Schlesinger, Jr., is a charter member, as are Arthur C. Cole, Richard McCormick, E. M. Carroll, Louis Hartz, Ulrich Phillips, and Glyndon Van Deusen. Alert to every revisionist tremor, today's Jacksonians, Edward Pessen, Lee Benson, Charles Sellers, Frank O. Gatell, Major L. Wilson, and John William Ward, have turned the field so continuously that laymen have become impatient about the harvest. Until the wave of the Bailyn thesis passes through this field of American history, students will have to rely, as I have done, on compendia of the contenders, like A. Cave's *Jacksonian Democracy and the Historians* (Gainesville, Fla.: University of Florida Press, 1964), or E. Pessen's *New Perspectives on Jacksonian Parties and Politics* (Boston: Allyn and Bacon, 1969). Whig rhetoric was well summarized recently by Daniel Howe in *The Political Culture of the American Whigs* (Chicago: University of Chicago Press, 1979) but to find a Whig biography sympathetic to the anti-Jackson ideology, one must go to the nineteenth century, or to G. Van Deusen's Clay (Boston: Little, Brown, 1937), G. Lipsky's J. Q. Adams (New York: Apollo Editions, 1950), or R. Morgan's Tyler (Lincoln, Nebr.: University of Nebraska Press, 1954).

The generational connection between Whigs and Republicans, on the other hand, is so untouched that there is reason to overstress it here. David Donald's article "A Whig in the White House," reprinted in *Lincoln Reconsidered* (enlarged ed., New York: Vintage, n. d.), ought to be the stimulus here.

As for the Radical Republicans, the province of Civil War and Reconstruction specialists, historians have displayed zest and thoroughness but little quantitative method or Jacksonian contentiousness. Most useful are Hans Trefousse's *The Radical Republicans* (New York: Knopf, 1969), Patrick Riddleberger's *1866* (Carbondale, Ill.: Southern Illinois University Press, 1979), David Donald's *The Politics of Reconstruction* (Baton Rouge: Louisiana State University Press, 1965), which analyzes voting patterns, and particularly Eric Foner's *Free Soil, Free Labor, Free Men* (New York: Oxford University Press, 1970), a history of the ideology of all Republican factions which I think neglects the resonance of the party's name, but which seems to neglect nothing else. The day-to-day workings of the Thirty-Ninth and Fortieth Congresses have been well presented by a sympathetic Englishman who knows how parliaments function, W. R. Brock, to whose *An American Crisis* (New York: Harper, 1963) I owe the enumeration of the twenty-eight leaders of the American Long Parliament.

On the subject of Thaddeus Stevens, contention not only continues but flourishes. Four fascinating and often incompatible biographies by Fawn Brodie (New York: Norton, 1959), Ralph Korngold (New York: Harcourt, Brace, 1955), Richard N. Current (Madison: University of Wisconsin Press, 1942), and James Woodburn (Indianapolis: Bobbs Merrill, 1913) have all been composed from the major source, the Stevens Papers preserved at the Library of Congress. I am indebted to Current for Stevens's views in 1847, to Korngold for a concurrent interpretation, and to Brodie for a sounding of the personal sources of Stevens's greatness.

NOTES

1. *Harper's Weekly*, March 14, 1868.

2. Fawn Brodie, *Thaddeus Stevens, Scourge of the South* (New York: Norton, 1959), p. 196.

3. Georges Clemenceau, *American Reconstruction*, ed. F. Baldensperger (New York: Da Capo, 1969), p. 165. The volume is unindexed. For Stevens, see pp. 125, 132, 138, 149, 153ff., 161, 224ff.

4. David Donald, *Lincoln Reconsidered*, enlarged ed. (New York: Vintage, n. d.), has a chapter on Lincoln as a Whig. See also Lincoln to Herndon (1848) in *Works of Abraham Lincoln*, eds. A. Nicolay and J. Hay (New York: Century, 1922), vol. 1, p. 111.

5. John Wilkes Booth, by the way, was named, like Wilkes-Barre, Pa., for

the great English radical whig, John Wilkes. His brother was named for Junius Brutus. Whatever the son may have become, the father was clearly a republican.

6. This is the accomplishment. Stevens's intention, as he put it in a speech at Lancaster, Pa., on September 6, 1865, was "to inflict condign punishment on the rebel belligerents and so . . . reform their municipal institutions as to make them republican in spirit as well as in name" (*New York Tribune*, September 11, 1865), quoted in R. Current, *Old Thad Stevens* (Madison: University of Wisconsin Press, 1942), pp. 214–216. I doubt that "republican" refers to the G.O.P.

7. Charles Sumner's long and erudite effort to redefine "republic" was delivered to a skeptical Senate on February 5 and 6, 1866. See Sumner, *Works* (New York: Negro Universities Press, 1969), vol. 13, pp. 115–269, and Wiecek, *The Guarantee Clause of the Constitution* (Ithaca, N. Y.: Cornell University Press, 1980).

8. Alexander Stephens's view is expressed at length in his *Constitutional View of the Late War Between the States* (Philadelphia: National Publishing Company, 1868); cf. vol. 2, p. 668.

9. Jacobus Ten Broek, *Equal Under Law* (New York: Collier, 1965), pp. 73, 74, 90.

10. S. E. Morison, *Oxford History of the American People* (New York: Oxford University Press, 1965), p. 456. U. Phillips, C. Sellers, L. Hartz, and L. Benson can be approached through Benson, *Jacksonian Democracy, New York as a Test Case* (Princeton, N. J.: Princeton University Press, 1961).

11. Meeting the Whig fear of the unrepublican Catholic immigrant, Archbishop Hughes, in 1856, cited the example of the democratic republic of San Marino in the middle of Catholic Italy: "Though Catholic, she is against one-man power." "Lecture on the Present Conditions and Prospects of the Catholic Church in the United States," in M. Abell, ed., *American Catholic Thought* (Indianapolis, Ind.: Bobbs-Merrill, 1968), p. 18.

12. W. R. Brock, *An American Crisis: Congress and Reconstruction, 1865–1867* (New York: Harper, 1963) short-lists twenty-eight leaders of the Thirty-ninth and Fortieth Congresses on the basis of their influence on the parliamentary process. I give his list here, followed by years of birth, years of entry into politics (in my judgment), and indications of which party each one entered: "w" for Whig, "d" for Democrat, "am" for Anti-Mason, "l" for Liberty or Free-Soil, and "r" for republican. In addition, JCR stands for membership in the cabinet-like Joint Committee on Reconstruction, and CC stands for chairmanship of a major standing committee of either House.

HOUSE

John Bingham (Ohio)	1815, 1840, w, JCR
James G. Blaine (Maine)	1830, 1848, w
Benjamin Franklin Butler (Mass.)	1818, 1840, d
George Boutwell (Mass.)	1818, 1842, d, JCR
Schuyler Colfax (Indiana)	1823, 1848, w
Joshua Giddings (Ohio)	1795, 1826, w
George W. Julian (Indiana)	1817, 1845, w, CC
William (Pig Iron) Kelly (Penna.)	1814, 1856, d
Justin Morrill (Vermont)	1810, 1854, w, JCR, CC
Henry J. Raymond (New York)	1820, 1841, w (editor of *New York Times*)
Samuel Shellabarger (Ohio)	1817, 1852, ?
Thaddeus Stevens (Penna.)	1792, 1833, am, JCR, CC
Elihu Washburne (Illinois)	1816, 1844, w, JCR, CC
James Wilson (Iowa)	1828, 1856, r, CC
Roscoe Conkling (New York)	1828, 1855, w, JCR

SENATE

Zachariah Chandler (Michigan)	1813, 1851, w
William Pitt Fessenden (Maine)	1806, 1830, w
Lafayette S. Foster (Conn.)	1806, 1830, w, President Pro Tempore
James Grimes (Iowa)	1816, 1838, w, JCR
J. H. Howard (Michigan)	1805, 1838, w, JCR
Timothy Howe (Wisconsin)	1816, 1845, w
Henry Lane (Indiana)	1811, 1840, w
John Sherman (Ohio)	1823, 1848, w
Charles Sumner (Mass.)	1811, 1846, w
Lyman Trumbull (Illinois)	1813, 1840, d
Benjamin Wade (Ohio)	1800, 1830, w
George Williams (Oregon)	1823, 1847, d, JCR
Henry Wilson (Mass.)	1812, 1841, w

13. James Madison, *Notes of Proceedings in the Federal Convention* (1787), ed. A. Koch (New York: Norton, 1969), pp. 45, 46, 53, 60, 357, 368, 651.

14. H. Richardson, ed., *Messages and Papers of the Presidents* New York: Bureau of National Literature and Art, 1907), vol. 3, p. 1145. The veto message is in this volume, as are other addresses referred to in this chapter by Harrison and Tyler.

15. *Washington Weekly Chronicle*, August 22, 1868, as quoted in Brodie, *Thaddeus Stevens*, pp. 24–25.

16. H. Richardson, ed., *Messages and Papers of the Presidents*, vol. 4, pp. 1860–1876, for Harrison's Inaugural Address.

17. O. P. Chitwood, *John Tyler* (New York: Appleton-Century, 1939), p. 215. The story, alas, is not well vouched for.

18. Current, *Old Thad Stevens*, p. 82.

19. John Clayton (Delaware) in *Congressional Globe*, 29th Congress, 1st Session, p. 786, as quoted in John Schroeder, *Mister Polk's War* (Madison, Wis.: University of Wisconsin Press, 1973), p. 17.

20. *Congressional Globe*, 29th Congress, 1st Session, Appendix, p. 294, as quoted in Schroeder, *Mister Polk's War*, p. 27.

21. *Ibid.*, p. 950, as quoted in Schroeder, *Mister Polk's War*, pp. 27–28.

22. *Congressional Globe*, 29th Congress, 2nd Session, Appendix, p. 294, as quoted in Schroeder, *Mister Polk's War*, p. 79.

23. Corwin's full speech is in a hundred anthologies, and in D. Howe, ed., *The American Whigs* (New York: Wiley, 1973), pp. 203–217.

Chapter 11: Léon Gambetta

BIBLIOGRAPHICAL ESSAY

The originality of the Third Republic as the mother of parliamentary republics is not a theme for any of its historians, who concentrate on how the British constitutional monarchy served as its progenitor. Other periods in French history have more glamor, even for French historians. The best short history seems to be by an Englishman (D. W. Brogan, *France Under the Republic, 1870–1939*, New York: Harper, 1940), and the new French surveys by J. M. Mayeur (*Les débuts de la Troisième République*, Paris: Seuil, 1975), Madeleine Rébérioux (*La République radicale?* Paris: Seuil, 1975), and Philippe Bernard (*La fin d'un monde, 1914–1929*, Paris: Seuil, 1975) have little to add to the multivolume histories of a generation ago by Jacques Chastenet (7 vols., Paris: Hachette, 1952–1962) and Georges Bonnefous (Paris: Presses Universitaires de France, 1956–1957). The thesis that the Third Republic was essentially an accident is shared by all who have studied its birth, so much so that one gets suspicious of the pleasure of its ironies. As a thesis it has had the effect of obscuring the ways in which the new republican ideology was formed after the 1851 coup. L. Tchernoff's *Le Parti républicain sous le Second Empire* (Paris: A. Pedone, 1906) says little about ideas, and John Scott's *Republican Ideas and the Liberal Tradition in France, 1870–1914* (New York: Columbia University Press, 1951) makes it seem as if the definition of republic followed its creation by a full generaion. Claude Nicolet's new *L'Idée républicaine en France* (Paris: Gallimard, 1982) does indeed hark back to the First Republic but curiously gives only one chapter, Chapter 10, to purely political definitions of the term *république*.

In any case, the best short book on how the constitution worked is David Thomson's *Democracy in France: The Third Republic* (New York: Oxford University Press, 1946).

On the origins of the Third there is an absolutely charming narrative by Daniel Halévy (*La fin des notables*, Paris: Grasset, 1930, and *La République des ducs*, Paris: Grasset, 1937), a detailed electoral study by Jacques Gouault (*Comment la France est devenue républicaine, 1870–1875*, Paris: Colin, 1954), and American analysis by Frank Brabant (*The Beginning of the Third Republic*, London: Macmillan, 1940), and a study by Allan Mitchell of *The German Influence in France After 1870: The Formation of the French Republic* (Chapel Hill, N. C.: University of North Carolina Press, 1979). For the provisional Government of National Defense there is little beyond J. P. T. Bury's exhaustive *Gambetta and the National Defense* ([1936], New York: H. Fertig, 1970), but for the Commune there is a gratifying host of studies, headed by that of Charles Rihs (*La Commune de Paris*, Geneva: Droz, 1955; reedition, Paris: Seuil, 1973).

Gambetta has had three biographers of importance in this century: J. P. T. Bury, whose indispensable *Gambetta and the Making of the Third Republic* (London: Longman's, 1973) brings his 1936 study to a conclusion; Jacques Chastenet, whose *Gambetta* (Paris: Fayard, 1968) is a sympathetic but wary portrait; and Georges Wormser, whose *Gambetta dans les tempêtes, 1870–1877* (Paris: Sirey, 1964) is the nearest thing we have to a republican hagiography. Wormser also wrote the most republican study of Clemenceau, whom he once served as Cabinet Secretary (*La République de Clemenceau*, Paris: Presses Universitaires, 1961), while Jaurès has been most carefully sounded by the American historian Harvey Goldberg (*The Life of Jean Jaurès*, Madison, Wis.: University of Wisconsin Press, 1962).

NOTES

1. Karl Marx, *The Eighteenth Brumaire of Louis Napoleon Bonaparte* (New York, 1852), ed. C. P. Dutt (New York: International Publishers, 1963), p. 15.

2. Leon Gambetta, "Address" (Belleville, February 15, 1876), in *Discours et Plaidoyers*, ed. J. Reinach (Paris: Charpentier, 1906), vol. 5, p. 155.

3. Gambetta (September 4, 1870), in J. P. T. Bury, *Gambetta and the National Defense* (1936) (New York: H. Fertig, 1970), p. 61.

4. David Thomson, *Democracy in France: The Third Republic* (New York: Oxford University Press, 1946).

5. J. Delafosse, *Figures contemporaines* (Paris: Calmann-Lévy, 1899), p. 191.

6. Emile Ollivier, *L'Empire libéral* (Paris: Garnier, 1907), vol. 11, pp. 497ff. Significantly, Gambetta's speech giving what came to be known as the

Belleville Program of 1869 is not reprinted in the collected works edited by his friend Reinach.

7. J. P. T. Bury, *Gambetta and the National Defense,* p. 224.

8. Gambetta, "Letter" (January 22, 1871), in *Dépêches,* ed. J. Reinach (Paris: Charpentier, 1886), vol. 1, p. 76.

9. This view of Gambetta, though plausible, is based on inference rather than evidence. The evidence we do possess does not contradict it in any way, however.

10. This was Thiers. Quoted in D. Halévy, *La fin des notables* (1930) (Paris: Livre de Poche, 1972), p. 43.

11. *Ibid.,* p. 91.

12. *Ibid.,* p. 186.

13. Gambetta, "Interview," in New York *Herald* (Paris, January 27, 1873). Reprinted as an Appendix to J. P. T. Bury, *Gambetta and the Third Republic* (London: Longman's, 1973).

14. Gambetta, "Address" (Belleville, February 14, 1876), in *Discours,* vol. 6, p. 169.

15. Halévy, *La République des ducs* (1937) (Paris: Livre de Poche, 1972), p. 272.

16. Bury, *Gambetta and the Third Republic,* p. 461.

17. J. Hampden-Jackson, *Clemenceau and the Third Republic* (New York: Macmillan, 1948), p. 156.

18. *Ibid.,* p. 161.

19. *Ibid.,* p. 140.

20. Jean Jaurès, "Address" (January 12, 1894), in H. Goldberg, *Jean Jaurès* (Madison, Wis.: University of Wisconsin Press, 1962), pp. 117, 157.

21. *Ibid.,* p. 267.

22. Hampden-Jackson, *Clemenceau,* p. 86.

23. See note 2 above.

Chapter 12: Gustav Noske

BIBLIOGRAPHICAL ESSAY

For a long time Weimar was a republic without republicans. Today's German republicans find the episode painful; though Karl Dietrich Bracher (*Die Auflösung der Weimarer Republik,* Stuttgart: Ringverlag, 1955) and Martin Borszat (*Der Staat Hitlers* and *Die Weimarer Republik,* tr. J. Hiden, New York: Longman's, 1981), with other younger historians have begun at least to analyze the disaster. Their work supplements the forlorn narrative of Weimar by democratic deputy Erich Eyck (*History of the Weimar Republic* [1954–1956], 2 vols., New York: Wiley, 1967).

Two historiographical introductions are helpful to interlopers in German history: J. Flemming *et al.*, eds., *Die Republik von Weimar* (2 vols., Düsseldorf: Athenäum-Verlag, 1979) and George Castellan, *L. Allemagne de Weimar* (Paris: Colin U, 1969); and it is a welcome discovery for anyone who reads English better than German that the works most sympathetic to republicanism are most often by Americans. Among these are Richard M. Watt, *The Kings Depart* (New York: Simon & Schuster, 1968) and the more scholarly F. M. Watkins, *The Failure of Constitutional Emergency Powers under the German Republic* (Cambridge, Mass.: Harvard University Press, 1939), W. H. Kaufman, *Monarchism in the Weimar Republic* (New York: Octagon, 1973), and Robert Waite, *Vanguard of Nazism* (Cambridge, Mass.: Harvard University Press, 1952).

Historians of the critical first two years of the Republik do include Germans, like Bracher, conservative Koppel Pinson, and Communist Eric Waldman; but the only accounts I have found which neither damn nor excuse Noske are Arthur Rosenberg's old *History of the German Republic* (trs. I. Morrow and L. Sieveking, London: Methuen, 1936), Klaus Epstein's articles (e.g., in *World Politics* XI, 1959), and A. J. Ryder's *The German Revolution of 1918* (London: Cambridge University Press, 1967). Only Ryder, and specialists like David Morgan (*The Socialist Left and the German Revolution*, Ithaca, N. Y.: Cornell University Press, 1980) are kind to those unembarrassed but ineffective republicans of the USPD. Richard Hunt's Heath pamphlet, *The Creation of the Weimar Republic* (Lexington, Mass.: D. C. Heath, 1969), collects many of the above writers; and for documents there is an excellent paperback compendium by G. Ritter and S. Miller (*Die Deutsche Revolution 1918–1919*, Hamburg: Hoffmann u. Campe, 1975).

There is not even a full-length biography of Noske, despite what I think of as his potential to have been the Gambetta of Weimar. A short German essay, U. Czisnik's *Gustav Noske, Ein Sozialdemokratiker Staatsman* (Göttingen: Musterschmidt, 1969), is useful, and so are Noske's own memoirs, still untranslated, *Von Kiel bis Kapp* (Berlin: Verlag für Politik u. Wirtschaft, 1920) and *Aufsteig und Niedergang der deutschen Sozialdemokratie* (Zürich: Aeroverlag, 1947). Many of Noske's colleagues have found scholars worthy of them: Klaus Epstein for Erzberger (Princeton, N. J.: Princeton University Press, 1959), George Kotowski for Ebert (Wiesbaden: Steiner, 1963), J. P. Nettl for Luxemburg (New York: Oxford University Press, 1966); and even the surprisingly constitutional Hindenburg has found a student in Andreas Dorpalen (Princeton, N. J.: Princeton University Press, 1964). Scheidemann has only his excellent memoir (tr., J. Michell, 2 vols., New York: Appleton, 1929) as does the remarkable General Groener (Osnabrück: Biblio-Verlag, 1972); but they and Noske have no real biographers as yet, possible because neither Marxists, nor Nationalists, nor moderate modern republicans can forgive them. Indeed, there are some who cannot forgive Noske his mistake of surviving the Third Reich.

NOTES

1. Phillip Scheidemann, *Memoirs*, tr. J. Michell, 2 vols. (New York: Appleton, 1929), vol. 2, p. 264.

2. For the Prussian version of German history, the most egregious source is Heinrich von Treitschke, particularly his *Deutsche Geschichte im Neunzehnten Jahrhundert* (1879–1894), trs. E. Paul and C. Paul, 4 vols. (New York: McBride, Nast & Co., 1915–1919). For a more whiggish view, one may begin with F. L. Carsten, *Princes and Parliaments in Germany* (Oxford: Clarendon Press, 1959).

3. Michael Balfour, *The Kaiser and His Times* (Boston: Houghton-Mifflin, 1964), pp. 277, 140, 157, 119, 158. Balfour is the fullest of many biographies.

4. Martin Kitchen, *The Silent Dictatorship* (New York: Holmes and Meier, 1976), describes the war monarchy of Ludendorff—what Ludendorff himself baptized *Totaler Krieg* or total war—and pays particular attention to its constitutionality and legal structure.

5. August Bebel to Friedrich Engels (July 12, 1891), in *Briefwechsel mit Friedrich Engels*, ed. K. Blumenberg (The Hague, Mouton, 1965), p. 424.

6. Gustav Noske, "Address" (April 25, 1907). See Carl Schorske, *German Social Democracy* (Cambridge, Mass.: Harvard University Press, 1955), pp. 77ff.

7. The Weimar Constitution can be found in volume 3 of the large document collection, H. Michaelis et al., eds., *Ursachen und Folgen vom Deutschen Zusammenbruch* (Berlin: Dokumenten-Verlag, 1959ff.), no. 740, pp. 464–493.

8. Gambetta's achievement was, however, recognized by contemporary Germans. See C. von der Goltz, *Gambetta et ses armées* (Paris: Sandoz et Fischbacher 1877), quoted by Jacques Chastenet, *Histoire de la IIIe République* (Paris: Hachette, 1955), vol. 1, p. 49.

9. Gustav Noske, *Von Kiel bis Kapp* (1920), in G. Ritter and S. Miller, eds., *Die Deutsche Revolution 1918–1919* (Hamburg: Hoffmann u. Campe, 1975), p. 181.

10. Robert G. L. Waite, *Vanguard of Nazism, The Free Corps* (Cambridge, Mass.: Harvard University Press, 1952), describes in full the activities of the "bloodhound."

11. G. von Lossow, "Testimony," in *The Hitler Trial* (1924), trs. H. Freniere, L. Karcic, P. Fandek (Arlington, Va.: University Publications of America, 1976), vol. 2, p. 138. See Joachim Fest, *Hitler*, Trs., R. Winston and C. Winston (New York: Harcourt, Brace, Jovanovich, 1974), pp. 177, 192.

Chapter 13: Five Senators

BIBLIOGRAPHICAL ESSAY

My work here is largely from scratch. Generations of legislators may quote each other in the same ringing words, but historians have yet to pronounce the magic word "tradition." Excellent new biographies exist for Norris (Richard Lowitt, Syracuse, N. Y.: Syracuse University Press, 1963, and Urbana, Ill.: University of Illinois Press, 1971) and Taft (James T. Patterson, Boston: Houghton-Mifflin, 1972), and there is an old, delightfully stuffy one for Hoar (F. H. Gillett, Boston: Houghton-Mifflin, 1934); but Wheeler's extraordinary case is carried only by his as-told-to memoir (*Yankee from the West*, Garden City, N. Y.: Doubleday, 1962), and Sam Ervin, the only one of the five still living, is at the mercy of quick-dab journalism. Ervin prefers Paul Clancy's version of his career (*Just a Country Lawyer*, Bloomington, Ind.: University of Indiana Press, 1974) and writes that Dick Dabney's (*A Good Man*, Boston: Houghton-Mifflin, 1976) is "based on his imagination" (Ervin to the author, April 3, 1979).

Surely, the most useful works on the subject of the antirepublican executive in this century are the key treatises in constitutional law and politics, including one by a Senator, Jacob Javits, who put his name to a useful compilation on *Who Makes War* (New York: William Morrow, 1973). Most important among these books are Corwin on *The President, Office and Powers* ([1940], 4th ed., New York: New York University Press, 1958), Raoul Berger on *Impeachment* and *Executive Privilege* (Cambridge, Mass.: Harvard University Press, 1973 and 1974), Clinton Rossiter on *The Supreme Court and the Commander-in-Chief* ([1951], 2nd ed., Ithaca, N. Y.: Cornell University Press, 1976), Louis Fisher on *The Presidential Spending Power* (Princeton, N.J.: Princeton University Press, 1975), Nathan Grundstein's 1947 article on *Presidential Delegation of Authority* (reprinted as a book, Pittsburgh, Pa.: University of Pittsburgh Press, 1961), Leonard W. Levy on the abuse of the Justice Department (*Against the Law*, New York: Harper, 1974), and the grandaddy of them all, Radical Republican William Whiting's *The War Powers of the President*, which began as a pamphlet in 1862 and is still going stong (Glorieta, N. M.: Rio Grande Press, 1971).

Next to these, histories of Congress (there are a few) seem anemic; and republican-sounding muckrakers, even those of genuine stature like David

Wise (*The Politics of Lying* and *The American Police State*, New York: Vintage, 1973 and 1976), Morton Halperin (*The Lawless State*, New York: Penguin, 1976), or the great Henry Steele Commager (*The Defeat of America*, New York: Simon & Schuster, 1974) lack perspective. As for the histories, they are, with few exceptions (Maeva Marcus, *Truman and the Steel Seizure Case*, New York: Columbia University Press, 1979; Geoffrey Smith, *To Save a Nation*, New York: Basic Books, 1973; Ronald Radosh, *Prophets on the Right*, New York, Simon & Schuster, 1975), so bespangled with president-worship, American provincialism, and war patriotism that even the most careful, detailed, and skeptical among them (Arthur Schlesinger, James M. Burns) make it seem as if the controversy over executive power were minor, muted, and ultimately worthless. Perhaps one can get some sense of the seriousness of the opposition from the left wing of the profession, and the revisionist histories of American foreign policy: Richard van Alstyne's *The Rising American Empire* (Oxford; Basil Blackwell, 1960), William A. Williams, *The Tragedy of American Diplomacy* (New York: Random House, 1972), Gabriel Kolko's *Politics of War* (New York: Vintage, 1968), and Walter Karp's new book of the same title (New York: Harper, 1979), which contains the following sad cry:

> The triumph of Wilson and the war party [in 1917] struck the American Republic a blow from which it has never recovered. (p. 324)

NOTES

1. *Hearings Before the Select Committee on Presidential Campaign Activities of The United States Senate*, 93rd Congress, 1st Session (Washington, D. C.: Government Printing Office, 1973), Book 6, p. 2595.

2. *Congressional Record* (November 15, 1954), p. 16021

3. F. H. Gillett, *George Frisbie Hoar* (Boston: Houghton-Mifflin, 1934), p. 91.

4. Woodrow Wilson, *Congressional Government* (1884) (New York: Meridian Books, 1956): "scheme," p. 28; "standing committees," p. 56; "decline," p. 48. For Wilson's ambition to be senator, see R. S. Baker, *Woodrow Wilson, Life & Letters* (New York: Doubleday, Page, 1927), vol. 1, p. 104.

5. Wilson, *Congressional Government*, "Preface" (1900) (New York: Meridian Books, 1956), p. 23.

6. *Congressional Record* (January 9, 1899), p. 494.

7. *Ibid.*, and E. S. Creasy, *Six Decisive Battles of the World* (1851), chap. 2 (Harrisburg, Pa.: Stackpole, 1960), p. 39. For Hoar's gestures as a speaker, see Gillett, *Hoar*, p. 239.

8. *Congressional Record* (April 17, 1900), p. 4280.

9. *Congressional Record* (May 22, 1902), pp. 5788ff.

10. *Congressional Record* (March 3, 1916), p. 3485.

11. *Congressional Record* (March 2, 1917), p. 4777, 8322.

12. *Congressional Record*, 64th Congress, 2nd Session (1917), p. 5007. For Cummins's words, see *ibid.*, p. 4912.

13. *Ibid.*, p. 5008.

14. Woodrow Wilson (March 4, 1917), in R. S. Baker, *Woodrow Wilson* (New York, Doubleday, Page, 1937), vol. 6, p. 481. For the subsequent fate of this and other "little bands," see H. Peterson and G. Fite, *Opponents of War 1917–1918* (Seattle, Wash.: University of Washington Press, 1968).

15. *Congressional Record* (August 23, 1928), p. 6967.

16. *Congressional Record* (August 12, 1940), p. 10119.

17. For an introduction to the long debate on FDR's responsibility, see Joseph Lash, *Roosevelt and Churchill* (New York: Norton, 1976), and Charles Beard's opening shot, *American Foreign Policy in the Making 1932–1940* (New Haven, Conn.: Yale University Press, 1946). Details of the laws FDR evaded are in Robert Divine, *The Illusion of Neutrality* (Chicago: Quadrangle, 1962).

18. Burton K. Wheeler (with P. F. Healy), *Yankee from the West* (Garden City, N. Y.: Doubleday, 1962), p. 198.

19. *Ibid.*, p. 319.

20. *Ibid.*, p. 333.

21. *Ibid.*, p. 325.

22. *Congressional Record* (March 8, 1938), p. 3020. FDR (March 30, 1938), in *New York Times*, March 31, 1938, p. 1. On the bill itself, see Richard Polenberg, *Reorganizing Roosevelt's Government* (Cambridge, Mass.: Harvard University Press, 1966).

23. Wheeler, *Yankee from the West*, p. 31.

24. Franklin Roosevelt, "Fireside Chat (September 3, 1939), in B. Zevin, ed., *Nothing to Fear* (1946) (New York: Popular Library, 1961), pp. 192, 194, 193.

25. Wheeler, *Yankee from the West*, p. 29. "Hard to shake" is right. According to W. Stevenson, *A Man Called Intrepid* (New York: Ballantine, 1976), they were inspired and led by British intelligence operating illegally in the United States with Roosevelt's tacit agreement. Fortunately for Roosevelt's reputation, this book, which describes acts that make Watergate look like a fish fry, is not entirely trustworthy.

26. Wheeler, "Radio Address" (January 11, 1940), quoted with FDR's reply in Wheeler, *Yankee from the West*, p. 27.

27. *Congressional Record* (March 1, 1941), pp. 1607, 1608.

28. Wheeler, *Yankee from the West*, pp. 387, 417ff.

29. J. T. Patterson, *Mister Republican* (Boston: Houghton-Mifflin, 1972), p. 157.

30. *Ibid.*, pp. 241, 243.

31. *Congressional Record* (August 14, 1940), pp. 10300–10301. See also Taft's speech in Vienna, Ill., in *Congressional Record*, 1939 Appendix, pp. 75–77.

32. *Congressional Record* (April 22, 1947), p. 3786. *C. R.* (March 12, 1948), p. 2642. *C. R.* (July 1949), pp. 9208, 9278.

33. *Congressional Record* (June 28, 1950), p. 9320.

34. Sam J. Ervin on tests, *Congressional Record* (September 13, 1967), pp. 25409ff.; safe streets, *C. R.* (May 20, 1968), pp. 14018–14028; data banks, *C. R.* (February 3, and September 8, 1970), pp. 30797ff.; army spying, *C. R.* (July 29, 1970), pp. 26321ff.; drug busts, *C. R.* (January 26, 1970), p. 1159; and D. C. crime, *C. R.* (July 17, 1970), pp. 24836–24888.

35. *Congressional Record* (May 21, 1965), pp. 11215–11220.

36. For early appearances of "noonday sun" and "Gabriel's horn," see *Congressional Record*, 89th Congress, 1st Session, pp. 8983–8984, and November 15, 1954, p. 16021.

37. *Hearings Before the Select Committee on Presidential Campaign Activities*, Book 6 (July 24, 1973), p. 2576.

38. *Hearings*, Book 6 (July 25, 1973), pp. 2597, 2594, 2577 (Ehrlichman's view), 2595 (Baker's view).

39. Benjamin Franklin, Thomas Jefferson, John Adams, et al., *Declaration of Independence* (July 2, 1776), various editions. The original was reported by an *ad hoc* committee, adopted after intense debate as a resolution of Congress, and signed by the then-President of the United States, John Hancock, and the rest of his colleagues.

Chapter 14: Conclusion

BIBLIOGRAPHICAL ESSAY

Since John Adams wrote his *Defence of the Constitutions of America* in 1787–1788, no one has tried to combine the writing of republican history with the elucidation of its political science. Perhaps attention ought to be called to the long whig tradition in nineteenth-century historiography, beginning with Sismondi's enormous work (J. C. L. Simonde de Sismondi, *Histoire des républiques italiennes du moyen-âge*, Paris: H. Nicolle, 1809–1818), which so impressed the liberals of the 1820s and 1830s. In the field of jurisprudence, which is closely related, monarchy tends to survive in the concept of "sovereign," but Carl Friedrich's *Constitutional Reason of State* (Providence, R. I.: Brown University Press, 1957) skillfully reverses this effect and illuminates ali of republican legal thought. Political science can offer at least two major works on republican problems: Clinton Rossiter's old attack on *Constitutional Dictatorship* (Princeton, N. J.: Princeton University Press, 1948) and Robert Dahl's complex analysis of *Polyarchy* (New Haven, Conn.: Yale University Press, 1971). Economics is also relevant, and Mancur Olson's *The Logic of Collective Action* (Cambridge, Mass.: Harvard University Press, 1971) gives a fascinating analysis of the uses of pluralism and of the practical limits of what the ancient republicans would have called virtue.

NOTES

1. George McGovern to *New York Times*, January 21, 1973.

2. For this capsule history I am indebted to Jonathan Schell, *The Time of Illusion* (New York: Vintage, 1975); Elizabeth Drew, *Washington Journal* (New York: Vintage, 1974); *The Pentagon Papers*; and Richard Nixon, *Presidential Transcripts* (New York: Dell, 1974).

3. Machiavelli himself doubted it. He wrote in the *Discourses*, Book 1, chap. 39, tr. L. Ricci and E. Vincent (New York: The Modern Library, 1950), p. 216, that: "... it is easy, by diligent study of the past to foresee what is likely to happen in the future of any republic, and to apply those remedies that were used by the ancients, or, not finding any that were employed by them, to devise new ones from the similarity of the events. But as such considerations are neglected or not understood by most of those who read, or, if understood by these, are unknown by those who govern, it follows that the same troubles generally recur in all republics."

4. James Madison, *Federalist* 52 (1787), puts it this way: "The greater the power is, the shorter ought to be its duration."

5. Stéphane Rials, *La Présidence de la République* (Paris: Que-sais-je, 1981), is an introduction. Unlike the Third or Fourth Republics, the Fifth is presidential. It is instructive to compare the tiny but now expanding bibliography on the French presidency with the enormous size of the one of the American presidency.

6. *The Right to Keep and Bear Arms* (Washington, D. C.: Government

Printing Office, 1982) contains a history of this view in the United States. It was published for the Senate Judiciary Committee.

7. Charles-Louis le Secondat, Baron de Montesquieu, *De l'esprit des lois* (1748), Book 2, chaps. 1 and 2, in *Oeuvres complètes* (Paris: Seuil, 1964), p. 532.

8. Polybios, *The Histories*, Book 6, tr. W. R. Paton (Cambridge, Mass.: Loeb Classical Library, 1922, vol. 3.

9. Niccolò Machiavelli, *Discourses* I:17 (New York, 1950), p. 167.

10. Royall Tyler, *The Contrast*, "Prologue" (New York: AMS Press, 1970).

11. Machiavelli, *Discourses* I:25 (New York: 1950), p. 183.

12. Machiavelli, *Discourses* I:6, *ibid.*, p. 127.

13. Senator Alan Cranston proposed something like this in the aftermath of Watergate and the beginnings of a debate on this point may be found in *Hearings of the House Subcommittee on International Security and Scientific Affairs* (94th Congress, 2nd Session) (Washington, D. C.: Government Printing Office, 1976), pp. 16, 24, 25, 39, 48, 49, 50, 51, 71, 72, 128, 129, 178, 181, 182, 184, 185, 212–223. See also Senator Jacob Javits, *Who Makes War* (New York: William Morrow, 1973), and Arthur S. Miller, "Nuclear Weapons and Constitutional Law," in *Nova Law Journal*, vol. 7, no. 1, Fall 1982, pp. 29–32. Also, the current (1983) debates on military action in Central America and the Bland Amendment.

14. No one knows who made this wise comparison. Bartlett, *Familiar Quotations*, says he was first quoted by Andrew Fletcher of Saltoun, who omitted to credit him by name.

15. For a note on republican iconography, see above, Chapter. 9, note 9.

Index

355